CW00662131

Conduct and Acc
in Financial Services:
A Practical Guide

Conduct and Accountability in Financial Services:
A Practical Guide

Stacey English

Susannah Hammond

Bloomsbury Professional

LONDON · DUBLIN · EDINBURGH · NEW YORK · NEW DELHI · SYDNEY

BLOOMSBURY PROFESSIONAL
Bloomsbury Publishing Plc
41–43 Boltro Road, Haywards Heath, RH16 1BJ, UK

BLOOMSBURY and the Diana logo are trademarks of Bloomsbury Publishing Plc

First published in Great Britain 2018

Copyright © Bloomsbury Professional, 2018

Cover design © Two Associates

British Library Cataloguing-in-Publication Data

A catalogue record for this book is available from the British Library.

ISBN: PB: 978-1-52650-520-0
         ePDF: 978-1-52650-522-4
         ePub: 978-1-52650-521-7

Typeset by Evolution Design and Digital
Printed and bound by by CPI Group (UK) Ltd, Croydon, CR0 4YY

To find out more about our authors and books visit www.bloomsburyprofessional. com. Here you will find extracts, author information, details of forthcoming events and the option to sign up for our newsletters

Preface

What this guide is and what it isn't

This guide is aimed primarily at senior managers and practitioners in financial services firms operating in, from, or into, the UK. It provides a plain English overview of evolving regulatory expectations, obligations and resulting potential liability which will be of benefit to staff in financial services firms, including risk and compliance professionals. It sets out practical insight as to what senior individuals can and should do to identify, mitigate and manage their own personal regulatory risk.

The authors are experienced compliance and risk professionals with the best part of 50 years of practical experience between them as practitioners in regulated firms, advisers and regulators. The book demystifies and takes the undue complexity out of the seemingly profound changes arising from the introduction of the Senior Managers and Certification Regime (SM&CR) in the UK.

The book assumes a working knowledge of the financial services sector and its regulation. The guide is not by, or for, lawyers, rather it focuses on the qualitative aspects relating to personal liability and accountability.

> 'People capabilities are becoming more and more important to having the right culture. It's not enough to be motivated to behave in a new way; people also need to understand how to be successful with the new behaviours.
>
> The accountability regime reinforces this view of culture and its key drivers. It sets a standard for the outcomes of culture and has an important impact on senior managers, on how a firm is governed and on people's capabilities.'
>
> Source: 'Culture and conduct – extending the accountability regime', speech by Jonathan Davidson, Director of Supervision – Retail and Authorisations, FCA (September 2017)

There is no substitute for expert advice tailored to a firm's specific circumstances, and for all senior managers in financial services the mantra should continue to be 'if in doubt speak to compliance'. That said, the guide will inform, up-skill and raise awareness to enable senior managers to spot potential issues earlier, ask key questions and to understand the possible implications of certain courses of (in)action. At the heart of the SM&CR is the crystal-clear intention that senior individuals are, and will be held, accountable for compliance in the area under their responsibility. The robust and consistent mitigation of personal regulatory risk has been made more challenging by the evolving regulatory focus on culture and conduct risk – the 'how' business is done as well as the 'what'.

This means that senior managers need to have a comprehensive awareness of not only their part of the business but also how good customer outcomes are assured and their accountability is demonstrably discharged. Senior managers need to be seen to be playing their part to embody and promote the appropriate 'tone from the top' culture. This is not set out in any black and white set of rules, but is inherent in the codes of conduct, principles and a judgement-based approach to supervision which is informed by regulatory speeches, enforcements and thematic reviews.

To help senior managers navigate the brave new regulatory world of increased personal liability, the guide covers the practical impact of the SM&CR on a sector-by-sector basis, an analysis of the key changes from the previous regime, some specifics based on particular roles such as non-executive directors, practical challenges and how to overcome them, the now critical role of culture and conduct risk, how to learn lessons from enforcement actions and examples of better risk mitigation. The book also gives guidance on regulatory relationship management, the role of technology and an overview of related global developments. At the end of each chapter is a checklist of questions. Not as a test, but rather issues or areas for senior managers to consider.

The guide will also be of interest to, and useful for, anyone working or seeking a career in financial services given the extension of conduct risk requirements to all staff. Aspects relating to the evolving expectations around onboarding, performance management and the focus on the role of incentive and compensation schemes as a possible driver of misconduct will be relevant to specific people-related functions within firms, including human resources.

For regulators themselves, together with academics, the guide deals with how the SM&CR has been interpreted in practice and what 'good' is beginning to look like in terms of personal regulatory risk management and compliance. The SM&CR, although still in its relative infancy, has already been deemed a success by a number of non-UK regulatory bodies with personal accountability regimes beginning to be considered and rolled out modelled on the UK approach. To give just one example, in January 2018 the Central Bank of Ireland stated that it 'strongly recommends' that reforms to assign responsibility to senior personnel should be adopted and that such reforms 'should be modelled on the Senior Managers and Certification Regime in the UK'. The Central Bank of Ireland further noted the UK Financial Conduct Authority has found the new approach 'effective' and that 'great benefit has been found in other jurisdictions in relation to the adoption of this policy'.

Personal accountability and individual senior manager liability is here to stay.

We hope you find it useful!

Stacey English & Susannah Hammond
September 2018

Dedication

For Stacey's much loved Dan, Alice and Florence and Susannah's wonderful boys Chris, Fred and Tom.

Thank you for supporting us through the juggling act of book, life and work.

Dedication

About the authors

Stacey English

https://www.linkedin.com/in/stenglish/

@regexperts

Stacey has over 20 years' regulatory risk, compliance and audit experience within the financial services as a regulator, practitioner and adviser, giving her an extensive and unique view of conduct in the industry.

Stacey began her regulatory career with the UK regulator, now the FCA, where she led supervisory inspections and mis-selling investigations within banks and insurers and developed new rules and guidance for the financial services industry. She also spent two years as an internal auditor inspecting the conduct of the UK regulator itself. As an industry practitioner she specialised in risk management predominantly within the insurance sector, developing and embedding enterprise-wide risk management at Aviva and Lloyd's of London, and as an adviser to start up Lloyd's managing agents. She joined Barclays as head of governance, reporting and intelligence shortly before the global financial crisis unfolded.

As head of global regulatory intelligence for Thomson Reuters, Stacey is responsible for expert analysis of regulatory developments from global regulators and providing insight, industry thought leadership and benchmarking to tens of thousands of compliance, risk and regulatory professionals worldwide. Stacey joined Thomson Reuters through the acquisition of the compliance regtech start up Complinet. She is also a non-executive director of Dublin-based regulatory risk regtech firm, Corlytics.

Stacey is a Chartered Certified accountant with the highest results worldwide; she has first class degrees in BSc (Hons) Applied Accounting and BA (Hons) Business Administration; she also holds the Chartered Insurance Institute's Certificate in Financial Planning and is a Member of the Chartered Institute of Securities and Investments, the Personal Finance Society and the Chartered Insurance Institute.

Susannah Hammond

https://www.linkedin.com/in/susannahhammond/

@SannaHamm

Susannah has over 25 years' wide-ranging experience in international and UK financial services.

A chartered accountant and chartered fellow of the Chartered Institute for Securities and Investment, Susannah began her compliance career at SG Warburg where she became head of European compliance. She was the global head of compliance and a founding employee of Caspian Securities before joining PricewaterhouseCoopers as a consultant. Susannah was also head of international regulatory risk for the Halifax Group and became head of retail regulatory risk for HBOS plc upon Halifax's merger with Bank of Scotland. Before joining Thomson Reuters, she was head of compliance at GE Capital Bank.

In her role as senior regulatory intelligence expert, Susannah shares her extensive experience with Thomson Reuters Regulatory Intelligence customers writing some of the most-read articles on the site. She is co-author of a series of special survey reports which have been downloaded by tens of thousands of firms, regulators, lawyers and consultancies around the world. Susannah regularly attracts large audiences at events and webinars and is a much sort after speaker and commentator on financial services regulation.

Well known and highly respected throughout the industry, Susannah brings a deep understanding of the unique challenges facing today's senior managers in financial services and the need for clarity on their risk management and compliance obligations in order to identify, manage and mitigate the daily challenges faced.

Contents

Preface   v
Dedication   vii
About the authors   ix
Abbreviations   xvii

Chapter 1 Context and drivers for the new accountability regime   **1**
The financial crisis   1
    The financial crisis and the response: timeline of events   4
    Key parties in driving legislative and regulatory reform   6
The Approved Persons Regime   12
Need for accountability and the new regime   13
Checklist   14

Chapter 2 Key changes from previous regime   **15**
Introduction   16
'Fit and proper'   16
    Honesty, integrity and reputation   18
    Competence and capability   19
    Financial soundness   20
    Due diligence and documentation   20
    Banking Standards Board   22
'Reasonable steps'   23
    Senior Manager Conduct Rules   23
    Effective control   24
    Compliance with relevant requirements and standards   25
    Delegation   26
    Cooperation with regulators   27
Individual Conduct Rules   27
    Integrity   29
    Due skill, care and diligence   29
    Open and cooperative with regulators   30
    Treating customers fairly   30
    Proper market conduct   31
Checklist   31

Chapter 3 Specifics of the Senior Managers and Certification Regime as it applies to banks and large investment firms   **33**
Introduction   34
Who is a 'senior manager'?   35
Senior Managers Regime   36
    Senior Management Functions   36
    Applying the regime to smaller firms   42
Certification Regime   42

'Employees' subject to the Certification Regime   43
Territorial scope   44
PRA certification functions   44
FCA significant harm functions   46
Fit and proper   49
Content of certificates   56
Moving functions during the year   57
What happens if the employee is not fit and proper?   57
Emergency appointments   58
Temporary UK role   59
Checklist   59

Chapter 4 Specifics of the Senior Managers and Certification Regime for insurers   **61**
The new regime for insurers   61
Scope of extended regime   62
Which employees are impacted?   62
What is changing for insurers?   64
The Senior Managers Regime for insurers   65
The Senior Management Functions   65
Handover   67
Duty of responsibility   68
Prescribed Responsibilities   68
Practical implementation   70
Statements of Responsibilities   71
Management Responsibilities Map   72
The Certification Regime   73
Who it applies to   73
Certification functions   73
Fitness and propriety requirements   74
Regulatory references for senior managers and certified staff   75
The Conduct Rules   76
The Individual and Senior Manager Conduct Rules   77
Training and notification   78
Outsourcing under the SMR   79
Checklist   79

Chapter 5 Extension of SM&CR to (almost) all financial services firms   **81**
Introduction   81
What type of SM&CR firm will yours be?   82
The Senior Managers Regime   84
Statements of Responsibilities (SoRs)   85
Duty of responsibility   86
Prescribed responsibilities   86
Fit and proper   87
Certification Regime   89
Conduct Rules   94
How the Senior Managers Regime applies to limited scope firms   95

How the Senior Managers Regime applies to core firms 98
How the Senior Managers Regime applies to enhanced firms 100
Transition between the Approved Persons Regime and SM&CR 104
    Transition for core, limited scope firms and branches 106
    Transition for enhanced firms 108
Checklist 111

Chapter 6 Key roles in embedding and overseeing the SM&CR 113
Introduction 113
Board challenges 113
Risk management and assurance – three lines of defence 114
Key functions in overseeing the SM&CR, culture and conduct risk 115
    Roles of the three lines of defence 115
    Lines of defence in practice 117
Liaison between control functions 118
Human Resources 119
Non-executive directors 124
Internal audit 128
    Good practices for internal audit 130
    Internal audit reviews 132
    Practical questions about culture 134
Legal function 135
Checklist 136

Chapter 7 Practical aspects of better risk mitigation 137
Responsibilities Maps and reasonable steps in action 137
    Statements of Responsibilities 138
    Management Responsibilities Map 140
    Allocation of responsibilities 143
    Applying the regime to smaller firms 147
    Reasonable steps 148
    Evidencing 'reasonable steps' – oversight in action 149
    Training for boards and senior managers 151
Checklist 154

Chapter 8 Practical challenges to overcome 155
Introduction 156
Line of sight 156
Conflicts of interest 157
Outsourcing 160
Skill sets 162
Evidence of qualitative risk management 166
Checklist 168

Chapter 9 Role of culture and conduct risk 169
Regulatory expectations and industry practices 169
    Why culture has become such a focus 169
    What good looks like 173
Conduct risk programmes 183

Approaches to implementing conduct risk management | 183
Conduct risk framework | 184
Good practices in risk management | 184
Measurement and metrics | 189
Misconduct risk monitoring | 190
Checklist | 192

Chapter 10 Other areas personal liability can arise | **195**
Money laundering | 195
The 2017 Regulations | 196
Governance | 199
Bribery and corruption | 201
'Adequate procedures' | 202
Foreign Corrupt Practices Act | 203
Market abuse | 205
Corporate governance | 211
OECD/G20 Principles of Corporate Governance | 213
BCBS Corporate Governance Principles for Banks | 214
Checklist | 215

Chapter 11 Enforcement | **217**
Purpose of enforcement and priorities | 218
Enforcement and the SM&CR | 220
Duty of responsibility | 220
Reasonable steps | 220
Conduct Rules | 225
Penalties | 226
Investigations and cases | 227
Publication of findings and learning the lessons | 228
Examples of enforcement action | 231
Co-operation | 233
Checklist | 234

Chapter 12 Overarching principles for how to manage personal regulatory risk | **235**
Introduction | 235
External environment | 236
Misconduct and incentives | 237
The final guidance | 238
Lobbying | 242
Internal environment | 245
Tone from the top and mood in the middle | 245
Understanding the business and its risks | 245
Management information and evidence | 247
Personal archive | 247
Decision registers | 247
Skills | 248
Evidence, evidence and more evidence | 248
Checklist | 249

Chapter 13 Regulatory relationship management   **251**
Dealing with regulators   251
Internal investigations   254
Regulatory (external) investigations   258
   Dawn raids   259
What to do if another group company is under investigation   261
Checklist   263

Chapter 14 Technology   **265**
Cyber resilience   266
   Good and better practice cyber resilience   268
   Board responsibility   270
   Case study: Ransomware attacks and what to do about them   270
Data protection   272
Nuisance calls   275
Fintech, regtech and insurtech   276
Checklist   281

Chapter 15 Overview of related global developments   **283**
The Financial Stability Board   283
Asia   284
   Hong Kong   284
   Singapore   286
Australia   287
   Case study for compliance and prevention of money laundering breaches   290
Europe   291
   Holland   291
   Republic of Ireland   292
Middle East   295
   United Arab Emirates (UAE)   295
North America   298
   Canada   298
   USA   300
Checklist   303

Appendix 1 Full timeline   **305**
The financial crisis   305
The reviews   306
The LIBOR scandal becomes public   307
Reviews and recommendations   307
New regulatory structure   308
Industry consultation on new accountability regime   308
The new Senior Managers Regime takes effect   310
Extending the Senior Managers Regime to all firms   311

Appendix 2 Useful sources for senior managers of UK financial services firms   **313**
UK regulators/policymakers   313
   Financial Conduct Authority (FCA)   313

Contents

Prudential Regulation Authority (PRA)   314
Financial Ombudsman Scheme (FOS)   315
Financial Services Compensation Scheme (FSCS)   315
Information Commissioner's Office (ICO)   316
Financial Reporting Council (FRC)   316
Banking Standards Board (BSB)   317
Supranational policy makers   317
   G20   317
Financial Stability Board (FSB)   318
Bank for International Settlements (BIS) and the Basel Committee on
    Banking Supervision (BCBS or Basel)   319
International Organisation of Securities Commissions (IOSCO)   320
International Association of Insurance Supervisors (IAIS)   321
Organisation for Economic Co-operation and Development (OECD)   321
Financial Crime   321
Financial Action Task Force (FATF)   322
The Wolfsberg Group   322
European bodies   323
European Central Bank (ECB)   323
European Banking Authority (EBA)   324
European Securities and Markets Authority (ESMA)   325
European Insurance and Occupational Pensions Authority (EIOPA)   325
Thought leadership   325
Culture and Conduct Risk 2018: benchmarking five years of
    implementation   326
State of Regulatory Reform 2018   326
Cost of Compliance 2018   326
Five key risks for 2018   327

Index   329

Abbreviations

AFMs	Authorised Fund Managers
AML/CTF	Anti money laundering and counter terrorist financing
APR	Approved Persons Regime
APRA	Australian Prudential Regulatory Authority
ASIC	Australian Securities and Investment Commission
BCBS	Basel Committee on Banking Supervision
BEAR	Banking Executive Accountability Regime (Australia)
BIS	Bank for International Settlements
BSB	Banking Standards Board
BSRC	Banking Standards Review Council
CEO	Chief Executive Officer
CFDs	Contracts for differences
COCON	Code of Conduct (section of FCA handbook)
COO	Chief Operations Officer
CRR	Capital Requirements Regulations
DBS	Disclosure and Barring Service
DFSA	Dubai Financial Services Authority (United Arab Emirates)
DIFC	Dubai International Financial Centre (United Arab Emirates)
DNB	Dutch Central Bank
EBA	European Banking Authority
EBSM	EEA Branch Senior Manager
ECB	European Central Bank
EIOPA	European Insurance and Occupational Pensions Authority
ESMA	European Securities and Markets Authority
ExCo	Executive Committee
FATF	Financial Action Task Force
FCA	Financial Conduct Authority
FCPA	Foreign Corrupt Practices Act 1977 (US)
FEMR	Fair and Effective Markets Review
FI	Financial institution
FICC	Fixed Income, Currency and Commodities
FINRA	Financial Industry Regulatory Authority (US)
FOS	Financial Ombudsman Scheme
FRC	Financial Reporting Council
FSCS	Financial Services Compensation Scheme
FSB	Financial Stability Board

FSF	Financial Stability Forum
GDPR	General Data Protection Regulation
G-SIFIs	Global Systemically Important Financial Institutions
HKMA	Hong Kong Monetary Authority
IA	Internal audit
IAIS	International Association of Insurance Supervisors
ICO	Information Commissioner's Office
IFPRU	The Prudential Sourcebook for Investment Firms
IMF	International Monetary Fund
IOSCO	International Organisation of Securities Commissions
ISPV	Insurance special purpose vehicles
LIBOR	London Inter-bank Offered Rate
MAS	Monetary Authority of Singapore
MI	Management information
MIC	Managers in Charge (Hong Kong)
MiFID II	Markets in Financial Instruments Directive II
MiFIR	Markets in Financial Instruments Regulation
MLRO	Money laundering reporting officer
MRT	Material risk taker
MTF	Multilateral trading facility
NCA	National Crime Agency
NDF	Non-directive firms
NED	Non-executive director
OECD	Organisation for Economic Co-operation and Development
ORSA	Own Risk and Solvency Assessment
OTF	Organised trading facility
RAP	Relevant authorised person
P&L	Profit and loss
PCBS	Parliamentary Commission on Banking Standards
PDMRs	persons discharging managerial responsibilities
PECR	Privacy and Electronic Communications Regulation
PRA	Prudential Regulation Authority
SFC	Securities and Futures Commission (Hong Kong)
SFO	Serious Fraud Office
SHF	Significant harm functions
SIF	Significant influence functions
SIMFs	Senior Insurance Management Functions
SIMR	Senior Insurance Managers Regime
SM&CR	Senior Managers and Certification Regime
SMF	Senior management function
SMR	Senior Managers Regime
SoR	Statement of Responsibilities
STOR	Suspicious transaction and order reporting

Chapter 1

Context and drivers for the new accountability regime

Chapter summary

This chapter covers:

- Context, events and developments which led to new conduct and accountability requirements

- Individuals and organisations involved in developing new rules and requirements

- The existing Approved Persons Regime

- The need for accountability and a new regime

'Too many bankers, especially at the most senior levels, have operated in an environment with insufficient personal responsibility. Top bankers dodged accountability for failings on their watch by claiming ignorance or hiding behind collective decision-making. They then faced little realistic prospect of financial penalties or more serious sanctions commensurate with the severity of the failures with which they were associated.'

Source: PCBS Report on 'Changing Banking for Good' Volume 1:
Summary, and conclusions and recommendations (June 2013)

The financial crisis

1.1   The failure of Northern Rock in September 2007 and the global financial crisis that followed throughout 2008 and 2009 triggered major changes in the regulation of financial services. The immediate post-financial crisis priorities were to minimise the likelihood that firms would fail and to ensure that if a failure did occur there would be no bail out from governments and taxpayers. Accordingly, urgent measures were drawn up in order to stabilise and repair firms' balance sheets and implement liquidity and capital reforms.

The financial crisis also exposed deep systemic failures in the governance and culture within firms. It became evident that the behaviour and culture within banks had played a fundamental role in enabling the conditions which led to the crisis and conduct scandals, from a lack of individual accountability to incentives for excessive risk-taking. Understandably, regulators soon concentrated their attention and resources on behaviours, in particular those of senior individuals, and how they conducted their business.

'Ultimately, the events of the past few years – from the crisis itself, to PPI, to Libor – can be laid at the feet of individuals.'

Source: 'Enforcement and credible deterrence in the FCA', Tracey McDermott, FCA director of enforcement and financial crime, at the Thomson Reuters Compliance and Risk Summit (June 2013)

Without doubt, reform was urgently needed to create lasting change that would prevent such systemic failure ever happening again and, accordingly, unprecedented levels of resources across the industry have been devoted to try and put things right. A decade on from the financial crisis, much has been achieved, but much still remains to be addressed, understood and implemented by firms and individuals within financial services.

'Here and overseas a culture had developed in many areas of financial services where the pursuit of revenue – often short-term revenue – was the primary focus of people's activities and energies. Whether that revenue was derived from selling the wrong products to the wrong people; seeking to manipulate an industry-wide benchmark to suit your own book; or, from using inside information to benefit yourself or your firm is, to a large degree, irrelevant. People within the industry had forgotten why financial services firms existed in the first place. Rewards flowed to those who were seen to make money not to those who built long-lasting client relationships, so people, naturally, thought that was what institutions valued.'

Source: 'Enforcement and credible deterrence in the FCA', Tracey McDermott, FCA director of enforcement and financial crime, at the Thomson Reuters Compliance and Risk Summit (June 2013)

Public confidence in the system remains low because some banks continue to behave improperly, putting short-term profit ahead of serving their customers and communities. Society is still reeling from, and feeling the impact of, the financial crisis. Its trust in banking and financial services further erodes every time another incident of misconduct emerges, from the several billion settlement agreed by Deutsche Bank at the end of 2016 for mis-selling toxic mortgages, to the millions of accounts created without customers' permission to hit sales targets at Wells Fargo.

The regulators continue to take action against firms and levy enormous fines. However, despite the crises and scandals and the impact they have had on customers, shareholders and taxpayers worldwide, it has proved virtually impossible to hold any individuals to account. Certainly, no senior bankers or executives have faced prison for the worst financial failures since the Wall Street crash in 1929. Instead, prosecution has centred on more junior traders who have received custodial sentences for manipulating the London Interbank Offered Rate (LIBOR), including Tom Hayes from Citi Group, whose prison sentence was reduced to 11 years following appeal.

While previous iterations of rulebooks did enable regulators to enforce against senior managers it was often a costly exercise in terms of both time and money. Firms were seen as much easier to enforce against. UK regulators had control over individuals working in the industry through the Approved Persons Regime, but responsibilities within firms were not, in practice, attributed to anyone. This meant there was little realistic prospect of enforcement action against them. Martin Wheatley, former Chief Executive of the UK Financial Conduct Authority (FCA), summed up the problem to the UK Treasury Select Committee in September 2013:

> 'It has been hard to nail an individual against responsibility because matrix organisation structures … means that individuals always diffuse responsibility … evidence is hard to gather in a way that would allow you to take action.'

Fast forward ten years since the financial crisis and there is now a very definite focus on the personal liability and accountability of individuals, with the regulatory approach shifting from rules-based compliance to behaviour and specifically culture and conduct. The regulators' unrelenting focus on changing behaviours, improving standards and ensuring greater alignment between risk and individual reward, to discourage excessive risk-taking and short-termism, are all designed to improve culture.

Each wave of widespread misconduct within firms, ranging from the mis-selling of PPI to retail customers through to LIBOR manipulation in wholesale banking have triggered surges of regulatory, legislative and operational reform across financial services. What is central to the new rules and requirements that have, and are, being developed is making individuals more accountable to regulators. Crucially, the new Senior Managers and Certification Regime (SM&CR) will significantly increase the number of people who are subject to FCA rules and enforcement powers, making it more important than ever for those who work in financial services to understand exactly what is expected of them and to be able to manage their own personal liability.

'Ultimately, we need more individual accountability. Good corporate governance is forged by the ethics of its individuals. That involves moving beyond corporate "rules-based" behavior to "values-based" behavior. We need a greater focus on promoting individual integrity.'

Source: Christine Lagarde, managing director, International Monetary Fund, during a conversation with Janet Yellen, chair of the Board of Governors of the Federal Reserve System (May 2015)

The financial crisis and the response: timeline of events

1.2 Understanding how the relevant global developments have unfolded throughout the decade and the ongoing regulatory and legislative response by UK authorities ever since, is important context to the direction, priorities and spirit of regulatory reform today. Firms within the financial services sector have needed to stay on top of a continuous stream of proposals to respond to, final rules to implement and lessons to learn, in order to strengthen accountability. All whilst there has been no let up in other areas of regulation which have been equally critical to the safety and soundness of the sector ranging from MiFID II through to cyber resilience.

Table 1.1 outlines key events and developments as they have continuously unfolded over the decade. Full details of the timeline of events and relevant publications are set out in **Appendix 1**.

Table 1.1 – Financial crisis – key developments

The financial crisis – a decade of key developments	
Late July/early August 2007	The credit crunch begins as banks begin to stop lending to each other due to fears over exposure to potential losses on high-risk US mortgages.
October 2008	The UK Government unveils an unprecedented £500bn rescue package for the banking industry including £50bn to part-nationalise major UK banks, £200bn into a Special Liquidity Scheme and a further £250bn under a debt guarantee scheme.
March 2009	The Tripartite review Preliminary Report is published which reviews the UK's Tripartite regulatory structure in relation to financial stability, requested by the Shadow Chancellor.
The reviews	
June 2010	The UK Chancellor announces a review of the UK banking industry in his Mansion House speech by an independent commission chaired by Sir John Vickers and the intention to reform the UK regulatory system and replace the tripartite system.
September 2011	The Independent Commission on Banking published its final report 'Changing banking for good' following an interim report including proposals on ring-fencing in April.
Reviews and recommendations	
July 2012	The UK Chancellor announced action in response to the LIBOR scandal becoming public, including the setting up of the Wheatley Committee to undertake a review of the structure and governance of LIBOR and determine legal reforms to incorporate into the Financial Services Bill.

December 2012	The Parliamentary Commission on Banking Standards (PCBS) published its first report focused largely on the structural ring-fencing proposed by the Vickers Commission.
New regulatory structure	
April 2013	The new regulatory structures take effect with three new bodies: The Financial Policy Committee, The Prudential Regulation Authority (PRA) and the Financial Conduct Authority (FCA).
June 2013	The PCBS published its final report also entitled 'Changing Banking for Good' proposing a new framework for individuals including making senior individuals more accountable for their responsibilities.
June 2014	The Fair and Effective Markets Review (FEMR) was launched by the Chancellor and the Governor of the Bank of England to reinforce confidence in the wholesale Fixed Income, Currency and Commodities (FICC) markets following serious misconduct and to influence the international debate on trading practices.
Industry consultation on new accountability regime	
June 2015	The FEMR published its final report, providing an analysis of the root causes of misconduct and other sources of perceived unfairness in FICC markets. It recommended that: • individuals active in FICC markets should be more accountable for their actions; • the UK authorities should extend the regulatory perimeter, broaden the regime to hold senior management to account and toughen sanctions against misconduct.
The new senior managers regime	
March 2016	The Senior Managers Regime (SMR) takes effect for banks.
July 2017	The FCA and PRA publish proposals to extend the SMR to all firms, replacing the Approved Persons Regime with the new Senior Managers and Certification Regime.
December 2018	The extension of the Senior Managers and Certification Regime effective for insurers.
December 2019	Extension of the SM&CR to all financial services firms including investment firms, asset managers, mortgage brokers and consumer credit firms.
December 2020	Conduct Rules apply to staff not holding a senior management function (SMF) or a certification function.

Key parties in driving legislative and regulatory reform

1.3   Development of the new rules and reforms to existing legislation and regulatory requirements have been borne out of a myriad of political intervention, reviews, committees and consultations. Understanding the organisations and people critical to driving the major changes in regulation, and their role and influence, provides the context for the politics, priorities and future direction.

Independent Commission on Banking: 'The Vickers Commission'

> 'Though corporate culture cannot be directly regulated, the structural and governance arrangements proposed here should consolidate the foundations for long-term customer-oriented UK retail banking.'
>
> Source: Independent Commission on Banking Final
> Report Recommendations (September 2011)

1.4   In response to the financial crisis the Chancellor announced a review of the UK banking industry. An Independent Commission on Banking ('the Vickers Commission') was set up in September 2010 to:

- review the structure of the UK banking sector, look at measures to reform the banking system and make recommendations to reduce systemic risk, mitigate moral hazard;
- reduce the likelihood and impact of firm failure; and
- promote competition.

The Commission's Final Report in September 2011 made it clear that national measures were required to enhance the international reform already underway, particularly Basel III and the EU regulatory initiatives. Its recommendations covered: the retail ring fence, loss absorbency and competition. Critically, it recommended that banks' UK retail activities should be carried out in separate subsidiaries which would be legally, economically and operationally separate from the rest of the banking groups to which they belonged and would have distinct governance arrangements and cultures.

> 'The UK retail subsidiaries would be legally, economically and operationally separate from the rest of the banking groups to which they belonged. They would have distinct governance arrangements and should have different cultures.'
>
> Source: Independent Commission on Banking Final
> Report Recommendations (September 2011)

Wheatley Committee

1.5   In response to the LIBOR scandal, the Chancellor announced on 5 July 2012 the establishment of the Wheatley Committee to report on:

- necessary reforms to the current framework for setting and governing LIBOR;

- the adequacy and scope of sanctions to appropriately tackle LIBOR abuse; and

- whether analysis of the failings of LIBOR has implications on other global benchmarks.

LIBOR is the most frequently utilised benchmark for interest rates globally but disturbing events uncovered in the manipulation of LIBOR severely damaged trust and eroded its credibility as a benchmark. The system needed a complete overhaul and the Committee's recommendations covered:

(1) *Regulation* – Introducing a new regulatory structure for LIBOR, including criminal sanctions for those who attempt to manipulate it.

(2) *Governance* – Transferring the oversight and governance role from the British Bankers' Association.

(3) *The rate itself* – A range of technical changes to make the system work better, including streamlining a lot of the currencies and maturities currently used.

Parliamentary Commission on Banking Standards (PCBS)

'Banks in the UK have failed in many respects. They have failed taxpayers, who had to bail out a number of banks including some major institutions, with a cash outlay peaking at £133 billion, equivalent to more than £2,000 for every person in the UK. They have failed many retail customers, with widespread product mis-selling. They have failed their own shareholders, by delivering poor long-term returns and destroying shareholder value.'

Source: PCBS Report on 'Changing Banking for Good' (June 2013)

1.6   Following the LIBOR scandal, further calls for an independent inquiry to examine professional standards in the UK banking industry led to the establishment of the PCBS. It was appointed by both Houses of Parliament to report on professional standards and culture of the UK banking sector, taking account of regulatory and competition investigations into the LIBOR rate-setting process, lessons to be learned about corporate governance, transparency and conflicts of interest, and their implications for regulation and for government policy and to make recommendations for legislative and other actions.

> 'Serious regulatory failure has contributed to the failings in banking standards. The misjudgement of the risks in the pre-crisis period was reinforced by a regulatory approach focused on detailed rules and process which all but guaranteed that the big risks would be missed. Scandals relating to mis-selling by banks were allowed to assume vast proportions, in part because of the slowness and inadequacy of the regulatory response.'
>
> Source: PCBS Report on 'Changing Banking for Good' (June 2013)

The PCBS's first report at the end of 2012 focused on the structural separation or ring-fencing in the banking sector which had been proposed by the Vickers Commission. Its final report in June 2013, 'Changing Banking for Good', arguably led to the most significant transformation of the industry. It criticised both the lack of accountability at senior level and the Approved Persons Regime, which meant that effective enforcement action could not be taken, proposed a new framework for individuals and recommended that banks put in place mechanisms to allow their employees to raise concerns internally. The Commission's proposals were centred on five areas:

- making individual responsibility in banking a reality, especially at the most senior levels. It proposed a new regulatory framework for individuals, a new Remuneration Code and a new approach to sanctions and enforcement against individuals;

- reforming governance within banks to reinforce each bank's responsibility for its own safety and soundness and for the maintenance of standards. It set out reforms to governance to reinforce individual responsibility;

- creating better functioning and more diverse banking markets in order to empower consumers and provide greater discipline on banks to raise standards;

- reinforcing the responsibilities of regulators in the exercise of judgement, replacing mechanical data collection and box ticking;

- specifying the responsibilities of the Government and of future Governments and Parliaments.

Banking Standards Board/Banking Standards Review Council

1.7   On 19 September 2013, Sir Richard Lambert was asked by chairmen of banks to develop proposals for a new organisation to raise standards in UK banking and examine the need for standardised skills and qualifications and consider how to raise overall standards. The Banking Standards Review Council (BSRC) published a consultation in February 2014 and recommendations on 19 May 2014 containing nine recommendations for the BSRC's structure and remit. The body, The Banking Standards Board, began its work in 2015 to promote high standards of behaviours and competence across UK banks and building societies. It is a private sector body funded by members.

'All of those in the financial services industry have a legal, as well as social and ethical, responsibility to act with integrity. We expect to hold them to that standard. Trust and confidence in financial services is at an all-time low. Both the industry and the regulator have an interest in changing this.'

Source: 'Credible deterrence: here to stay', Tracey McDermott, FCA director of enforcement and financial crime at the FSA's Enforcement Conference (July 2012)

Fair and Effective Markets Review

1.8   The FEMR was established by the Chancellor in June 2014, to conduct a review of the way wholesale financial markets operate, to help restore trust in those markets in the wake of a number of recent high-profile abuses, and influence the international debate on trading practices. In line with the recommendations of the PCBS, the FEMR made it clear that it viewed individual integrity and responsibility as fundamental and recommended that elements of the SM&CR should be extended to cover firms active in FICC markets.

On 10 June 2015, the FEMR published its Final Report, setting out 21 recommendations to:

- raise standards, professionalism and accountability of individuals;
- improve the quality, clarity and market-wide understanding of FICC trading practices;
- strengthen regulation of FICC markets in the UK;
- launch international action to raise standards in global FICC markets;
- promote fairer FICC market structures while also enhancing effectiveness;
- promote forward-looking conduct risk identification and mitigation.

'Frankly, until individuals have a meaningful sense of responsibility for their actions – particularly in a high-reward environment – governance issues are unlikely to be reduced.'

Source: 'Confidence to crisis and back', speech by Martin Wheatley, CEO, FCA (June 2015)

Tripartite review

1.9   In Autumn 2008, the shadow Chancellor asked Sir James Sassoon to carry out a review of the UK's Tripartite regulatory structure for handling matters of financial stability. The preliminary report was published in March 2009 and recommended a significant overhaul in the UK, setting out five options for restructuring the regulatory system.

- *Option 1.* The FSA should retain its responsibilities but move to a new structure with Prudential and Conduct of Business divisions rather than its focus on Retail and Wholesale divisions.

- *Option 2.* The FSA should be reorganised as in option 1 but there should also be new statutory powers for the Bank of England to take direct action in respect of individual regulated firms where there was a threat to overall financial market stability.

- *Option 3.* The FSA should be abolished and replaced by two separate regulators, one with responsibility for prudential regulation and one for conduct of business regulation.

- *Option 4.* A combination of options 2 and 3, with the Bank of England or Tripartite having power to step in over the head of the micro-prudential regulator (ie the supervisors of individual firms) in exceptional circumstances.

- *Option 5.* Under options 3 and 4, the micro-prudential regulator of banks, or of the whole financial sector, could be folded into the Bank of England.

It was highly critical of the current system stating that:

'The financial authorities did not have clearly defined powers (or responsibilities) to take pre-emptive action in response to the threats to systemic stability, as opposed to the stability of individual firms, which emerged over a number of years leading up to the 2007 crisis; the authorities lacked appropriate instruments to mitigate these risks; there was inadequate enforcement of existing prudential regulation; and the authorities were poorly coordinated and inadequately equipped to handle the crisis when it hit.'

UK regulators: the Prudential Regulation Authority (PRA) and the Financial Conduct Authority (FCA)

1.10   In April 2013, a new regulatory framework came into force under the Financial Services Act 2012. The FSA, which had previously been responsible for the regulation of financial firms from both a prudential and conduct perspective ceased to exist.

The PRA became part of the Bank of England, responsible for the microprudential regulation of deposit-takers, insurers and major investment firms. The FCA, a separate institution, became responsible for the conduct regulation of all financial services firms. This includes acting to prevent market abuse and ensuring that financial firms treat customers fairly. In doing so, its aim is to advance the protection of consumers, the integrity of the UK financial system and promote effective competition. The FCA is also responsible for the microprudential regulation of those financial services firms not supervised by the PRA including asset managers, hedge funds, many broker-dealers and independent financial advisers.

The new regulators developed the new rules and guidance relating to conduct and accountability underpinned by the Financial Services (Banking Reform) Act 2013 legislative framework. The Bill set out the new structure for banking, specifically ring-fencing retail deposits and lending from investment banking activities and amendments were introduced to implement the PCBS's recommendations. The Senior Persons Regime was re-named the Senior Managers Regime and the licensing regime was termed the Certification Regime.

In May 2016, the Government introduced the Bank of England and Financial Services Act 2016 which made changes to the SM&CR for banks and extended it to all Financial Services and Markets Act authorised firms.

'Earlier this month, we introduced the new Senior Managers Regime. The aim of this regime is to establish clear responsibilities for senior managers, including chairs of Board Committees. This is not to create new responsibilities, but rather to be clear on what those responsibilities are, and then to supervise to hold individuals to those responsibilities. In the previous regime, we had too many examples of individuals shirking their responsibilities. My strong view is that senior figures cannot delegate responsibilities. We will then direct our supervision to support this new regime operating effectively.'

Source: 'Defining the objectives and goals of supervision', speech by Andrew Bailey, Chief Executive, PRA (March 2016)

The Financial Stability Board (FSB)

1.11   The FSB was established in April 2009 as the successor to the Financial Stability Forum (FSF) with a broadened mandate to promote financial stability. The FSB has assumed a key role in promoting the reform of international financial regulation. Its predecessor institution was founded in 1999 by the G7 Finance Ministers and Central Bank Governors following recommendations for a new structure for enhancing cooperation among the national and international supervisory bodies and international financial institutions so as to promote stability in the international financial system.

In November 2008, the leaders of the G20 countries called for a larger membership of the FSF to strengthen its effectiveness as a mechanism for national authorities, standard-setting bodies and international financial institutions to address vulnerabilities and to develop and implement strong regulatory, supervisory and other policies in the interest of financial stability. The FSB has been calling for improved corporate governance and supervisory structures within banks since 2010, and has published a number of papers on the subject.

> 'You must take responsibility for understanding and managing the risks in your business, you cannot delegate and forget, and you cannot hide in labyrinthine structures where it is all too easy for everyone to say it was not me.'
>
> Source: 'Wholesale markets and risk: FEMR and beyond', speech by Tracey McDermott, acting CEO, FCA, at the British Bankers' Association Conference (July 2015)

The Approved Persons Regime

1.12   Individuals who work in the financial services industry have been regulated through the Approved Persons Regime. Under this regime, financial services firms cannot employ a person to perform a 'controlled function', unless the individual has been approved by the PRA or the FCA following an application by the firm concerned.

Approved persons have to comply with the statements of principle which are binding standards of professional conduct issued by the regulators. The regulators can take enforcement action where there have been breaches of the statements of principle. They may also take enforcement action against approved persons for being knowingly concerned in a breach of regulatory requirements by the firm.

This regulatory regime was in place for the approval and oversight of individuals at the time of the financial crisis. It has operated alongside the new Senior Managers and Certification Regime, applying to firms which fall outside the scope of the SMR and Senior Insurance Managers Regime (SIMR). The main purpose of the Approved Persons Regime is the protection of consumers and the UK financial system by ensuring the calibre of individuals carrying on activities within the financial services industry.

The PCBS was very critical of the Approved Persons Regime and took the view that it was too broad and insufficiently focused on senior management. It was also only used when a person was entering the industry, changing jobs, or as a result of enforcement action, by which time it was too late. In contrast it needed to be relevant for a financial services employee's entire career.

It concluded that:

- the Approved Persons Regime acted mainly as an initial gateway rather than as a system for the effective ongoing supervision of the most important individuals in firms;
- there was a lack of clarity of the responsibilities of individuals at senior level;

- institutions did not take enough responsibility for the fitness and propriety of their own staff at more junior levels;

- there were gaps in the regulators' enforcement powers.

The serious flaws identified in the regime in practice have been the catalyst for the new individual accountability regime. The PCBS anticipated that the issues it had identified in relation to the Approved Persons Regime were unlikely to be confined to the banking sector, but were concerned that extending the proposed reforms across all sectors would delay implementation in banks. For that reason, the reforms were prioritised for the banking sector.

> The existing framework – the 'Approved Persons' regime ... was, the [Banking Standards] Commission concluded, a complex and confused mess. It failed to perform any of its varied roles to the necessary standard: it was the mechanism through which individuals could notionally be sanctioned for poor behaviour, but its coverage was woefully narrow and it did not ensure that individual responsibilities were adequately defined, restricting regulators' ability to take enforcement action; and it operated mostly as an initial gateway to taking up a post, rather than serving as a system through which the regulators could ensure the continuing exercise of individual responsibility at the most senior levels within banks.'
>
> Source: Statement by former Members of the Parliamentary
> Commission on Banking Standards (November 2014)

Need for accountability and the new regime

1.13

> 'One thing that the introduction of the Senior Managers Regime will do is hard-wire responsibility for good conduct into the firm's governance.'
>
> Source: Speech by Tracey McDermott, FCA director of supervision, investment,
> wholesale and specialists, delivered at the British Bankers' Association
> Conference 'Wholesale Markets and Risk: FEMR and beyond' (July 2015)

The new regime was designed to reintroduce and reinforce professional accountability to the industry. Firms' senior managers have a crucial role in delivering effective governance. This includes taking personal responsibility and being accountable for their decisions and exercising rigorous oversight of the business areas they lead. The SMR is about being clearer on its expectations of individuals within firms and being able to hold them personally to account if they do not meet these expectations.

The new framework for individuals proposed by the PCBS recommended the following elements:

- a Senior Persons Regime, which would ensure that the key responsibilities within banks are assigned to specific individuals, who are made fully and unambiguously aware of those responsibilities and made to understand that they will be held to account for how they carry them out;

- a Licensing Regime alongside the Senior Persons Regime, to apply to other bank staff whose actions or behaviour could seriously harm the bank, its reputation or its customers;

- the replacement of the Statements of Principles and the associated codes of practice, which are incomplete and unclear in their application, with a single set of Banking Standards Rules to be drawn up by the regulators; these rules would apply to both senior persons and licensed bank staff and a breach would constitute grounds for enforcement action by the regulators.

The SMR and individual accountability does not replace other forms of governance within firms or mean that senior managers can no longer delegate activities or that they must clear everything with their compliance team. It simply requires that businesses are run well and that senior managers must take responsibility for understanding and managing the risks in their business. Senior managers cannot simply delegate and then have no further oversight of risks. Nor can they operate or hide within a complex structure that allows them to avoid responsibility because it is unclear who is responsible and accountable.

Checklist

1.14   The checklist below offers practical questions for compliance practitioners, senior individuals and financial services professionals to consider.

Checklist

- Have you implemented a process for staying on top of announcements and developments from regulators, including emerging thinking through speeches, in relation to the individual accountability requirements?

- Do you have a mechanism for understanding best practices within the industry in relation to practical implementation of the new regime and to compare and benchmark your approach to peers within the industry?

- Are you clear which requirements apply to both your firm and to different individuals?

- Could you explain to a regulator how your firm has adopted the spirit of the rules and demonstrate that staff understand that it is a regulatory priority?

Chapter 2

Key changes from previous regime

Chapter summary

The shift from the previous Approved Persons Regime to the Senior Managers and Certification Regime (SM&CR) has introduced a wealth of changes for firms and senior managers. Three key changes and their practical ramifications are covered in this chapter:

- Requirement for firms to certify employees as fit and proper
- Requirement for senior managers to take 'reasonable steps'
- Application of Conduct Rules to all employees

'The essence of the regime is a statutory provision created by the Bank of England and Financial Services Act 2016 which created what is called the duty of responsibility. The duty of responsibility imposes an obligation on senior managers to take such steps as a person in their position could reasonably be expected to take to avoid the firm from contravening a relevant requirement. It is the first statutory duty of its kind and it is significant for that fact alone because previously conduct rules for senior management were the result of regulatory rather than parliamentary processes. In enforcing this duty, the FCA must establish, first that the firm committed a relevant contravention of our requirements; secondly that the defendant was the senior person responsible for the activities in question and thirdly the defendant failed to take such reasonable steps to avoid or prevent the firm from contravening.

While the FCA's Handbook included Conduct Rules for individuals in authorised firms, the key difference under the Senior Managers Regime is that specific senior management responsibilities have now been mapped to identify individuals within firms, with Statements of Responsibility which make it clear what each senior manager, in fact, has responsibility for. The regime is also supported by Conduct Rules that apply to all staff in the firm and employees who undertake roles which could pose a risk of significant harm to the firm or its customers are also required to be certified by the firm as fit and proper.'

Source: 'The expanding scope of individual accountability for corporate misconduct', speech by Mark Steward, Director of Enforcement and Market Oversight at the FCA (March 2017)

Introduction

2.1   UK financial services regulators have always had the power to enforce against individuals, but in practical terms it was found to be easier to hold firms to account. More often than not authorised firms settled early, undertook the required remedial action and paid the ever-increasing fines as simply another cost of doing business. Individuals, on the other hand, were seen to fight tooth and nail as their professional reputation, and possibly even livelihood, was on the line should a regulatory sanction be imposed. Pre-financial crisis the sense was that the required 'good customer outcomes' could be achieved with the Approved Persons Regime. Post financial crisis the political climate changed radically with a public clamour for senior individuals to be, and seen to be, held responsible for the actions (or inactions) of their firms.

As has been discussed earlier (see **1.2** above) the SM&CR came into force in March 2016 for banks, building societies, UK branches of non-EEA banks, credit unions and PRA-designated investment firms, and enhanced significantly the expectations around the responsibility and accountability of not only senior individuals but also almost all employees of the firms covered. A parallel SM&CR regime for insurers will come into force in December 2018 and a tiered approach to SM&CR will be rolled out to (almost) all other financial services firms in December 2019.

Over and above the previous Approved Persons Regime, there are three key changes consistent to all versions of SM&CR, with a series of practical consequences, for firms and their senior managers to consider:

- requirement for firms to certify employees as fit and proper;
- requirement for senior managers to take 'reasonable steps';
- application of individual Conduct Rules to all employees.

'Fit and proper'

2.2   The SM&CR places an explicit requirement on firms to certify, both on recruitment and then annually, as fit and proper any individual who performs a function that could cause significant harm to the firm or its customers.

The Certification Regime requires that all employees who could cause significant harm are duly identified and then certified as fit and proper for their role. Certified persons perform either an FCA-specified significant harm function or a PRA certification function. The introduction of the Certification Regime puts the regulatory focus back onto the firms themselves. In what could be seen as a reversal of approach, the Certification Regime expects firms to self-certify and monitor continuously that its employees are, and remain, fit and proper. Under the previous Approved Persons Regime, all persons performing a 'controlled function' were subject to regulatory approval with, in effect, the regulator being seen to certify employees.

Senior managers need to be aware that the standards of fitness and propriety are both quantitative and qualitative and apply to individuals subject to the Certification Regime as well as those caught under SM&CR. In all instances the firm itself must be satisfied, and be able to evidence, that an individual is deemed fit and proper for the role or function to be performed. The regulators have set out a number of designated assessment criteria but these should be seen as only high-level guidance with the need to ensure each case is treated on a separate basis with extensive, documented checks tailored to the position being filled and the candidate being considered.

The main assessment criteria for individuals are set out in the FCA's FIT ('fit and proper test for approved persons') sourcebook (available at www.handbook.fca. org.uk/handbook/FIT/1/?view=chapter) and make clear that the firm must have 'particular regard' to whether or not the candidate:

- has obtained a qualification; or
- has undergone, or is undergoing, training; or
- possesses a level of competence; or
- has the personal characteristics,

as required by the rules made by the regulators.

That said, in the FCA's view, the most important considerations will be the person's:

- honesty, integrity and reputation;
- competence and capability; and
- financial soundness.

In assessing fitness and propriety, the FCA will also take account of the activities, permissions and markets within which a firm operates and, in particular, consider:

- the nature, scale and complexity of its business, the nature and range of financial services and activities undertaken in the course of that business; and
- whether the candidate or person has the knowledge, skills and experience to perform the specific role that the candidate or person is intended to perform.

Where the person concerned is a candidate for a position in the management of the firm, there is an additional requirement to ensure that the management body, as a collective, possesses adequate knowledge, skills and experience to understand the firm's activities.

The FCA may choose to interview senior individuals as part of the assessment process. Both firms and the individuals concerned need to ensure that they are fully prepared or else risk the application being delayed or refused, although in practical terms, if it appears that an application is to be refused the firm usually chooses to withdraw it before a formal refusal is confirmed.

Honesty, integrity and reputation

2.3   When assessing honesty, integrity and reputation, the regulator will consider matters such as criminal convictions, adverse findings in civil proceedings and investigations or disciplinary proceedings. The FCA has produced something of a, non-exhaustive, shopping list of factors which may be considered 'adverse' when considering a person's honesty, integrity and reputation.

Potential adverse factors for firms to consider when assessing honesty, integrity and reputation:

- whether the person has been convicted of any criminal offence; this *must* include, where provided for by the Rehabilitation Exceptions Orders to the Rehabilitation of Offenders Act 1974 or the Rehabilitation of Offenders (Northern Ireland) Order 1978 (as applicable), any spent convictions; particular consideration will be given to offences of dishonesty, fraud, financial crime or an offence under legislation relating to companies, building societies, industrial and provident societies, credit unions, friendly societies, banking, other financial services, insolvency, consumer credit companies, insurance, consumer protection, money laundering, market manipulation and insider dealing, whether or not in the UK;

- whether the person has been the subject of any adverse finding or any settlement in civil proceedings, particularly in connection with investment or other financial business, misconduct, fraud or the formation or management of a body corporate;

- whether the person has been the subject of, or interviewed in the course of, any existing or previous investigation or disciplinary proceedings, by the appropriate regulator, by other regulatory authorities (including a previous regulator), clearing houses and exchanges, professional bodies, or government bodies or agencies;

- whether the person is, or has been, the subject of any proceedings of a disciplinary or criminal nature, or has been notified of any potential proceedings or of any investigation which might lead to those proceedings;

- whether the person has contravened any of the requirements and standards of the regulatory system or the equivalent standards or requirements of other regulatory authorities (including a previous regulator), clearing houses and exchanges, professional bodies, or government bodies or agencies;

- whether the person has been the subject of any justified complaint relating to regulated activities;

- whether the person has been involved with a company, partnership or other organisation that has been refused registration, authorisation, membership or a licence to carry out a trade, business or profession, or has had that registration, authorisation, membership or licence revoked, withdrawn or terminated, or has been expelled by a regulatory or government body;

- whether, as a result of the removal of the relevant licence, registration or other authority, the person has been refused the right to carry on a trade, business or profession requiring a licence, registration or other authority;

- whether the person has been a director, partner, or concerned in the management, of a business that has gone into insolvency, liquidation or administration while the person has been connected with that organisation or within one year of that connection;

- whether the person, or any business with which the person has been involved, has been investigated, disciplined, censured or suspended or criticised by a regulatory or professional body, a court or tribunal, whether publicly or privately;

- whether the person has been dismissed, or asked to resign and resigned, from employment or from a position of trust, fiduciary appointment or similar;

- whether the person has ever been disqualified from acting as a director or disqualified from acting in any managerial capacity;

- whether, in the past, the person has been candid and truthful in all his dealings with any regulatory body and whether the person demonstrates a readiness and willingness to comply with the requirements and standards of the regulatory system and with other legal, regulatory and professional requirements and standards.

Source: FCA FIT 2.1.3G available at www.handbook.
fca.org.uk/handbook/FIT/2/1.html#D3

Competence and capability

2.4   In determining a person's competence and capability, the regulator will again take a broad brush, judgement-based, approach when considering the fulfilment of training and competence requirements, whether the person has demonstrated experience and training designed to ensure that he or she has the requisite skills, knowledge and capacity and whether the person has adequate time to perform the function or role under consideration. The last point is particularly pertinent for non-executive directorship roles when the person may have other substantial calls on his or her time.

Financial soundness

2.5   In determining a person's financial soundness, the regulator will have regard to matters including, but not limited to, whether the person has been the subject of any judgment debt or award that remains outstanding or was not satisfied during the relevant annual period and whether the person has made arrangements with his or her creditors or filed for bankruptcy. That said, being of limited financial means does not, in and of itself, affect an individual's potential suitability to be authorised under the SMR or the Certification Regime.

Due diligence and documentation

2.6   Firms and their senior manager should not underestimate the range and nature of the checks expected to be undertaken on anyone subject to either SMR or the Certification Regime. This holds equally true if someone (either an internal or external candidate) is transferring from overseas where the same level of due diligence is expected to be undertaken. It should be stating the obvious that all checks should be meticulously documented together with the detailed assessment as to whether or not the person is deemed to be fit and proper. Senior managers need to be helpful, open and honest as part of the assessment of fitness and propriety and will need to ensure that any and all due diligence evidence gathered is correct and up to date.

As a matter of good practice, the compliance function should be involved alongside human resources in the setting of the fit and proper criteria for the firm as well as reviewing the documentation gathered and ultimate decision reached. If nothing else, the compliance function needs to ensure that the firm fulfils its legal requirement to undertake the required fit and proper assessments both upon recruitment and then also on an annual basis. It is critical that both the initial assessment and the annual review are documented in detail and stand up to both audit and any regulatory scrutiny. While the initial assessment of fitness and propriety is likely to be a one-off process, any annual review needs to take into consideration not only all changes to the person's role but also to the collective capability of any relevant management body. Firms may choose to undertake a skills audit of all management bodies alongside a continuing annual review and re-certification of senior individuals.

Once the firm has determined that a candidate is fit and proper, it should ensure that the relevant application has been completed by both the firm and the candidate, and accurately records and discloses all information. The relevant forms can be found in FCA SUP 10C Annex 2D Form A: Application to perform senior management functions (at www.handbook.fca.org.uk/handbook/SUP/10C/?view=chapter).

As just one example, the 'Long Form A' for UK relevant authorised persons and third country relevant authorised persons only runs to 21 pages and contains a series of questions (in section 5) which require 'yes' or 'no' answers relating to the candidate's fitness and propriety (at www.handbook.fca.org.uk/form/sup/ SUP_10C_ann_02_Long_A_NON-EEA_20171112.pdf). Supporting the application there should usually be a number of documents collected by the firm including (but not limited to):

- specifically defined regulatory references for all employment for the past six years;
- qualification certificates;
- credit checks;
- criminal record checks;
- directorship checks.

In assessing fitness and propriety, the regulators may grant permission outright or impose conditions, time limits and/or variations on senior management function approvals. Any conditions will apply on a case-by-case basis and only be applied to advance the regulators' respective objectives and seek to ensure that a firm remains in compliance with the threshold conditions for authorisation. Firms need to be aware that non or late fulfilment of a condition could mean a senior individual is deemed to have failed to observe minimum standards of fitness and propriety and may trigger disciplinary action, which could involve the relevant regulator withdrawing approval.

As with all regulatory processes, firms and their compliance officers in particular, should seek to build and maintain an open and constructive relationship with all relevant regulators. With regard to fitness and propriety questions, this would enable firms to discuss potential senior candidates with the regulator and to have early sight of any potential regulatory concerns or considerations.

While all senior individuals are subject to fitness and propriety checks, those subject to the Certification Regime will require the firm to issue a certificate which:

- states that the firm is satisfied that the person is fit and proper to perform the function to which the certification relates; and
- sets out the aspects of the affairs of the firm in which the person will be involved in performing the function.

The certificate is valid for 12 months, beginning on the day it is issued. If the firm refuses to issue (or renew) an individual's certificate, the firm must take reasonable care to ensure that the individual does not (or ceases) to perform the relevant significant harm function or PRA certification function.

As with those subject to SMR, the Certification Regime requires detailed documentation and a continuing assessment of fitness and propriety which may need to be invoked on a more than annual basis if the person's role and responsibilities change. Firms need to put in place suitable systems and controls infrastructure to ensure all changes to roles and responsibilities are both notified and then also expressly assessed to determine whether or not a change or update is required to the certificate in place. Critically, such an assessment must take place, and take place successfully, before the person takes up a new significant harm function or PRA certification function.

Senior individuals (including those subject to the Certification Regime) would be well advised to maintain a personal record of their own fitness and propriety as part of a suite of evidence to demonstrate the discharge of all regulatory accountabilities and, in turn, manage their personal regulatory risk. This is even more important when senior individuals change roles and/or firms. It is not necessarily fair, but yesterday's business will be judged by today's evolving cultural standards and, as such, the need to have contemporaneous evidence of compliance is an essential part of mitigating the added potential complication of hindsight.

Banking Standards Board

2.7   The Banking Standards Board (BSB) was established in April 2015 with the aim of promoting high standards of behaviour and competence across UK banks and building societies. The BSB is a private sector body funded by membership subscriptions and open to all banks and building societies operating in the UK. It is neither a regulator nor a trade association; it has no statutory powers, and it will not speak or lobby for the industry. It will, instead, provide challenge, support and scrutiny for firms committed to rebuilding the sector's reputation, and it will provide impartial and objective assessments of the industry's progress.

On that basis, in February 2017 the BSB published their 'Statement of Good Practice 1' (see www.bankingstandardsboard.org.uk/pdf/Assessing-F&P-Statement-of-Good-Practice.pdf) on the Certification Regime: fitness and propriety assessment principles setting out codified good, and better, practice intended to help firms implement the Certification Regime effectively, by providing a high-level set of principles relating to the assessment of fitness and propriety. A year later, in February 2018, the BSB followed up with additional guidance specifically dealing with the risks and issues together with 'pass/fail criteria' that may arise when firms are assessing the fitness and propriety of their staff (see www.bankingstandardsboard. org.uk/wp-content/uploads/2018/02/BSB-Certification-decision-guidance-draft-incorp-reg-comments-v0.3.pdf).

> 'BSB good practice guidance allows member firms and others in the sector to reference their own policies and practices against a set of aspirational guiding principles. It is developed in partnership with BSB members and through public consultation, and represents a pooling of knowledge and experience. It does not impose any legal or regulatory obligations on BSB members, nor does it replace regulation (and where relevant, this guidance should support both the letter and spirit of regulation). In the event of inconsistency, applicable laws,

> rules and regulations should prevail. This guidance is additional to all of the relevant regulatory requirements, and builds on, rather than substitutes for them.'
>
> Source: 'About this guidance', Supporting guidance: 'Establishing pass/fail criteria and evidencing the fitness and propriety assessment', BSB, (February 2018)

Firms would be well advised to look to bodies such as the BSB for benchmarked guidance and emerging good practice when seeking to comply with the requirements of the Certification Regime. Indeed, in the event of an issue, the regulators may well ask why a firm has not followed such practical and detailed industry guidance.

'Reasonable steps'

2.8   The requirement for senior managers to take 'reasonable steps' is not new but has been enhanced in the Senior Manager Conduct Rules which make crystal clear the expectations placed on those covered by SMR with a specific statutory requirement for senior managers to take reasonable steps to prevent regulatory breaches in their areas of responsibility and to cooperate with the FCA and PRA.

Senior Manager Conduct Rules

(1) You must take reasonable steps to ensure that the business of the firm for which you are responsible is controlled effectively.

(2) You must take reasonable steps to ensure that the business of the firm for which you are responsible complies with the relevant requirements and standards of the regulatory system.

(3) You must take reasonable steps to ensure that any delegation of your responsibilities is to an appropriate person and that you oversee the discharge of the delegated responsibility effectively.

(4) You must disclose appropriately any information of which the FCA or PRA would reasonably expect notice.

Senior Manager Conduct Rules

2.9   Senior managers are responsible, personally, for any breaches of the Conduct Rules. The practical ramifications of the Conduct Rules centre around the need for senior individuals to define the precise scope of their remit and the adequacy of the control and decision-making mechanisms in place. In the event of a regulatory breach, senior managers will be expected to have not only taken reasonable steps but to be able to evidence those steps. What constitutes 'reasonable' will be assessed on a case-by-case basis by the regulator. Two immediate practical actions which senior managers may wish to consider are:

- a thorough review of all management information flowing through the corporate governance and risk reporting mechanisms of the firm. This would include a review of any and all underlying assumptions, the basis on which risk reporting is undertaken (bearing in mind that the Financial Stability Board described board risk reporting as 'voluminous and not easily understood') and the quality of line of sight gained to emerging risks;

- the need to ensure that all risk, compliance and other meetings are minuted in detail and provide the required depth of evidence to show 'reasonable steps' in action.

The regulators have indicated that they will assess 'controls' put in place by senior managers with respect to the nature, scale and complexity of the business. This is particularly pertinent as it is for the regulator to establish (and not the senior individual) that the senior manager failed to take steps that were reasonable for a person in that position to take to prevent a regulatory breach.

A critical element of 'reasonable steps' begins before the senior manager has even started any new role or takes up new responsibilities. Firms themselves are required to take all reasonable steps to make sure that a person taking a senior manager role has 'all the information and materials they could reasonably expect to have to do their job effectively'. Firms are required to have a policy which shows how they comply with this requirement and to maintain adequate records to evidence compliance with the policy.

The FCA requires that any handover includes details about unresolved or possible breaches of the regulatory system and any unresolved concerns expressed by the FCA, PRA or other regulator. The emphasis is on the need for the handover to be a practical and helpful document and not just a record of activities undertaken. The supporting materials should include an assessment of what issues remain to be prioritised and should contain judgement and opinion as well as relevant facts and figures.

One obvious means of compliance is for the predecessor in a role to prepare a comprehensive handover note as part of an orderly transfer of responsibilities, although it is acknowledged that this is not always possible.

Effective control

2.10   Senior manager conduct rule 1 requires senior managers to take reasonable steps to ensure that the business of the firm for which they are responsible is controlled effectively. The FCA has given the following examples of conduct that would be in breach of the rule:

- failing to take reasonable steps to apportion responsibilities for all areas of the business under the senior manager's control;

- failing to take reasonable steps to apportion responsibilities clearly among those to whom responsibilities have been delegated;

- in the case of a manager who is responsible for dealing with the apportionment of responsibilities, failing to take reasonable care to maintain a clear and appropriate apportionment of responsibilities;

- failing to take reasonable steps to ensure that suitable individuals are responsible for those aspects of the business under the control of a senior conduct rules staff member.

The PRA guidance includes the following:

- Strategy and plans will often dictate the risk that the business is prepared to take on and high-level controls will dictate how the business is to be run. If the strategy of the business is to enter high-risk areas, then the degree of control and strength of monitoring reasonably required within the business will be higher. A person performing a senior management function should take this into account in organising the business for which they are responsible.

- The organisation of the business and the responsibilities of those within it should be clearly defined. Reporting lines should be clear to staff. Where staff have dual reporting lines there is a greater need to ensure that the responsibility and accountability of each individual line manager is clearly set out and understood.

Compliance with relevant requirements and standards

2.11   Senior manager conduct rule 2 requires senior managers to take reasonable steps to ensure that the business of the firm for which they are responsible complies with relevant requirements and standards of the regulatory regime. In this instance, 'standards' includes the evolving regulatory focus on, and approach to, culture and conduct risk. The FCA has given the following examples of conduct that would be in breach of the rule:

- Failing to take reasonable steps to implement (either personally or through a compliance department or other departments) adequate and appropriate systems of control to comply with the relevant requirements and standards of the regulatory system for the activities of the firm.

- Failing to take reasonable steps to monitor (either personally or through a compliance department or other departments) compliance with the relevant requirements and standards of the regulatory system for the activities of the firm in question.

- Failing to take reasonable steps to inform themselves adequately about the reason why significant breaches (suspected or actual) of the relevant requirements and standards of the regulatory system for the activities of the firm may have arisen (taking account of the systems and procedures in place).

- Failing to take reasonable steps to ensure that procedures and systems of control are reviewed and, if appropriate, improved, following the identification of significant breaches (suspected or actual) of the relevant requirements and standards of the regulatory system relating to the activities of the firm.

The PRA guidance includes the following:

- A person performing a senior management function should take reasonable steps both to ensure the firm's compliance with the relevant requirements and standards of the regulatory system, and to ensure that all staff are aware of the need for compliance.

- A person performing a senior management function role need not personally put in place the systems and controls in the business. Whether the senior manager does this depends on their specific role and responsibilities. The senior manager should, however, take reasonable steps to ensure that the business has operating procedures and systems which include well-defined steps for complying with relevant requirements and standards of the regulatory system and for ensuring that the business is run prudently.

Delegation

2.12   Senior manager conduct rule 3 requires senior managers to take reasonable steps to ensure that any delegation of their responsibilities is to an appropriate person and that they oversee the discharge of the delegated responsibility effectively. The FCA has given the following examples of conduct that would be in breach of the rule:

- Failing to take reasonable steps to maintain an appropriate level of understanding about an issue or part of the business that the senior conduct rules staff member has delegated to an individual (whether in-house or outside contractors). This includes:
  - disregarding an issue or part of the business once it has been delegated;
  - failing to require adequate reports once the resolution of an issue or management of part of the business has been delegated; and
  - accepting implausible or unsatisfactory explanations from delegates without testing their accuracy.

- Failing to supervise and monitor adequately the individual(s) (whether in-house or outside contractors) to whom responsibility for dealing with an issue or authority for dealing with a part of the business has been delegated. This includes any failure to:
  - take personal action where progress is unreasonably slow, or where implausible or unsatisfactory explanations are provided; or
  - review the performance of an outside contractor in connection with the delegated issue or business.

The PRA guidance includes the following:

- A person performing a senior management function should take reasonable steps to ensure that systems are in place that result in issues being addressed at the appropriate level. When issues come to the senior manager's attention, they should deal with them in an appropriate way.

- Delegating the authority for dealing with an issue or a part of the business to an individual(s) (whether in-house or outside contractors) without reasonable grounds for believing that the delegate had the necessary capacity, competence, knowledge, seniority or skill to deal with that issue, or to take authority for dealing with that part of the business, exemplifies a failure to comply with this conduct rule.

Cooperation with regulators

2.13   Senior manager conduct rule 4 requires a senior manager to disclose appropriately any information of which the FCA or PRA would reasonably expect notice. This is deemed to be a higher standard of cooperation than that set out in individual conduct rule 3 (see below). In determining whether or not a person's conduct complies with this rule, the FCA will take the following into account, whether:

- it would be reasonable for the individual to assume that the information would be of material significance to the regulator concerned;

- the information related to the individual personally or to his or her firm;

- any decision not to report the matter was taken after reasonable enquiry and analysis of the situation.

The PRA expects that in disclosing appropriately, the person will need to disclose:

- sufficient information for the regulators to be able to understand the full implications of the matter being disclosed;

- in a timely manner;

- to an appropriate contact at the PRA or FCA (or both), which may include the firm's usual supervisory contact.

Individual Conduct Rules

2.14   The Individual Conduct Rules are deceptively simple. From March 2017 the Individual Conduct Rules apply to all employees of banking firms excluding only those who are deemed to be ancillary, such as security guards or post room staff. The increased reach of the Individual Conduct Rules will, quite deliberately, give the regulators the capacity to hold to account almost every individual currently in a

SM&CR firm. Conduct Rules are to be similarly rolled out to almost all employees of all other regulated financial services firms.

Individual Conduct Rules

(1) You must act with integrity (PRA and FCA).

(2) You must act with due skill, care and diligence (PRA and FCA).

(3) You must be open and cooperative with the FCA, the PRA and other regulators (PRA and FCA).

(4) You must pay due regard to the interest of customers and treat them fairly (FCA only).

(5) You must observe proper standards of market conduct (FCA only).

In practical terms this means that staff at all levels can, and will, be held personally liable for breaches of the Individual Conduct Rules. Personal liability can, depending on the nature and severity of the breach, include a fine, a warning or a ban or a combination as part of regulatory enforcement action.

It is a specific responsibility of all firms to ensure that everyone subject to the Individual Conduct Rules is not only aware of that fact but also that reasonable steps are taken to ensure those affected understand the implications of how the rules apply to them. For firms this means a potentially substantial amount of training and, indeed, re-training for all members of staff to ensure an appropriate level of awareness is built and then maintained. Firms will need to take particular care with regard to record keeping so they can evidence robustly that all the required reasonable steps have been taken.

In July 2018 the regulators published policy statements with near final rules for the extension of SM&CR requirements to insurers and all other financial services firms. Experience has shown that it is likely that those firms which are to be brought into the scope of the regime will need to factor in a substantial investment in training on the final applicable Conduct Rules into their preparations.

The Individual Conduct Rules are high level but represent the baseline of expected behaviour in a UK financial services firm. Many firms are required to have risk appetite statements, set at the highest level, which articulate the firm's approach to risk taking and risk management. Any statement of risk appetite should, as a matter of course, reflect the core standards expected of all employees. Most firms should have considered a working definition of conduct risk and equally should ensure that the applicable Conduct Rules are appropriately reflected.

The regulators have given guidance on the practical implications of the Individual Conduct Rules with, in the main, examples of what would be considered to be in breach.

Integrity

2.15   Individual conduct rule 1 requires employees to act with integrity. The FCA has given the following examples of conduct that would be in breach of the rule:

- misleading (or attempting to mislead), the regulators, a client or the firm for who the person works, by act or omission;

- providing false or inaccurate information to the firm (or the firm's auditors) or the regulators;

- recommending an investment to a customer, or carrying out a discretionary transaction for a customer where the person knows that he or she is unable to justify its suitability for that customer;

- procuring the unjustified alteration of prices on illiquid or off-exchange contracts, or both;

- failings to disclose dealings where disclosure is required by the firm's personal account dealing rules;

- misusing the assets or confidential information of a client or of their firm.

Due skill, care and diligence

2.16   Individual conduct rule 2 requires employees to act with due skill, care and diligence. The FCA has given the following examples of conduct that would be in breach of the rule:

- staff recommending an investment to a customer, or carrying out discretionary transactions for a customer where they do not have reasonable grounds to believe that it is suitable for that customer;

- managers failing to take reasonable steps to ensure the business of the firm for which they have responsibility is controlled effectively or failing to adequately inform themselves about the affairs of the business for which they are responsible.

On the PRA side, the focus is on the second element articulated by the FCA such that:

- it is important for a manager (including, but not limited to, a person performing a senior management function) to understand the business for which he or she is responsible. A manager is unlikely to be an expert in all aspects of a complex financial services business. However, the manager should understand and inform himself or herself about the business sufficiently to understand the risks of its trading, credit or other business activities.

- Where unusually profitable business is undertaken, or where the profits are particularly volatile or the business involves funding requirements on the firm beyond those reasonably anticipated, a manager should require explanations from those who report to him or her. Where those explanations are implausible or unsatisfactory, the manager should take steps to test the veracity of those explanations.

Open and cooperative with regulators

2.17   Individual conduct rule 3 requires employees to be open and cooperative with the FCA, the PRA and other regulators. The FCA has given the following examples of conduct that would be in breach including:

- failing to report promptly in accordance with their firm's internal procedures (or, if none exist, direct to the regulator concerned), information in response to questions from the FCA, the PRA, or both;

- failing without good reason to:

    o   inform a regulator of information of which the person was aware in response to questions from the regulator;

    o   attend an interview or answer questions put by a regulator, despite a request or demand having been made; and

    o   supply a regulator with appropriate documents or information when requested or required to do so, and within the time limits attaching to that request or requirement.

The PRA has set out a number of factors to consider in assessing compliance with individual conduct rule 3 including:

- whether a person has provided information in an appropriate manner into the firm's mechanisms for reporting to the regulator(s);

- whether the person has taken steps to influence a decision so as not to report to the regulator concerned;

- whether the person has acted in a way intended to obstruct the reporting of the information to the regulator concerned;

- where relevant to the person's role, the way in which the person has operated, managed or overseen the mechanisms for reporting referred to above; and

- the way in which a person has responded to requests from a relevant regulator.

Treating customers fairly

2.18   Individual conduct rule 4 is only applied by the FCA and requires employees to pay appropriate attention to the interests of customers and treat them fairly. The FCA has given the following examples of conduct that would be in breach including:

- failing to inform a customer of material information in circumstances where they were aware, or ought to have been aware, of such information and of the fact that they should provide it;

- recommending an investment to a customer, or carrying out a discretionary transaction for a customer, where they do not have reasonable grounds to believe that it is suitable for that customer;

- undertaking, recommending or providing advice on a transaction without a reasonable understanding of the risk exposure of the transaction to a customer, including recommending transactions in an investment to a customer without a reasonable understanding of the liability (either potential or actual) of that transaction;

- failing to provide adequate control over a client's assets, including failing to segregate a client's assets, and failing to process a client's payments in a timely manner;

- providing a customer with a product that is different to the one applied for by that customer, unless the customer understands the differences and understands the product he or she has purchased;

- failing to acknowledge, or to seek to resolve, mistakes in dealing with customers;

- failing to provide terms and conditions to which a product or service is subject in a way that is clear and easy for the customer to understand.

As with so much of the practical implications of the regulatory regime in the UK, firms and senior individuals need to ensure that an appropriate level of documentation is built and maintained to evidence the discharge of all personal accountabilities, responsibilities and liabilities. The above 'treating customers fairly' breach list is a mixture of quantitative and qualitative elements each of which require a different approach to the initial policies, procedures, control infrastructure and testing all the way through to record keeping and evidence.

Proper market conduct

2.19   Individual conduct rule 5 is only applied by the FCA and requires employees to observe proper standards of market conduct. The FCA guidance states that firms and persons should consider relevant market codes and exchange rules in this context. The FX Code of Conduct, which came into effect in May 2017, is one such example. Proper market conduct failings also cover the criminal offences of manipulating or attempting to manipulate a benchmark or a market, such as a foreign exchange market.

It is oversimplifying, but if an individual can show that he or she complied with all relevant regulations and market codes, then the catch-all of proper market conduct should not apply.

Checklist

2.20   The checklist below offers practical questions for senior individuals to consider.

Checklist

- Have you built and maintained a suite of evidence designed to demonstrate your individual fitness and propriety together with all 'reasonable steps' taken in compliance with the Senior Manager Conduct Rules?

- Could you explain to a regulator how the firm ensures that all relevant staff are aware of, and comply, with the Individual Conduct Rules?

- Can you explain how the conduct requirements are incorporated into the firm's risk appetite statement and/or working definition of conduct risk?

- Are you comfortable that you fully understand the business for which you are responsible? In particular, do you understand sufficiently the risks of its trading, credit or other business activities?

Chapter 3

Specifics of the Senior Managers and Certification Regime as it applies to banks and large investment firms

Chapter summary

This chapter covers the specifics of how the Senior Managers and Certification Regime (SM&CR) applies in detail to banks and large investment firms and includes consideration of:

- Who is a 'senior manager'
- The senior manager functions
- Regulatory approval
- Statements of Responsibilities
- The Certification Regime
- Regulatory references

'We must move from an excessive reliance on punitive, ex post fines of firms to greater emphasis on more compelling ex ante incentives for individuals, and ultimately a more solid grounding in improved firm culture.'

Source: Mark Carney, Governor of the Bank of England, remarks at the Banking Standards Board Panel: 'Worthy of trust? Law, ethics and culture in banking' (March 2017)

Introduction

3.1   By design, the SM&CR applies to anyone who has a direct influence on a UK-authorised financial services firm. This chapter considers the regime aimed at banks and large asset managers, **Chapter 4** looks at insurers and **Chapter 5** at the extension of SM&CR to all other authorised firms. The key changes between the previous, Approved Persons Regime, and SM&CR are considered in **Chapter 2**.

The SM&CR replaced the Approved Persons Regime for banks, building societies, credit unions and dual-regulated (FCA and PRA regulated) investment firms in March 2016. There are three key parts to SM&CR:

- the Senior Managers Regime (SMR);
- the Certification Regime; and
- the Conduct Rules.

The SMR covers the most senior people in a bank who perform key roles ('senior management functions') and who need FCA approval before they can begin their roles. Every senior manager must have a 'Statement of Responsibilities' that clearly states what they are responsible and accountable for. In addition, there are some specific, 'prescribed' responsibilities that firms must allocate to their senior managers, to make sure there is a senior manager accountable for the SM&CR itself as well as key conduct and prudential risks. A senior manager must also be named as having 'overall' responsibility for each of the firm's business functions and activities.

Firms are also required to compile 'Responsibilities Maps' setting out the responsibilities of their senior managers covering the entire business together with their management and governance arrangements.

At least once a year firms need to certify that senior managers are suitable to do their jobs.

The Certification Regime applies to employees whose role means it is possible for them to cause significant harm to the firm or customers. These roles are called 'certification functions'. Those covered by the Certification Regime do not need to be approved by the regulator, but firms are required to check and certify, at least once a year, that they are fit and proper to perform their role.

The Conduct Rules are high-level standards of behaviour that apply to almost everyone in the banking sector. There are also some Conduct Rules that only apply to senior managers. Firms are required to make sure staff are trained in, and be aware that, the Conduct Rules apply to them, and to notify the regulator when someone breaches a Conduct Rule.

Who is a 'senior manager'?

3.2   The SMR element of the SM&CR applies to individuals who perform key roles (such as the chief executive) or have overall responsibility for whole areas of a firm. From 7 March 2016, the SM&CR has applied to UK banks, building societies, credit unions, UK branches of foreign banks and PRA-designated investment firms. The SMR requires the exact scope of the responsibilities of a senior manager to be accurately documented, and regulatory approval to be granted, *before* the senior manager may perform his or her role.

The associated Certification Regime came into effect from 7 March 2017 and requires the completion of a certification of those who perform either FCA-prescribed 'significant harm functions' or a PRA certification function.

The SM&CR applies at an individual legal entity basis. This is particularly pertinent for financial services groups as firms need to assess exactly which individual has responsibility for what and in which legal entity. There are different versions of the SM&CR depending on the type, nature and size of regulated financial services business conducted and in a group situation it is entirely possible that there will be firms which are subject to different tiers of the regime. That said, some groups may choose to apply the highest tier of the regime to all entities.

This responsibility or accountability for the activities of an authorised legal entity is not dependent on where (either geographically or legally) a senior individual is employed or based. For the absence of doubt, a senior manager could be more closely associated with another group company but may still be performing a senior management function directly on behalf of the firm. Any such senior individuals are not only subject to SMR, including UK regulatory approval, but also the Conduct Rules.

There is no 'one size fits all' and firms and their senior managers must exercise care and clarity to ensure that all appropriate approvals are obtained, documented, reviewed, reconciled and maintained.

Example

An Indian-based senior manager of a large multinational banking group is employed by one of the group's local Indian legal entities. She is responsible for the entire banking group's information technology, including the IT of the UK-authorised firm. Under this scenario, the Indian-based senior manager would be within the scope of SM&CR and classified as a Group Entity Senior Management Function 7 (SMF7). As such, she would need her responsibilities documented in detail, and regulatory approval granted, before she would be able to perform her role with regard to the UK-authorised firm.

Senior Managers Regime

Senior Management Functions

3.3   Senior managers are divided into broad categories, set by either the FCA or PRA, which cover the entire gamut of governance and oversight in an authorised firm. The full list of Senior Management Functions (SMF) for the SM&CR for banks is shown in **Table 3.1** below.

Table 3.1: List of Senior Management Functions for banks

SMF	Description	FCA or PRA Function?	Executive or non-Executive
SMF1	Chief executive function	PRA	Executive
SMF2	Chief finance function	PRA	Executive
SMF3	Executive director function	FCA	Executive
SMF4	Chief risk function	PRA	Executive
SMF5	Head of internal audit function	PRA	Executive
SMF6	Head of key business area function	PRA	Executive
SMF7	Group entity SMF	PRA	Executive
SMF8	Credit union SMF (small credit unions only)	PRA	Executive
SMF9	Chairman function	PRA	Non-Executive
SMF10	Chair of the risk committee function	PRA	Non-Executive
SMF11	Chair of the audit committee function	PRA	Non-Executive
SMF12	Chair of the remuneration committee function	PRA	Non-Executive
SMF13	Chair of the nominations committee function	FCA	Non-Executive
SMF14	Senior independent director function	PRA	Non-Executive
SMF16	Compliance oversight function	FCA	Executive
SMF17	Money laundering reporting function	FCA	Executive
SMF18	Other overall responsibility function	FCA	Executive
SMF19	Head of overseas branch function	PRA	Executive
SMF21	EEA branch senior manager function	FCA	Executive
SMF22	Other local responsibility function	FCA	Executive

A senior management function is one where the person undertaking the role is responsible for managing one or more aspects of the regulated business of the firm and those aspects may involve a risk of serious consequences for either the firm itself or other business or interests in the UK. As might be expected, SMFs cover the activities of the chief executive, chairman, chief financial officer, compliance oversight function and all other governance and senior business roles within the firms. For those covered by the former Approved Persons Regime, SMFs are a direct replacement for the previous significant influence functions. The twin regulatory regime means there is the potential need for multiple approvals depending on the nature of the SMF to be performed. Specifically:

- individuals seeking to perform a PRA-designated SMF will require the PRA's pre-approval and the FCA's consent in order to perform that role;

- individuals seeking to perform an FCA-designated SMF require only the FCA's pre-approval.

Senior individuals and their compliance officers need to ensure that anyone (whether in-house or external) who is a candidate for a SMF does not start to perform any of the activities of that function before approval is granted from the relevant regulator. Firms are required to take 'reasonable care' to ensure that no-one performs a SMF without the appropriate regulatory approval. As a matter of good practice and to minimise any potential delay, senior individuals should be prepared to work with the compliance officer to complete the application (including all supporting documentation) and submit it to the relevant regulator well in advance of the individual commencing the role.

While the need for regulatory approval may be obvious when considering external recruitment for senior roles, it is equally important for any changes to existing in-house roles and responsibilities. As such it should be a key consideration as and when there are any management reorganisations in a regulated firm.

There is a shopping list of possible banking SMFs but firms do not need to 'fill' all of the roles. The number of SMFs to be allocated will vary depending on the size, sophistication, structure and governance of the firm. For example, the chairman of the nominations committee function (SMF13) need only be allocated to a non-executive where the firm has a committee that performs this – if nominations are conducted by the board as a whole, there would be no need to allocate SMF13.

To help firms, the FCA has given an example of its own structure with allocated senior management functions which is reproduced in **Chapter 7** at **7.3**.

As a matter of course the regulators expect firms to nominate the most senior individual for each SMF. Once a designation has been approved by the regulator(s), individual SMFs are held personally liable for all of the responsibilities inherent in, or allocated to, that SMF.

Fit and proper

'Since codes are of little use if no one reads, follows or enforces them, the UK has instituted a unique Senior Managers Regime to embed cultures of risk awareness, openness and ethical behaviour. Based on its early successes, international authorities are now considering following the UK's lead.'

Source: Speech by Mark Carney, Governor of the Bank of England, 'The high road to a responsible, open financial system' (April 2017)

3.4 The detail of the fit and proper requirements is considered at **2.2** above. In a nutshell, before applying to the relevant regulator for approval, the firm must be satisfied that the candidate is a fit and proper person to perform the specific SMF. In deciding whether the person is fit and proper, the individual and the compliance officer should consider all relevant factors, including whether the candidate:

- has obtained a (relevant) qualification;
- has undergone, or is undergoing, training;
- possesses a level of competence; and/or
- has the personal characteristics required by the rules made by the regulator(s).

When the application has been submitted, the FCA will examine the candidate's honesty, integrity and reputation; competence and capability; and financial soundness.

Regulatory approval

3.5 Regulatory approval can come in a range of forms. In assessing fitness and propriety, the regulators may grant permission outright or impose conditions, time limits and/or variations on SMF approvals. The regulators have stated that any such application of conditions, time limits or regulator-initiated variations of SMF approval will apply on a case-by-case basis and only be applied to advance the regulators' respective objectives. If the regulator wants a variation of approval to take place immediately, it must give the firm and the senior manager in question the right to make representations. The firm may also apply to vary or remove the condition or to ask the relevant regulator to impose a new condition.

Example: Time-limited approval

A very large bank is going through a period of transition after the individual performing the chief finance function (SMF2) leaves the bank unexpectedly due to ill health. The bank believes that finding a suitable permanent replacement will take longer than 12 weeks. The bank proposes that the treasurer temporarily assumes the chief finance function until a suitable replacement is found. In this instance, the PRA considers the bank treasurer to be fit and proper, and authorises him to perform SMF2 with a time limit of six months. This gives the bank six months to find a new chief financial officer and get him/her approved to perform SMF2.

As highlighted in the above example, a firm may appoint an individual to perform a SMF without seeking regulatory approval where the appointment is for less than 12 consecutive weeks to provide cover for the SMF whose absence was temporary or reasonably unforeseen. That said, it would be good practice to inform the regulator(s) of any interim or temporary arrangements and the plans in place to fill any gaps on a permanent basis.

Any responsibility that the absent manager holds under the 'overall responsibility' requirement can be reallocated to someone who is not approved, during their absence.

Senior individuals and their firms need to take any time-limited approvals seriously – continuing to perform a SMF after the expiry of any approval would be deemed to be performing a SMF without approval and may be subject to enforcement action. The firm itself may also be liable for failing to take reasonable care to ensure that the individual does not perform a SMF without approval.

Example: (1) Conditional approval

A large asset manager would like to promote one of its senior fund managers to head up its entire Asian portfolio based out of London and is seeking approval for her to perform the head of key business area function (SMF6). The candidate has substantial experience in equities, fixed income and bonds but her knowledge of derivatives, which accounts for a significant part of the firm's portfolio, is somewhat out of date. In this case, the PRA decides to attach a condition to the individual's approval requiring her to undertake training to update her knowledge of derivatives and the associated regulatory and other risks by a specified date.

As with the time-limited approval, failure to observe a condition may, depending on the circumstances, amount to a breach by the firm and/or the relevant senior manager. Equally, non or late fulfilment of a condition may also mean the senior manager has failed to observe minimum standards of fitness and propriety and could trigger disciplinary action, which could involve the relevant regulator withdrawing approval.

Example: (2) Conditional approval

A medium-sized building society is seeking to appoint an executive director function (SMF3) knowing that the person already holds a number of non-executive directorships in different businesses. The regulator is concerned about the potential impact of these other commitments on the individual's ability to devote sufficient time to the proposed role. The regulator chooses to impose a condition requiring the individual to resign from some of the non-executive directorships before SMF3 approval will be granted.

Statement of Responsibilities

3.6   As an inherent part of the overall operation of SM&CR, firms are required to submit a 'Statement of Responsibilities' (SoR) with each application for approval of a senior manager and to update a SoR whenever there is a significant change in the senior manager's responsibilities.

Senior individuals need to take personal responsibility for their SoR which can be a useful exercise to distil and ensure clarity and consistency of understanding as to exactly what the senior person is, and is not, responsible for. SoRs are required to be practical, useable, without unnecessary detail, as well as succinct and clear. SoRs should be seen as a statement of what a senior manager is responsible for, and not a record of how they will discharge those responsibilities. The regulators expect that a SoR will show how the responsibility of a senior manager fits in with the overall system of governance and management within the firm and is consistent with the firm's own Management Responsibilities Map. When taken all together, the SoRs of all the firm's SMFs should present a seamless whole covering all aspects of the business and a comprehensive allocation of responsibilities.

The succinct point is borne out by the regulators having suggested (but not mandated) a word limit of 300. A template SoR is provided in SUP 10C Annex 5D of the FCA Handbook (see www.handbook.fca.org.uk/handbook/sup/10c/annex5d.html).

The regulators have specified 30 'prescribed responsibilities' which need to be assigned to individuals who hold SMFs to ensure that someone is accountable for the fundamental responsibilities inherent in a particular SMF.

Where a responsibility is prescribed by the FCA, it is set out in SYSC 4.7.7R (see www.handbook.fca.org.uk/handbook/SYSC/4/7.html#D383). The PRA's prescribed responsibilities are set out in its rulebook in Allocation of Responsibilities, Part 4.1 (see www.prarulebook.co.uk/rulebook/Content/Part/212514/05-07-2018#212514).

The process is as follows:

(1) identify those individuals that hold SMFs 1–17;

(2) allocate 'prescribed responsibilities' that are relevant to the firm's activities to individual senior managers; and

(3) identify the 'overall responsibilities' of senior individuals for any other activities, functions or business areas of the firm – if there are any which are not already assigned as SMF 1–17, which will require approval as a SMF 18.

As a matter of course, firms will need to agree all allocation of responsibilities with the relevant senior managers and record the allocation on individual SoRs with a summary provided in the firm's Management Responsibilities Map.

SoRs should include the FCA and PRA 'prescribed responsibilities' allocated to the SMF as well as any allocation of overall responsibility for the firm's activities, business areas and management functions. The PRA has noted that, in many cases, simply allocating a prescribed responsibility to a senior manager should be enough to identify that person, clearly and formally, as responsible for that area with no further elaboration required. While a SoR must be a stand-alone document it should tie in with the senior individual's personal objectives and any other supporting documentation as to how the allocated responsibilities are meant to be discharged.

In July 2018 the FCA confirmed that it would be introducing a new prescribed responsibility for the Conduct Rules under which all firms, banks included, will be required to allocate a senior manager to make sure the firm trains its staff in the Conduct Rules and complies with the FCA notification requirements. The new prescribed responsibility for the Conduct Rules, and the need to appoint a named senior manager, came into force for banking firms on 1 November 2018.

'The Conduct Rules and this PR aim to drive up standards of individual behaviour in financial services. We aim to improve individual accountability and awareness of conduct issues. This will in turn achieve the culture change that we are seeking. We want to make sure a senior individual is accountable for ensuring adequate training and accurate reporting of breach information to the regulator. As a result, having considered respondents' feedback, we believe that introducing this PR will help achieve our aims.

Firms must decide which Senior Manager is the best person to hold this PR. It should be given to the Senior Manager who is the most senior person responsible for the Conduct Rules training and notification requirements. They must also have sufficient authority and an appropriate level of knowledge and competence to do this properly. In larger firms, this may be the individual accountable for ensuring that activities undertaken across different parts of the firm (eg HR, legal and compliance) enable the firm to comply with our requirements. It doesn't mean this person needs to be personally involved in these activities day to day.

This PR should normally be held by only one person. Firms will only be able to share this PR in limited circumstances. They must be able to show that this is appropriate and justifiable. If a firm decides it is appropriate to share this PR, they must show why this is justified and confirm that this does not leave a gap.'

Source: Feedback on proposal to introduce a new prescribed responsibility for the Conduct Rules, PS 18/14 'Extending the Senior Managers & Certification Regime to FCA firms' (July 2018)

A firm must also provide the relevant regulator with a revised SoR if there has been any significant change in the responsibilities of an approved SMF. Examples of what constitutes a 'significant change' may include:

- a variation of the senior manager's regulatory approval resulting in the imposition, variation or removal of a condition or time limit;

- sharing or dividing a SMF that was originally performed by one person between two or more persons;
- the addition, re-allocation or removal of any SMF; and
- ceasing to perform any SMF that was originally shared with another, or others.

Senior individuals need to work with human resources and/or compliance officers to monitor the evolving responsibilities of SMFs in order to detect any 'significant change' in remit. Given the seniority of those likely to be involved, board level oversight should be considered. As with other aspects of the SM&CR, the FCA has not set any threshold of what a 'significant change' may constitute so that must be assessed, and documented clearly, on a case-by-case basis.

In the event of regulatory breach, the SoRs will be critical in defining the limits of any liability incurred by a senior manager. If nothing else, this should be a driver to ensure SoRs are, and remain, up to date. As a matter of course, past versions of SoRs should be maintained and be accessible by both firms and senior individuals as a contingency against any future regulatory investigation.

Chapter 7 has more detail on how the required Statements of Responsibilities fit into the overarching firm Responsibilities Maps.

Applying the regime to smaller firms

3.7   The rules of the SM&CR have been adapted and, to an extent, have a lighter approach for smaller firms. The regulators are committed to applying the SMR proportionally based on the risk profiles of regulated firms.

Fewer requirements of the SM&CR apply to firms with gross total assets of £250m or less. This threshold is calculated over a rolling period of five years or, if the firm has been in existence for less than five years, over the period of its existence. This threshold means that fewer requirements of the SM&CR are applied to all credit unions and to a small number of existing banks and building societies (including new entrants to the market, such as 'challenger banks').

For small firms, the relevant prescribed responsibilities (including those that must be allocated to all firms and those that apply just for small firms) would be allocated in practice to a small number of senior managers. As is the case for all firms, in addition to allocating the required and relevant prescribed responsibilities, small firms must ensure that at all times, one or more of its approved senior managers has overall responsibility for each of the activities, business areas and management functions of the firm.

Certification Regime

3.8   The certification element of the banking SM&CR came into effect from 7 March 2017 and requires the completion of a certification of those who perform either FCA-prescribed 'significant harm functions' or a PRA certification function.

The Certification Regime applies to employees of firms who are employed in positions where they could pose a risk of significant harm to either the firm itself or any of its customers. The regulators have diverged, due to differing statutory objectives, on the nomenclature of, and approach to the implementation of, the Certification Regime. The FCA uses 'significant harm functions' (SHF) while the PRA refers to 'certification functions'. For ease of reference, this chapter uses 'SHF' to encompass all roles that require certification under the FCA and PRA rules.

The fundamental difference between the SMR and the Certification Regime is that while SMFs require regulatory approval, individuals performing SHFs do not, with firms themselves required to take reasonable care that no-one performs a SHF unless they have been assessed by the firm as fit and proper. To evidence the firm's finding, a certificate for each individual confirming him or her as fit and proper needs to be issued before that individual may commence performing the SHF.

In practice, this means that firms are responsible for their own Certification Regimes and must put in place systems, controls and procedures for the assessment of fitness and propriety. There are likely to be relatively few SMF even in a large firm but there may well be many more senior individuals who will fall under the Certification Regime. Firms need to ensure they build the appropriate systems and controls to verify, continually monitor and maintain the firm's up-to-date list of certified persons. This will not only be required when recruiting for roles which fall under the Certification Regime but also to fulfil the requirement for an annual re-assessment and re-confirmation of all employees subject to the regime.

The expectation is that the mandatory annual fitness and propriety assessments will become part of firms' existing performance appraisal cycles.

'Employees' subject to the Certification Regime

3.9   The Certification Regime applies to an 'employee' which has a wide definition as someone who:

- personally provides, or is under an obligation to personally provide, services to the firm in question under an arrangement made between the firm and the person providing the services or another person;

- is subject to (or to the right of) supervision, direction or control by the firm as to the manner in which those services are provided.

These characteristics of an 'employee' for the purposes of the Certification Regime are deliberately broad enough to encompass appointed representatives of the firm.

Senior managers in an authorised firm need to be fully aware of all aspects of due diligence, governance and oversight of any appointed representatives. This is not only to ensure that the regulatory obligations are fulfilled but also to be aware of in the event an appointed representative falls into the Certification Regime and therefore needs to be regularly assessed for fitness and propriety.

Unlike the previous Approved Persons Regime, the rules do not specifically say that the Certification Regime applies if the function is performed under an arrangement between the firm and a contractor. A contractor will only be in scope of the Certification Regime if they perform the function and meet the criteria above. For example, a contractor who has been seconded to work at the firm, under the supervision of the firm, may be required to be certified.

It is critical that senior managers have a clear line of sight to who is inside, and excluded from, the Certification Regime. As part of the governance arrangements, a senior manager from the firm must be allocated the 'prescribed responsibility' for the firm's performance of its obligations under the Certification Regime. It is likely that the senior manager appointed this responsibility will work closely with the compliance, risk and HR functions in the fulfilment of his or her obligations. Given the nature of the Certification Regime, the senior manager allocated responsibility may be the chief executive or another person with sufficient seniority to demonstrate the appropriate 'tone from the top'.

Territorial scope

3.10   The Certification Regime applies to regulated activities carried on from an establishment of the firm in the UK. This includes establishments of non-UK firms (referred to by the PRA as third-country firms).

The Certification Regime also applies to persons performing the FCA SHF of dealing with a client of the UK firm from an overseas part of that firm.

PRA certification functions

3.11   The PRA's rules in respect of the Certification Regime are based on functions that involve risk to the financial stability of the firm, and indirectly the market. The PRA defines certification functions in its rulebook (see www.prarulebook.co.uk) to generally encompass functions performed by a 'significant risk taker' to the extent that the function requires the person to be involved in one or more aspects of the firm's regulated activities. Anyone deemed to be caught by the definition of 'significant risk taker' will be subject to the Certification Regime and their firm will be required to undertake annual fitness and propriety certifications.

The PRA is required by EU Directives and the European Banking Authority's suitability guidelines to ensure that all board members are fit and proper. The European requirements cover UK banks, building societies and large investment firms but not credit unions.

For non-credit union firms, a 'significant risk taker' is defined as an employee whose professional activities have a material impact on the firm's risk profile, including any employee who is deemed to have a material impact on the firm's risk profile by being classified as a material risk taker (MRT).

For credit unions, a 'significant risk taker' is defined as any employee who:

- is a member of the governing body;

- is a member of the senior management;

- is responsible and accountable to the management body for the activities of the independent risk management function, compliance function or internal audit function; or

- heads a function responsible for legal affairs, finance including taxation and budgeting, human resources, remuneration policy, information technology or economic analysis.

Material risk takers

3.12   The definition of a 'material risk taker' is in the remuneration section of the PRA rulebook (see www.prarulebook.co.uk/rulebook/Content/Part/292166/29-11-2017) and, in turn, refers to the Material Risk Takers Regulation (Commission Delegated Regulation (EU) No 604/2014, see https://publications.europa.eu/en/publication-detail/-/publication/4c81143c-d376-4d1d-a9dc-67a7e02a22c1/language-en) which sets out the qualitative and quantitative criteria for identifying staff whose professional activities have a material impact on a firm's risk profile. The MRT Regulation comprises:

- a catch-all subjective definition covering all categories of staff whose professional activities have a material impact on an institution's risk profile (Article 2);

- a set of defined qualitative criteria (Article 3); and

- a set of defined quantitative criteria (Article 4), which can be overridden in specified circumstances.

The qualitative criteria include (but are not limited to) staff members who are heads of material business units or members of the management body or senior management. Some senior managers caught by these criteria will be automatically excluded from the Certification Regime as they will have already been caught by SMR.

An example of the quantitative criteria is where an employee was awarded total remuneration of €500,000 or more in the preceding financial year.

The range of criteria as to who falls to be a material risk taker, and is therefore a significant risk taker and subject to the Certification Regime, requires careful and continuous monitoring by both senior individuals and their compliance officers and HR.

It is possible that some employees classified as MRTs under the remuneration rules will not fall within the Certification Regime. For example, there may be MRTs who are not sufficiently involved in the regulated activities of the firm to meet the statutory test of certification. This could be the case where an individual is employed by an overseas subsidiary of the UK-authorised firm but has no involvement in the regulated activity of the UK-authorised firm. This person will be a MRT for remuneration purposes as the PRA's remuneration rules apply at a group, parent undertaking and subsidiary undertaking level, including subsidiaries outside the EEA. But if they have no involvement in a regulated activity of the UK-authorised firm, they would not be performing the PRA certification function.

FCA significant harm functions

3.13   The FCA has provided rules and guidance on the application of the Certification Regime to firms in Chapter 5.2 of the Senior Management Arrangements, Systems and Controls (SYSC) section of the FCA Handbook (see www.handbook.fca.org.uk/handbook/SYSC/5/2.html).

The FCA has specified nine SHFs which, if an employee is performing them in connection to the regulated activities of the firm, requires the firm to certify those employees as 'fit and proper' before they may commence their function. The FCA's SHFs are wider than the PRA's certification function, reflecting the FCA's focus on conduct regulation.

FCA-specified significant harm functions

3.14   To avoid duplication between the SMR and the Certification Regime, a function is not a FCA-specified SHF for a firm if it is carried out by a person performing a designated SMF for that firm.

Table 3.2 – FCA specified SHF

Number	Function	Description
1.	Client assets (CASS) sourcebook oversight (www.handbook.fca.org.uk/handbook/CASS/)	Each of the following is an FCA-specified significant harm function: • in CASS medium firms and CASS large firms: oversight of operational effectiveness function under CASS 1A.3.1AR; • in CASS large debt management firms: oversight of operational effectiveness function under CASS 11.3.4R.

Number	Function	Description
2.	Benchmark submission and administration – requirements in the Market Conduct (MAR) sourcebook (www.handbook.fca. org.uk/handbook/ MAR/)	Each of the following is a FCA-specified significant harm function: • acting as a benchmark manager under MAR 8.2.3R(1); • acting as a benchmark administration manager under MAR 8.3.5R(1).
3.	Proprietary trader	The function of acting as a proprietary trader whose activity involves, or might involve, a risk of significant harm to the firm or any of its customers.
4.	Significant management	The function of acting as a senior manager with significant responsibility for a significant business unit. For a non-UK relevant firm's branch in the UK, the significant management function is limited to business units of the UK branch. The function could include: • the head of a unit carrying on the activities of retail banking, personal lending, corporate lending, salvage or loan recovery or proprietary trading; • acting as a member of a committee making decisions in the above functions.
5.	Functions requiring qualifications – requirements in the Training & Competence (TC) sourcebook (www. handbook.fca.org. uk/handbook/TC)	Each function involving an activity that requires a qualification requirement as specified in TC appendix 1.1.1R is a FCA-specified significant harm function. For a non-UK relevant firm, each function involving an activity for which there would have been a qualification requirement if the firm had been a UK relevant authorised person, is a FCA-specified significant harm function.
6.	Managers of certification employees	The function of managing or supervising a certification employee, directly or indirectly, is a FCA-specified significant harm function. However, a function is not a FCA-specified significant harm function for a firm if it is performed by a SMF manager of that firm.

Number	Function	Description
7.	Material risk takers	Generally, each function performed by a member of a firm's remuneration code staff (eg earns more than €500,000) is a FCA-specified significant harm function.
8.	Client-dealing	A person (P) performs the client-dealing function for a firm if both: • P is carrying out any of the activities in the table in SYSC 5.2.45R; • those activities will involve P dealing with: ○ a person with or for whom those activities are carried out; or ○ the property of any such person; in a manner substantially connected with the carrying on of regulated activities by the firm. SYSC 5.2.45 R states that the function includes: • advising on investments other than a non-investment insurance contract and performing other functions relating to this, such as dealing and arranging; • dealing, as principal or agent, and arranging (bringing about) deals in investments; • acting in the capacity of an investment manager and functions connected with this; and • acting as a bidder's representative.
9.	Algorithmic trading	Each of the following is a FCA-specified significant harm function: • approving the deployment of: ○ a trading algorithm or a part of one; or ○ an amendment to a trading algorithm or a part of one; or ○ a combination of trading algorithms;

Number	Function	Description
		• each of the following functions: ○ having significant responsibility for the management of monitoring whether or not a trading algorithm; and ○ deciding whether or not a trading algorithm, is, or remains, compliant with the firm's obligations. The firm's obligations include the firm's regulatory obligations and the rules and requirements of the trading venues to which the firm's trading systems are connected.

Practice note

A FCA specified SHF does not cease to be so defined if the PRA also specifies that function as a PRA Certification Function. In practice, this means that certified persons may be performing one or more SHFs. For example, a team leader may be both a material risk taker (a PRA certification function) and a manager of certified persons (a FCA specified SHF).

As with all aspects of the SM&CR, senior individuals need to be aware of, and work with, the compliance and other functions within their firms' governance systems to ensure that everyone is, and remains, defined correctly with regard to those who fall in and out of scope of the PRA certification functions and the FCA-specified SHFs. The FCA gives extensive guidance as to what is considered 'significant' when it comes to, say, business units but an area where particular care may be needed is with regard to the management of a certified person as managers of certified persons are, themselves, deemed to be certified persons and performing either FCA specified SHF 6 (managers of certification employees) or, if at a more senior level likely to be, SHF 4 (significant management).

Fit and proper

3.15   A firm may only issue individuals who fall under the Certification Regime with the required certificate if the firm is satisfied that each individual meets the standards of fitness and propriety. The issue has been covered in detail at **2.2** above but are covered again here in part for context.

The fitness and propriety standards that apply to senior managers are broadly applicable to certified persons. The rules state that when deciding whether a person is fit and proper, a firm must be satisfied that the person has appropriate qualifications, training, competence and personal characteristics to perform his or her function effectively. Firms should have regard to the factors considered by both the FCA and the PRA with requirements which relate to a person's:

- honesty, integrity and reputation;
- competence and capability; and
- financial soundness.

Fitness and propriety should be assessed in view of the individual's role, or seniority. Firms would be well advised to create their own policies and procedures, approved by the board, for the operation of the Certification Regime. This could include designing firm-specific metrics for fitness and propriety with the inherent flexibility to adapt to the role, level, experience and responsibilities of the individual applying to perform a significant harm function. A key feature of any successful approach to the Certification Regime by senior and other managers will be investment in scrupulous record keeping.

There are a range of measures and metrics which can be tracked. Monitoring of technical competencies, such as the completion of training courses required for fitness and propriety can utilise online eLearning modules and employee-tracking software. For many firms, assessment of fitness and propriety will require access and review of more information about a candidate than was previously the case. For instance, firms will need to consider whether they should routinely check whether the candidate has any adverse finding or any settlement in civil proceedings, particularly in connection with financial services. In addition, firms may consider using screening, additional regulatory references, due diligence and/ or declarations by the candidate at the time of hire.

The assessment of the fitness and propriety of employees is a continuing obligation on firms. While most firms are used to checking new employees before hiring them, there has traditionally been less focus on continuous assessment of ongoing fitness and propriety for the role being undertaken. Firms should already have in place policies, procedures and systems for a regular cycle of appraisals and performance reviews for their staff which is used for, among other things, determining pay raises and bonuses. Those systems are likely to be an appropriate baseline for the fitness and propriety assessment with systems being updated and additional checks incorporated which take into account the nature and level of the individual's responsibilities within the firm.

Firms are expected to undertake due diligence on new employees, particularly with regard to a candidate's prior relevant experience, including previously performed approved or other functions. Specifically, regulators expect regulatory references (see further below) and checks of the Financial Services Register to be undertaken as they are an important independent source of information, not only of a person's past business conduct, but also as a potential source of evidence to support decision making regarding both employment and subsequent certification. The Financial Services Register has not proved to be infallible and is to be replaced by a new public 'Directory' of key individuals working in financial services by, most probably, the end of 2019.

It is entirely possible that firms may choose to make any offers of employment contingent on that person being approved by the regulator (where relevant) and found to be fit and proper.

Regulatory references

Regulatory references are a special kind of employment reference which are used to verify a candidate's fitness and propriety. The underlying purpose of regulatory references has been defined as to 'help firms prevent the "recycling" of individuals with poor conduct records between firms'. Instead of focusing on an employee's work experiences and abilities, regulatory references attest to the candidate's honesty, integrity and reputation, competence and capability, and financial soundness. Regulatory references are deliberately distinct from the usual employee references.

3.16   The mandatory use of regulatory references came into effect for banks on 7 March 2017 and will be required for both insurers and all other financial services firms subject to SM&CR.

FCA 'full scope regulatory reference firms' and PRA 'full scope regulatory references firms' (which includes banks, building societies, credit unions, PRA-authorised investment firms, incoming third-party branches) must take reasonable steps to acquire regulatory references before issuing a certificate under the Certification Regime or appointing a person to perform a controlled function, a senior management function or appointing a person as a non-executive director. Full scope regulatory references firms must request regulatory references from every one of the candidate's employers of the past six years. Full scope regulatory firms must request the required regulatory references, even if the previous employers are unauthorised firms or firms outside of the UK. If, however, the firm requesting the regulatory reference is part of a group which has centralised records or alternative means of sharing relevant information for candidates, that firm is not obliged to request references.

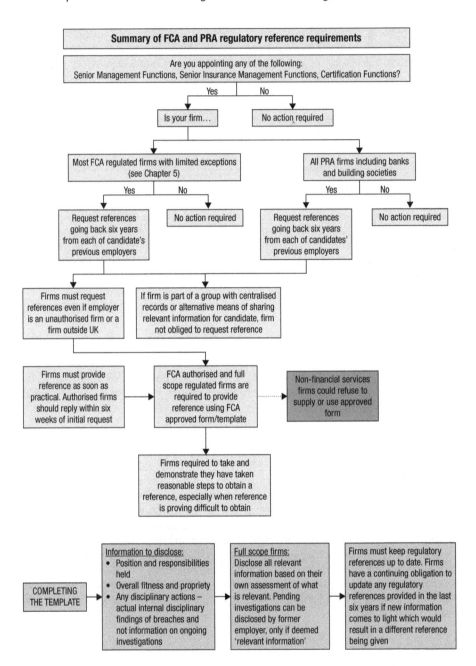

The previous employer is required to provide a regulatory reference only if it is an FCA-authorised firm or a full-scope regulatory reference firm. If the previous employer is a full-scope regulatory reference firm, it must provide the reference, even if the firm requesting it is not a full-scope regulatory reference firm. In practice, this means that non-financial services firms could simply refuse to provide a regulatory reference or provide a reference in a non-approved form. In which case, firms need to have a process to work with and assess the information provided.

Mandatory template for regulatory references

3.17   The FCA has provided a mandatory template for regulatory references which can be found in SYSC 22 Annex 1 Template for regulatory references given by relevant authorised persons and disclosure requirements (see www.handbook. fca.org.uk/handbook/SYSC/22/Annex1.html).

Part One: Form of Template

Guide to using this template:
Each question must be answered. Where there is nothing to disclose, this should be confirmed by ticking the 'No' box for the relevant question.
In this template:
• 'we'/'our firm' refers to the firm or firms giving the reference (as set out in either 1A or 1B below);
• 'individual' refers to the subject of the reference (as set out in 2 below);
• 'your' refers to the firm requesting the reference (as set out in 3 below).

Information requested		**Response**
1A	Name, contact details and firm reference number of firm providing reference; or	
1B	Names, contact details and firm reference numbers (where applicable) of group firms providing a joint reference	
2	Individual's name (ie the subject of the reference)	
3	Name, contact details and firm reference number of firm requesting the reference	
4	Date of request for reference	
5	Date of reference	
The answers to Questions A to F cover the period beginning six years before the date of your request for a reference and ending on the date of this reference		
Question A:		
Has the individual:		
(1)	performed a specified significant harm function for our firm; or	
(2)	been an approved person for our firm?	

Answer:	
Yes	
No	
Question B:	
Has the individual performed one or more of the following roles in relation to our firm:	
(1)	notified non-executive director;
(2)	credit union non-executive director; or
(3)	key function holder (other than a controlled function)?
Answer:	
Yes	
No	
Question C:	
If we have answered 'yes' to either Question A or B above, we set out the details of each position held below, including:	
(1)	what the controlled function, specified significant harm function or key function holder role is or was;
(2)	(in the case of a controlled function) whether the approval is or was subject to a condition, suspension, limitation, restriction or time limit;
(3)	whether any potential FCA governing function is or was included in a PRA controlled function; and
(4)	the dates during which the individual held the position.
Answer:	
Question D:	
Has the individual performed a role for our firm other than the roles referred to in Questions A and B above?	
Answer:	
Yes	
No	
If 'yes', we have provided summary details of the other role(s), eg job title, department and business unit, below.	
Question E:	
Have we concluded that the individual was not fit and proper to perform a function?	
Answer:	
Yes	
No	

If 'yes' and associated disciplinary action was taken as a result, please refer to Question F below.		
If 'yes', and no associated disciplinary action was taken as a result, we have set out below the facts which led to our conclusion.		
Question F:		
We have taken disciplinary action against the individual that:		
(1)	relates to an action, failure to act, or circumstances, that amounts to a breach of any individual conduct requirements that:	
	(a)	apply or applied to the individual; or
	(b)	(if the individual is or was a key function holder, a notified non-executive director or a credit union non-executive director for your firm) the individual is or was required to observe under PRA rules (including if applicable, PRA rules in force before 7 March 2016); or
(2)	relates to the individual not being fit and proper to perform a function.	
Answer:		
Yes		
No		
If 'yes', we have provided below a description of the breaches (including dates of when they occurred) and the basis for, and outcome of, the subsequent disciplinary action.		
Question G:		
Are we aware of any other information that we reasonably consider to be relevant to your assessment of whether the individual is fit and proper? This disclosure is made on the basis that we shall only disclose something that:		
(1)	occurred or existed:	
	(a)	in the six years before your request for a reference; or
	(b)	between the date of your request for the reference and the date of this reference; or
(2)	is serious misconduct.	
Answer:		
Yes		
No		
If 'yes', we have provided the relevant information below.		

Senior individuals need to be aware of the level of detail of the contents which includes a list of questions on the personal information of the candidate, the position and the responsibilities he/she has held, overall fitness and propriety and any disciplinary actions taken against him/her. The firm providing the reference is obliged to provide only actual internal disciplinary findings of breaches and not information on ongoing investigations. Additionally, full scope regulatory reference firms may disclose all relevant information based on their own assessment of what is relevant. Pending investigations can therefore be disclosed by the former employer, only if the former employer considers it to be 'relevant information' that should be disclosed.

There is an additional obligation to keep regulatory references up to date. When the current employer is a financial services authorised firm, full scope regulatory reference firms have a continuing obligation to revise a regulatory reference that they have already provided within the past six years, should new information become available that would result in a different content for the regulatory reference. The six-year limit does not apply for cases of serious misconduct of the candidate that may arise from 7 March 2017 onwards.

For example, if a firm is considering a candidate for the role of the executive director function (SMF 3), ie an FCA SMF, it must take all reasonable steps to obtain regulatory references from the candidate's employers of the past six years (even if some or all of these employers are unauthorised). If the former employer asked to provide the regulatory reference is any kind of UK financial services authorised firm, then it is obliged to provide a regulatory reference. If the previous employer is not FCA authorised or a full scope regulatory references firm, the unauthorised firm has a choice about providing a regulatory reference.

As part of any recruitment process or internal move, senior individuals should enquire as to the information likely to be needed as part of any firm-specific metrics and make every effort to comprehensively and swiftly complete (with full supporting evidence) any pre-employment questionnaires. Where a firm becomes aware of information of a person's past business conduct that may be relevant for the fit and proper assessment, the firm should make 'reasonable' enquiries to establish the circumstances of that conduct.

As a matter of course, firms should also undertake criminal record checks, checks of prior directorships, sanctions and credit checks in assessing fitness and propriety. On criminal record checks a firm (based in England or Wales) should get an application form from the Disclosure and Barring Service (DBS) or an umbrella body (which is a registered body that gives access to DBS checks). There is an equivalent procedure in Scotland (involving Disclose Scotland) and Northern Ireland (involving Access NI).

Content of certificates

3.18   Certificates issued by the firm to a person must both:

- state that the firm is satisfied that the person is fit and proper to perform the function to which the certification relates; and
- set out the aspects of the affairs of the firm in which the person will be involved in performing the function.

A certificate is valid for 12 months, which starts from the day on which it is issued. The FCA has stated that a certificate may be issued for less than 12 months in keeping with the spirit of the Certification Regime. A certificate must not be issued to be valid more than 12 months from the date of issue.

Where an employee performs multiple SHFs (including FCA specified SHFs or PRA certification functions), the firm must assess each function against applicable standards but need only issue one certificate to the employee. A certificate may also cover functions that a certified person is not currently performing, as long as the firm has assessed the employee's fitness for the additional functions. A certificate should not normally cover additional functions that are not being performed.

All certificates produced confirming the firm's assessment of fitness and propriety must be supported by detailed and up-to-date evidence. Part of that evidence could include the employee's job description which includes the firm's stance on fit and proper.

Moving functions during the year

3.19   If a person changes a SHF role during the 12-month period of their certificate there is not an automatic read across. There needs to be a re-assessment to ensure that the person is fit and proper for the new role and he or she must not start the new role until the assessment is complete and his or her fitness and propriety confirmed for the new activities.

Specifically, firms must not wait until the annual re-assessment of fit and proper to consider whether or not the employee is fit and proper for any new activities being undertaken.

Example

An employee is performing the algorithmic trading function (SHF 9). Three months after the issue of the employee's certificate, the employee is promoted to a client-facing role. This new role will necessitate the employee performing the client-dealing function (SHF 8). The employee's firm decides that the two SHFs are sufficiently different in terms of the standards of fitness and propriety. Accordingly, the firm does not permit the employee to commence the client-dealing function (SHF 8) until assessed as fit and proper. Once this process is completed successfully, the employee's certificate is updated accordingly and he/she is able to take up his/her new role.

What happens if the employee is not fit and proper?

3.20   If a firm decides that a person is not fit and proper, the firm must refuse to renew (or issue) that person's certificate of fitness and propriety in the case of individuals undertaking functions under the Certification Regime. If the firm refuses to renew an individual's certificate, the firm must take reasonable care to ensure that the individual ceases (or does not perform) the certification function in question.

In practical terms, any decision taken by a firm whereby an employee is not deemed to be fit and proper is likely to lead to the termination of the employee's contract of employment. After all, without the required fit and proper certificate the firm is not permitted to allow the individual concerned to undertake any of SHF activities. Employment contracts will make clear that continuing fitness and propriety is a condition of employment in a certified or SMF role.

In order to manage this potentially difficult process, some firms have instituted an internal right to appeal against a finding that the individual is not fit and proper. This may then lead to a hearing at a (very) senior level of the firm. Depending on the outcome of any appeal, disciplinary action may continue up to and including dismissal.

Emergency appointments

3.21   If a relevant firm appoints an individual to perform a function that is a significant harm or certification function, then the performance by that individual of the function does not constitute a significant harm or certification function if both of the following conditions are met:

- the appointment is to provide cover for a certification employee whose absence is reasonably unforeseen; and
- the appointment is for less than four weeks.

In practice, the exemptions cover situations where temporary cover is provided for holidays or where certified persons are absent for, say, bereavement leave. The function will not, in the four weeks, be treated as a certification function so the firm will not be required to issue a fit and proper certificate.

The four-week rule exemption does not apply to an FCA-specified significant harm function that requires a qualification. Where there is an unforeseen absence of an employee performing a function for which there is a qualification requirement:

- the firm should take reasonable care to ensure that no employee performs that function without a valid certificate; and
- the certificate should be issued before an employee starts to perform the function.

Wherever temporary measures are put in place it does not absolve the firm of the need for strong consistent governance of the activities undertaken. Given the potential for personal liability, senior individuals would be well advised, whenever possible, to have detailed handovers at each end of any temporary period of cover.

Temporary UK role

3.22 For FCA-designated SHFs, there is a 30-day grace period so that anyone entering the UK for a short period does not need to be certified as fit and proper. This grace period was introduced by the FCA to allow for the smooth functioning of cross-border business and to ensure that the FCA rules are applied proportionally to staff based outside the UK.

The 30-day rule only applies to the extent that the individual is appropriately supervised by either:

- one of the firm's SMF managers; or

- one of the firm's certification employees whose certificate covers the FCA designated SHF that is being dis-applied.

The FCA expects an individual from overseas using the temporary UK-role grace period to be accompanied on a visit to a customer in the UK. The exception being that the 30-day grace period does not apply to MRTs, as MRTs employed by UK firms have no territorial limitation.

Checklist

3.23 The checklist below offers practical questions for senior individuals to consider.

Checklist

- Do you know exactly:
    - which SMF you hold (if any);
    - whether there are any conditions applied to your regulatory approval (if any);
    - which SHF (FCA) or certification function (PRA) you hold (if any);
    - which prescribed responsibilities have been allocated to you;
    - the basis on which you have been deemed fit and proper?
- How do you evidence your continuing fitness and propriety?
- Can you explain the governance process around your firm's SM&CR compliance, fitness and propriety certifications and how it ties into not only the group structure but also the annual appraisal process?

Chapter 4

Specifics of the Senior Managers and Certification Regime for insurers

Chapter summary

- The specifics of the Senior Managers and Certification Regime (SM&CR) which apply to insurers

- An overview of key changes from previous accountability regimes

- Insight into the scope, implementation and required processes and documentation

'The new rules will give consumers peace of mind that those at the top of the big insurers will be held personally responsible for any wrongdoing. The rules will also ensure that a code of conduct is set out for all staff, and that employees who do a job where they could do significant harm to consumers, or to the UK's financial stability, are approved annually by their firm.'

Press release: 'New accountability rules for insurers', HM Treasury and John Glen MP the Economic Secretary to the Treasury and City Minister (January 2018)

The new regime for insurers

4.1   A new accountability regime for the largest and most complex insurers took effect in early 2016 to coincide with the introduction of the SM&CR in the banking sector. The regime only applied to insurers subject to the EU Solvency II Directive. The PRA introduced a brand new Senior Insurance Managers Regime (SIMR) and the FCA amended its existing Approved Persons Regime to both implement the governance requirements of the EU Solvency II Directive and raise accountability standards in insurers.

The PRA and the FCA aligned these new and amended requirements for insurers as closely as they could with the SM&CR for banks. However, as the SIMR and the revised Approved Persons Regime do not include key elements of the SM&CR for banks, and only applied to 'Solvency II insurers', the SM&CR is being extended to cover all insurance companies, replacing the existing SIMR and Approved Persons Regime requirements. Both the FCA and the PRA have responsibility for implementing the extended regime across the entire insurance sector through their respective rules and guidance.

Scope of extended regime

4.2   All insurers and reinsurers regulated by the FCA and the PRA need to comply with the SM&CR rules. The requirements affect almost all staff in those firms, including existing approved individuals. That includes:

- all firms in scope of the UK rules implementing Solvency II (known as Solvency II firms);

- the Society of Lloyd's;

- managing agents;

- UK branches of third-country firms and European Economic Area (EEA) firms;

- insurance special purpose vehicles (ISPVs);

- all insurers outside the scope of Solvency II (referred to as Non-directive firms or NDFs) regardless of size, categorised as:

  ○ 'small NDFs' where the value of assets for all regulated activities it carries out is £25,000,000 or less;

  ○ 'large NDFs' where the value of assets for all regulated activities it carries out exceeds £25,000,000.

The full SM&CR set out here applies to Solvency II firms and large NDFs. A streamlined version of it with fewer requirements applies to other insurers including small NDFs, small run-off firms and ISPVs. This proportionality reflects the scope of the regime covering the very largest household name product providers through to high street dentists offering dental insurance policies as a tiny proportion of their business. Aspects of the regime will also apply to both UK branches of EEA firms (EEA branches) and third-country branches (non-EEA branches).

Which employees are impacted?

4.3   In line with the SM&CR in the banking sector, there is a baseline set of requirements or 'core regime' that will apply to staff in each and every firm. The three core elements of the SM&CR that firms will need to comply with are:

(1) the Senior Managers Regime;

(2) the Certification Regime;

(3) the Conduct Rules.

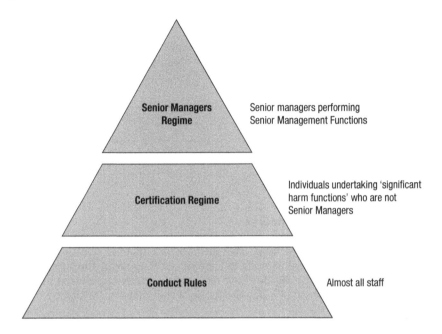

Snapshot of the regime for insurers

(1) The Senior Managers Regime

This focuses on the most senior people, the senior managers, in the firm who perform 'Senior Management Functions' roles which are defined by regulators.

Anyone who holds a Senior Management Function needs regulatory approval and firms are responsible for ensuring senior managers are suitable to do their jobs (with a review at least once a year). Every senior manager is required to have:

(i) A **Statement of Responsibilities** setting out what they are responsible and accountable for.

(ii) A **duty of responsibility** meaning that if something goes wrong in an area they are responsible for, the FCA will consider if they took 'reasonable steps' to stop it from happening.

(iii) **Prescribed Responsibilities** which are new responsibilities firms need to give their senior managers.

---

(2) The Certification Regime

This covers individuals who are not senior managers, but whose jobs (called 'significant harm functions') mean they can have a big impact on customers, markets or the firm.

These roles are defined by regulators. The individuals do not need regulatory approval, but firms need to check and confirm ('certify') that they are suitable, ie fit and proper to do their job at least once a year.

---

(3) The Conduct Rules

These are basic rules to improve the behaviour of all staff in and apply to almost everyone working in financial services firms.

What is changing for insurers?

4.4   The Solvency II and large NDF insurance companies already operating within the SIMR regime will already be familiar with some of the fundamental elements of the extended SM&CR. However, the key difference between the SIMR and the new regime is the much broader scope of staff that the SM&CR covers.

The key changes and requirements for insurance companies include the following:

Key changes and requirements

• All insurers will need to both identify and allocate clearer accountabilities including new Prescribed Responsibilities to senior managers, and articulate them in formal Statements of Responsibilities. Senior managers will also be subject to a statutory duty of responsibility.

• All insurers will be subject to the Certification Regime for the first time which includes a requirement for insurers to satisfy themselves every year that employees within this regime are fit and proper.

• The vast majority of employees working for insurers will become subject to directly enforceable Conduct Rules.

• There are increased obligations around obtaining and providing references including the need to obtain regulatory references from past employers when seeking to appoint an individual as a certified person.

• Insurers (excluding small NDFs, small run-off and ISPVs) will need to produce Management Responsibilities Maps, albeit this is predominantly a renaming exercise for Solvency II and large NDF firms who produced governance maps under the prior regime.

- A new handover requirement for Solvency II firms and large NDFs.

- A new requirement for Solvency II insurers and large NDFs to have a policy to consider a broad set of competencies and to promote diversity when recruiting board members.

The Senior Managers Regime for insurers

4.5   The first fundamental component of SM&CR focuses on the most senior individuals in a firm, the 'senior managers' who perform key roles or 'Senior Management Functions' specified by the regulators. They have the greatest potential to cause harm. There is no territorial limitation on the Senior Managers Regime which means that it applies to anyone who performs a senior manager role, whether they are based in the UK or overseas.

There are multiple aspects to this part of the regime to ensure that senior managers are, and continue to be, both suitable and accountable for their responsibilities:

(1) Senior managers performing Senior Management Functions need prior regulatory **approval** before starting their roles.

(2) At least once a year firms need to **certify** that senior managers are suitable to do their job – '**Fit and Proper** tests'.

(3) Every senior manager must have a '**Statement of Responsibilities'** that clearly states what he or she is responsible and accountable for.

(4) **A Duty of Responsibility** – a senior manager may be held accountable if he or she did not take 'reasonable steps' to prevent or stop a breach.

(5) Firms need to give senior managers specific responsibilities, known as '**Prescribed Responsibilities'** to make sure there is a senior manager accountable for the SM&CR and key conduct and prudential risks.

(6) Solvency II firms and large non-directive firms need to provide '**Responsibilities Maps'** which replace the former 'governance maps' but have a similar function.

(7) A senior manager must be responsible for each of the firm's business functions and activities. These responsibilities are called '**overall responsibilities'**.

The Senior Management Functions

4.6   The number and type of Senior Manager Functions a firm has depends on how it is organised. It would not need to restructure the business or recruit new staff to fill specific SMF roles. Instead, if a firm does not have anyone fulfilling these roles, the functions will not apply. That said, there are certain functions which are required to meet other rulebook obligations, for example, the requirement to have a client assets oversight function.

Table 4.1 lists a full set of SMFs. They include both the FCA's new set of SMFs which replace the former significant influence functions (SIFs) under its revised Approved Persons Regime and the PRA's SMFs which are renamed versions of Senior Insurance Management Functions (SIMFs) to provide consistency with the regime for banks. Only **Non-executive Directors** (NEDs) that perform specific roles will be senior managers.

Table 4.1 – Senior Management Functions

Reference	Function
SMF 1	Chief Executive Officer
SMF 2	Chief Finance Officer
SMF 3	Executive Director
SMF 4	Chief Risk Officer
SMF 5	Head of Internal Audit
SMF 6	Head of Key Business Area
SMF 7	Group Entity Senior Manager
SMF 8	Credit Union Senior Manager
SMF 9	Chair of the Governing Body
SMF10	Chair of the Risk Committee
SMF11	Chair of the Audit Committee
SMF12	Chair of the Remuneration Committee
SMF13	Chair of the Nomination Committee
SMF14	Senior Independent Director
SMF15	Chair of With Profits Committee
SMF16	Compliance Oversight
SMF17	Money Laundering Reporting Officer (MLRO)
SMF18	Other Overall Responsibility
SMF19	Head of Third Country/Overseas Branch
SMF20	Chief Actuary
SMF20a	With Profits Actuary
SMF21	EEA Branch Senior Manager (EBSM)
SMF22	Other Local Responsibility
SMF23	Chief Underwriting Officer
SMF23a	Underwriting Risk Oversight (Lloyd's)
SMF23b	Conduct Risk Oversight (Lloyd's)
SMF24	Chief Operations
SMF25	Small Insurer Senior Management Function

Reference	Function
SMF26	Head of Small Run-off Firm
SMF27	Partner

Practical implementation

4.7

- **Separation of roles:** To ensure independence and autonomy, the Chair function (SMF9) and CEO function (SMF1) roles cannot be held by a single individual at 'large firms'. Similarly, a non-executive director (NED) oversight SIMF role at a 'large firm' that is part of a group cannot be performed by a group executive to ensure large insurance firms have independence and autonomy from their parents.

- **Holding more than one Senior Management Function:** An individual may hold more than one FCA Senior Management Function, in which case they only need one Statement of Responsibilities clearly describing all their responsibilities. If an individual performs both a PRA and FCA Senior Management Function, an overlap rule enables a single application to the PRA for approval to covers both roles.

- **Temporary cover:** This can be provided for a role where there is a temporary or reasonably unforeseen absence and the appointment is for less than 12 consecutive weeks. The individual covering the role would not require regulatory approval.

- **Overall responsibility function:** If the most senior person with overall responsibility for an area is not already a senior manager, he or she will need to be approved as a senior manager under the Other Overall Responsibility Function. Situations where this could apply include:

  (i)   an individual with overall responsibility for a direct sales force;

  (ii) the person with senior responsibility for legacy life business;

  (iii) individuals with overall responsibility of functions such as product pricing (if separate from underwriting), complaints, claims, IT (including systems to support back office and front office functions);

  (iv) where new lines of business offered or expansion into new products.

Handover

4.8   All Solvency II firms and large NDFs need to ensure that when an individual takes on a senior manager role he or she has all the information, materials and documentation needed in order to do his or her job effectively. This is likely to include a handover note produced by the role's predecessor.

In practice, firms should encourage handover notes to be as practical and helpful as possible and not simply a factual record. This means they should include judgement and opinion as well as facts, metrics and figures. They should include information relating to relevant past incidents such as potential regulatory breaches or unresolved issues, with an assessment of how issues should be prioritised.

The firm must also have a policy explaining how it complies with the requirement. In practice, this would set out the handover process for both incoming and outgoing senior managers and how situations are managed where a senior manager departs abruptly. Firms also need to keep records to demonstrate the steps it has taken.

Duty of responsibility

4.9   Every senior manager has a duty of responsibility which crucially means that in the event of a breach of regulatory requirements by a firm, the senior manager responsible for the relevant area could be held accountable if he or she did not take reasonable steps to prevent or stop the breach; that is, steps that a person in their position could reasonably have been expected to take to avoid the breach occurring again (or continuing to take place). Whilst in practice the burden of proof lies with the FCA to show that the senior manager did not take the reasonable steps, it is critical that senior managers maintain a continuous suite of evidence of decisions made and actions taken to be able to evidence to regulators the discharging of their responsibilities.

> '... a senior manager is not liable just because the firm has breached a requirement. The senior manager's liability arises because he or she has failed to take reasonable steps to prevent the firm from being in breach and the firm is in breach.'
>
> Source: Mark Steward, Director of Enforcement and Market Oversight at the FCA, at the New York University Program on Corporate Compliance and Enforcement (April 2017)

Prescribed Responsibilities

4.10   Prescribed Responsibilities are the specific responsibilities that the FCA and the PRA have defined and that a firm must allocate to a senior manager. The senior manager to which a Prescribed Responsibility is allocated must be the most senior person responsible for that area in the firm.

- Seven Prescribed Responsibilities are shared between the PRA and the FCA demonstrating areas where both regulators have a significant interest, although each will be allocated to a single SMF.

- Three Prescribed Responsibilities are FCA only, covering:

- ○ Code of Conduct (COCON) obligations including ensuring the firm trains its staff in the Conduct Rules and complies with FCA notification requirements;

- ○ CASS (applicable where a firm has an obligation to comply); and

- ○ financial crime prevention.

- The Prescribed Responsibilities allocated by the PRA focus on its prudential soundness objectives.

Table 4.2 – Full list of Prescribed Responsibilities

Prescribed Responsibility Reference	Regulator	Prescribed Responsibility
A	FCA and PRA	Responsibility for the firm's performance of its obligations under the **Senior Managers Regime**
B	FCA and PRA	Responsibility for the firm's performance of its obligations under the **Employee Certification Regime**
B1	FCA	Responsibility for the firm's obligations in relation to **Individual Conduct Rules for training and reporting**
C	FCA and PRA	Responsibility for compliance with requirements of the regulatory system relating to the **Management Responsibilities Map**
D	FCA	Overall responsibility for the firm's policies and procedures for countering the risk that the firm might be used to further **financial crime**
F	FCA and PRA	Responsibility for leading the development of and monitoring the effective implementation of policies and procedures for the **induction, training and professional development** of all members of the firm's **governing body**
G	FCA and PRA	Responsibility for monitoring the effective implementation of policies and procedures for the **induction, training and professional development** of all of the firm's **senior managers**
J-2	FCA and PRA	Responsibility for providing **oversight** of Internal Audit (IA) at firms that **outsource their IA** to a third party

Prescribed Responsibility Reference	Regulator	Prescribed Responsibility
H	PRA	Responsibility for overseeing the adoption of the firm's **culture in the day-to-day management** of the firm
I	PRA	Responsibility for leading the development of the firm's **culture by the governing body** as a whole
M	FCA and PRA	Responsibility for overseeing the development of, and implementation of the firm's **remuneration** policies and practices
N	FCA and PRA	Responsibility for the independence, autonomy and effectiveness of the firm's policies and procedures on **whistleblowing**
O	PRA	Responsibility for managing the allocation and maintenance of the firm's **capital, funding and liquidity**
Q	PRA	Responsibility for the production and integrity of the firm's **financial information and its regulatory reporting**
T	PRA	Responsibility for the development and maintenance of the firm's **business model** by the governing body
T2	PRA	Responsibility for the performance of the firm's **Own Risk and Solvency assessment** (ORSA)
U	PRA	Responsibility for the firm's performance of its obligations under **Fitness and Propriety** in respect of notified non-executive directors and those who perform a key function (where applicable for insurers)
X	PRA	Responsibility for the firm's **outsourced operational functions** including systems and technology
Z	FCA	Overall responsibility for the firm's compliance with **CASS**

Practical implementation

4.11

- When allocating Prescribed Responsibilities, firms need to determine who in practice is the most senior person responsible.

- A Prescribed Responsibility:

    - must be allocated clearly;

    - will normally be held by a single person, except where the firm can show that it is appropriate and justifiable to divide (ie give responsibility for separate parts) or share (ie give jointly accountability for) a responsibility. Where that is the case, it must be clearly explained in relevant Statements of Responsibilities;

    - cannot be allocated to individuals approved under the Other Overall Responsibility Function (SMF18), except for the CASS responsibility.

- Where a Prescribed Responsibility moves from one senior manager to another, relevant Statements of Responsibilities will need updating to reflect the changes but the re-allocation will not require regulatory approval.

Statements of Responsibilities

4.12   At all times firms must have a complete set of current Statements of Responsibilities (SoR) for all their SMF managers. A SoR is a document that all senior managers need to have, which clearly sets out their role and what they are responsible and accountable for. They rename and replace the 'scope of responsibilities' documents produced by Solvency II and large NDF firms under the SIMR regime. The statement needs to be:

- submitted with a senior manager's application for approval;

- maintained and kept up to date once approval is granted; and

- re-submitted whenever there is a significant change in responsibilities including:

    - where a senior manager has a Prescribed Responsibility added or removed from his or her responsibilities; or

    - where there is a change to how responsibilities are shared between senior managers.

The accuracy and clarity of statements is not to be underestimated. Where enforcement action is taken against a senior manager, the regulator will take into account the individual's Statement of Responsibilities when determining the extent of the senior manager's responsibilities. Senior managers will need to agree the description of their role and wider responsibilities and sign the statement.

The statements should:

- be practical and useable without unnecessary detail and be succinct and clear and not heavily caveated;

- be a single, self-contained document without cross-reference to other documents, attachments or links;

- clearly and succinctly set out each responsibility within 300 words, without unnecessary detail;

- focus on and contain enough information to understand what the senior manager is actually responsible for and which business functions and activities fall into the SMF manager's overall responsibilities;

- make it clear how any responsibilities or functions are divided between senior managers;

- show how the senior manager's responsibilities fit with the firm's overall governance and management arrangements;

- be consistent with the firm's Management Responsibilities Map and collectively demonstrate that there are no gaps in the allocation of responsibilities among SMF managers.

> '... your statement of responsibility is first and foremost the areas for which you are accountable, not the day-to-day tasks you are responsible for. To be precise, you are responsible for taking reasonable steps to ensure that the decisions made by the people that you lead are appropriate.'
>
> Source: Jonathan Davidson, Director of Supervision – Retail and Authorisations, City and Financial Summit, London (September 2017)

Management Responsibilities Map

4.13   The Management Responsibilities Map sets out the firm's management and governance arrangements in a single comprehensive document that shows details of:

- how Prescribed Responsibilities have been allocated;

- how any responsibilities are shared or divided;

- who has overall responsibility for the firm's activities, business areas and management functions;

- individuals' and committees' reporting lines.

The Management Responsibilities Map replaces the 'governance map' which Solvency II firms and large NDFs prepared and maintained under the former regime. Its purpose and design is to give a complete view of the allocation of responsibilities across a firm and demonstrate that the senior managers' SoR collectively do not leave any gaps in responsibility. It is therefore crucial that the responsibilities map is consistent with the collective statements of responsibilities.

Whilst there are requirements concerning the contents of the map, there is no prescribed format to follow. The map should provide adequate information about the firm's governance arrangements, including how they relate to, and fit within, the firm and a group as a whole. It should demonstrate that there is a clear organisational structure and help the regulator to identify which individual to speak to about issues and who is accountable where something goes wrong.

It is therefore important that they are continuously kept up to date and submitted with any FCA application for approval. In addition, the PRA requires maps to include a record of any matter reserved to the governing body (including its committees' terms of reference).

The Certification Regime

4.14   The introduction of the Certification Regime is one of the biggest changes for insurers compared to the former SIMR and revised APR regimes. It applies to employees who perform certain functions, known as certification functions. These employees are not senior managers but their role means it is possible for them to cause significant harm to the firm or its customers. They do not need regulatory approval. This means that firms themselves are responsible for ensuring that their employees who fall within the Certification Regime are fit and proper to perform their roles, rather than the regulators having this responsibility.

Who it applies to

4.15

The Certification Regime:

- applies only to employees;

- does not apply to non-executive directors;

- does not apply to senior managers approved to perform SMFs;

- applies to those performing a certification function who are either based in the UK or, if based outside the UK, have contact with UK clients;

- for material risk takers under Solvency II regulations on remuneration, there is no territorial limitation and the regime will apply even if they are based overseas and do not deal with a UK client.

Certification functions

4.16   Firms need to identify employees who perform a certification function. The same list of certification functions applies to all firms, although some, such as algorithmic trading, are unlikely to be relevant in practice to insurers. The regulators have set out a number of certification functions which reflect their different objectives. The FCA functions are called 'significant harm functions' whilst the PRA refers to 'certification functions'. In small firms, there may be no-one in the Certification Regime if there is only a handful of senior managers supported by administrative staff.

FCA certification functions

- Anyone who supervises or manages a certified person (directly or indirectly), but is not a senior manager
- Material risk takers
- The client dealing function
- Proprietary traders
- CASS Oversight function (current CF10a)
- Algorithmic trading

PRA certification functions

- All key function holders – individuals who are responsible for a 'key function' at Solvency II insurers, ie risk, actuarial, internal audit, compliance and finance
- Material risk takers – whose professional activities have a material impact on the firm's risk profile as per the Solvency II remuneration requirements
- Individuals who are managing a material risk taker

Fitness and propriety requirements

4.17   Firms must issue employees holding one of these roles with a certificate that confirms they are fit and proper, and firms must re-assess employees and renew the certificates at least once a year. In practice, firms may coordinate the annual certification with wider year-end performance management processes.

Firms must do this assessment:

- at the point of recruitment (or before a person performs a certification function); and
- on an ongoing basis, and at least once a year.

The **Fit and Proper Test** should take into account relevant FCA rules around the qualifications, training, competence and personal characteristics required for that role, specifically:

- honesty, integrity and reputation, ie they will be open and honest in their dealings and be able to comply with the requirements imposed on them;

- competence and capability, ie that they have the necessary skills, experience, training and time to carry on the function they are to perform;

- financial soundness with regard to judgment debts or awards, arrangements with creditors or bankruptcy.

The **certificate** that needs to be issued to employees:

- must state that the firm is satisfied that the person is a fit and proper person to perform the function the certificate relates to;

- must set out what aspect of the firm's affairs the person will be involved in as part of performing his or her function.

If the firm completes a fit and proper assessment and then decides not to issue a certificate to someone, the firm must give the person a notice in writing setting out what steps (if any) the firm proposes to take in relation to the person as a result of the decision and the reasons for the proposal.

The **evidence** that firms need to collect and steps they need to take when assessing fitness and propriety of individuals includes:

- a criminal record check for each senior manager approval application. This will ensure the information the candidate has given to the firm is accurate and complete. This also applies to NEDs who are not senior managers;

- firms have to register with the Disclosure and Barring Service (DBS) (and the equivalent agencies in Scotland and Northern Ireland), who run the checks;

- where a candidate has spent a considerable amount of time working or living outside the UK, firms should carry out an equivalent check with the appropriate overseas regulatory body, where possible;

- criminal record checks for certified staff are not mandated but firms may choose to undertake them where legally allowed.

Regulatory references for senior managers and certified staff

4.18   All insurers seeking to appoint someone to a senior manager or a certified role need to request a regulatory reference from the candidate's past employer(s). The requirement also applies to all non-executive directors who are not senior managers. Specifically, firms need to:

- request a reference from all previous employers in the past six years for individuals applying for senior manager, certification and non-approved non-executive director roles;

- share information with other firms in a standard template;

- disclose certain mandatory information going back six years, including details of disciplinary action taken due to breaches of the Conduct Rules including the basis and outcome, and any findings that the individual was not fit and proper;

- disclose any other relevant information for assessing whether a candidate is fit and proper (eg the number of upheld complaints) covering the previous six years. For serious misconduct there is no time limit;

- retain records of disciplinary and fit and proper findings going back six years;

- not enter into non-disclosure or other arrangements that conflict with the disclosure obligations;

- update regulatory references where new and significant information comes to light.

The Conduct Rules

4.19 Under the SM&CR, the FCA and PRA's enforceable Conduct Rules apply to a wide range of staff working in insurers. This includes:

- all senior managers in the SMR;

- all non-executive directors who are not senior managers;

- all certification staff in the Certification Regime;

- all other employees, except ancillary staff.

The ancillary staff out of scope of the rules are receptionists, switchboard operators, post room staff, reprographics/print room staff, property/facilities management, events management, security guards, invoice processing, audio-visual technicians, vending machine staff, medical staff, archive records management, drivers, corporate social responsibility staff, data controllers and processors, cleaners, catering staff, personal assistants, secretaries, information technology support (ie helpdesk) and human resources administrators/processors.

The aim of the rules is to:

- set basic standards of good personal conduct, against which regulators can hold individuals to account;

- deter people from doing something that could damage the firm or its customers given the possibility of enforcement;

- shape the culture, standards and policies of a firm as a whole;

- drive up standards of individual behaviour in financial services;

- improve individual accountability and awareness of conduct issues across firms;

- achieve cultural change across organisations.

The Individual and Senior Manager Conduct Rules

4.20   The tables below illustrate the Individual Conduct Rules and the Senior Managers Conduct Rules.

Table 4.3 – Individual Conduct Rules

Individual Conduct Rules		
	Conduct rule	*Regulator*
Rule 1	You must act with integrity	PRA/FCA
Rule 2	You must act with due skill, care and diligence	PRA/FCA
Rule 3	You must be open and cooperative with the FCA, the PRA and other regulators	PRA/FCA
Rule 4	You must pay due regard to the interests of customers and treat them fairly	FCA
Rule 5	You must observe proper standards of market conduct	FCA

In addition to the Individual Conduct Rules, SMFs must comply with additional Conduct Rules for senior managers.

Table 4.4 – Senior Manager Conduct Rules

Senior Manager Conduct Rules	
SC1	You must take reasonable steps to ensure that the business of the firm for which you are responsible is controlled effectively
SC2	You must take reasonable steps to ensure that the business of the firm for which you are responsible complies with the relevant requirements and standards of the regulatory system
SC3	You must take reasonable steps to ensure that any delegation of your responsibilities is to an appropriate person and that you oversee this effectively
SC4	You must disclose appropriately any information of which the FCA or PRA would reasonably expect notice

The five Individual Conduct Rules and the Senior Manager Conduct Rule 4 also apply to non-executive directors.

The rules apply to both a firm's regulated and unregulated financial services activities (including any ancillary activities carried on in connection with a regulated activity) such as property investment for both life and non-life insurers.

Training and notification

4.21

> '...the rules look like common sense, so it is easy to skate over them without thinking how they apply to each job. So we have introduced a requirement to train all employees about what they might mean for them.'
>
> Source: Jonathan Davidson, FCA Director of Supervision – Retail and Authorisations, City and Financial Summit, London (September 2017)

The Conduct Rules create obligations for a firm relating to training and notification, which in practice will require insurers to implement a significant programme of communications and training to ensure they meet the requirements. Responsibility will sit with the senior manager to which the Prescribed Responsibility for the firm's obligations for Conduct Rules notifications and training has been allocated.

(1) *Firms need to make individuals aware of the Conduct Rules that apply to them.* They need to train them to understand how the rules apply to them and to ensure they have a broad awareness and understanding of what the rules mean in practice in the context of their organisation and work. Firms will also need to track completion of training and follow up where necessary to be able to demonstrate meeting this obligation.

To provide efficient and effective training, firms may choose to adapt the type and style to the distinct categories of individuals within the SM&CR: senior managers, certified persons and other staff, and to roles, so that it can be tailored to needs. For example:

- staff dealing directly with customers may require additional training on Rule 4: You must pay due regard to the interests of customers and treat them fairly;

- individuals who trade in the markets would require bespoke training on Rule 5: You must observe proper standards of market conduct would apply to their day-to-day activities.

(2) *Firms need to notify regulators when disciplinary action has been taken against a person because of any action, failure to act or circumstance that amounts to a breach of the Conduct Rules.* Therefore, firms will also need to have procedures and systems in place to enable the monitoring and reporting of breaches:

- for senior managers, firms need to notify the regulator within seven business days of the firm becoming aware of the matter;

- for other staff, the notification needs to be made once a year in a report covering a 12-month period to the end of August. Where there are no breaches of the Conduct Rules to report, firms should still submit a nil return.

Outsourcing under the SMR

4.22   Where a firm relies on a third party for operational functions of the firm, it remains fully responsible for all of its regulatory obligations. This means that while firms may outsource the function, they cannot outsource the responsibility for this function. For example, for internal audit or claims handling functions undertaken by third parties, firms will be required to explain clearly how responsibility for oversight of these outsourced functions is allocated among its senior managers.

Checklist

4.23   The checklist below offers practical questions for insurers to consider.

Checklist

- Have you identified the most senior and appropriate individuals to hold senior management functions and how responsibilities are allocated between them?

- Do you have a process for the annual fit and proper certification of senior managers, staff in certification roles and non-executive directors?

- Have all staff been adequately trained in how the Conduct Rules apply to them?

- Are statements of responsibilities in place for each manager in the firm holding a SMF?

- Is there sufficient information about governance arrangements to ensure regulators will understand how the firm is managed and governed?

Chapter 5

Extension of SM&CR to (almost) all financial services firms

Chapter summary

The Senior Managers and Certification Regime (SM&CR) will be rolled out to almost all financial services firms with effect from 9 December 2019. In this chapter the preparations for, and implications of, the roll-out are considered:

- Categorisation of SM&CR FCA solo-regulated firms

- Application of the Senior Managers Regime (SMR)

- Application of the Certification Regime

- Application of the Conduct Rules

- Transition between the Approved Persons Regime and the SM&CR

Introduction

5.1   The extension of the SM&CR to firms other than banks and insurers completes the implementation of the SM&CR to financial services business in the UK. The FCA has, as flagged in the consultation process, chosen to take a tiered approach separating out firms by size and activity and then applying elements of the three-pronged approach (Senior Managers Regime, Certification Regime and Conduct Rules) on a proportional basis.

Senior managers will need to be front and centre in resourcing, overseeing and championing the required SM&CR implementation project for their firm with a critical first step being to ensure that all the appropriate people in their business are in the correct approved functions before approved individuals are converted from the current Approved Persons Regime to the SM&CR. As the FCA puts it, 'this will help to make the move to the new regime as effective as possible'.

In order to help firms with the move to SM&CR, the FCA has published 'The Senior Managers and Certification Regime: Guide for FCA solo-regulated firms' (at www.

fca.org.uk/publication/policy/guide-for-fca-solo-regulated-firms.pdf) which pulls together a summary of rules and guidance, although 'it is not a substitute for reading the relevant Handbook requirements'.

What type of SM&CR firm will yours be?

5.2   The FCA has defined three types or classifications of SM&CR for solo-regulated firms with a fourth type of firm being exempted from the SM&CR regime. The three types of firm with a sliding scale of requirements are:

- limited scope;
- core;
- enhanced.

A firm is not subject to the SM&CR if it is currently exempt from the Approved Persons Regime.

A 'limited scope' firm will be subject to fewer requirements than a 'core' firm. The limited scope categorisation covers all firms that currently have a limited application of the Approved Persons Regime including:

- limited permission consumer credit firms;
- all sole traders;
- authorised professional firms whose only regulated activities are non-mainstream regulated activities;
- oil market participants;
- service companies;
- energy market participants;
- subsidiaries of local authorities or registered social landlords;
- insurance intermediaries whose principal business is not insurance intermediation and who only have permission to carry on insurance mediation activity in relation to non-investment insurance contracts; and
- authorised internally managed alternative investment funds.

Example

A small dental practice is a limited company and has 1,200 registered patients. It is a limited permission consumer credit firm and is therefore a limited scope firm under SM&CR.

A 'core' firm is one which currently is subject to the Approved Persons Regime with no limitations. It will have a baseline of SM&CR requirements applied which will be more than a limited scope firm and less than an enhanced one.

Example

A medium-sized independent financial advisor and mortgage broking firm has been a limited company for more than 10 years and has 40 staff. There are two executive directors and 30 advisers, all of whom give investment or mortgage advice. The remaining staff either do not advise but undertake various roles connected with financial services or are not involved in financial services activities at all. The firm's board has three non-executive directors, one of whom acts as the chair. The firm is currently subject to the Approved Persons Regime and will be a core firm under the SM&CR.

An 'enhanced' firm is one of the small proportion of solo-regulated firms that will have to apply extra rules. If a firm meets one or more of the six listed criteria below it will be considered an enhanced firm. The criteria are as follows:

1. A firm that is a significant investment firm that is not a collective portfolio management investment firm (ie an IFPRU firm) as defined by the FCA (see www.handbook.fca.org.uk/handbook/IFPRU/1/2.html) whereby it meets, at any time, one or more of the following conditions:

   - its total assets exceed £530m;

   - its total liabilities exceed £380m;

   - the annual fees and commission income it receives in relation to the regulated activities carried on by the firm exceeds £160m in the 12-month period immediately preceding the date the firm carries out the assessment under this rule on a rolling basis;

   - the client money that it receives or holds exceeds £425m; and

   - the assets belonging to its clients that it holds in the course of, or connected with, its regulated activities exceed £7.8bn.

2. A firm that is a CASS large firm as defined by the FCA (see www.handbook. fca.org.uk/handbook/CASS/1A/2.html#DES43) whereby the highest total amount of client money held during the firm's last calendar year or, as the case may be, that it projects it will hold during the current calendar year, is more than £1bn or the highest total value of safe custody assets held by the firm during the firm's last calendar year or, as the case may be, that it projects it will hold during the current calendar year, is more than £100bn.

3. Firms with assets under management of £50bn or more on a three-year rolling average.

4. Firms with an annual intermediary regulated business revenue of £35m calculated on a three-year rolling average.

5. Firms with annual revenue generated by regulated consumer credit lending of £100m or more calculated on a three-year rolling average.

6. Mortgage lenders and administrators (that are not banks) with 10,000 or more regulated mortgages outstanding at the latest reporting date.

Example

A separate legal entity is solo-regulated by the FCA and part of a large global banking group. Another entity within the same group is subject to the banking SM&CR and the entities have a number of directors in common. The solo-regulated entity has a thriving business with total assets of more than £700m. The entity will be an enhanced firm under SM&CR.

The SM&CR applies at legal entity level and it will be entirely possible that within financial services groups there will firms in different tiers of the regime. For ease of governance and oversight, senior managers may choose to apply the highest tier of the regime to all entities in a group. The regulator has made clear that there is 'no expectation or requirement' to do this but it may be one way in which firms can seek to streamline their regulatory obligations.

The Senior Managers Regime

5.3 In outline, the SMR applies to all firms and specifies what senior management functions need to be identified and allocated, what firms and their senior managers then need to do about the SMR, the allocation of prescribed responsibilities and the additional requirements imposed on enhanced firms.

The FCA has adapted the SMR to be more proportionate for solo-regulated firms but the same principles apply whereby firms need to allocate senior individuals to hold senior management functions. The functions are set out by the FCA and must be the most senior people in a firm with the greatest potential to cause harm or impact upon market integrity. Specifically, the FCA expects to know who a firm's most senior decision makers are and to have line of sight to the allocation of responsibilities within a firm.

There is no territorial limitation on SMR, so anyone deemed to be performing a senior management function, whether based in the UK or overseas, will be subject to the regime.

Working out your firm's type

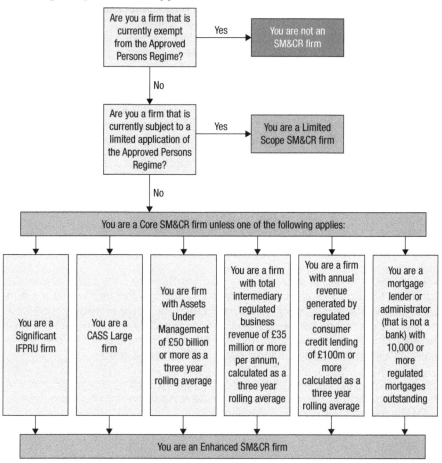

Source: 'The Senior Managers and Certification Regime: Guide for FCA solo-regulated firms', FCA (July 2018)

Critically, anyone who is allocated a senior management function must be approved by the FCA *before* he or she can start their role.

The FCA can impose time limits or other conditions as part of the approval process for senior managers. Firms can utilise the 12-week rule which allows someone to cover for a senior management function without being approved where the absence is temporary or reasonably unforeseen.

Statements of Responsibilities (SoRs)

5.4   Every individual allocated a senior management function must have a single written Statement of Responsibilities which sets out their role and responsibilities. SoRs are discussed in more detail in **Chapter 3** but each SoR is required to state what each senior manager is responsible and accountable for – it does not cover 'how' those responsibilities are carried out. It is expected that each SoR will be self-contained, clear and succinct and will not refer to any other documents although there may well be a suite of underlying documents which themselves refer to the SoR.

If someone holds more than one senior management function in a single legal entity they only need to have one SoR, but it must clearly articulate the scope of allocated responsibilities. The SoR is one of the documents which must be submitted as part of the FCA approval process for an individual to hold a senior management function.

Firms need to keep all SoRs up to date and, if there has been a significant change, then it will need to be resubmitted to the FCA.

Duty of responsibility

5.5   Every holder of a senior management function in a financial services firm has a legal duty of responsibility. In practical terms this means that if a firm breaches one of the regulatory requirements then the senior manager responsible for that area could be held responsible for the breach if he or she did not take the appropriate 'reasonable steps' to prevent or stop the breach. The concept of reasonable steps is discussed in more detail in **Chapters 2** and **7**.

The burden of proof lies with the FCA to show that the senior manager did not take the steps a person in his or her position could reasonably be expected to take to avoid the breach occurring or continuing.

Prescribed responsibilities

5.6   The FCA has defined a series of prescribed responsibilities which are specific to senior managers and cover key conduct and prudential risks. Firms are required to allocate the prescribed responsibilities as they see fit with the expectation that they will be given to the most senior person responsible for that activity or area. Those allocated prescribed responsibilities need to have sufficient authority and an appropriate level of knowledge and competence to carry out the responsibility properly.

Before senior managers agree to take on a prescribed responsibility they must be comfortable that, in practice, they are the most senior person and that they, in reality, have the authority to discharge the accountability.

Normally, only one person can hold a prescribed responsibility but there are limited circumstances in which it can be divided or shared. If a firm chooses to share a prescribed responsibility, it will need to be able to show why the share is justified and confirm that the share does not leave a gap. Examples of circumstances under which a prescribed responsibility might be shared are:

- as part of a job share;
- where a departing and incoming senior manager work together temporarily as part of a handover; or
- where a particular area of a firm is run by two senior managers.

Where responsibilities are shared or divided then this must be explained in the relevant Statement of Responsibilities and the senior managers concerned will be seen to be jointly accountable.

It should be noted that Prescribed Responsibilities do not apply to limited scope firms or EEA branches.

Fit and proper

5.7   Firms must make sure all senior managers and people performing certification functions (ie people under the Certification Regime) are fit and proper to perform their role. This must be done on appointment and at least once a year.

A central thread of the SM&CR is the need for firms to take responsibility for their staff being fit and proper to do their jobs. As part of the extension of the SM&CR, the FCA extended the application of the fit and proper guidance in the FIT part of the Handbook to cover certification staff, as well as senior managers and non-approved non-executive directors (see www.handbook.fca.org.uk/handbook/FIT/1/?view=chapter). FIT sets out detailed guidance about the types of things firms should consider as part of assessing a person's fitness and propriety including:

- honesty, integrity and reputation;
- competence and capability, including whether the person satisfies any relevant FCA training and competence requirements; and
- financial soundness.

Table 5.1 – Summary of senior manager fit and proper requirements

	New hire	Internal hire (including intra-group hires)	Annual Assessment
Regulatory reference	Yes	No	No
Fit and proper assessment	Yes	Yes	Yes
FCA approval before starting role	Yes	Yes	No
Criminal record check	Yes	Yes	No

5.7   *Extension of SM&CR to (almost) all financial services firms*

Under the SM&CR, firms must collect extra evidence when assessing candidates for senior manager positions, certification functions or non-executive director roles (even if they are not a senior management function).

Criminal record checks are required for senior managers and candidates for senior management functions must declare any criminal record (to the maximum extent allowed by law). Firms must also undertake a criminal record check as part of each senior manager application for approval. This requirement also applies to non-executive directors who are not senior managers.

One upshot of this is that firms will have to register with the Disclosure and Barring Service (DBS), and the equivalent agencies in Scotland and Northern Ireland, who run the checks. Smaller firms may need to use an umbrella organisation as an intermediary. Where a candidate has spent a considerable amount of time working or living outside the UK, firms should consider undertaking an equivalent check with the appropriate overseas regulatory body where available.

Criminal record checks are not mandatory for certification functions, but firms may choose to conduct these checks for other staff where they are legally allowed to do so – this is for firms to decide.

Firms also need to take up (and be prepared to give) regulatory references and must request a reference from the senior management and certification function candidates' past employers. This again applies to non-executive directors who are not senior managers.

The regulatory reference rules require firms to:

- Request a reference from all previous employers in the past six years for people applying for senior manager, certification and non-approved non-executive director roles.

- Share information between firms in a standard template.

- Disclose certain information going back six years. This includes details of any disciplinary action taken due to breaches of the Conduct Rules and any findings that the person was not fit and proper.

- Disclose any other information relevant to assessing whether a candidate is fit and proper (eg the number of upheld complaints), covering the previous six years (unless it relates to serious misconduct, in which case there is no time limit). Firms will need to use their judgement when considering what is relevant, on a case-by-case basis.

- Retain records of disciplinary and fit and proper findings going back six years.

- Not enter into arrangements that conflict with their disclosure obligations (eg non-disclosure agreements).

Firms will also need to update regulatory references where new, significant information comes to light. As part of the allocation of prescribed responsibilities, a senior manager will be accountable for the firm's regulatory reference obligations.

Table 5.2 – Summary of certification function fit and proper requirements

	New hire	Internal hire (including intra-group hires)	Annual Assessment
Regulatory reference	Yes	No	No
Fit and proper assessment	Yes	Yes	Yes
Certification for function	Yes	Yes	Yes

Note: The application of the fit and proper requirements to limited scope firms is slightly different in some areas:

- Sole traders are not required to seek regulatory references or criminal records checks for themselves, even where they also hold a senior management function.

- Sole traders with employees should consider whether any of these individuals meet the definition of a senior manager or perform one of the certification functions. If so, the fit and proper requirements apply.

- Non-approved board directors (both executive and non-executive) at limited scope firms are not subject to the fit and proper requirements, including regulatory references and criminal records checks.

Certification Regime

5.8   The Certification Regime sits underneath that for senior managers. Certification covers specific functions that are not senior management functions, but can have a significant impact on customers, the firm and/or market integrity.

The most immediate distinction between the Senior Managers Regime and the certification one is that under the Certification Regime the FCA does not approve the individuals but instead requires firms to check and confirm (certify) at least once a year that these people are suitable to do their job. As part of the certification firms should take into account whether the individual:

- has obtained a qualification;

- has undergone, or is undergoing, training;

- possesses a level of competence.

Certificates issued by firms should both state that the authorised person is satisfied that the person is a fit and proper person to perform the certification function and set out the aspects of the firm's business in which the individual will be involved.

Certification functions apply where the firm has individuals (specifically employees) performing relevant roles. This means it is possible that in very small firms there could be a situation where no-one falls within the Certification Regime, for example, where there are only a handful of senior individuals (who are all senior management functions) who are in turn supported by administrative staff. Equally, if a sole trader has no employees, then the Certification Regime will not apply.

The following functions will be certification functions under the SM&CR.

Table 5.3 – Overview of certification functions

Certification function	Overview
Significant management function (previously CF29)	This includes individuals with significant responsibility for a business unit.
Proprietary traders CASS operational oversight function (previously CF10a)	These important roles can seriously impact the way the firm conducts its business and are not limited to revenue-generating business areas. All proprietary traders are covered by the Certification Regime. The CASS operational oversight certification function covers oversight of the operational effectiveness of a firm's systems and controls for client money and assets.
Functions subject to qualification requirements	This includes, for example, mortgage advisers, retail investment advisers and pension transfer specialists. The full list is set out in the FCA's Training and Competence Sourcebook at www.handbook.fca.org.uk/handbook/TC.pdf.
The client dealing function	This function will be expanded from the current CF30 function to apply to any person dealing in or arranging investments with clients, including retail and professional clients and eligible counterparties. This will include: • financial advisers; • people who are involved in corporate finance business; • people who are involved in dealing or arranging deals in investments; • investment managers.

Certification function	Overview
Anyone who supervises or manages a certified function (directly or indirectly), but is not a senior manager	This will make sure that people who supervise certified employees are held to the same standard of accountability. It also makes sure a clear chain of accountability between junior certified employees and the senior manager ultimately responsible for that area. For example, if a firm employs a customer-facing financial adviser, every manager above him/her in the same chain of responsibility will have to be certified (until the senior manager approved under the SMR is reached).
Material risk takers	The concept of material risk takers (also known as Remuneration Code staff) already exists for firms under the FCA remuneration rules (SYSC 19 itemises the requirements for AIFMD, UCITS, IFPRU and BIPRU firms). These firms need to consider all types of risk when identifying their material risk takers, including those of a prudential, operational, conduct and reputational nature. All of these material risk takers will be covered by this certification function.
Algorithmic trading	This function includes people with responsibility for: • approving the deployment of a trading algorithm or a material part of one; • approving the deployment of a material amendment to a trading algorithm or a material part of one, or the combination of trading algorithms; • monitoring or deciding whether the use or deployment of a trading algorithm is or remains compliant with the firm's obligations.

Not all of the functions in the above table will apply to all firms and firms are only required to apply those that are relevant.

If someone performs more than one certification function, a firm must certify that the person is fit and proper to carry out each function. For example, someone might carry out a function requiring a qualification and also carry out the significant management function. There might be different competencies required for the different functions, so firms must assess that the person is fit and proper to do each role (but this could be done as part of a single assessment process).

The significant management certification function (which replaces CF29 in the Approved Persons Regime) applies to people below senior managers who are responsible for business units that, because of their size, nature or impact, are considered significant by the firm. The intention of the significant management certification function is to provide broad coverage of a firm's main activities below the senior manager layer. It is up to the judgement of firms themselves as to whether a business unit is deemed to be 'significant'. The FCA has set out a number of factors for firms to consider, including:

- the size and significance of the firm's business in the UK;
- the risk profile of the unit;
- the unit's contribution to the firm's capital requirements;
- its contribution to the profit and loss account;
- the number of employees, certification functions or senior managers in the unit;
- the number of customers served by the unit.

A business unit is not limited to one that carries on commercial activities with customers and third parties or that generates revenue. A business unit can also be an internal support department (eg human resources, operations or information technology).

The Certification Regime is limited to people performing a certification function who are either based in the UK or, if based outside the UK, are dealing (ie have contact with) with UK clients. This means that if a person based overseas does not deal with UK clients, but would otherwise have been carrying out one of the functions listed in the table of certification functions, the Certification Regime will not apply to them.

The exception to this is where an individual is a material risk taker under one of the remuneration codes as set out in SYSC 19. For these individuals, there is no territorial limitation. This means that if an individual is a material risk taker, the Certification Regime will apply even if they are based overseas and do not deal with a UK client.

The diagrams below explain how territoriality applies to UK firms and branches in the context of the Certification Regime.

Territoriality and the Certification Regime for UK firms

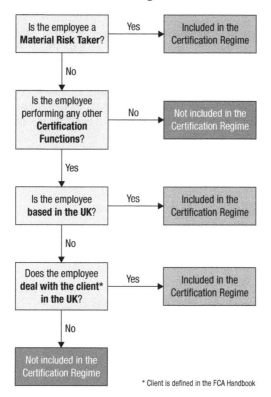

* Client is defined in the FCA Handbook

Territoriality and the Certification Regime for branches

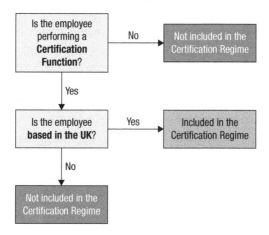

Source: 'The Senior Managers and Certification Regime: Guide for FCA solo-regulated firms', FCA (July 2018)

Conduct Rules

5.9   The third element of the SM&CR, after the Senior Manager Regime and the Certification Regime, is the application of Conduct Rules. The FCA's Conduct Rules are in the COCON Chapter of the Handbook (at www.handbook.fca.org. uk/handbook/COCON/1/?view=chapter) and apply to all employees in a firm. The FCA sees the Conduct Rules as a 'meaningful change' in the standards of conduct expected from those working in financial services and, by applying them to all staff, the aim is to improve individual accountability and awareness of conduct issues.

There are two tiers of Conduct Rules which apply to a firm's regulated and unregulated financial services activities, including any related ancillary activities.

The first tier of Conduct Rules applies to all individuals:

First tier of Conduct Rules:

1.   You must act with integrity.

2.   You must act with due care, skill and diligence.

3.   You must be open and cooperative with the FCA, the PRA and other regulators.

4.   You must pay due regard to the interests of customers and treat them fairly.

5.   You must observe proper standards of market conduct.

The second tier of Conduct Rules applies to senior managers:

Second tier of Conduct Rules:

SC1. You must take reasonable steps to ensure that the business of the firm for which you are responsible is controlled effectively.

SC2. You must take reasonable steps to ensure that the business of the firm for which you are responsible complies with the relevant requirements and standards of the regulatory system.

SC3. You must take reasonable steps to ensure that any delegation of your responsibilities is to an appropriate person and that you oversee the discharge of the delegated responsibility effectively.

SC4. You must disclose appropriately any information of which the FCA or PRA would reasonably expect notice.

The Conduct Rules apply to all senior managers, all certified functions, all non-executive directors who are not senior managers and all other employees who are not ancillary staff. The FCA has produced something of a shopping list of those considered to be 'ancillary' by not performing a role specific to financial services (see 'The Senior Managers and Certification Regime: Guide for FCA solo-regulated firms', pp 44–45 at www.fca.org.uk/publication/policy/guide-for-fca-solo-regulated-firms.pdf).

The FCA is clear that the Conduct Rules apply to the vast majority of people working in financial services firms as a broad range of staff have the potential to cause harm.

Firms are required to train staff on the Conduct Rules and to have a senior manager allocated the relevant prescribed responsibility. Senior managers and those covered by the Certification Regime are expected to have been trained and to abide by the Conduct Rules as from the start of the extended regime on 9 December 2019. Firms will have a further 12 months to put in place processes to comply with the training and reporting requirements and training all other staff on the Conduct Rules.

It should be noted that the Conduct Rules prescribed responsibility does not apply to limited scope firms.

The FCA requires notification by firms when disciplinary action has been taken against a person for a breach of the Conduct Rules. In addition, firms need to make an annual notification about Conduct Rules even if there have not been any breaches.

How the Senior Managers Regime applies to limited scope firms

5.10   There are three required senior management functions within the limited scope tier:

• **SMF29 Limited Scope function:**

This replaces the apportionment and oversight function (CF8) from the Approved Persons Regime and is the person who deals with the apportionment of responsibilities under SYSC 4.4.3.R such that:

'A firm must take reasonable care to maintain a clear and appropriate apportionment of significant responsibilities among its directors and senior managers in such a way that it is clear who has which of those responsibilities and the business and affairs of the firm can be adequately monitored and controlled by the directors, relevant senior managers and governing body of the firm.'

Table 5.4 – Summary of SM&CR tools

Tool	Limited Scope	Core	Enhanced	EEA Branches	Third Country Branches
SMFs	SMF29 – Limited Scope Function SMF16 – Compliance Oversight SMF17 – MLRO	SMF1 – CEO SMF3 – Executive Director SMF9 –Chair SMF27 – Partner SMF16 – Compliance Oversight SMF17 – MLRO	SMF1 – CEO SMF2 – CFO SMF3 – Executive Director SMF27 – Partner SMF4 – CRO SMF5 – Head of Internal Audit SMF9 – Chair SMF10 – Chair of the Risk Co SMF11 – Chair of the Audit Co SMF12 – Chair of the Remuneration Co SMF13 – Chair of the Nominations Co SMF14 – Senior Independent Director SMF16 – Compliance Oversight SMF17 – MLRO SMF18 – Other Overall Responsibility SMF24 – COO	SMF21 – EEA Branch Manager Function SMF17 – MLRO	SMF19 – Head of Third Country Branch SMF3 – Executive Director SMF16 – Compliance Oversight SMF17 – MLRO
PRs	None apply	5 (+1 for AFMs) apply	12 (+1 for AFMs) apply	None apply	8 (+1 for AFMs) apply
Duty of Responsibility	Applies to all firms				
Statements of Responsibilities	Applies to all firms				
Responsibilities Maps	✗	✗	✓	✗	✗
Handover Procedures	✗	✗	✓	✗	✗
Overall Responsibility	✗	✗	✓	✗	✗
Certification Regime	Applies to all firms				
Fit and Proper	Applies to all firms				
Conduct Rules	Applies to all firms				

Source: 'The Senior Managers and Certification Regime: Guide for FCA solo-regulated firms', p 72, FCA (July 2018).

It is also the person that oversees the establishment and maintenance of controls under SYSC 4.1.1.R such that:

> 'A firm must have robust governance arrangements, which include a clear organisational structure with well defined, transparent and consistent lines of responsibility, effective processes to identify, manage, monitor and report the risks it is or might be exposed to, and internal control mechanisms, including sound administrative and accounting procedures and effective control and safeguard arrangements for information processing systems.'

- **SMF16 Compliance oversight:**

  This is the person responsible for the compliance function in the firm and reporting to the governing body on this.

- **SMF17 Money laundering reporting officer:**

  This is the person who has responsibility for overseeing the firm's compliance with the FCA's rules on systems and controls against money laundering.

The number of functions that a limited scope firm will need will depend on its specific permissions and activities. The FCA has summarised the application of the limited scope rules for a number of common firm types – see **Table 5.5**.

Table 5.5 – Limited scope rules

Firm type	Senior Management Functions
Limited permission consumer credit firms that have a CF8 under the Approved Persons Regime.	SMF29 – Limited Scope Function
Sole traders with no employees – in practice, a sole trader with no employees is only required to have an SMF16 where required by relevant rules. It is possible that further core-tier senior management functions may apply where a sole trader with employees has a governance body comprising of individuals who perform relevant roles, but the FCA believes 'that this will be rare in practice'.	SMF16 – Compliance Oversight
Authorised professional firms whose only regulated activities are non-mainstream regulated activities.	SMF16 – Compliance Oversight SMF17 – Money Laundering Reporting Officer SMF29 – Limited Scope Function

Firm type	Senior Management Functions
Oil market participants, service companies, energy market participants, subsidiaries of local authorities or registered social landlords.	SMF16 – Compliance Oversight SMF17 – Money Laundering Reporting Officer SMF29 – Limited Scope Function
Insurance intermediaries whose principal business is not insurance intermediation and who only have permission to carry on insurance mediation activity in relation to non-investment insurance contracts.	SMF29 – Limited Scope Function

It should be noted that no prescribed responsibilities apply to limited scope firms.

How the Senior Managers Regime applies to core firms

5.11   There are six senior management functions applied to core firms: four governing functions and two required functions. The functions are summarised in **Table 5.6**.

Table 5.6 – Senior Management Functions

Governing functions:		
SMF1	Chief Executive	This is the person(s) with responsibility, under the immediate authority of the governing body, for the conduct of the whole of the business (or relevant activities). **Note:** Although the chief executive is the most senior member of an executive team, it does not mean that a firm's governing body cannot allocate specific responsibilities to other senior managers.
SMF3	Executive Director	A director of a firm, other than a non-executive director.
SMF27	Partner	A partner in a firm, other than a limited partner in a partnership registered under the Limited Partnership Act 1907.

SMF9	Chair	The person with responsibility for chairing, and overseeing the performance of the role of, the governing body of the firm. The SMF9 Chair is the only approved function that can be held by a non-executive director. Other non-executive directors who hold the CF2 function under the Approved Persons Regime will no longer need to be approved by the FCA, and their existing approval will lapse at the start of the new regime. The non-executive directors will be subject to the Conduct Rules, fit and proper requirements and regulatory reference rules.
Required functions:		
SMF16	Compliance oversight	This is the person responsible for the compliance function in the firm and reporting to the governing body on this.
SM17	Money laundering reporting officer	This is the person who has responsibility for overseeing the firm's compliance with the FCA's rules on systems and controls against money laundering.

The FCA has allocated five prescribed responsibilities that must be given to senior managers in core firms and an additional responsibility for Authorised Fund Managers (AFMs).

Table 5.7 – Prescribed Responsibilities

Prescribed Responsibility reference	Description
(a)	Performance by the firm of its obligations under the SMR, including implementation and oversight.
(b)	Performance by the firm of its obligations under the Certification Regime.
(b-1)	Performance by the firm of its obligations in respect of notifications and training of the Conduct Rules.
(d)	Responsibility for the firm's policies and procedures for countering the risk that the firm might be used to further financial crime.
(z)	Responsibility for the firm's compliance with CASS (if applicable).

For AFMs only, the additional prescribed responsibility (za) for an AFM's value for money assessments, independent director representation and acting in investors' best interests.

How the Senior Managers Regime applies to enhanced firms

5.12 There are 17 senior management functions applied to enhanced firms. Ten governing functions, three required functions and four systems and controls functions.

Table 5.8 – Senior Management Functions

Governing functions:		
SMF1	Chief Executive	This is the person(s) with responsibility, under the immediate authority of the governing body, for the conduct of the whole of the business (or relevant activities). NB: Although the chief executive is the most senior member of an executive team, it does not mean that a firm's governing body cannot allocate specific responsibilities to other senior managers.
SMF3	Executive Director	A director of a firm, other than a non-executive director.
SMF7	Group entity senior manager	This is someone with significant influence on the management or conduct of the affairs of the UK-regulated entity and is employed by, or is an officer of, another member of its group.
SMF9	Chair	The person with responsibility for chairing, and overseeing the performance of the role of, the governing body of the firm.
SMF10	Chair of the risk committee	The person with responsibility for chairing, and overseeing the performance of, any committee responsible for the oversight of the risk management systems, policies and procedures of the firm.
SMF11	Chair of the audit committee	The person with responsibility for chairing and overseeing the performance of any committee responsible for the oversight of the internal audit system of the firm.
SMF12	Chair of the remuneration committee	The person with responsibility for chairing and overseeing the performance of any committee responsible for the oversight of the design and the implementation of the remuneration policies of a firm.
SMF13	Chair of the nominations committee	If a firm has a nomination committee, this person is the person who chairs that committee.
SMF14	Senior independent director	The person with particular responsibility for leading the assessment of the chair's performance.
SMF27	Partner	A partner in a firm, other than a limited partner in a partnership registered under the Limited Partnership Act 1907.

Only those non-executive directors who hold a chair role (including the chairs of committees) or the senior independent director role will need to be approved under the SM&CR. Non-approved non-executive directors will be subject to the Conduct Rules, fit and proper requirements and regulatory reference rules.

Required functions:		
SMF16	Compliance oversight	This is the person responsible for the compliance function in the firm and reporting on this to the governing body.
SMF17	Money laundering reporting officer	This is the person who has responsibility for overseeing the firm's compliance with the FCA's rules on systems and controls against money laundering.
SMF18	Other overall responsibility	This function applies where a senior executive is the most senior person responsible for an area of the firm's business, but they do not perform any other senior management function. The FCA has stated that many firms will not need this function as the people ultimately responsible for everything the business does will already be captured by other SMFs. However, it gives flexibility and recognises the diversity of business structures in different types of firms.
Systems and controls functions:		
SMF2	Chief finance function	The person responsible for managing the financial resources of the firm, including reporting to the governing body on the firm's financial affairs.
SMF4	Chief risk function	The person with overall responsibility for managing the firm's risk controls.
SMF5	Head of internal audit	The person responsible for managing the internal audit function of a firm and reporting to the governing body on this.
SMF24	Chief operations function	The most senior person responsible for managing the internal operations (including HR), systems and technology of a firm.

For an enhanced firm there are 12 prescribed responsibilities. The FCA expects that a firm will normally allocate the prescribed responsibilities to an executive, with the exception of responsibilities (j), (k) and (l), which should be allocated, where possible, to a senior manager who is a non-executive director of the firm or a partner who does not have management responsibilities. However, as not all firms have non-executive directors, this may not always be possible and, if this is the case, the prescribed responsibility must be allocated to another appropriate senior manager.

Table 5.9 – Prescribed Responsibilities

Prescribed Responsibility reference	Description
(a)	Performance by the firm of its obligations under the SMR, including implementation and oversight.
(b)	Performance by the firm of its obligations under the Certification Regime.
(b-1)	Performance by the firm of its obligations in respect of notifications and training of the Conduct Rules.
(d)	Responsibility for the firm's policies and procedures for countering the risk that the firm might be used to further financial crime.
(z)	Responsibility for the firm's compliance with CASS (if applicable).
(c)	Compliance with the rules relating to the firm's responsibility map.
(j)	Safeguarding and overseeing the independence and performance of the internal audit function (in accordance with SYSC 6.2).
(k)	Safeguarding and overseeing the independence and performance of the compliance function (in accordance with SYSC 6.1).
(l)	Safeguarding and overseeing the independence and performance of the risk function (in accordance with SYSC 7.1.21R and SYSC 7.1.22R).
(j-3)	If the firm outsources its internal audit function, taking reasonable steps to ensure that every person involved in the performance of the service is independent from the persons who perform external audit, including: • supervision and management of the work of outsourced internal auditors; • management of potential conflicts of interest between the provision of external audit and internal audit services.
(t)	Developing and maintaining the firm's business model.
(s)	Managing the firm's internal stress test and ensuring the accuracy and timeliness of information provided to the FCA for the purposes of stress testing.

For AFMs only, the additional prescribed responsibility (za) for an AFM's value for money assessments, independent director representation and acting in investors' best interests.

There are a number of elements – overall responsibility, Responsibilities Maps and handover requirements – which apply only to enhanced firms in the extension of the SM&CR.

The overall responsibility requirement means that an enhanced firm will need to make sure that every activity, business area and management function has a senior manager assigned as having overall responsibility for it. Overall responsibility means a senior manager:

- has ultimate responsibility for managing or supervising a function;

- briefs and reports to the governing body about their area of responsibility;

- puts matters for decision about their area of responsibility to the governing body.

Having overall responsibility does not mean that the person needs to have day-to-day management control of that function. They need to be the most senior person responsible for managing the area overall and be sufficiently senior and credible, and with sufficient resources and authority, to be able to exercise their management and oversight responsibilities effectively.

As with all elements of the SM&CR, a senior manager who has designated overall responsibility needs to be comfortable that he or she does, in practice, have the resources and authority to discharge the accountability. At its heart the intention of the overall responsibility designation is to ensure that it is clear who the governing body of a firm has delegated responsibility to for each area of the firm's business. The allocation of responsibilities will differ from one firm to another.

The scope of the overall responsibility requirement is the same as the scope of the Conduct Rules and, as such, applies to a firm's regulated and unregulated financial services activities. Under the overall responsibility rule, firms must allocate responsibility to a senior manager for each of the firm's activities, business areas and management functions of the whole firm, including those carried out from a branch overseas. This includes all transactions that take place overseas (whether in full or in part).

Unlike other senior management functions an 'overall responsibility' cannot be divided because they are specific to a firm's structure and the roles of the people running it. Senior managers need to make sure that each individual Statement of Responsibilities sets out what they are responsible for in a clear and accurate way. Two or more senior managers may have overall responsibility for the same area or activity and, if that is the case, it should be clearly stated in the relevant SoRs.

Enhanced firms must prepare and maintain a Responsibilities Map setting out the firm's management and governance arrangements. This includes, for example, how the Prescribed Responsibilities have been allocated, details on who has overall responsibility for the firm's activities, business areas and management functions, details of individuals' and committees' reporting lines, and how any responsibilities are shared or divided between different people.

Responsibilities Maps are designed to give a collective view of the allocation of responsibilities across a firm, and to make sure that there are no gaps in the aggregated senior managers' SoRs. Responsibilities Maps also help the regulator to identify who to speak to about particular issues and who is accountable if something goes wrong. Where an enhanced firm is part of a group, the firm should explain, in the Responsibilities Map, how their governance arrangements fit with the rest of the group (where applicable).

Last, but not least, enhanced firms are required to take all reasonable steps to make sure that a person taking a senior manager role has all the information and materials he or she could reasonably expect to have in order to do the job effectively. One way of doing this could be for the predecessor to prepare a handover note. Firms are required to have a policy which explains how it complies with this requirement, and maintain adequate records of the steps it has taken.

Transition between the Approved Persons Regime and SM&CR

5.13   The extension of the SM&CR comes into effect on 9 December 2019. The FCA has stated that it will contact firms ahead of the transition to the SM&CR with its assessment of their status (ie enhanced, core or limited) based on the information held by the regulator. Any assessment made by the FCA should be seen as indicative with firms themselves still responsible for deciding into which tier they fall.

The FCA has set out two transitional provisions which, while providing additional time to firms and their senior managers, should not be used as a reason to delay consideration of the impact of SM&CR. The two transitional provisions are:

- firms are required to have identified those staff who will be covered by the Certification Regime by 9 December 2019, but will have until 9 December 2020 to complete the initial certification process;

- all senior management function and certification staff must be trained and abide by the Conduct Rules by 9 December 2019 but, again, will have until 9 December 2020 to train all other staff on the Conduct Rules.

There is also an element of grandfathering with firms not being required to obtain regulatory references for existing employees and who will be performing the same role after the start of the new regime.

Timelines for moving to the SM&CR

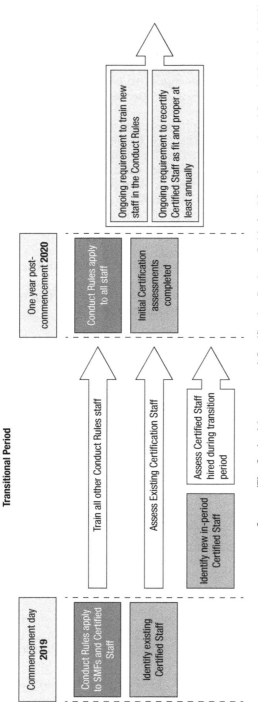

Source: 'The Senior Managers and Certification Regime: Guide for FCA solo-regulated firms', FCA (July 2018)

Transition for core, limited scope firms and branches

5.14   The FCA is seeking to streamline the implementation of the new regime as much as is feasible. Individuals at core and limited scope firms will be automatically converted wherever possible, with no action required by firms. To facilitate the automatic conversion, the FCA has recommended that firms consider whether any changes to their approvals are required ahead of 9 December 2019.

Specifically, firms will not have to apply for re-approval for currently approved individuals where there is no substantive change in the individual's role before and after the introduction of the extended SM&CR. This means that no extra checks are required (for example, criminal record checks and regulatory references). The FCA has made crystal clear that firms already have to make sure that these individuals are, and continue to be, fit and proper. That said, senior managers would be well advised to check the quality and completeness of the suite of evidence maintained by the firm to demonstrate the required fitness and propriety.

Table 5.10 – Function mapping for core, limited scope firms and branches

Controlled function under the Approved Persons Regime	Corresponding senior management function under SM&CR
CF1 – director	SMF3 – executive director
CF2 – non-executive director	SMF9 – chair (NB: non-executive directors at core and limited scope firms who are not the firm's chair will no longer be approved by the FCA.)
CF3 – chief executive	SMF1 – chief executive SMF19 – head of third country branch
CF4 – partner	SMF3 – executive director (for third country branches only) SMF27 – partner
CF5 – director of unincorporated association	SMF3 – executive director
CF6 – small friendly society function	SMF3 – executive director
CF8 – apportionment and oversight (for limited scope firms only)	SMF29 – limited scope
CF10 – compliance oversight	SMF16 – compliance oversight
CF11 – money laundering reporting officer	SMF17 – money laundering reporting officer
CF29 – significant management function (EEA branches only)	SMF21 – EEA branch senior management function

If an individual holds more than one convertible function under the Approved Persons Regime then all of the relevant functions will be converted in line with the approaches detailed below. If an individual is not approved, or requires additional approvals, they will need to apply for each new function (if an application is for multiple functions this can be done at the same time and using the same form for those functions).

Each senior manager is required to have a SoR. Firms are not required to submit these to the FCA for converted individuals, but they must be able to provide a senior manager's SoR to the FCA on request. Senior managers of core and limited scope firms would be well advised to ensure they are completely comfortable with, and can support, the required succinct SoR and could, if required, discuss the contents with the regulator.

A number of existing functions at core and limited scope firms won't be automatically converted as those roles will no longer require approval by the FCA. Some of these roles will, depending on the firm however, fall into the Certification Regime.

The functions disappearing are:

- CF2 – non-executive director (with the exception of the SMF9 – chair);

- CF10a – CASS oversight function;

- CF28 – systems and controls function;

- CF29 – significant management function (although this can be converted to the new EEA branch manager function for EEA Branches);

- CF30 – customer function.

To enable the automatic conversion of the relevant non-executive director (CF2 under the Approved Persons Regime) to SMF9 – chair, firms with a non-executive chair will need to submit a Form K to the FCA. As noted above, core firms are not required to submit senior manager's SoR to the regulator. The FCA has made clear that if the appropriate Form K is not submitted for the conversion of the role of chair, then the individual's approval will lapse when the new regime starts. If the chair continues to perform the role without approval, he or she will be in breach of the rules. The exception and requirement only applies to a conversion to a non-executive chair, all other non-executive directors at core firms will no longer be approved by the FCA.

Some core firms have an executive chair. In this scenario there will be an automatic conversion of the director (CF1) to executive director (SMF3) and the firm will then have to use Form A to apply for the additional SMF9 – chair function.

Most core and limited scope firms do not need to take any action ahead of conversion, but if firms wish to change their approved individuals, the following principles apply:

- the existing processes for individual applications continue to apply as usual until the start of the new regime;

- the SM&CR application forms will be available from the FCA for submission before 9 December 2019, however, these approvals will only be effective from the start of the new regime;
- an APR application submitted, but not determined before the start of the new regime, will be converted to an application for the relevant senior management function at commencement.

The FCA has given a table of scenarios and details of the relevant forms to be used for additional applications and where the firm has a chair (see the 'Guide for FCA solo-regulated firms', page 60 at www.fca.org.uk/publication/policy/guide-for-fca-solo-regulated-firms.pdf).

Transition for enhanced firms

5.15   As with core, limited scope firms and branches, the FCA is seeking to streamline the transition between the APR and the SM&CR. Enhanced firms will have to inform the FCA who they want to assign to the new senior management functions but firms will not have to re-apply for approval if the proposed SMFs can be mapped directly (see **Table 5.11** below) from the Approved Persons Regime.

There is no need for firms to do extra checks on these individuals when they are converted as firms are already required to make sure that these individuals are, and continue to be, fit and proper. There are additional obligations on enhanced firms and they will need to submit the following, as part of a Form K submission:

- details of all of the approved persons converted to SMFs as at 9 December 2019;
- Statements of Responsibilities for all of the SMFs covered by the Form K (note that for core firms, while SoRs have to be produced for each senior manager they are not required to be submitted to the regulator);
- a Responsibilities Map.

Where firms wish to make changes to their approvals prior to the start of the new regime, Forms A and E should also be submitted, and the details included in Form K, for new or transferred individuals respectively.

Table 5.11 – Function mapping for enhanced firms

Controlled function under the Approved Persons Regime	Corresponding possible senior management function under SM&CR
CF1 – director	SMF2 – chief finance officer SMF3 – executive director SMF4 – chief risk officer SMF5 – head of internal audit SMF7 – group entity senior manager SMF24 – chief operations

Controlled function under the Approved Persons Regime	Corresponding possible senior management function under SM&CR
CF2 – non-executive director	SMF9 – chair SMF10 – chair of the risk committee SMF11 – chair of the audit committee SMF12 – chair of the remuneration committee SMF14 – senior independent director SMF7 – group entity senior manager
CF3 – chief executive	SMF1 – chief executive SMF2 – chief finance officer SMF4 – chief risk officer SMF5 – head of internal audit
CF4 – partner	SMF27 – partner SMF2 – chief finance officer SMF4 – chief risk officer SMF5 – head of internal audit
CF5 – director of unincorporated association	SMF3 – executive director SMF2 – chief finance officer SMF4 – chief risk officer SMF5 – head of internal audit
CF6 – small friendly society function	SMF3 – executive director SMF2 – chief finance officer SMF4 – chief risk officer SMF5 – head of internal audit
CF10 – compliance oversight	SMF16 – compliance oversight
CF10a – CASS operational oversight function	SMF18 – other overall responsibility (NB: If an enhanced firm chooses not to convert an individual performing a CF10a (CASS oversight) function to SMF18 (other overall responsibility) function, then this individual will be expected to be certified under the Certification Regime. The CASS prescribed responsibility should then be allocated to the senior manager to whom to the individual reports.)
CF11 – money laundering reporting officer	SMF17 – money laundering reporting officer
CF28 – systems and controls function	SMF2 – chief finance officer SMF4 – chief risk officer SMF5 – head of internal audit
CF29 – significant management function	SMF18 – other overall responsibility SMF24 – chief operations

The FCA has stated that conversion only applies for the controlled functions and corresponding senior management functions listed above. For other controlled functions (such as CF30 – customer function) regulatory approval will not be needed and existing approvals will lapse when SM&CR comes into effect. Depending on the firm, the roles not mapped across are likely to fall into the scope of the Certification Regime.

Enhanced firms need to ensure that they submit a comprehensive and complete conversion notification (Form K) to the FCA ahead of 9 December 2019. Consideration will need to be given to any APR functions which had previously 'rolled up' into governing functions as well as the need (similar to that of core firms) to submit an additional form for any executive chair role. The FCA has made clear that enhanced firms that do not submit the required Form K will be in breach of regulatory requirements. The existing APR approvals will lapse and the enhanced firm will not have any of the Senior Managers Regime approvals needed – in other words, there will be no-one at the enhanced firm approved to undertake regulated financial services activities. As the FCA put it:

> '... we will consider what further regulatory action needs to be taken, including possible enforcement action. Firms in this situation would have to re-apply for approval of individuals through the full [SM&CR] application process, including mandatory criminal records checks and regulatory references.'

Senior managers for enhanced firms need to be fully engaged with all elements of the conversion process from the Approved Persons Regime to SM&CR. Consideration should be given to having a board-sponsored project including firm-wide training and explicit board sign-off to the conversion Form K (and others as required) before submission to the FCA.

Where enhanced firms wish to change their approved individuals, the following principles apply:

- The existing processes for individual applications continue to apply as usual until the start of the new regime. Individuals approved under the Approved Persons Regime should be included on the firm's Form K if they are to be converted.

- The SM&CR application forms will be available for submission before 9 December 2019 but these approvals will only be effective from the start of the new regime.

- An Approved Persons Regime application submitted, but not determined, before the start of the new regime, will be converted to an application for the relevant senior management function at commencement as long as it is included on the firm's Form K.

The FCA has given a table of scenarios and details of the relevant forms to be used for additional applications for enhanced firms in the guide for FCA solo-regulated firms at pages 68–69 (at www.fca.org.uk/publication/policy/guide-for-fca-solo-regulated-firms.pdf). The FCA has also given a summary list of regulatory forms in Annex 3 to the guide on page 74.

Checklist

5.16   The checklist below offers practical questions for senior managers to consider.

Checklist

- Do I know how my firm will be categorised after 9 December 2019? Do I know whether it will be limited scope, core or enhanced? And am I fully aware of the reasons for, and implications of, the categorisation?

- Am I clear on my personal status, and associated responsibilities, under the new SM&CR?

- Has my firm considered the SM&CR readiness checklist in Annex 2 of the FCA guide to solo-regulated firms? (See www.fca.org.uk/publication/ policy/guide-for-fca-solo-regulated-firms.pdf.)

- Have sufficient skilled resources been devoted to ensure a successful transition between the Approved Persons Regime and the SM&CR?

Chapter 6

Key roles in embedding and overseeing the SM&CR

Chapter summary

This chapter covers:

- Key roles in implementing, embedding and overseeing the Senior Managers and Certification Region (SM&CR)

- Important considerations for HR and internal audit

- The status of the legal function

- The role of non-executive directors

Introduction

6.1 The scope of the SM&CR requires almost all staff within a financial services firm to comply with some or all of the requirements of the regime. It requires significant changes to firms' training, employment documentation, policies and procedures, and for senior managers to understand the impact on them personally. Certain functions, particularly those with governance, assurance or oversight responsibilities, also have an important role to play in helping an organisation both embed and demonstrate that it is meeting the requirements of the SM&CR and, critically, in supporting Senior Managers to understand and discharge their responsibilities.

Board challenges

6.2 Conduct risk, culture and the SM&CR have been recognised as a specific compliance challenge for boards of financial services firms. The challenges set out by over 800 banks, insurers and asset managers from around the world in response to Thomson Reuters' annual Cost of Compliance survey specifically highlight preparations for the UK SM&CR in parallel with the global focus on greater accountability and oversight, culture, personal liability and corporate governance as key current challenges. The biggest challenge of having to deal with continuing regulatory change includes the development of global accountability regimes around the world.

The greatest compliance challenges the board expects to face in 2018 is/are:

Source: Thomson Reuters Regulatory Intelligence – Cost of Compliance 2018 survey

Risk management and assurance – three lines of defence

6.3 All boards will need assurance on meeting the requirements of accountability regimes and managing conduct risk across their organisations. They will need support from specialist roles and functions across the three lines of defence, a model which sets out the roles for managing risks across an organisation. Ownership, responsibility and accountability for directly assessing, controlling and mitigating risks sits with operational management in the first line of the business. The specialist control functions which monitor and facilitate risk management by the first line and ensure risk information flows up and down the organisation sit in the second line. Internal audit provides independent assurance in the third line of defence.

The second and third line functions need to have appropriate independence, authority and skills in order to provide effective risk management and assurance to boards and senior managers. The Parliamentary Commission on Banking Standards had criticised the implementation of the model in preventing the financial crisis because 'the lines were blurred and the status of the front-line, remunerated for revenue generation, was dominant over the compliance, risk and audit apparatus'. It specifically recommended for:

'… the lines to be separate, with distinct authority given to internal control and give particular non-executive directors individual personal responsibility for protecting the independence of those responsible for key internal controls. This needs to be buttressed with rigorous scrutiny by the new regulators of the adequacy of firms' control frameworks'.

'The financial crisis, and multiple conduct failures, have exposed serious flaws in governance. Potemkin villages were created in firms, giving the appearance of effective control and oversight without the reality. Non-executive directors lacked the capacity or incentives to challenge the executives ... Responsibilities have been blurred, accountability diluted, and officers in risk, compliance and internal audit have lacked the status to challenge front-line staff effectively.

Source: 'Changing banking for good', Report of the Parliamentary Commission on Banking Standards (June 2013)

Key functions in overseeing the SM&CR, culture and conduct risk

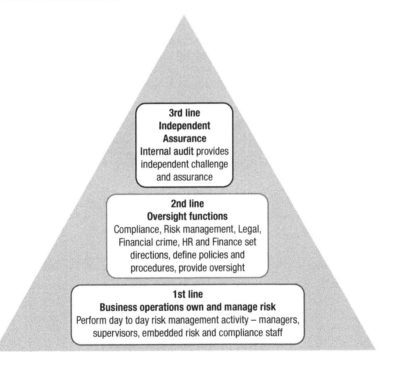

Roles of the three lines of defence

6.4 The first three lines of defence as taken from the IIA Policy Paper, 'Internal audit, risk and corporate governance – the Three Lines of Defence Model', are as follows:

115

(1) **The first line of defence (functions that own and manage risks)** is formed by managers and staff who are responsible for identifying and managing risk as part of their accountability for achieving objectives. Collectively, they should have the necessary knowledge, skills, information, and authority to operate the relevant policies and procedures of risk control. This requires an understanding of the company, its objectives, the environment in which it operates, and the risks it faces.

(2) **The second line of defence (functions that oversee or who specialise in compliance or the management of risk)** provides the policies, frameworks, tools, techniques and support to enable risk and compliance to be managed in the first line, conducts monitoring to judge how effectively they are doing it, and helps ensure consistency of definitions and measurement of risk.

(3) **The third line of defence (functions that provide independent assurance)** is provided by internal audit. Sitting outside the risk management processes of the first two lines of defence, its main roles are to ensure that the first two lines are operating effectively and advise how they could be improved. Tasked by, and reporting to the board/audit committee, it provides an evaluation, through a risk-based approach, on the effectiveness of governance, risk management, and internal control to the organisation's governing body and senior management. It can also give assurance to sector regulators and external auditors that the appropriate controls and processes are in place and are operating effectively.

Source: www.iia.org.uk/media/1042665/three-lines-of-defence-march-2015.pdf

The three lines of defence in an organisation:

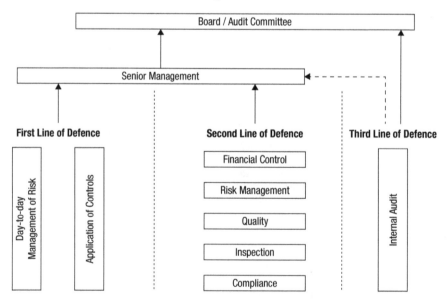

Source: IIA Policy Paper, 'Internal audit, risk and corporate governance
– the Three Lines of Defence Model' (March 2015)

Lines of defence in practice

6.5   All employees will need to adhere to conduct and behavioural expectations and it is the managers in the first line of the business who will have primary responsibility for overseeing delivery of expected conduct, behaviour and accountability. Some firms have created new First Line of Defence (front office) roles with titles such as 'Chief Conduct Officer' or 'Head of Culture and Conduct' with a specific mandate to develop a holistic approach to the firm's conduct programmes, and have developed or expanded tools to help improve monitoring and oversight (at   www.fca.org.uk/publication/market-studies/5-conduct-questions-industry-feedback-2017.pdf).

The compliance and risk management functions in the second line will set standards, monitor adherence and provide advice to the front-line and senior management on conduct, culture and the accountability regime, in conjunction with relevant functions such as human resources (HR) and legal as necessary. Compliance and risk will lead the relationship with the firm's regulator but responsibility for compliance with regulatory standards and rules remains the responsibility of all employees. As noted by the Parliamentary Commission on banking standards report (at www.parliament.uk/documents/banking-commission/Banking-final-report-volume-i.pdf):

> 'Responsibility for acting in accordance with the letter and spirit of regulation should lie with every individual in a bank. This responsibility should not be outsourced to a compliance function, any more than to the regulator itself, particularly in the light of the fact that, owing to the complexity of banks, the compliance function would face a very difficult task were this responsibility to lie solely with it.'

Internal audit in the third line will need a clear mandate to test adherence to the firm's standards, expectations and regulatory requirements. It is important that all these functions have the requisite skills and resources to make difficult judgements on behaviour, risks and breaches.

Timely and relevant reports and management information is an important tool in assisting senior management and the board to meet their governance responsibilities to oversee conduct and accountability. Compliance, risk and internal audit functions will need to provide senior management and the board with regular, comprehensive and, as far as possible, aligned reports, to enable them to understand firm-wide adherence to conduct and accountability expectations as well as areas of risk and the actions needed to address exposure.

The oversight provided by control functions is critical to assurance and the effectiveness of these functions needs to be a priority. Two out of the top three control failures identified by Corlytics resulting in the largest fines by regulators in the last two years are compliance monitoring and oversight together with third-party oversight, which indicates that there is more work to do to ensure their effectiveness (see www.corlytics.com/corlytics-barometer). The fourth control failure identified is record keeping which is likely to feature more prominently in future as senior managers strive to evidence the discharge of their personal accountability under the SM&CR.

In practice, precisely how firms implement and manage different aspects of conduct, culture and their accountability framework will depend on the structure, size and complexity of the firm. Firms will need to agree roles and responsibilities for implementing and overseeing SM&CR and managing conduct risk and culture, including what involvement the HR, legal, and assurance functions will have. There is no single blueprint and, as illustrated, accountability for embedding and implementing firms conduct risk policy varies across the financial services industry (see the diagram below).

Who is accountable for implementing and embedding the conduct risk policy in your organization?

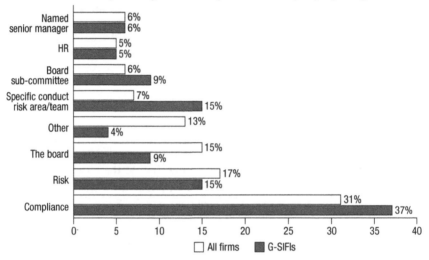

Source: Thomson Reuters Regulatory Intelligence – Culture and Conduct Risk 2018 survey

Liaison between control functions

6.6   An important feature of effective governance and oversight is an alignment of approach between a firm's control functions. It is essential that internal audit, compliance, risk management and legal functions are aligned to help ensure there is a consistent, integrated and holistic approach to risk identification, management and mitigation. Only then will the business be able to focus on addressing the most significant areas of risk.

Thomson Reuters Regulatory Intelligence explored how much time control functions spend liaising with each other. The alignment in terms of the interaction between the compliance function and legal, internal audit and risk has been limited with the number of compliance teams who spend less than an hour a week with other control functions a potential concern (see below). The control functions in a firm will all have distinct roles and remits but greater liaison and cooperation can bring benefits. Firms can seek to make the best use of in-house skills by optimising the alignment, cooperation and coordination between the risk and control functions to ensure there is coverage of the key risks to the organisation and that associated reporting to senior management is consistent particularly in terms of culture and conduct risk.

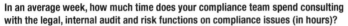

In an average week, how much time does your compliance team spend consulting with the legal, internal audit and risk functions on compliance issues (in hours)?

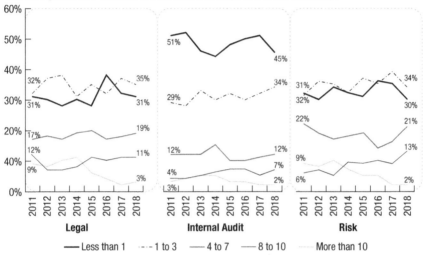

Source: Thomson Reuters Regulatory Intelligence – Cost of Compliance 2018 survey

Human Resources

6.7   As one of the strictest accountability regimes across all industries, the SM&CR leaves staff and senior managers open to financial, reputational and potentially criminal penalties for breaches and failings. The regime also shifts the responsibility for ensuring that individuals are fit and proper from the regulator to firms themselves, meaning that existing processes such as performance management need to be able to evidence how individuals' competencies and behaviours have been assessed. The HR function therefore has a critical role to play in managing processes that underpin compliance with the SM&CR and in providing support to individuals impacted by the new regime.

Implementing and embedding the requirements requires significant change throughout all aspects of the employee lifecycle, from the initial recruitment of staff through to providing references to new employers after staff members have left the organisation. Given the increased burden on firms, early involvement of the HR function in preparations for SM&CR is critical to ensuring there is adequate time to implement or update all the relevant HR processes, systems and controls.

The key stages and processes across the employee lifecycle where HR are likely to be engaged in collaboration with risk, compliance and legal functions include the following:

Recruitment, resourcing and onboarding	• Ensuring job descriptions and adverts specifically refer to responsibilities under the SM&CR and reflect where a role will require regulatory approval or certification prior to undertaking the position. • Promoting the firm's commitment to standards to attract individuals who fit with the firm's culture. • As part of the selection process, including criteria to assess candidates' approach to conduct risk, good customer outcomes and adherence to regulatory rules. • Making clear that job offers are conditional on meeting SM&CR requirements including regulatory approval and fit and proper test where relevant. • As part of the on-boarding process, ensuring all relevant background checks are undertaken and references obtained (covering employment in the previous six years) prior to an individual taking on a role. In circumstances where a reference cannot be obtained, documenting the reasonable steps taken in trying to obtain it. • Maintain evidence of the candidate's competence and qualifications as part of the interview process. • Include conduct and cultural expectations and requirements in the onboarding and induction of new staff.
Identifying and engaging with relevant staff	• Identification of Senior Management Functions (SMFs), certified employees and staff falling within the scope of the Conduct Rules, including any relevant individuals based overseas. • Providing additional support to and engagement with staff to ensure they are comfortable with roles and responsibilities and understand their accountabilities. • Helping identify and resolve any potential gaps or overlaps in responsibilities between roles and individuals. • Providing support for any required changes to resources, governance arrangements, legal structures of groups and their entities to ensure they are fit for SM&CR purposes.
Developing important documentation	• Identifying the overall governance structure within the organisation and who is responsible for what at the most senior levels to determine whether job descriptions are aligned.

	• Clarifying and agreeing roles and responsibilities with employees, including negotiation with and allocation of Prescribed Responsibilities to senior managers.
	• Developing or updating job descriptions for senior managers and certified staff including responsibilities to minimise conduct risk and adhere to regulatory requirements.
	• Developing Statements of Responsibilities in line with SM&CR requirements.
	• Determining and documenting Responsibilities Maps in line with SM&CR obligations.
	• Revising employee contract terms, for example, to include references to Statements of Responsibilities, adherence to Conduct Rules, duty of responsibility, fitness and propriety requirements, an obligation to notify the firm if any doubt relating to ongoing fitness and propriety, training obligations and handover requirements.
Remuneration and reward strategy	• Advising on remuneration, incentive and bonus schemes, to drive the right behaviours, ensuring alignment between risk and reward and complying with regulatory requirements on remuneration.
Performance management	• Aligning performance review or management processes with the requirements of the SM&CR firms and the obligation to ensure relevant employees are 'fit and proper'.
	• Implementing processes and systems for recording and evidencing the fitness and propriety assessment, enabling firms to track when certificates are due for annual renewal and record the decision making underpinning each certification made. Processes also need to be in place to manage situations where an individual fails to meet the fitness and propriety criteria required for a role.
	• Firms may consider the frequency of existing annual performance review processes and whether periodic assessments are needed to maintain more up-to-date records to rely on. They may also reconsider which parties need to be involved in conducting appraisals and build in steps for involvement or oversight by the senior manager responsible for ensuring the fitness and propriety of individuals and certified staff.
	• Developing balanced scorecards that include qualitative conduct measures as well as commercial metrics.

Role changes and promotions	• Ongoing monitoring of staff changing roles or taking on promotions to determine whether certification or fitness and propriety assessments are required.
	• Ensuring a handover policy is in place and relevant staff are aware.
Training	• Ensuring that staff are notified that Conduct Rules apply to them, understand how the rules apply and the potential consequences of breaches.
	• Developing and providing suitable training to ensure staff have an awareness and broad understanding of all of the Conduct Rules and also a deeper understanding of the practical application of the specific rules which are relevant to their work.
	• Ensuring staff understand how Conduct Rules apply to their role, potentially through separating training into distinct categories for senior managers, certified individuals and staff covered by Conduct Rules in order for it to be tailored rather than generic.
	• Training staff responsible for fitness and proper assessments on the identification of certification risks and on discussing the outcome of an assessment.
	• Training for line managers to identify when certification is required following an individual being promoted or taking on new responsibilities.
	• Ensuring awareness of whistleblowing processes, how to recognise a whistleblowing disclosure and ensuring that whistleblowers are protected.
Disciplinary	• Ensuring policies and systems are in place to support the internal monitoring and reporting of breaches of the Conduct Rules and for notifying regulators of disciplinary action for breach of a Conduct Rule.
Record keeping	• Supporting the SM&CR programme with accurate record keeping and audit trails.
	• Maintaining records on fit and proper assessments, certification and training.
	• Ensuring recording and reporting systems enable an audit trail to be maintained of actions taken if a breach of the Conduct Rules occurs and any disciplinary action and outcomes.
	• Maintaining records of regulatory submissions and notifications.
	• Ensuring processes and systems are in place to store employees' records including Statements of Responsibilities and references.

	• Keeping track of references given about past employees, so they can be updated where further information comes to light.
Termination and departures	• Re-allocation of an outgoing senior manager's responsibilities and revisions to Statements of Responsibilities and Responsibilities Maps.
	• Ensuring there is a process in place for departing senior managers to hand over responsibilities and communicate relevant information.
	• Determining whether a regulatory notification is required, particularly if termination is linked with misconduct.
Providing References	• Establishing a process for providing and updating references.
	• Ensuring appropriate policies are in place to determine the appropriateness of information to be included in a regulatory reference.
	• Keeping track of references given in the past six years about past employees, so they can be updated where further information comes to light that would cause the reference to be drafted differently.
	• Ensuring any failures to meet the fitness and propriety requirements for certification roles are recorded, along with relevant breaches of the Conduct Rules, to enable the accurate provision of regulatory references.
	• Utilising regulatory templates where required to improve the consistency of disclosures across firms.
	• Providing references as soon as reasonably practicable and within six weeks of being asked.

Training is a key indicator for a regulator that a firm has taken its compliance obligations seriously and has maintained and updated the knowledge and skill sets of all staff. Accordingly, the SM&CR includes specific training requirements on Conduct Rules. There is a mixed picture of training across the financial services industry with two-fifths of respondents to the Thomson Reuters Culture and Conduct Risk survey stating that they have not undertaken training conduct training but know that it is needed.

Year-on-year analysis: Has your firm implemented training on conduct risk?

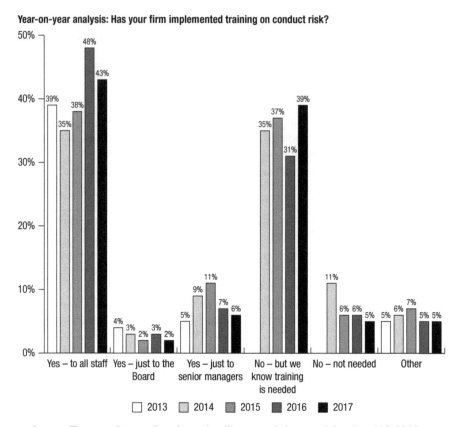

Source: Thomson Reuters Regulatory Intelligence – Culture and Conduct Risk 2018 survey

Non-executive directors

6.8   Non-executive directors (NEDs) do not manage a firm's business in the same way as executive directors; therefore, the responsibilities for which NEDs are accountable are more limited. However, NEDs have important responsibilities requiring them to not only support and oversee executive management but to critically challenge executive management and effectively hold them to account. Weaknesses in this role in the lead up to the financial crisis were criticised by the PCBS which revealed that 'non-executive directors lacked the capacity or incentives to challenge the executives' (www.parliament.uk/documents/banking-commission/Banking-final-report-volume-i.pdf).

All non-executive directors now fall within the scope of the SM&CR to some extent. The SMR element applies to a specific population of non-executive directors, including: chairman; senior independent director; and the chairs of the Risk, Audit, Remuneration and Nominations Committees who require regulatory pre-approval for roles. Others need to adhere to the Conduct Rules.

> 'Non-executive directors in systemically important financial institutions have a particular duty to take a more active role in challenging the risks that businesses are running and the ways that they are being managed.'
>
> Source: 'Changing banking for good', Report of the Parliamentary Commission on Banking Standards (June 2013)

According to Annex 1 of the *FCA Handbook* (www.handbook.fca.org.uk/handbook/COCON/1/Annex1.html?date=2016-03-07), the general role of non-executive directors is to:

- provide effective oversight and challenge;
- help develop proposals on strategy through:
  - attending and contributing to board and committee meetings and discussions;
  - taking part in collective board and committee decisions, including voting and providing input and challenge;
  - ensuring they are sufficiently and appropriately informed of the relevant matter prior to taking part in board or committee discussions and decisions;
- scrutinise the performance of management in meeting agreed goals and objectives;
- monitor the reporting of performance;
- satisfy themselves on the integrity of financial information;
- satisfy themselves that financial controls and systems of risk management are robust and defensible;
- scrutinise the design and implementation of the remuneration policy;
- provide objective views on resources, appointments and standards of conduct; and being involved in succession planning.

Where non-executive directors have the role of chair of the board or a committee they will also need to:

- ensure that the board or committee meets with sufficient frequency;
- foster an open, inclusive discussion which challenges executives;
- ensure that the board or committee devotes sufficient time and attention to the matters within its remit;
- help to ensure that the board or committee and its members have the information necessary;
- report to the main board on the committee's activities;
- facilitate the running of the board or committee to assist it in providing independent oversight of executive decisions;

- in relation to the nomination committee, safeguard the independence and oversee the performance.

To fulfil the crucial role of providing and demonstrating effective challenge across the firm's major business lines and key strategic decisions, there are important aspects that need to be met to ensure NEDs are able to fulfil their roles. NEDs should collectively have:

- up-to-date and relevant knowledge and experience to understand the key activities and risks involved in the business;

- enough time to fulfill their duties;

- adequate support to enable them to carry out their duties, including induction, ongoing training and expert advice;

- timely, accurate, complete and relevant management information and reports supplied by executive management.

In addition, the chairman will need to ensure that all views are heard and that the executives are not able to control the board discussion. They are also required to lead the development and monitoring of policies and procedures for the induction, training and ongoing professional development of NEDs.

In helping develop proposals on strategy, NEDs in all firms will need to ensure that conduct is taken into account and remains firmly on the agenda. As many as 75% of the 600+ firms who took part in Thomson Reuters Regulatory Intelligence's research said they considered, or in part considered, conduct risk factors when discussing business strategy. Culture and conduct risk concerns are also affecting decision making with a quarter of firms reporting that they had declined potentially profitable business opportunities due to culture and/or conduct risk concerns. Firms would be well advised to maintain detailed documentation on those opportunities declined as a critical part of their suite of evidence on a positive compliant culture in action.

Year-on-year analysis: Are conduct risk factors considered when business strategy is being discussed?

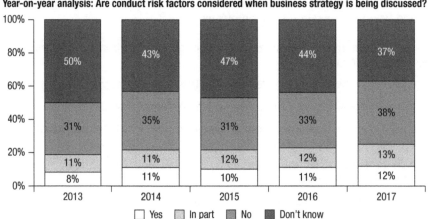

Source: Thomson Reuters Regulatory Intelligence – Culture and Conduct Risk 2018 survey

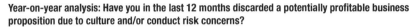

Year-on-year analysis: Have you in the last 12 months discarded a potentially profitable business proposition due to culture and/or conduct risk concerns?

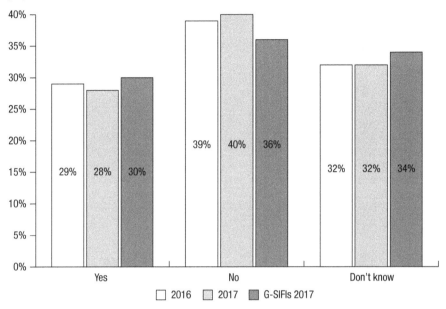

Source: Thomson Reuters Regulatory Intelligence – Culture and Conduct Risk 2018 survey

As discussed in **Chapter 14**, technology is having a greater impact on financial services than ever before, bringing both opportunities and challenges. Both the impact of new technology, arising from the unprecedented pace and scale of innovation, and potential weaknesses in existing systems which can expose them to outages, data breaches and cyber-attacks, can increase conduct risk. If technology is not safely implemented and managed, then there is a real risk of disruption and harm to customers. Given the increasing scrutiny by regulators on firms' use of technology and operational resilience, the impact of technology equally needs to be a priority for boards including NEDs. As illustration, the view of over 800 financial services firms into the involvement of their board in the firm's approach to new technology innovation indicates that it needs continued attention when determining strategy and conduct risk.

Does your board have enough involvement in your firm's approach to fintech, regtech and insurtech?

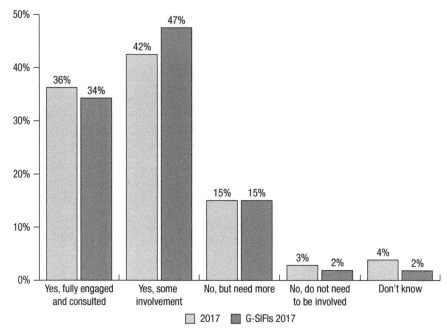

Source: Thomson Reuters Regulatory Intelligence – Fintech, Regtech and the Role of Compliance 2017

Internal audit

6.9   The internal audit function is in an exceptional position to provide assurance to the board and senior management on the effectiveness of conduct and accountability processes across the firm. It is able to provide independent and objective insight on the key conduct challenges that boards and senior managers face, including how well it is managing risks and the adequacy of its internal controls.

The greatest conduct risk challenges you expect the board to face in the next 12 months are:

External economic factors
Training and awareness Embedding an appropriate culture
Consistency in approach to culture and conduct risk   Cost and availability of skilled resources
Balancing commercial and compliance demands   Cyber resilience
Conflicts of interest
Establishing and embedding an appropriate conduct risk framework
Information security   **Don't know** AML and fraud   Reputation
Political uncertainty Changing most in the middle **Appropriate metrics and management information**
Renumeration   Incentives   Technological innovation Senior management accountability
Competition Tax evasion **Changing business model**
Changing regulatory environment   Treating customers fairly
Budgetary complaints **Corporate governance and tone from the top**
Compensation and redress
Third party risk   Bribery and corruption

Source: Thomson Reuters Regulatory Intelligence – Culture and Conduct Risk 2018 survey

128

The Heads of Internal Audit are designated as SMFs under the SM&CR and must be approved by regulators before taking up their position. The Head of Internal Audit has explicit responsibility for: 'management of the internal audit function of a firm and for reporting directly to the governing body of the firm on the internal audit function'.

The role of internal audit had previously been criticised following the financial crisis which has led to increased regulatory scrutiny and new guidance to protect the organisation.

> '... internal audit functions of firms must be active and able to push their case strongly. To be frank, I think one of the relatively untold stories of the financial crisis concerns how little attention these functions have attracted. Boards and senior management ... must be supported by robust ... audit functions (internal and external). Unfortunately, when I look across the landscape, I don't believe that we are in the right place today in terms of the role and influence of these ... functions.'
>
> Source: 'Why Prudential Regulation matters', speech by Andrew Bailey
> – Director of UK Banking Supervision, PRA (October 2011)

There are still areas for internal audit to focus on to ensure they are most effective in being able to provide assurance. As noted by Stephen Brown, Head of Internal Audit, Bank of England ('Increasing the Relevance of Internal Audit', December 2016), these include internal audit needing to:

- stand its ground more;

- invest in developing talented internal auditors who can go 'toe-to-toe' with senior management on key issues;

- provide reports that are more concise and more readable and focus on the key risks to the business;

- be more forward looking and focus more on 'emerging risks'; and

- invest more in quality assurance and in challenging themselves.

No internal audit function can be effective without sufficient and visible support from the board, audit committee and senior managers. This is not just a question of the provision of adequate resources but also ensuring that the 'tone from the top' emphasises that the internal audit function is a valued and inherent part of the risk management of the firm.

The need for firms to be aware of emerging risks and to use limited resources as efficiently and effectively as possible should encourage compliance and internal audit functions in particular towards close and continuous liaison. Regulators expect regulatory risks to shape internal audit's monitoring plans, so it is important that there is a consistent and joined-up approach within the firm.

Good practices for internal audit

6.10   What 'good' looks like for internal audit, will vary from firm to firm as the risk management arrangements must be tailored to the exact business being undertaken by each firm. One size definitely does not fit all but there are several features of best practice which are universal.

- ***Terms of reference:***

  Clearly defined terms of reference, reviewed annually and approved by the audit committee, setting out the role, remit and scope of the internal audit work. Individual elements in the terms of reference could include both specific and broad assurance work, investigations and the statement that the internal audit function has an untrammelled right of access to all areas of the business encompassing all property, records and staff throughout the firm as well as any outsourced areas of business. The terms of reference should be seen as a part of the firm's corporate governance infrastructure and should be sufficiently detailed so that they not only set expectations unambiguously but also to act as a template for other terms of reference set within the firm. In this, as in other areas of corporate governance, the internal audit function needs to consider how best to lead by example.

- ***Scope of work programmes:***

  The work plans of the internal audit function cannot be static but need to evolve with changes to the business and the developing regulatory environment. Audit plans will necessarily vary by firm but they should all focus on the main risks to the business including:

  - highest impact risks identified by any of the risk management functions;

  - areas that regulators already do, or intend to, focus on;

  - weaknesses and risks that have crystallised in peer firms, including regulatory enforcement action taken against them;

  - corporate governance and whether or not it is operating effectively. Review measures can include unannounced attendance at meetings, assessment of the quality of the argument on risk as evidenced in the minutes of key committees, a sense check of the practical ramifications of the 'tone from the top' in terms of culture and risk awareness and a detailed assessment of the quality of management information.

- ***Evidence:***

  The quality and accessibility of internal audit work papers has always been essential, but never more so than after the high-profile regulatory failures and the subsequent increased risk and control scrutiny. It is crucial for future follow-up audits, monitoring the implementation of remedial action and to maintain intelligence gathered through audit work that all historical and current working papers and outcomes are not only securely and readily accessible, but also supported by a full suite of solid evidence.

- ***Reporting:***

  Internal auditors need to cast a critical eye over the clarity, quality and timeliness of their own reporting. It is well understood that internal auditors need to have the independence and authority to report all material findings, risks and weaknesses without interference and undue pressure to alter or omit points. Internal auditors now also need to consider how their reporting fits into, and supports, the effective corporate governance of the firm. Reporting to the board and audit committee needs to be clear and consistent with other risk and compliance reporting to enable an overall view of risk management and governance to be formed. Meetings with the business, external auditors, other risk and compliance functions as well the function's planning meetings all need to be documented thoroughly to show how risks were raised, discussed and, where required, followed up.

- ***Skills and resources:***

  An effective assessment of skills and resources in both the internal audit function and represented on the audit committee. Consideration should be given to whether there are sufficient experts in preventative, detective and transactional controls and control frameworks as well as corporate governance on the audit committee.

- ***Regulator relationship management:***

  The internal audit function of the future may well need to build relationships with the firm's regulator or regulators. A firm of any size is likely to have a lead regulatory relationship manager (often in the compliance function) and the internal auditor should ensure that it works within the existing relationship management framework to build its access to and understanding of the changing supervisory expectations. Often the independent and valuable work of internal audit has been taken into account as a mitigating factor when determining enforcement decisions and penalties, so there is tangible value in regulators having the confidence to rely on internal audit to ensure issues are addressed.

What are the key challenges to the organization when managing conduct risk in the year ahead?

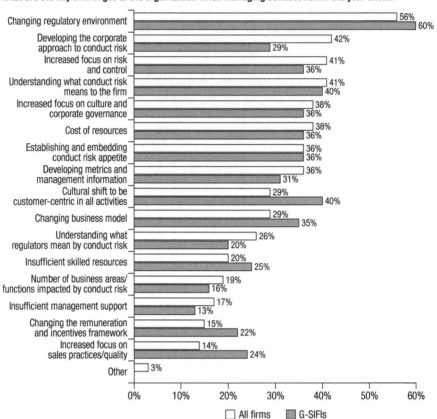

Source: Thomson Reuters Regulatory Intelligence – Culture and Conduct Risk 2018 survey

Internal audit reviews

6.11   There are multiple challenges for firms in managing conduct risk and accountability regimes (see the chart above) which internal audit functions should be aware of in scoping and developing their work plans. Firms implementing the SM&CR for the first time will need to plan ahead by building assessment into their audit plan well ahead of the commencement date of the regime; other firms will need to ensure that important aspects of the regime remain in plan in order to provide ongoing assurance to senior managers and the board. Examples of important areas where internal audit can assess and review the adequacy and effectiveness of procedures and processes, completeness and accuracy of documentation, and systems and outcomes in order to provide assurance to senior managers, include:

- approach to ongoing identification of SMFs and certified Individuals;

- adequacy and completeness of fit and proper assessments;

- allocation of all relevant areas of responsibility within the business to an appropriate SMF;

- whether the Management Responsibilities Map contain the required information;

- whether Individual Statements of Responsibilities clearly set out exactly what the individual is responsible for;

- allocation of Prescribed Responsibilities to ensure overlaps and underlaps are highlighted in the current organisational responsibilities;

- whether the Management Responsibilities Map and the Individual Statements of Responsibilities fit together to form a complete and consistent picture of the firm's overall governance framework;

- processes for ensuring the most up-to-date documentation has been submitted to the regulators;

- identification, recording and reporting of any breaches of Conduct Rules;

- criteria for what constitutes a Conduct Rule breach;

- policies and procedures in place to underpin critical processes within the SM&CR including handover requirements and requests for, and provision of, regulatory references;

- the effectiveness of all policies affecting the employee lifecycle from recruitment to termination;

- adequacy and appropriateness of training;

- the reasonable steps framework, particularly in terms of 'what good looks like', consistency and evidence;

- communication of the regime to SMFs, key function holders and other relevant individuals;

- where deficiencies are identified, assessing whether similar issues exist in other areas of the firm;

- outsourcing (see **8.4**);

- whistleblowing;

- remuneration policies and practices together with a judgement call as to whether the policies are fit for purpose and being appropriately adhered to in practice to ensure that the approach to compensation is not a driver of misconduct; and

- key regulatory areas of focus that can impact customers, including resilience of technology and systems.

Year-on-year analysis: For conduct risk matters, are reports to the board from the compliance, risk and internal audit functions aggregated?

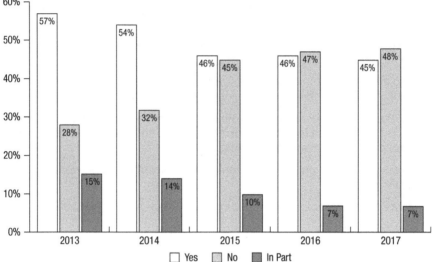

Source: Thomson Reuters Regulatory Intelligence – Culture and Conduct Risk 2018 survey

Practical questions about culture

6.12   The Institute of Risk Management (IRM) has identified useful questions for a board to ask itself about the organisation's culture and for control functions to consider in order to determine where to focus:

> • Have we as a board fully articulated the risk appetite of the organisation such that the culture of the organisation can deliver effectively?
>
> • Do we have a blame culture operating at any level of the organisation?
>
> • Does the organisation's structure support or detract from the development of organisation wide sociability?
>
> • Do we really acknowledge and live the values we publish at every level within the organisation in everything we do?
>
> • Do we have multiple subcultures within the organisation and do they support social exchange or are they subcultural barriers to our cultural development?
>
> • A communal culture requires time and investment. Do we as a board invest consistently and wisely to develop and maintain an effective communal culture?
>
> • Are there identifiable stories and values that are commonly referenced and shared within the organisation? If so, what do they say about the culture?

- Is there a common theme to organisational artefacts found within the communal spaces of the organisation?

- Is there a strong set of published values that are regularly referenced, taught to new joiners and reinforced by management? What do those values say about the culture of the organisation?

- Is there a common set of terms or accepted organisational language frequently used within the organisation over and above the terminology common to the industrial sector that the organisation operates in?

- Is expertise respected alongside seniority?

Legal function

6.13 The in-house legal function has a key role to play in helping firms and their staff meet the requirements of the SM&CR. There are many aspects of the HR lifecycle covered within the HR section where legal will provide support and advice, particularly relating to employee contracts, disciplinary action, provision of regulatory references and termination.

For the legal function itself there is ongoing uncertainty relating to whether the SM&CR should apply to general counsels and others responsible for a bank's internal legal function. Whilst the regulators did not specify the head of legal function in its list of SMFs, they took the view that the role would be covered by another SMF. This could mean that firms would identify the role as an 'overall responsibility' senior management function if it was not covered by another specific SMF such as a head of compliance or head of risk.

Some of the key arguments for excluding legal function heads from the accountability regime include:

- that heading the legal function is often not regarded as 'an activity, business area or management function', and that the role is considered fundamentally advisory rather than involving 'management' of the firm's affairs.

- the potential to prejudice legal professional privilege, which protects the confidentiality of client-lawyer communications, and would compromise the independence of the advice the internal legal function provides.

On the other hand, arguments for including the function are:

- the requirement for a firm to assign overall responsibility for every aspect of its business, including the legal function, to a senior manager. This ensures there are no gaps in responsibility in line with the view of the Parliamentary Commission on Banking Standards that without complete coverage of a firm at the senior level, key responsibilities or accountabilities could remain unallocated, potentially undermining the regime when a firm failed; and

- that despite the legislation underpinning the SMR not covering the giving of legal advice, the role of managing the legal function, rather than that of providing legal advice, brings the legal function head into the SMR.

It is a contentious issue which remains with the regulators to determine the approach. Firms that have made decisions on their approach ahead of final policy by regulators do not need to change their approach in the interim.

'There has been a question raised in the context of the Senior Managers Regime about whether general counsel should be a responsible function. That isn't an easy question, because obviously it raises big issues about the role of legal advice and so on in firms, but it has been raised, including by lawyers, I should say. We were going to do some work on that. We will do some work in the future on that, but it isn't going to happen in the next year.'

Source: FCA Business Plan: Press Conference (April 2018)

Checklist

6.14 The checklist below offers practical questions for firms and their senior managers to consider:

Checklist

- Are culture, conduct and important SM&CR processes and requirements included in compliance monitoring, risk assessments and internal audit plans?

- Have all employees received training to understand how Conduct Rules are relevant to their role?

- Does reporting and management information from compliance, risk management and internal provide the board and senior managers with an up-to-date, accurate and complete view of conduct and accountability risks and issues across the organisation and remedial actions needed to address them?

- Are HR and legal functions sufficiently engaged to ensure that all aspects of the employee lifecycle incorporate SM&CR requirements and conduct and culture values and standards?

- Do employees across second and third lines of defence have the requisite skills to identify and make judgements about conduct issues and breaches?

Chapter 7

Practical aspects of better risk mitigation

Chapter summary

It is considered a core competency that senior managers understand how to identify, manage and mitigate all risks arising in the business under their control. This chapter covers a number of practical areas of better risk mitigation including:

- Further detail on the need for lucid Responsibilities Maps and reasonable, evidenced steps

- What 'good' may look like for appropriate management oversight of the business

- The requirement for regular, relevant, evidenced training

'In some cases, we have seen evidence of overlapping or unclear allocation of responsibilities. In other cases firms appear to be sharing responsibility amongst more junior staff, obscuring who is genuinely responsible. This goes against the intention of the Senior Managers and Certification Regime and should not continue.'

Source: Andrew Bailey, FCA CEO, 'FCA supervisory review of SMR' (September 2016)

Responsibilities Maps and reasonable steps in action

7.1   The SMR codifies the concept that senior managers in financial services firms must take 'reasonable steps' to prevent regulatory breaches from both occurring and continuing to occur in their particular area of responsibility. As part of the discharge of this obligation, senior managers are required to produce and maintain a 'Statement of Responsibilities' (SoRs) which sets out the role undertaken and the areas of the business for which they are responsible.

Firms are required to maintain a 'Management Responsibilities Map' which pulls together all the Statements of Responsibilities to show the firm's overall management and governance arrangements. This is to ensure there are no gaps between the individual Statements of Responsibilities and all areas of the business are seen to be appropriately covered and allocated to a senior manager. Firms should not underestimate the resources that may need to be devoted to the maintenance of up-to-date and coherent Management Responsibilities Maps which accurately reflect the current structure and activities of the business.

Statements of Responsibilities

7.2   Firms are required to submit a SoR with each application for approval as a senior manager and to update SoRs whenever there is a significant change in the senior manager's responsibilities. Specifically, there must be an up-to-date SoR covering each senior management function (SMF).

SoRs are required to be practical, useable, without unnecessary detail, as well as succinct and clear. Senior managers need to be aware that SoRs are 'only' a statement of what they are responsible for – the need to have a comprehensive suite of evidence showing how those responsibilities have been discharged is for each senior manager to build and maintain as a separate document or documents.

A template SoR is provided in SUP10C Annex 5D of the *FCA Handbook* with additional guidance to be found in SUP10C.11. The template can be found at www.handbook.fca.org.uk/handbook/SUP/10C/Annex5D.html.

The instructions given in the template set out the expected criteria including:

> 'A *statement of responsibilities* should be drafted to clearly show the responsibilities that the *candidate* or senior manager is to perform as part of their *controlled function and* how they fit in with the *firm's* overall governance and management arrangements. A *statement of responsibilities* should also be consistent with the *firm's management responsibilities map.*
>
> A *statement of responsibilities* should be drafted in such a way as to be practical and useable by regulators. The *FCA* and the *PRA* consider that this would be achieved by succinct, clear descriptions of each responsibility which avoid unnecessary detail. Firms have the opportunity to provide details of each responsibility allocated to an individual using the free text boxes in this form, however, the PRA and FCA would not usually expect the description of each responsibility to exceed 300 words.
>
> A *statement of responsibilities* must be a self-contained document. There should be one statement per senior manager per firm. Where an individual performs a senior management function on behalf of more than one firm within a group, one *statement of responsibilities* is required for each firm. Any supplementary information may be provided in section 4 (or if submitting electronically, in a single attachment). A statement of responsibilities must not cross refer to other documents, attachments or links.

A *statement of responsibilities* should include responsibilities held in relation to FCA controlled functions that are included in a *PRA controlled function* under *SUP* 10C.9 (Minimising overlap with the *PRA* Approved Persons Regime).

(SUP 10C.11)

If the appropriate regulator considers that the *statement of responsibilities* is not sufficiently clear to be practical and usable, it could be challenged as part of a candidate's application for approval, or in ongoing supervision.

Details of the individual's responsibilities should be set out in sections 3.2 to 3.4, as appropriate:

- Section 3.2 covers prescribed responsibilities required by regulators to be allocated to one or more senior managers.

- Section 3.3 covers having overall responsibility for each of the business areas, activities, and management functions of the firm.

- Section 3.4 covers anything else, not otherwise included, for which a candidate or senior manager is to be responsible as part of their *FCA* and/or *PRA* senior management function(s) role.'

Source: UK RAP (or firm) version of Statement of Responsibilities form from SUP 10C Annex 5D

As a matter of course, SoRs should include the FCA and PRA prescribed responsibilities allocated to the SMF as well as any allocation of overall responsibility for the firm's activities, business areas and management functions. The PRA has noted that in many cases simply allocating a prescribed responsibility to a senior manager should suffice to identify that person, clearly and formally, as responsible for that area with no further elaboration required.

SoRs must be kept up to date with any significant changes in the responsibilities of an approved SMF provided to the relevant regulator. Examples of what constitutes a 'significant change' may include:

- a variation of the senior manager's regulatory approval resulting in the imposition, variation or removal of a condition or time limit;

- sharing or dividing a SMF that was originally performed by one person between two or more persons;

- the addition, re-allocation or removal of any SMF; and

- ceasing to perform any SMF that was originally shared with another, or others.

While compliance officers in conjunction with Human Resources will need to have systems to monitor the responsibilities of SMFs in order to detect any significant change, senior managers themselves need to track the actual scope of all work undertaken in order to detect any potentially significant changes. All jobs morph over time and, as the regulators have not set any threshold as to what constitutes 'significant', it is incumbent on senior managers to remain vigilant and review individual roles and remits on a regular and case-by-case basis.

An additional incentive for keeping a SoR up to date is that it will be used as a critical document by the regulator to define (and limit) any liability incurred by a senior manager in the event of a regulatory breach. SoRs not only define what a senior manager is responsible for but also (by omission) what he/or she is not responsible for. Senior managers (and firms) should maintain all past copies of SoRs to ensure that any historic breach coming to light can be appropriately allocated in terms of accountability.

Management Responsibilities Map

7.3 A firm's Management Responsibilities Map describes its management and governance arrangements and should show how all activities and associated responsibilities are shared or divided between different senior managers.

The contents of a Management Responsibilities Map are prescribed in the *FCA Handbook* at SYSC 4.5.7, to include not only the following, but to also provide details on how the elements all fit together:

- names of the relevant authorised person's (or firm's) key personnel (including executive, board, etc – whether or not all these persons perform an SMF);
- all responsibilities described in any current SoRs;
- details of the management and governance arrangements relating to Prescribed Responsibilities;
- reasons why (if so done), the firm has allocated/divided responsibility for Prescribed Responsibilities to more than one person or different persons;
- details about the overall responsibility functions allocated based on the firm's activities, business areas and management functions;
- matters reserved to the governing body (generally, the board) such as the terms of reference of its committees;
- details of how the firm's management and governance arrangements fit together with any group or person;
- details of any reporting lines and lines of responsibility (if any) between the firm and other members of its group or third parties (including their employees, officers and committees);
- reasonable information about the persons described or identified in the map including whether they are employees or certified persons and what their responsibilities are in relation to other group members.

The aim of the map is to provide clarity as to how the responsibilities allocated in a particular SoR fit into the overall system of management and governance of a firm. The allocation of responsibilities should be seamless with no gaps and as simple as is feasible. Wherever possible, dotted, dual or complex reporting lines should be avoided or explained to ensure that there is clarity of decision making and accountability throughout the firm.

The regulators themselves have produced their own suite of SMR documentation designed to be used as an example by the financial services industry.

The FCA's own structure chart and management responsibilities are shown below and intended to be used by firms as a template.

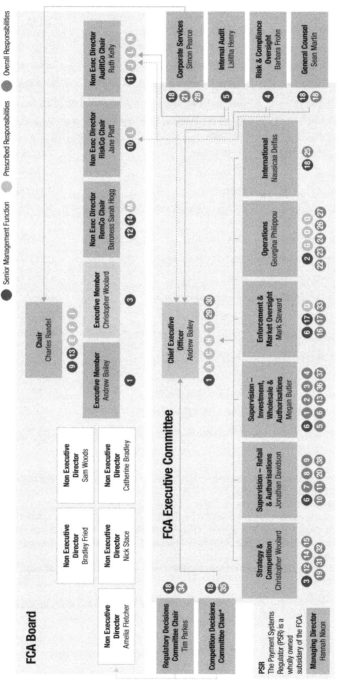

141

7.3   *Practical aspects of better risk mitigation*

Senior Management Function	Allocation – FCA role	Allocation – name
❶ Chief Executive Function	Chief Executive Officer	Andrew Bailey
❷ Chief Finance Function	Chief Operating Officer	Georgina Philippou
❸ Chief Executive Function	Executive Board Members	Christopher Woolard
❹ Chief of Risk Function	Director of Risk & Compliance Oversight	Barbara Frohn
❺ Head of Internal Audit	Director of Internal Audit	Lalitha Henry
❻ Head of Key Business Area[1]	Director of Enforcement & Market Oversight	Mark Steward
	Director of Supervision – Retail & Authorisations	Jonathan Davidson
	Director of Supervision – Investment, Wholesale & Specialists	Megan Butler
❼ Group Entity Senior Manager	Not applicable[2]	Not applicable
❽ Credit Union SMF	Not applicable[2]	Not applicable
❾ Chairman	Chair	Charles Randell
❿ Chair of Risk Committee	Chair of the External Risk & Strategy Committee (Risk Co)	Jane Platt
⓫ Chair of Audit Committee	Chair of the Audit Committee (AuditCo)	Ruth Kelly
⓬ Chair of Remuneration Committee	Chair of the Remuneration Committee (RemCo)	Baroness Sarah Hogg
⓭ Chair of Nominations Committee	Chair	Charles Randell
⓮ Senior Independent Director	Senior Independent Director	Baroness Sarah Hogg
⓯ Compliance Oversight	Not applicable[3]	Not applicable
⓰ Money Laundering Reporting	Director of Enforcement & Market Oversight	Mark Steward
⓱ Other Overall Responsibility function	General Counsel[4]	Sean Martin
	International	Nausicaa Delfas
	Head of Corporate Services	Simon Pearce
	Chair of the Regulatory Decisions Committee	Tim Parkes
	Chair of the Competition Decisions Committee	Appointed by the Chair when a CDC is formed[5]

Notes:
1. SMF6 has been applied to reflect the nature of the FCA business areas whilst recognising they do not meet the quantitative criteria that applies to firms.
2. No roles in the FCA reflect this SMF.
3. SMF16 relates to the individual responsible for reporting to a firm's Board about the firm's compliance with the regulations and rules that apply to firms as set out in the FCA and PRA Handbooks. This is not applicable to the FCA.
4. Role is within scope as a result of responsibility for FCA Handbook. The application of a SMF to legal counsel is subject to consultation.
5. The Chair of the Competition Decisions Committee is appointed by the FCA Chair on each occasion that the committee is formed.

Source: 'Senior Managers Regime', FCA 2018

Allocation of responsibilities

> 'The key principle of that regime is to establish clearly appropriate responsibility for the governance of firms. Put like that, it is not meant to be radical or life-changing, despite whatever you may hear and read .... clarity of responsibility is, I hope, unobjectionable.'
>
> Source: Andrew Bailey, then CEO of the PRA (May 2015)

7.4   There are 30 prescribed responsibilities which need to be assigned to individuals who hold SMFs to ensure that someone is accountable for the fundamental responsibilities inherent in a particular SMF.

A list of the minimum Prescribed Responsibilities that must be allocated can be found in **Table 7.1** below. Senior managers should note that this is the minimum list of Prescribed Responsibilities and further Prescribed Responsibilities will need to be allocated based on firm size and characteristics. Where a responsibility is prescribed by the FCA, it is set out in SYSC 4.7.7R (at www.handbook.fca.org.uk/handbook/SYSC/4/7.html?date=2016-06-30). The PRA's associated Prescribed Responsibilities are set out in Allocation of Responsibilities Part 4.1 (at www.prarulebook.co.uk/rulebook/Content/Chapter/212518/16-01-2017).

Firms are also required to ensure that, at all times, they have allocated to senior managers the overall responsibility for each of the activities, business areas and management functions of the firm. There is some flexibility, mainly designed to avoid undue overlap or repetition and, as such, a firm is not required to allocate overall responsibility for an activity, business area of management function where it is included in an existing SMF or managed by the following SMFs:

(a) the chief finance function;

(b) the chief risk function;

(c) the head of internal audit function;

(d) the head of key business area function; or

(e) the group entity senior manager function.

In the majority of cases the person who has overall responsibility for an area will be the most senior employee (or officer) responsible for managing that area. It does not necessarily mean the person has day-to-day management control of that function but rather the person who has overall responsibility is someone who has:

- ultimate responsibility (under the governing body) for managing or supervising that function; and

- primary and direct responsibility for:

  - briefing and reporting to the governing body about that function; and

  - putting matters for decision about that function to the governing body.

7.4   *Practical aspects of better risk mitigation*

Firms need to be aware that SMR has no territorial limitation and the person with overall responsibility (as defined) could well be located outside the UK.

Table 7.1 – List of mandatory (and minimum) prescribed responsibilities

Description of prescribed senior management responsibility	FCA-prescribed?	PRA-prescribed?
Applies to all firms (RAPs)		
Responsibility for the firm's performance of its obligations under the SMR. The responsibility includes compliance: • With conditions and time limits on approval. • With requirements about the Statements of Responsibilities (but not the allocation of responsibilities recorded in them). • By the firm with its obligations under section 60A of the Financial Services and Markets Act 2000 (vetting of candidates by relevant authorised persons).	SYSC 4.7.7R(1)	4.1(1)
Responsibility for the firm's performance of its obligations under the employee Certification Regime.	SYSC 4.7.7R(2)	4.1(2)
Responsibility for compliance with the requirements of the regulatory system about the management responsibilities map. This responsibility does not include allocating responsibilities recorded in it.	SYSC 4.7.7R(3)	4.1(3)
Overall responsibility for the firm's policies and procedures for countering the risk that the firm might be used to further financial crime. The firm may allocate this responsibility to the money laundering reporting officer (MLRO) but does not have to. If the firm does not allocate it to the MLRO, this prescribed senior management responsibility includes responsibility for supervision of the MLRO.	SYSC 4.7.7R(4)	—
Acting as the firm's whistleblowers' champion.	SYSC 4.7.7R(4A)	—
Responsibility for the allocation of all prescribed responsibilities in accordance with Allocation of Responsibilities 3.1.	—	4.1(20)

Other prescribed responsibilities to be allocated focus on governance in the widest sense and includes, explicitly, both a responsibility for overseeing the adoption of the firm's culture in the day-to-day management of the firm and the responsibility for leading the development of the firm's culture by the governing body as a whole.

Table 7.2 – Other prescribed responsibilities

Description of prescribed senior management responsibility	FCA-prescribed?	PRA-prescribed?
Applies to all firms except for small Capital Requirements Regulations (CRR) firms and credit unions		
Responsibility for: (a) leading the development of, and (b) monitoring the effective implementation of policies and procedures for the induction, training and professional development of all members of the firm's governing body. (To be held by approved non-executive directors (NEDs) rather than executives.)	SYSC 4.7.7R(5)	4.1(13)
Responsibility for monitoring the effective implementation of policies and procedures for the induction, training and professional development of all persons performing designated SMFs on behalf of the firm other than members of the governing body.	SYSC 4.7.7R(6)	4.1(5)
Responsibility for overseeing the adoption of the firm's culture in the day-to-day management of the firm.	—	4.1(6)
Responsibility for leading the development of the firm's culture by the governing body as a whole.	—	4.1(14)
Responsibility for (a) safeguarding the independence of, and (b) oversight of the performance of, the internal audit function, in accordance with SYSC 6.2 (Internal Audit). (To be held by approved NEDs rather than executives.)	SYSC 4.7.7R(7)	4.1(15)
Responsibility for (a) safeguarding the independence of, and (b) oversight of the performance of, the compliance function in accordance with SYSC 6.1 (Compliance). (To be held by approved NEDs rather than executives.)	SYSC 4.7.7R(8)	4.1(16)

Description of prescribed senior management responsibility	FCA-prescribed?	PRA-prescribed?
Responsibility for (a) safeguarding the independence of, and (b) oversight of the performance of the risk function, in accordance with SYSC 7.1.21R and SYSC 7.1.22R (Risk control). (To be held by approved NEDs rather than executives.)	SYSC 4.7.7R(9)	4.1(17)
Responsibility for overseeing the development of, and implementation of, the firm's remuneration policies and practices in accordance with SYSC 19D (Remuneration Code) / SYSC 19A (Remuneration Code). (To be held by approved NEDs rather than executives.)	SYSC 4.7.7R(10)	4.1(18)
Responsibility for the independence, autonomy and effectiveness of the firm's policies and procedures on whistleblowing, including the procedures for protection of staff who raise concerns from detrimental treatment.	—	4.1(19)
Responsibility for managing the allocation and maintenance of the firm's capital, funding and liquidity.	—	4.1(7)
Responsibility for the firm's treasury management functions.	—	4.1(8)
Responsibility for the production and integrity of the firm's financial information and its regulatory reporting under the regulatory system.	—	4.1(9)
Responsibility for developing and maintaining the firm's recovery plan and resolution pack and for overseeing the internal processes regarding their governance.	—	4.1(10)
Responsibility for managing the firm's internal stress tests and ensuring the accuracy and timeliness of information provided to the PRA and other regulatory bodies for the purposes of stress testing.	—	4.1(11)
Responsibility for the development and maintenance of the firm's business model by the governing body.	—	4.1(4)

Applying the regime to smaller firms

7.5 The rules of the SMR have been adapted and, to an extent, have a lighter approach for smaller firms. Fewer requirements of the SMR apply to firms with gross total assets of £250m or less. This threshold is calculated over a rolling period of five years or, if the firm has been in existence for less than five years, over the period of its existence. This threshold means that fewer requirements of the SMR are applied to all credit unions and to a small number of existing banks and building societies (including new entrants to the market, such as 'challenger banks').

The SMR applies to small firms as follows:

- All credit unions will be required to have one credit union senior manager approved by the PRA who performs functions akin to those of a CEO or executive chairman. Credit unions are able to have more than one individual approved as credit union senior manager if they wish.

- The FCA also requires small firms to have a senior manager performing the compliance oversight function (SMF 16) and MLRO function (SMF 17).

- Other smaller firms (those with gross total assets of £250m or less) will be required to have a CEO, CFO and a chairman, reflecting EU-defined requirements to have at least two individuals who 'effectively direct the business of a firm' and restrictions on combining the roles of chairman and CEO.

- Smaller firms are subject to a single, customised, shorter and simplified set of Prescribed Responsibilities but which must reflect the firm's size, complexity and governance structure.

Table 7.3 –Prescribed Responsibilities for small firms

Description of prescribed senior management responsibility	FCA- prescribed?	PRA- prescribed?
Applies to small firms only (firms that have assets of £250m or less)		
Responsibility for implementing and management of the firm's risk management policies and procedures.	—	5.2(3)
Responsibility for managing the systems and controls of the firm.	—	5.2(4)
Responsibility for managing the firm's financial resources.	—	5.2(5)
Responsibility for ensuring the governing body is informed of its legal and regulatory obligations.	—	5.2(6)

Reasonable steps

'...for senior managers, most of the steps you'd expect them to take appear common sense, frankly. Behave with integrity; delegate appropriately; make sure you understand your business area; and comply with common law, existing rules and legal obligations.'

Source: Martin Wheatley, then FCA Chief Executive (March 2015)

7.6   Once responsibilities have been allocated, senior managers need to take, and be seen to take, 'reasonable steps' to prevent regulatory breaches from occurring, or continuing to occur in their areas of responsibility. Senior managers need to be able to ensure that they not only have full control over their areas of responsibility but also have full and clear line of sight to all activities.

'Reasonable steps', as defined by both the FCA and PRA, are also listed in **Chapter 3** but are worth repeating here.

(1) You must take reasonable steps to ensure that the business of the firm for which you are responsible is controlled effectively.

(2) You must take reasonable steps to ensure that the business of the firm for which you are responsible complies with the relevant requirements and standards of the regulatory system.

(3) You must take reasonable steps to ensure that any delegation of your responsibilities is to an appropriate person and that you oversee the discharge of the delegated responsibility effectively.

(4) You must disclose appropriately any information of which the FCA or PRA would reasonably expect notice

For many senior managers 'reasonable steps' are simply what they do day to day in managing their part of the business. Taking decisions on resource allocation, attending governance meetings and contributing to the decision making and oversight, setting goals for staff and reviewing their performance, reviewing management information, attending compliance briefings and reading and writing reports could all be considered to be reasonable steps taken in the appropriate discharge of allocated responsibilities. The deemed adequacy of such reasonable steps will depend on the appropriateness of the individual actions taken and the ability to evidence those actions.

The regulators will be ultimate arbiters of what was, in all the circumstances (and potentially with hindsight), reasonable. The FCA and PRA have indicated that where there is a regulatory breach they will review and assess the steps taken by the senior manager responsible for the area against the steps that they, as regulators, consider that a senior manager could reasonably have been expected to take to avoid the contravention occurring or continuing to occur. In order to manage their own personal regulatory risk, senior managers need to take responsibility for capturing and evidencing their own individual actions with as much context as is feasible. In an already well-run firm this is likely to be a matter of simply collating existing information but may be more challenging in a diverse firm with inconsistent or patchy standards of governance.

The regulators are committed to continue with their proportionate approach with SMR. The perceived reasonableness of steps taken will be in line with the size, nature, scale and complexity of a firm. A large international bank with numerous products and a diverse customer base would be expected to have a substantially more sophisticated and comprehensive suite of systems and controls than a small mono-line firm. As such, a senior manager in a large bank would be expected to be fully aware of, and operate within, the specific risk control infrastructure for his or her business area(s).

Other considerations which the regulators may take into account when assessing the ramifications of a breach could include the following:

- The fitness and propriety assessment carried out as part of the competency to undertake the specific SMF role – put another way, how robust was the assessment of the skills, knowledge and expertise of the senior manager to discharge the allocated responsibilities?

- What due diligence was undertaken by the senior manager when taking on the SMF role? Was there a formal handover including an update on any historic regulatory, conduct or other issues? What compliance or internal audit monitoring findings were outstanding when the role was taken up?

- What did the senior manager know, or ought to have known, taking into account all relevant circumstances?

- What steps did the senior manager take and what alternatives were available at the time?

Evidencing 'reasonable steps' – oversight in action

7.7   Before taking on a SMF, a senior manager must have confidence that he or she can fulfil the obligations, requirements and accountabilities of the role or, at the very least, be aware of any potential knowledge or competency gaps and have a plan to fill them. There is not a prescriptive and exhaustive list of all the elements needing to be evidenced to show the discharge of the reasonable steps expectation, but the following should be considered:

- *The level of detail involved in the handover or induction for the SMF role.* As a matter of course, all handover and induction materials should be read thoroughly and an assessment made as to which area(s) need further information or questions raised to ensure clarity of understanding. All assessments and questions should be documented together with the follow-ups and responses. It is entirely possible that this will be an iterative process in the early days of a new role. A critical feature of any briefing will be an in-depth analysis of the current risks facing the business together with any issues and concerns previously raised by a regulator and how those have (or are being) remediated.

- *A review of the capacity and capabilities of the resources available as well as an assessment of personal bandwidth.* When taking on a new role or new responsibilities, a critical assessment needs to be made as to whether there are sufficient resources in place to discharge all of the obligations, risks and management of the business. Any resourcing concerns should be escalated as a matter of urgency and remediated as soon as is feasible. Any concerns about limitations on skilled or other resources should, again, be documented.

- *Understand the need to maintain and improve on skills and knowledge.* There are likely to be myriad ways of fulfilling the objective but it will require time, on a consistent and regular basis, to be devoted to it. Industry seminars or conferences (whether internal or external) can be a useful way of ensuring that knowledge of both business developments and regulatory issues stay up to date. Senior managers (and specifically board members) are not expected to be experts in everything, but they do need to have sufficient knowledge and to have an appropriate range of skills to understand the issues, able to set an appropriate risk appetite, drive a strong compliant culture, understand and challenge all risk and compliance reports, as well as engage appropriately with regulators. Collective senior manager and/or board knowledge needs as much care and attention as individual skill sets. In particular, as a SMF, an example should be set and time should similarly be made available for all team members to build and maintain their skills and knowledge. (For further discussion on training, see **7.8** below.)

- *Good quality management information is the life blood of a firm.* Senior managers need to understand the precise basis on which management information has been extracted, collated and summarised with a critical focus on any assumptions or presumptions inherent in the source data. All reporting should remain under review on a regular basis with a view to ensuring the management information needed is being received rather than relying on what is currently available or being used. Any new business areas, acquisitions or significant changes should trigger a comprehensive review of management information flows and reporting to ensure that consistency of coverage of all key risks and issues remains. Any review of the quality of reporting needs to ensure that information flowing both in and out of a business area is concise and easy to understand.

- *Regulatory issues management needs to become a core competency for all senior managers.* In the first instance, senior managers need the ability to recognise a regulatory issue or breach and to take action. Inaction is not an option even if the only 'reasonable steps' taken are to make others in the governance structure aware of the issue. Where necessary, build and resource action plans to remediate the issue ensuring that the plans are fully resourced, have assigned owner(s) and deadlines together with appropriate internal and external reporting on progress. All actions should be tracked through to completion and then followed up to ensure that the steps taken have, in practice, remediated the issue. A final step should be for all lessons to be learned with an assessment of the weaknesses which led to the issue, the potential for root cause analysis to assess whether the weakness(es) could be systemic and hence a trigger point for issues elsewhere in the business and to use the issue identification, remediation and follow up as part of future senior manager training.

- *Group structure and reporting lines need to remain under review.* It ties in with having appropriate resources available to discharge the risk management and other obligations and, as such, where senior managers have members of their team with dual or matrix reporting lines, then it needs to be made clear exactly what this means in practice. It may require additional documentation, but there must be clarity as to who is accountable for what and to whom. Equally, where tasks are delegated they need to be clearly allocated with appropriate oversight for the delivery of the work. As part of any delegation, expectations as well as milestones need to be set with, say, daily reports, weekly meetings with all tasks completed being verified and documented. All discussion of key steps, discussions and decisions made should be evidenced including senior managers' constructive challenge. When a task is complete all documentation should be reviewed for completeness and to ensure that the contribution and actions of senior managers (and specifically SMFs) are captured fully and accurately.

- *There is a renewed regulatory focus on incentives with the supranational Financial Stability Board (FSB) making the overt link between incentives and misconduct.* The FSB has focused on the post-financial crisis need to strengthen financial institutions' governance and also, following continued high-profile misconduct cases, on the governance of (mis)conduct more broadly. The FSB has made the specific point that misconduct may further indicate that firms are unable to get their employees to adhere to other standards, including those for sound risk management. There are several elements for reading across into the required 'reasonable steps', the first being that it is made crystal clear that the accountability for any, and all, misconduct 'lies first with the board of directors'. Firms must not, and cannot, simply push the management of misconduct and the associated governance and compensation expectations down and away from the board table. Senior managers need to ensure that when setting objectives and key performance indicators for their team that they are not encouraging or being seen to support inappropriate risk taking. (As to incentives, see further **Chapter 12**.)

Training for boards and senior managers

7.8 A fundamental part of being able to understand and then discharge the regulatory risk and other obligations which come with being a SMF is to have the requisite up-to-date skills and knowledge and to be prepared to continue to invest in those skills in a changing regulatory environment. A key part of that investment should be in training. Put simply, an effective training program is one which gives individuals the tools with which to competently do their job. The opposite is equally true with a significantly increased likelihood of enforcement action for any unprepared or unaware individual.

151

'People capabilities are becoming more and more important to having the right culture. It's not enough to be motivated to behave in a new way; people also need to understand how to be successful with the new behaviours.

The accountability regime reinforces this view of culture and its key drivers. It sets a standard for the outcomes of culture and has an important impact on senior managers, on how a firm is governed and on people's capabilities.'

Source: Jonathan Davidson, Director of Supervision – Retail and Authorisations at the UK FCA. Speech – 'Culture and conduct – extending the accountability regime' at the City and Financial Summit, London (September 2017)

Training should not just be on quantitative topics but also on the qualitative concepts of culture and conduct risk. The challenges associated with robust training on culture should not be underestimated, that said, it is becoming an essential feature of the continuing professional development of all directors and senior managers and needs potentially considerable and consistent investment to pay dividends.

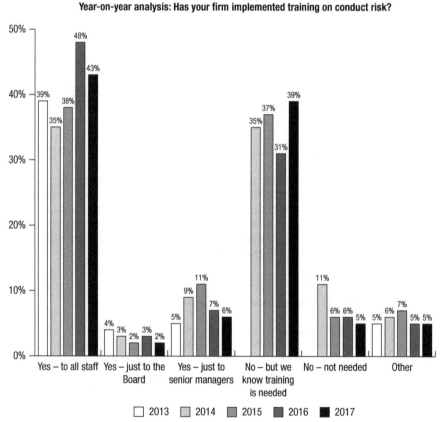

Year-on-year analysis: Has your firm implemented training on conduct risk?

Source: Thomson Reuters Regulatory Intelligence – Culture and Conduct Risk 2018 survey.

There are a number of hallmarks of an effective training program which above all else should be tailored to the audience. Given the seniority and diversity of experience at the board and senior manager level, bespoke training tends to be used with regular, often face-to-face, bite-sized updates to accommodate busy schedules. It is critical that any and all training is robustly and consistently captured and recorded with any absences from training course(s) followed up and completed in a timely manner. Specifically, training needs to be seen as a key mechanism, by which individuals (senior or otherwise) can use to identify, manage and mitigate any and all personal regulatory risks.

Training and awareness need to be considered in the round and subject-specific training should seek to fill any potential gaps in the wider information flow in and around a firm. Other elements to consider as factors in building a robust approach to training include the following:

- A robust, wide-ranging and regular review of all board member and senior manager skill sets as well as an assessment of the collective knowledge. The gap analysis should be documented in detail and have well-resourced remedial action plans with specific skill or knowledge gaps filled by training and/or targeted recruitment. All boards need to be able to demonstrate that they are individually and collectively fit, proper and competent for the roles they perform. Equally, the senior managers who operate below board level need to be individually and collectively fit, proper and competent to discharge their regulatory obligations.

- Job descriptions only used to be considered in detail when a person was new to a role and even then it was all too often a high-level and general document. Until SMR, routine interlinking between roles, job descriptions and accountabilities was rarely considered. One immediate area for consideration is for all senior managers to link their training requirements to their detailed prescribed responsibilities and to highlight how the training will support the discharge of their allocated obligations. This activity needs to be done on a firm-wide basis to ensure that the resulting aggregation of all the (much) more detailed job descriptions and training requirements come together into a seamless whole. For the whole process to be effective it then needs to be kept up to date. The aggregation of job descriptions and training can be usefully interlinked with the board and senior manager review of skills with a separate board-level aggregation to demonstrate how the board members, collectively and individually, discharge their personal accountability.

- While the firm should maintain its own training records, senior managers also need to build and maintain their own personal archive of evidence to demonstrate the full and complete discharge of their regulatory obligations. A quick win for some could be the collation of all training undertaken, continuing personal or professional development certifications together with attendance records for industry briefings.

- The information flows within a firm are a form of training and awareness in and of themselves. As noted above, good management information is the life blood of any firm and, in the current regulatory environment, management information could be seen as the need for 'evidence, evidence and more evidence' that a firm and the senior managers running it have done all the right things in all the right ways. Boards and senior managers must have the skills needed to constructively challenge the assumptions, scope and limitations on all reporting. In today's world the challenge needs to extend to all areas of the business and not just those that are overtly or directly regulated.

- The need to raise awareness about the external regulatory environment may mean changes to reporting and the inclusion of a standing update item on key meeting agendas. Firms need to be aware that it is not just mainstream financial services regulatory changes which may have an impact on the business – a case in point is data protection, which has numerous ramifications for firms. The impact of data protection requirements is considered at **14.5** below. All relevant regulatory information needs to be, and to be seen to be, considered, such as supranational or cross-border regulatory changes, the lessons to be learned from enforcement actions against firms undertaking similar business activities as well as the messages from speeches and other regulatory publications.

- Senior individuals need to have sufficient knowledge and awareness to be able to discuss competently all key relevant regulatory changes with the supervisor as well as to understand the likely impact on the firm and its customers.

- All board members and senior managers need to fundamentally understand the business being conducted. It ought to be stating the obvious that a firm needs thorough in-depth understanding of all products, activities and processes, but all too often enforcement actions show that as people and businesses change, knowledge levels become severely depleted with the inevitable regulatory consequences. Particular care needs to be taken over any new areas of business or products whether the change is by acquisition or internal development. The assessment of training needs should be an inherent part of any business change process.

Checklist

7.9   The checklist below offers practical questions for senior managers to consider.

Checklist

- How up to date is your training? Are you confident that you could evidence your skill set and demonstrate that it is fit for purpose for your role?

- Does your Responsibilities Map reflect the current business structure and does it capture all the areas for which you are responsible?

- When did you undertake the last comprehensive review of all management information? How would you explain to a regulator the basis and assumptions on which all management decisions are taken?

- Are you comfortable that when setting objectives and key performance indicators for your team that they are not encouraging or being seen to support inappropriate risk taking?

Chapter 8

Practical challenges to overcome

Chapter summary

Over and above the additional regulatory requirements associated with the Senior Managers and Certification Regime (SM&CR), senior managers need to ensure that they take a sufficiently wide view of their obligations and know what 'good' looks like, in practice, for a number of key areas. This chapter covers:

- The need for a clear, well-informed line of sight to the issues and concerns in the business under their control

- The identification, mitigation and management of all conflicts of interest arising

- Challenges associated with outsourcing

- The ability to robustly and consistently evidence qualitative risk management in action

'I am going to talk this morning about LIBOR. That often causes an intake of breath! LIBOR, or more precisely the London Interbank Offered Rate, has been given many column inches over the past ten years. Before the financial crisis, most people hadn't heard of LIBOR, even though it is a key part of the functioning of financial markets. It grew up so to speak with the eurocurrency markets, and like a number of things that came to be a focus of attention in the financial crisis, before then it was largely taken for granted, part of the financial landscape.

My remarks today will not go over the details of LIBOR's past scandals, but instead examine important questions about the sustainability of the LIBOR benchmarks, the way that LIBOR is used now and in the future, and give an insight into the work that we, and our domestic and international partners, have been doing to reform the interest rate benchmark landscape.

Can I also be very clear about one other related point. What I will say this morning does question the sustainability of LIBOR in its current form, but this is not because we suspect further wrongdoing or have any evidence of such.

In short – my remarks will concern the future of LIBOR.'

Source: 'The future of LIBOR', speech by Andrew Bailey,
Chief Executive of the FCA (July 2017)

Introduction

8.1   For senior individuals there are myriad practical challenges in balancing the commercial demands of a financial services business and the evolving compliance issues arising from the focus on culture and conduct risk overlaid with increased personal accountability. As with all complex tasks, clarity is needed as to exactly what is in scope, which begins with line of sight to the issues under the designated remit of individual concerned. It is not enough to simply have the required 'Responsibilities Map' discussed in **Chapter 7** – in order to be able to ensure that the 'reasonable steps' have been taken and the business is under the appropriate degree of management and control, there needs to be a granular break down of all elements of the business together with mapped interconnectivity. This granular analysis needs to expressly include any outsourced or overseas parts to the business. If an issue occurs in an overseas part of the business under the management line, whether or not delegated, of a SM&CR individual, it is more than likely that the issue will open the door to a closer examination of all areas of that individual's responsibility no matter where in the world they arise.

Line of sight

8.2   The London Interbank Offered Rate (LIBOR) and the associated misuse and abuse of the benchmark is a critical example of the importance of 'line of sight' to both the business practices at the front end and the potential risks and issues arising. Anecdotally, in all too many firms the contributions made to the LIBOR calculation process were out of sight and out of mind for senior individuals and almost nowhere was the efficacy of the submissions routinely reported on as part of the corporate governance framework of a firm. Theoretically, the argument could have been made that as LIBOR only became directly regulated by the FCA in 2013, before that it would have been outside of the regulatory obligations and/or expectations imposed on senior managers. The regulatory stance taken since has shown that all areas of an authorised firm need to be under the overt management and control of the relevant senior individual as all activities of the firm are deemed to be covered by, among other things, the overarching focus on culture and conduct risk.

The precise line of sight required will depend on, and need to be tailored to, the exact remit of the senior individual concerned though there are some common requirements:

- The line of sight should be considered the next level of granular detail from the Responsibilities Maps and job descriptions and should be documented with, where necessary, links into the corporate governance and risk and control framework of the firm.

- The review of line of sight should be conducted on a regular basis – in a fast-moving business environment where personnel and business activities change frequently, consideration should be given to a review once a quarter. In environments where the change is less frequent, an annual review conducted in line with, say, the fit and proper certification and the appraisal cycle could be deemed appropriate.

- All reporting which enables line of sight should be considered with a critical eye to ensure all assumptions, manual workarounds and limitations in the management information flow are understood fully and documented. Senior individuals should bear in mind that some reporting may need to be questioned, constructively challenged and/or tested independently and, where issues are found, a separate piece of work may be required. A continuing thread is for senior managers to seek to develop and maintain a suite of succinct management information which not only gives a clear line of sight to the business under their control but which can also form the basis for strategic and other decision making.

- Last, but certainly not least, but often one of the more challenging areas, is for the senior manager to ask questions and to keep asking questions until all areas under his or her control are explained to his or her satisfaction. Any questions asked, and the answers received, should all be documented as part of the 'reasonable steps' taken in the discharge of senior manager responsibilities.

Line of sight to key issues, whilst of critical importance to senior managers, needs to be explicitly facilitated by their firms. While senior managers are responsible for the business under their remit, there is an obligation on the firm to keep its management informed of key issues. A point reiterated in the August 2017 warning notice statement in which the FCA stated that it did 'not consider that IBUK's senior management or other staff were aware that its systems and controls fell short of required standards until an FCA visit to IBUK in December 2014' (see www.fca.org.uk/publication/warning-notices/warning-notice-statement-17-5-firm.pdf).

As part of the evaluation of line of sight and whether or not further work is required, senior individuals need a sense of what constitutes good or better risk and compliance practice. Again, the specifics will relate to the particular remit of the individual concerned but two areas which may be applicable to many are conflicts of interest and outsourcing.

Conflicts of interest

8.3   The financial services industry was born and built on firms' ability to identify and manage conflicts of interest. Nascent financial services firms would not have been entrusted with potential client's monies and assets if they could not be trusted to robustly, consistently and visibly manage any and all conflicts of interest arising. Small firms would not have grown into the international conglomerates we know today without having developed a reputation for looking after their clients, at least in part, through the diligent management of conflicts of interest.

Much of the current rulebook running to thousands of pages around the world is devoted to seeking to ensure that conflicts of interest between client and firm do not damage the client. An inherent part of the 'good customer outcomes' required by regulators requires that the firm puts the interests of the client at the centre of business strategy. The shifting regulatory expectations around culture and conduct risk are again focused on driving firms towards treating their customers and their customers' interests fairly.

Too many of the recent major regulatory breaches have at their heart been the result of either ignoring or the mis-management of conflicts of interest. The mis-selling of payment protection insurance and interest-rate hedging products in the UK, sub-prime mortgages in the US and the Lehman mini-bond product in Hong Kong are all examples of where firms put their own interest ahead – way ahead – of their customer. In a similar, but different, vein the benchmark and FX market scandals are both market abuse and also further examples of where firms were putting their own interests first to the ultimate detriment of the underlying client.

Regulators are clamping down and clamping down hard on the widespread mis-management of conflicts of interest. In the UK, for instance, the FCA asked the chief executives of asset managers to sign a personal attestation to state that all conflicts of interest were being appropriately managed. Policy has also been revamped. The revised Markets in Financial Instruments Directive, applicable to all investment activities in the EU and implemented on 3 January 2018, contains wide-ranging investor protection measures. On conflicts of interest, some of the specific detail is set out in the MiFID II (Organisational Requirements and Operating Conditions for Investment Firms) Regulation (EU) 2017/565). In a nutshell, the improvements to the existing framework include a number of additional safeguards:

- by creating an explicit requirement for conflicts of interest policies to be reviewed at least annually;

- by making it clear that disclosure of a conflict, as a means (or alternative) to managing it, should be an option of last resort. Any disclosure made must be specific and enable the client to make an informed decision as to whether to carry on with the service/investment offered; and

- an additional requirement to consider conflicts caused by inducements and incentives.

All in all, senior managers need to recall the origins of financial services firms. They were built on the ability to successfully manage conflicts between themselves and their clients. Firms of all shapes and sizes would do well to rebuild their core competency in the effective management of conflicts of interest. Senior managers and firms that excel at conflicts management are likely to find all stakeholders, clients and regulators in particular, are distinctly more supportive of all aspects of the business.

The continuing spotlight on conflicts of interest should encourage all firms and their senior managers, regardless of jurisdiction, to not only review their governance and control arrangements but also to raise awareness on all aspects of conflicts of interest. The need for consistently better customer outcomes is another driver for firms to check that they have taken, and can evidence they have taken, an appropriate approach to conflicts of interest. There are a range of measures which senior managers may wish to consider undertaking, including the following:

- First and foremost a fully resourced, board-sponsored review of the current arrangements in place for the effective management of conflicts of interest. Part of the work should include a detailed examination of all the poor practices highlighted. Perhaps the most powerful indicator of good practice and which was picked out by the FCA as being an overall positive force to drive appropriate behaviours and associated good customer outcomes is the express inclusion of conflict of interest considerations in a board or equivalent committee headed up by a non-executive, independent director.

- Culture has become a central tenet of regulatory approach around the world. As part of any consideration of culture within a firm, conflicts of interest need to be included with a strong correlation being seen between a firm's culture and its ability to recognise conflicts of interest. Good practice examples include firms where management was aware of the possibility of conflicts and trained staff to look for and report them and where the formal checks within product development and change management processes forced the firm to consider whether new activities created new conflicts or undermined the mitigation of pre-existing conflicts.

- The best control frameworks for the identification and management of conflicts of interest tend to be designed jointly by business and compliance functions. Firms doing so tended to have standards that were relevant to the nature of the conflict, and were operationally effective and accepted by business staff. Many of these standards were also aligned to regulatory expectations and good market practice.

- Monitoring conflicts is more effective when conducted by both business and compliance functions. In work which was again carried out by the FCA, firms that relied on monitoring performed by the compliance department as the only form of control over conflicts were unable to demonstrate robustly how compliance staff credibly challenged investment and trading decisions made by senior investment professionals.

- Monitoring conflicts is more effective when boards receive adequate management information. Examples of good practice of compliance monitoring work did not just consist of routinely checking specific procedures; it also looked at whether controls continue to meet their objectives and whether compliance standards used to manage conflicts reflect developments in market practices and new regulations.

- Conflicts are better managed when boards have committees dedicated to conflicts of interest management. Such governance bodies challenged and approved conflict identification and controls design work undertaken by others defined the management information they wished to receive and reviewed the implications of materials presented to them. Issues can arise in international firms and firms would be well advised to operate globally to a single high transparent standard.

- Conflicts are also better managed pre-emptively. In a corporate finance situation for example, firms would be wise to have a transparent protocol which sets out the process by which it is decided which client the firm will act for in the event that one client bids for another. Without the protocol in place, the firm is in danger of creating additional conflict of interest issues as part of an after the event, decision-making process.

Outsourcing

8.4 Senior individuals need to be involved in the oversight of all significant outsourcing arrangements which operate under their remit. Outsourcing can be an efficient and cost-effective way to supplement in-house resources, but it must be delivered appropriately to be of real benefit.

The issue of outsourcing came to the fore for all the wrong reasons in the recent past with fines and a regulatory risk alert. Western Union in Eire and Raphael & Sons in the UK were both sanctioned for specific outsourcing failures and, in the US, a risk alert was issued warning of the dangers of outsourcing any or all of the required compliance functionality.

PRA fines Raphaels Bank £1,278,165 for outsourcing failures

In November 2015, the PRA fined R Raphael & Sons Plc ('Raphaels') £1,278,165 for potentially putting its safety and soundness at risk by failing to properly manage its outsourcing arrangements.

As at April 2014, Raphaels owned 334 ATMs in the UK for public use in locations such as bureaux de change, railway stations and airports. Raphaels also owns mobile ATMs which are used at major sporting and other events. In September 2006, Raphaels agreed to enter into a joint venture with another company in its parent's group ('the Group') (Company C) to provide ATMs in various locations around the UK. Raphaels outsourced its ATM finance function to a team within Company C but did not have appropriate controls around this arrangement. Raphaels failed to enter appropriately into suitable written agreements or undertake suitable due diligence around the outsourcing.

From 2007 to 2014, Company C employees in the team responsible for managing the outsourced functions improperly transferred funds without the knowledge or consent of Raphaels and took steps to conceal their actions. The PRA has seen no evidence that anyone else in the Group was aware of their actions. The funds were transferred from Raphaels to deal with cash flow problems in Company C. This meant that Raphaels was exposed to Company C, which would have led to severe financial repercussions if Company C had become insolvent.

As a result of the failings around its outsourcing, these breaches meant that Raphaels had inadequate oversight and control over its regulatory capital position. Specifically, from May 2011 to November 2013, Raphaels failed to understand and accurately report its capital requirement and failed to understand that it had a large exposure to the Group of more than 25% of its capital resources.

Andrew Bailey, then Deputy Governor for Prudential Regulation and CEO of the PRA, said:

'You can delegate or outsource work but you cannot delegate or outsource responsibility. Raphaels put its safety and soundness at risk by failing to have adequate controls in place over their outsourcing. The lack of controls meant that Raphaels did not know what its capital position was or who it was exposed to. This behaviour could have had severe consequences for Raphaels which is why the PRA has taken the relatively unusual step of levying a fine in this case.'

Raphaels agreed to settle at an early stage of the PRA's investigation and therefore qualified for a 30% stage 1 discount under the PRA's Settlement Policy. Were it not for this, the PRA would have imposed a financial penalty of £1,825,950.

The golden rule for successful outsourcing is that while activities can be moved to a different group, company, or a third party, the skills to manage those activities must be retained in-house. This may be less obvious in an intra-group outsourcing scenario – but for a separate legal entity with a separate licence, it is essential. Equally, if there is a branch or other structure involved, then the firm needs to consider the efficacy of the outsourcing arrangements and the skills, governance and local responsibilities of the branch.

'Banks also need to maintain an adequate level of control. We see that many banks outsource, standardise and optimise business processes in order to achieve more agile and flexible ways of working. Our concern is that this might impact the quality of their controls. Under no circumstances should banks cut costs at the expense of risk management and of the quality of risk data aggregation and reporting. On the contrary, they should fortify their operational management, risk control and compliance, as well as their independent internal audit function. They should make sure that, for each risk, accountability and ownership are defined and well understood throughout the organisation.'

Source: 'Good governance – an asset for all seasons', keynote speech by Danièle Nouy, Chair of the Supervisory Board of the European Central Bank (June 2018)

As part of their oversight, and indeed 'reasonable steps' seen to be taken, senior managers should ensure that the risk, compliance and internal audit functions all include outsourcing in all their monitoring plans. Elements to consider for testing are:

- the need for upfront due diligence on the outsourcer (even when it is a group company), together with a detailed written agreement specifying all aspects of the outsourced arrangements. Among other things the detailed written agreement should cover the practical measures involved in exiting the outsourced arrangement;

- the ability to access physically the offsite outsource location: every effort should be made to carry out at least an annual on-site visit to all major or material outsourcers to assess the level, timeliness and quality of the information flows;

- the practical ramifications of data protection legislation particularly with regard to the security of data and any international data transfers. This became even more critical after the implementation of the European General Data Protection Regulation in May 2018 with its enhanced consent, data governance and 'right to be forgotten' requirements;

- the resilience of the outsource company: while most firms will undertake comprehensive due diligence at the start of the relationship with an outsourcer, it is less common to undertake continuing checks to ensure that the outsourcer remains effective. All firms should have comprehensive, tested contingency plans to deal with the failure of an outsource provider;

- the inclusion of outsourced arrangements in any dawn raids policy: firms need to remember that regulators, law enforcement agencies and others may seek to gain access to data and information through outsourced arrangements;

- the right (as should be set out in the outsource contract) to be informed before any of the firm's data or activity is outsourced from the outsourcer. Too many firms have found that their data has been passed on and away from their original outsourcer to numerous other entities, thereby increasing possible loss, contagion, reputational and concentration risks;

- the inclusion of outsourced arrangements in any recovery and resolution plans: this is particularly pertinent for any firm required to create a 'living will' but will also be critical for all business continuity and disaster recovery plans;

- the maintenance of all in-house skills and expertise to oversee the activities outsourced.

As a matter of course, any review undertaken on outsourced activities should be reported to the board as part of the firm's overall risk reporting.

Skill sets

'As a financial sector, we too need to play our part, and seek innovative ways to develop additional talent. It is no longer sustainable to rely on experienced

> hires attracted by ever larger compensation packages – we need to grow the talent pool.'
>
> Source: 'Expect the unexpected: cyber security in 2017 and beyond', speech by Nausicaa Delfas, Executive Director of the FCA (April 2017)

8.5   It should be stating the entirely obvious that everyone and anyone in a senior role should have the requisite skill set to both understand the ramifications of the role and to discharge all obligations arising. For very senior managers (directors expressly included), the question of skill sets is not just a matter of individual assessment but also a consideration of the collective skills needed for effective governance committees and boards.

The development and maintenance of a relevant skill set is one of the best insurance policies a senior individual can have against the increased personal liability arising out of SM&CR. Given that regulatory personal liability is here to stay, senior individuals increasingly need to assess for themselves what 'good' looks like in terms of their own personal regulatory risk management. A fundamental element of personal regulatory risk management is the need for continuing training and awareness without which senior individuals will not be able to stay up to date with either all applicable requirements or changing regulatory expectations.

Board members and other senior individuals are not expected to be experts in everything, but they do need to have sufficient knowledge and to have an appropriate range of skills to understand the issues, able to set an appropriate risk appetite, drive a strong compliant culture, understand and challenge all risk and compliance reports as well as engage appropriately with regulators.

Collective managerial knowledge needs as much care and attention as individual skill sets. A particular case in point was the January 2016 UK Treasury Committee correspondence between Rt Hon Andrew Tyrie MP, Chairman of the Treasury Committee, and RBS, HSBC, Barclays, the FCA and PRA, Bank of England, in relation to IT system failures at each of the banks during the period June to November 2015.

The correspondence published gives at least a partial insight into a range of IT issues all of which had varying degrees of customer impact. In the words of Andrew Tyrie:

> 'The current situation cannot be allowed to continue. IT risks need to be accorded the same status as credit, financial and conduct risk. They are every bit as serious a threat to customers and overall financial stability. More and higher quality, investment is probably required'.

With that background the Treasury Committee had made three, what it has called, 'suggestions' which will, in effect, steer the future regulatory and supervisory approach to IT in financial services. In outline, the three suggestions are:

• banks need greater IT expertise at main board and subsidiary board level;

- much greater resources should be put towards modernising, managing and securing banks' IT infrastructures;

- legal, regulatory, structural and cultural changes are needed to the way that banks manage their cyber security risks.

All firms have IT risks. Equally, all firms need to be aware of the Treasury Committee's suggestions on IT even though the discussion is, in the first instance, aimed at UK banks. The point on IT skills is particularly pertinent given the focus on fintech and cyber resilience combined with the expressed concern about the use of consultants with regard to IT. Specifically, the Treasury Committee makes the point that firms 'need enough skilled people throughout their IT management structure to enable them to be largely independent of consultants for crucial expertise'.

> 'The collective knowledge of boards can still be improved. In-depth knowledge is particularly important for challenging senior management on more technical topics such as digitalisation, IT, internal models and regulation.'
>
> Source: 'Good governance – an asset for all seasons', keynote speech by Danièle Nouy, Chair of the Supervisory Board of the European Central Bank (June 2018)

Firms would be well advised to undertake an IT skills audit to not only highlight and begin to remediate any key gaps, but also to be prepared when the regulators ask about skills at the board and other levels together with the potential (over)use of consultants. It is not just IT skills within the IT department itself, but should include the entire firm, the board expressly included, with all functions seen as having the appropriate levels of IT expertise needed for their roles.

Service disruption at TSB

The need for IT skills at the highest levels of firms is not merely theoretical. The IT troubles faced by TSB in the spring of 2018 have put the focus not only on the role of technology in delivering good customer outcomes but also raised the spectre of personal liability for senior managers.

The depth and nature of the IT problems at TSB led to the Treasury Committee launching an inquiry under which it will consider the preparation for, implementation of, and results of, the system migration, and TSB's handling of the problems that ensued (see www.parliament.uk/business/committees/committees-a-z/commons-select/treasury-committee/inquiries1/parliament-2017/tsb-sabadell-17-19).

The potential for personal liability has already been made clear with, in June 2018, the chair of the Committee publishing a letter expressing a 'loss of confidence' in the chief executive of the bank:

> 'As a result, the Committee considers that the TSB Board should give serious consideration as to whether Dr Pester's position as Chief Executive of TSB is sustainable. The Committee has lost confidence in his ability to provide a full and frank assessment of the problems at TSB, and to deal with them in the best interests of its customers. It is concerned that, if he continues in his position, this could damage trust not only in TSB, but in the retail banking sector as a whole. I ask that the Board consider the Committee's view as a matter of urgency.'

Board members together with other senior individuals need to see the benefit in continuing investment in building and maintaining knowledge and awareness of the changing regulatory environment. Put simply, an effective training program is one which gives individuals the tools with which to competently do their job. The opposite is equally true with a significantly increased likelihood of enforcement action for any unprepared or unaware individual. Further specifics on training and skill sets are considered in **Chapter 7**.

Case study – prospective compliance officer rejected by regulator for lack of detailed knowledge

In August 2017, the FCA published a final notice stating that Gregory Rupert Nathan lacked fitness and propriety to be given controlled functions CF10 (compliance oversight) and CF11 (money laundering reporting officer) of Goldenway Global Investments (UK) Limited.

It is unusual for the FCA to issue a formal final notice to decline controlled function applications as often the application is withdrawn before it gets to that stage, thus avoiding the adverse publicity for both the firm and, in particular, the individual concerned. In this instance, it was not made clear why Nathan's application was not withdrawn earlier. Possibly the firm did not appreciate the importance of doing so, or possibly there was a feeling that the regulator could be convinced to change its mind with Nathan undertaking some compliance training.

The final notice does give an insight into the importance the regulator places on detailed relevant knowledge and an appropriate skill set needed to undertake a controlled function (and by association any role caught by the SM&CR).

Goldenway's core business is the sale of contracts for differences (CFDs) through its Internet platform. The CFDs transacted are primarily foreign exchange and commodities. Nathan was interviewed twice by the FCA and failed to impress in a number of critical areas. The regulator's overarching concern was that Nathan 'failed to provide sufficiently detailed responses to the Authority's questions in relation to the compliance and AML responsibilities that he wished to assume…'.

In a similar vein, Nathan characterised Goldenway's business model as 'very, very simple'. The FCA interpreted this to mean:

'[He] failed to recognise the complex nature of the CFD products offered by the Firm to retail clients and the complexities arising from the composition of the Firm's client base, the reliance on other parties, the concern over managing the risk of offering inappropriate products to clients and the implications of the Firm's being authorised in a different jurisdiction to the majority of its client base.'

Other question marks on Nathan's practical knowledge and awareness included issues with regard to client verification, appropriateness, financial crime risks, risk mitigation and the key elements of an effective compliance programme.

There are a number of key lessons for firms and senior individuals from the Nathan case. A spotlight is shone on the need for an up-to-date, relevant and detailed skilled set for any approved person or SMR role. This is combined with the need for anyone applying for authorisation to be rigorously prepared for a possible interview by the FCA. In preparing a candidate, firms need to be aware that the FCA is a judgement-based regulator and considers regulated firms as being potential risks to it, the FCA, being able to fulfil its regulatory mission to protect consumers, ensure market integrity and promote competition.

(See www.fca.org.uk/publication/final-notices/goldenway-global-investments-uk-limited.pdf)

Evidence of qualitative risk management

8.6   The vast majority of firms have mastered quantitative risk management with the hard numbers and calculations involved in pricing, valuation and risk-adjusted capital or solvency a widespread competency. The effective capture and evidencing of qualitative risk management in action is still evolving as firms work to define and measure culture, conduct risk and good customer outcomes.

Regulators have tackled qualitative risk issues in a number of different ways with the global policy stance being set by the Financial Stability Board (which operates under the aegis of the G20). It is now somewhat dated having been first published in 2014, but the FSB's indicators of a sound risk culture remain a good place for firms to start in beginning to frame conduct risk and culture identification, management and mitigation. If nothing else, it provides a useful benchmark for senior managers to ensure the key culture and (mis)conduct risk issues have been captured.

The FSB has undertaken extensive further work on risk culture and associated misconduct risk. Guidance on the use of incentives and compensation to help manage and mitigate misconduct risk is considered in **Chapter 12** and the FSB 'toolkit' on misconduct is discussed in **Chapter 9**.

Indicators of a sound risk culture

Tone from the top

Leading by example:
- Integrity
- Open exchange of views encouraged
- Decision making not dominated by one individual
- Senior management subject to same expectations as other staff

Assessing espoused values:
- Board ensure tone from the "middle" and further down consistent with tone from the top
- Board and senior management assess that risk appetite framework and business strategy is clearly understood and embraced

Ensuring common understanding and awareness of risk:
- Risk appetite, strategy, risk management effectively aligned and embedded in decision making and ops at all levels
- Board and senior management have clear views on most risky business lines – risk/return balance
- Board and senior management monitor how promptly and effectively issues raises are addressed by management

Learning from past experience:
- Root cause analysis of deficiencies conducted
- Assessment and communication of lessons learned from past events (failures and successes) seen as opportunity to enhance risk culture

Accountability

Ownership of risk:
- Clear expectations set re: monitoring/reporting of risk
- Information-sharing mechanisms in place on emerging risks, etc
- All held accountable where their actions do not align with core values, risk appetite and culture

Escalation process:
- Processes in place to support risk management, and clear consequences for non compliance
- Assessments done to ensure employees are aware
- Mechanisms in place for employees to elevate and report concerns
- Clear whistleblowing policy that is followed in practice

Clear consequences:
- Consequences are clearly established, articulated and applied
- Breaches in internal policies, procedures and risk limits, as well as nonadherence to internal codes of conduct, are understood to have a potential impact on an individual's compensation and responsibilities, can affect career progression and, depending on severity, may result in termination

Effective communication and challenge

Open to alternate views:
- Alternative views and questions from individuals and groups are encouraged, values are respected and occur in practice
- A culture of open communication and collaboration is constantly promoted to ensure that each employee's view is valued and the institution works together to strengthen risk-related decision making

Stature of control functions:
- Risk management, internal audit, compliance share the same stature as the business lines, actively participate in committees and are proactively involved in all relevant risk decisions and activities
- Control functions operate independently, have appropriate direct access to the board and senior management
- Control functions, including their respective representatives, have sufficient stature not only to act as advisors, but to effectively exert control with respect to the institution's risk culture

Incentives

Remuneration and performance:
- Remuneration and performance metrics consistently support and drive the desired risk-taking behaviours, risk appetite and risk culture – encourage employees to act in the interest of the greater good of the company, rather than themselves or their business line
- Annual performance reviews, objectives-setting and processes are links to promoting the institution's desired core values and behaviours as well as compliance with policies and procedures
- Incentive compensation programs systematically include individual and group adherence to the financial institution's core values and risk culture, including treatment of customers, cooperation with internal control functions and supervisors, respect of risk limits and alignment between performance and risk

Talent development:
- Understanding key risks, essential elements of risk management and the institution's culture is considered a critical skill set for senior employees and reflected in the their development plans
- Job rotations between control functions and business lines in considered a virtuous cycle for bringing business knowledge to the control functions and introducing risk awareness to the decision-making process of the business line
- Training programs are available for all staff to develop risk management competences and the elements supporting a sound risk culture, including effective challenge and open communication

Source: Derived from the FSB's 'Guidance on Supervisory Interaction with Financial Institutions on Risk Culture' (April 2014)

Checklist

8.7 The checklist below offers practical questions for senior individuals to consider.

> ## Checklist
>
> - Can you explain how you have line of sight to all key risks and issues in the business under your control?
>
> - Has your skill set been assessed both individually and on a collective basis with regard to committee and other senior meeting memberships? And if so, have any gaps been remediated?
>
> - Can you explain your firm's approach to the assessment of risk-culture indicators as set out by the FSB?
>
> - Are you aware of all significant outsourcing arrangements? And are you aware of how they are overseen, managed and reported on?

Chapter 9

Role of culture and conduct risk

Chapter summary

This chapter covers:

* Regulatory focus on culture and conduct

* Defining culture and conduct risk

* Regulatory expectations and what firms are doing in practice

* Conduct risk programmes and frameworks

* Measurement and metrics

> 'The crisis exposed significant shortcomings in the governance and risk management of firms and the culture and ethics which underpin them. This is not principally a structural issue. It is a failure in behaviour, attitude and in some cases, competence. ... firms need to have an appropriate culture and one which is focused on the firm delivering the right long-term obligations to society. The right cultures are rooted in strong ethical frameworks and the importance of individuals making decisions in relation to principles rather than just short-term commercial considerations.'
>
> Source: 'Delivering effective corporate governance: the financial regulator's role', Hector Sants, FSA Chief Executive, at Merchant Taylors' Hall (April 2012)

Regulatory expectations and industry practices

Why culture has become such a focus

9.1   The importance of culture in financial services has been widely acknowledged in recent years following recognition across the industry that the financial crisis was as much a conduct crisis as it was a prudential one. Ever since the crisis, the role of culture has continued to be a critical feature in the findings published by regulators around the world. High-profile events from PPI mis-selling to LIBOR manipulation have shown culture to be at the root of scandals and abuses of the system. The incentivising of misconduct and excessive risk-taking through remuneration have reinforced a culture where poor standards, practices and outcomes became the norm.

The financial and operational impact on firms which result from regulatory enforcement action, ranging from stratospheric financial penalties to customer redress and remediation programmes, should in themselves be a huge disincentive to prevent further misconduct. However, the continued waves of systemic misconduct has led to recognition by regulators that, for the issue to be taken seriously within firms, it has to be personal to individuals too. That means having individuals within firms held personally accountable for their work and is the driver for the UK regulator's Accountability Regime which it says is directly targeted at the culture of firms.

> 'We are entering a world where the cultivation and maintenance of a robust institutional culture will be a key determinant of implementing a successful business strategy. Culture is critically important to the health of an institution and in turn the health of the whole financial system.'
>
> Source: Speech by John A Fraser, Secretary to the Treasury, Australia, 'The Importance of Culture', addressed to the ASIC Annual Forum (March 2016)

Closely related to culture is conduct and specifically conduct risk. The term 'conduct risk' was created by the UK Financial Services Authority (FSA) and has continued to underpin the agenda of its successor, the Financial Conduct Authority (FCA) in its determination to ensure that firms do the right thing for their customers whilst ensuring the integrity of the markets in which they operate. It has become increasingly evident that culture and conduct are inextricably linked and therefore a holistic approach to dealing with myriad conduct risks across firms is needed. Good conduct risk management is dependent on culture. It follows that changes in conduct cannot happen without cultural change.

In a survey by Thomson Reuters Regulatory Intelligence in 2018, over 600 financial services firms were asked whether their organisation recognised an interrelationship between culture and conduct risk. Almost half considered culture and conduct to be intrinsically linked. Firms also recognised that culture was a predominant factor in managing conduct risk:

Driven by tone from the top
Recognised as important but not linked
Culture predominates in managing conduct risk
Intrinsically linked _{Unclear}
Not formally discussed
Still in development **Conduct risk is a subset of culture**
Focus on treating customers fairly
No interrelationship

Source: Thomson Reuters Regulatory Intelligence – Culture and Conduct Risk 2018 survey

Broadly, the expectations from the regulators in achieving good conduct requires firms to move away from the following behaviours:

- prioritising profits and commercial interests over ethics and consumer interests;

- a tick-box and narrow legal approach to compliance;

- the view that point of sale disclosure absolves a firm from its responsibility to ensure its product or service represents a good outcome for the customer; and

- complying with only the letter of laws and regulations rather than the spirit.

> 'A firm's culture is the key driver behind the behaviour of those in it. In many cases, where things have gone wrong in a firm, a cultural issue is at the heart of the problem.'
>
> Source: Chairman's foreword, FCA Business Plan 2015/16

The widespread regulatory recognition that cultural change is essential is matched by the recognition that culture cannot be changed by regulation alone. Regulators cannot prescribe what culture firms should adopt, which means firms have an enormous challenge in defining their culture through to measuring the change. The purpose of this chapter is to provide a view of what 'good' looks like based on industry practices and regulatory expectations so that employees and senior managers can benchmark the practices within their own firms. As firms worldwide continue to deal with the challenges of conduct risk, the practical guidance can be leveraged across sectors and geographies.

Defining culture and conduct risk

> 'However much compliance officers may wish it, there is no off-the-shelf FCA-approved culture package that you can download and install in your business ('click here for good culture').
>
> Source: Jonathan Davidson, Director of Supervision – Retail and Authorisations at the FCA, delivered at City and Financial Summit, London (September 2017)

9.2 Defining what culture and conduct risk mean to an organisation is an essential first step in managing, monitoring and measuring it. In practice, firms find this particularly challenging and complex. Not least because of the qualitative nature of culture and conduct but because of the scale. Culture and conduct encompass the activities of the entire organisation. There are also no agreed definitions. Regulators have purposely not defined them because every firm is different and culture will be unique to individual organisations. Firms must develop their own conduct risk definition and strategy in line with the specific risks they are exposed to.

The FCA has expressly stated that there is no single approved culture that will suit every organisation, explaining that: 'Each firm will have a different culture. And that's fine – it is not the FCA's role to dictate a firm's culture any more than it would dictate its business model or strategy'.

In parallel, the FCA has confirmed that 'a firm's conduct risk profile will be unique to it, and there is no 'one size fits all' framework that can be put in place to assess it'.

That said, in 2016, Jonathan Davidson, Director of Supervision – Retail & Authorisations at the FCA, described culture as being 'the mindsets and behaviours that are typical for staff in each firm. These tiny, everyday acts by individuals are what make up the overarching culture of the firm in which they take place'. Similar insight into the regulator's view of conduct risk was set out in its Retail Conduct Risk Outlook 2011 where it referred to conduct risk as '… the risk that firm behaviour will result in poor outcomes for customers'.

Despite there being no agreed or industry-wide definitions, there is some consensus of the elements of those definitions. The FCA has said that the definitions it has seen typically refer to:

- client outcomes;
- factors such as sustainability of their business and market integrity;
- the FCA's competition objective 'to promote effective competition in the interest of consumers'; and
- the danger of actions or behaviours, or the conduct of business, that may: harm clients; cause the firm reputational damage; or risk undermining the integrity of the financial markets.

In the research undertaken by Thomson Reuters Regulatory Intelligence, only 21% of firms (36% in the previous year) had a working definition of conduct risk. There was a marked difference for Global Systemically Important Financial Institutions, where 68% (57% in the previous year) had a working definition of conduct risk. There is growing international agreement about the key components that define it.

The top three key components that make up conduct risk were identified as:

- culture, ethics and integrity (54%);
- corporate governance and tone from the top (44%); and
- conflicts of interest (41%).

Firms should consider what are their key components of conduct risk.

Strategy **Reputation**
Good customer outcomes
Management practices and 'mood in the middle' **Conflicts of interest**
Culture, ethics, integrity_{Fraud}
Evolving regulatory expectations Competition
Technology
Other External economic factors Vendor management **Information security**
Anti-money laundering Whistle-blowing Incentives **Sales and advice practices**
Corporate governance, tone from the top
Bribery & corruption Product governance Market abuse
Remuneration
Continued product suitability

Source: Thomson Reuters Regulatory Intelligence – Culture and Conduct Risk 2018 survey

The FCA has also given the example of cyber resilience and information security as having a 'huge conduct element – including basics like clear desk policies and phishing scams' and noted conduct risk emerging in areas such as algorithms and how they are used, reinforcing that conduct risk is as much an issue for wholesale firms as it is for retail firms. The FCA is equally focused on the role of wholesale conduct in protecting the integrity of the markets. It is clear that conduct is all encompassing and any aspects that could potentially adversely impact customers or markets should be considered.

> 'Neither best practices nor laws nor regulations can guarantee a lack of bad behavior. Recent failures illustrate the adverse consequences that behavioral weaknesses can have for those who rely on financial services. It also underscores the importance of adopting a culture that creates an environment in which laws, regulations and best practices are valued and upheld. To that end, regulators and supervisors in various jurisdictions have heightened their focus on firms' corporate governance programs and emphasized the need for instilling values that promote proper behavior and sound decision making throughout the firms.'
>
> Source: Speech by Simon Potter, Executive Vice President at the Federal Reserve Bank of New York, 'The Role of Best Practices in Supporting Market Integrity and Effectiveness', 2016 Primary Dealers Meeting, New York (September 2016)

What good looks like

9.3   Even though regulators will not define culture and conduct risk and neither expect nor want firms to have identical cultures, they have provided practical guidance and insight into their expectations. The following questions are used by the FCA to assess what management is doing to manage culture. Senior management must consider and be able to demonstrate and answer the following about their business:

(1) True purpose:

Is there a clearly communicated sense of purpose and approach? Clear communication of 'what' and 'how' are needed for a firm to work effectively and efficiently. But far more important is a well communicated 'why' so that all employees have a shared understanding of the company's true purpose. This sense of meaning is often found within strategic plans but not always articulated clearly in formal mission statements and values.

(2) Tone from the top:

What do staff hear and see from senior management? What are the behaviours that senior managers demonstrate as role model to employees?

'Setting the tone is all about creating a culture where everyone has ownership and responsibility for doing the right thing, because it is the right thing to do. It is about setting values and translating them into behaviours. This can only be established by the CEO and other members of the senior management team, who need to not only set out the key company values, but also personally demonstrate they mean them through their actions.'

Source: 'The importance of culture in driving behaviours of firms and how the FCA will assess this', speech by Clive Adamson, FCA Director of Supervision at the Chartered Financial Analyst Society – UK Professionalism Conference (April 2013)

---

(3) Governance:

What formal governance processes and structures, and policies and systems are in place which set out expectations related to behaviours and decision making? Is there a well thought through conduct risk framework in place? Are conduct risks clearly set out along with systems and controls for mitigating them and risk indicators for monitoring them?

(4) People related practices and capabilities:

These include a firm's incentives including remuneration, promotion and recognition criteria.

- Does the firm's pay structure reward misconduct?

- Is there pressure to meet sales or profit targets which discourage employees from acting in consumers' interests?

- Do employees have the right capabilities? These are increasingly important so that staff understand how new standards of behaviour will lead to success.

'...good conduct culture is about having the right capabilities as well as the right motivation.'

Source: Speech by Jonathan Davidson, Director of Supervision
– Retail and Authorisations at the FCA, delivered at City and
Financial Summit, London (September 2017)

The approach firms take to managing and mitigating conduct risk should be tailored to the risks to which they are exposed and the needs of their organisation. Broadly, the FCA expect firms to make positive outcomes for customers and integrity a priority. Regulators will not prescribe the approach that should be taken but have provided insight to what 'good' looks like within the industry, what questions firms should be asking themselves and what will be important to regulatory supervisors.

The FCA has set out five overarching questions which every firm will be expected to answer. The framework enables the regulator to compare and contrast practices in the industry and will assist firms in determining how effective their own practices are and in deciding whether they are doing enough.

UK Financial Conduct Authority – Five conduct questions	
1.	How do you identify the conduct risks inherent within your business?
2.	Who is responsible for managing the conduct of your business?
3.	What support mechanisms do you have to enable people to improve the conduct of their business or function?
4.	How does the board and executive committees gain oversight of the conduct of the organisation?
5.	Do firms have any perverse incentives or other activities that may undermine any strategies put in place?

Source: Tracey McDermott, Director of Supervision, Investment, Wholesale And Specialists, FCA, 'Wholesale Markets and Risk: FEMR and beyond' (July 2015)

Management of all levels should be asking themselves the five conduct questions and be ready to respond to regulators with answers.

The following sets out additional questions and areas for consideration plus an overview of what action other firms are taking in practice.

(1) What proactive steps do you take to identify conduct risks in your business?

- How are conduct risks inherent within the business identified? Risks cannot be mitigated if firms do not know they exist.

- Does the firm consider the root causes of misconduct within both the industry and the firm to ensure the same issues do not exist within the firm or another business area, rather than assuming that it could not happen here? For example, the FCA has noted that:

  'The root causes of much that goes wrong in wholesale markets are constant – risks exist in managing information flows, conflicts of interest and trader controls. However, time and again we see firms failing to identify where these might crystallise and manage these appropriately'.

What firms are doing in practice:

There are three main approaches that firms are taking to identifying conduct risk; the majority use a combination of the first two approaches:

(1) A top-down model where centrally defined key conduct risks are mapped to specific business activities, products and processes.

(2) A bottom-up approach where individual business units analyse their own business activities and processes end to end, and identified conduct risks are aggregated.

(3) A reverse-engineered approach where the firm's processes are reviewed to identify threats to desired firm-level conduct outcomes and the design of controls that could mitigate the risks to these desired outcomes.

Firms have adopted different approaches to collaboration and challenge in the risk identification process. These include:

- a business-led approach with the front-line business identifying conduct risks before challenge by the second-line control functions;

- the front-line business and the wider second-line control functions working together to identify conduct risks;

- the control functions such as compliance risk leading the identification of conduct risks. This approach has tended to make the least progress or needing to be repeated to be effective;

- some firms have held sessions led by senior business line staff to discuss conduct risks, grey areas, dilemmas and difficult issues. These help to reinforce expectations, uncover additional conduct risks and to produce guidelines for the business.

Different firms are at different stages of embedding their approaches to conduct risk identification with more advanced firms now having a process that has been in place for several years.

(2) How do you encourage people in front, middle, back office, control and support functions to feel responsible for managing conduct?

- Who is responsible for managing conduct in the business?

- How are individuals encouraged to feel and be responsible for managing the conduct of their business?

- Employees outside of risk and control functions need to understand that ensuring good conduct is part of their job and are helped to do it well. Given there are more people on the front-line than in compliance functions and that they tend to understand the business better than anyone else, they will know where the risks are and should have the greatest interest in managing them.

What firms are doing in practice:

- Many firms believe that the 'tone from the top' is key and use multiple channels to share top-down messages including:

  o senior management cascades, webcasts and 'town hall' meetings to communicate the firm's values and expectations of staff regarding the treatment of customers and behaviour in markets;

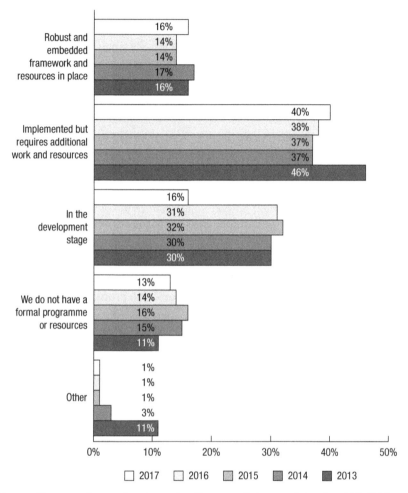

Year-on-year analysis: How mature is your organization's approach to culture and conduct risk management?

Source: Thomson Reuters Regulatory Intelligence – Culture and Conduct Risk 2018 survey

- ○ all-staff video messages from the CEO to underline the importance of maintaining good conduct and appropriate culture;
- ○ poster campaigns and screensavers to reinforce top-down messages;
- ○ videos with staff and/or clients highlighting the behaviours expected of staff;
- ○ specific programmes with a wide range of events such as a 'conduct week' to raise awareness.

- Many firms have made good conduct and culture an explicit priority for lines of business. In some cases this includes a periodic challenge process between the head of the business and the board on how all risks are managed.

- In the event that conduct incidents happen, firms are now taking into account the role of senior staff, supervisors, control functions, and bystanders who may have been aware, but did not speak up.
- Firms have firm-wide codes of conduct or specific conduct policies. These include:
  - different codes of conduct for supervisors, recognising their specific responsibilities;
  - confirmations of compliance from relevant staff members on an annual basis;
  - a focus on requiring supervisors to attest they have fulfilled their supervisory roles.
- Firms and management are reminding staff of the need to take individual responsibility for their conduct and that of their direct reports:
  - emphasising the requirements introduced by the Senior Managers and Certification Regime;
  - reinforcing personal ownership through individual objectives, remuneration, recruitment and promotion processes;
  - one firm sent some staff to watch part of a LIBOR trial;
  - using actual examples of inappropriate staff behaviour and email traffic to encourage all staff to set the right example.

(3) What support mechanisms do you put in place to help staff improve the conduct of their business or function?

- There are a large number of possible answers to this question because mechanisms are necessarily specific to individual businesses. For most firms a combination of practices are needed to create the environment expected by regulators, for example:
  - Do firms provide management information for supervisors that is useful, timely and genuinely helps them supervise their staff?
  - Are committees able to form and discuss issues?
  - Are new product and new business approval committees robust and appropriately represented by the control functions?
  - Do training and induction programmes set out a firm's expectations of its staff?
- Is there a culture of appropriate escalation, where people can and are willing to speak up when they observe poor behaviour or are unsure about what to do, knowing they will not be penalised if they do.
- Are there firm-wide policies and training to support good conduct and set out clear expectations? For example, clear desk policies and phishing scam awareness to support cyber resilience and information security.

What firms are doing in practice:

Providing management information:

- Most firms have developed conduct risk management information capturing metrics about individuals' conduct and policy breaches. These bring together disparate pieces of information to give supervisors a clearer picture of the risk and compliance culture of their area so they can manage it more effectively. Much activity is underway by firms to develop and refine metrics including:

  o developing risk tolerances for breaches with any breaches of those tolerances highlighted in dashboards;

  o identifying business-specific management information (MI) related to conduct with specified recipient action and escalation at relevant limits;

  o reviewing metrics after conduct incidents occur to determine if revisions are needed to ensure such an event would be identified in future;

  o developing metrics tailored to the outcomes they want to achieve.

Providing governance related mechanisms:

- New or stronger conduct risk challenge in existing new product approval or new business approval processes, and reputational risk committees.

- Post-deal or transaction analysis including input from clients to determine integrity and conduct performance based on specific events.

- Creation of governance and oversight structures to focus on conduct risk.

- Inclusion of conduct and culture questions in staff and client satisfaction surveys to check the value of integrity and reputation to clients and staff.

- Attempts to ethically hack the firm's own systems and controls as upgrades are rolled out to ensure they are genuinely effective.

Implementing a range of training and awareness activities to both identify and manage conduct risk including:

- Highly visible programmes with small groups of staff led by experienced business practitioners who draw on personal experiences.

- Leadership or manager-specific training focused on the firm's business, conduct and culture.

- Ethical decision-making training to help staff identify the right thing to do and decision making in grey areas.

- Advertising campaigns that connect everyday morality to employees' day jobs.

- Implementing a decision-making tool to help staff make responsible and ethically sound decisions.

- Testing staff on their knowledge of procedures and expected behaviour in conduct scenarios.

- Rolling programmes of supervisory reviews to check standards are met and providing support where poor behaviour is detected.

- Internal exams tailored for functional lines so that new staff are clear on what is, and is no,t acceptable in the new firm.

- 'Integrity Training' using the firm's own case study examples and past conduct issues.

- Assessment of candidates against the firm's values at the recruitment stage through situational judgement scenarios.

Implementing practices to encourage escalation of conduct issues:

- Highlighting and sharing positive examples of escalated issues and concerns, and also the consequences of non-escalation.

- Senior staff talking about mistakes made through their career to highlight that it is human to make mistakes and to encourage escalation of issues.

- One firm developed and trained their staff in an escalation framework followed by a fake internal 'rogue trade' to test the escalation procedures and reinforce that risk identification and escalation is a structured process and a necessary daily occurrence.

- Introduction of an escalation channel specifically for conduct risk issues, providing maximum assurance about preserving anonymity.

(4) How does your board, executive committee or senior management get oversight of conduct within the organisation? Equally, how does the board or executive committee consider the conduct implications of strategic decisions they make?

- Responsibility starts at the top so boards need to take account of the consequences of conduct risk in all its strategic decision making. What information does the board and executive team receive, and how do they take it into account in their decision making?

- Are conduct issues on board agendas? Are conduct implications brought into discussions and taken into account in every decision made, in recognition of the impact their decisions have on conduct.

- What is the information flow up the hierarchy of the organisation? Is the board able to stay aware of risks, and up to date with mitigation of those risks? For example, the FCA has stated that it will look to see:

  ○ whether the board of a firm probes high return products/services; and

  ○ the extent to which the board monitors whether products are being sold to the markets that they were designed for.

What firms are doing in practice:

- Including a conduct and culture report as a standing agenda item for board or executive committee (ExCo) meetings covering conduct incidents, strategic decisions that may increase conduct risk, an assessment of new and emerging conduct risks and conduct risk metrics for businesses and functions.

- Board and ExCo sitting on risk committees to ensure conduct and culture programmes are rolled out effectively.

- Undertaking external client surveys to highlight any potential conduct and culture issues.

- Conducting internal surveys which ask conduct-related questions such as whether staff have anyone they can confide in at work.

- Requiring the internal audit function to routinely consider conduct and culture in audits or undertake a stand-alone audit of the firm's conduct and culture programme.

- Managing conduct risks when exiting a business, for example, providing reasonable notice of the exit (longer than the contract terms if needed) and working proactively with customers to move them to a new provider.

- Recognising and revising budgets or targets that are overly ambitious and which may have caused staff to be pressured into meeting it.

- Deliberately downsizing the front office before control functions during significant strategic change to the business to ensure appropriate oversight during the process.

> 'I believe that incentives shape behavior, and behavior drives culture. If you want a culture that will support your long-term business strategy, you need to align incentives with the behaviors that will sustain your business over the long haul.'
>
> Speech by William C Dudley, President and CEO at the Federal Reserve Bank of New York, 'Remarks at the Culture Imperative – An Interbank Symposium', New York City (January 2017)

(5) Have you assessed whether there are any business activities that could undermine the work put in place to improve conduct?

- This is an all-encompassing question. The regulator expects firms to look throughout the organisation as well as externally to identify and assess the root causes of actual or potential conduct events.

- Firms should consider financial and non-financial incentives. For example, do staff members with a good profit and loss (P&L) get promoted or rewarded if they circumvent the rules? If employees see a colleague rewarded or promoted following behaviour that has not been consistent with the firm values, it does not send a clear message that such behaviour is not tolerated.

- Are positive role models identified and championed? Role models tend to be the stars of the firm, such as a top trader or desk head rather than the CEO or board members who employees never, or rarely, see.

- Where targets are raised or budgets cut, is the potential impact on conduct risk taken into account?

'Responsibility, accountability and governance in financial services firms and their impact on conduct has been and remains, a priority for the FCA with a focus on the most significant drivers of good or poor mindsets and behaviours. This includes incentives and remuneration, and the steps firms take which address associated risks.'

Source: FCA Press release – 'FCA proposes new measures to maintain firms' focus on culture' (September 2016)

What firms are doing in practice:

In practice, firms are linking values and standards to the objective setting, appraisal and promotion process by:

- using both financial and non-financial factors in setting variable remuneration for staff, specifically:

  o splitting grading systems into 'what was achieved' and 'how was it achieved'; and

  o being transparent to staff that their ultimate performance grade and reward will reflect not only financial and non-financial performance achievements but also their conduct;

- making an assessment of an individual's conduct and cultural characteristics when considering promotion and openly explaining this to staff;

- highlighting examples where possible of where staff have been held back from promotion because of conduct issues.

Assessing and rewarding behaviours through:

- sample reviews by senior management of appraisals and objectives to quality assure the system;

- gathering feedback from control functions and 360° input on individuals' conduct and behaviour for the remuneration and promotion process, particularly for more senior and risk-taking staff;

- rewarding staff for excellent conduct and culture, eg public acknowledgement, a financial reward, a 'thank you' dinner with senior management, utilising part of the annual bonus pool to reward staff for exemplary conduct and culture behaviours;

- applying penalties where staff fall short of the expected standards as opposed to rewarding it when it happens;

- developed 'scorecards' of conduct-linked metrics linked to promoting the firm's desired culture, strategy, values, reputation, quality of client relationships, stakeholder engagement and people. These are used to measure performance against conduct objectives, and reward and incentivise incremental improvements in behaviours.

Undertaking a wider analysis of different activities that could undermine efforts to improve conduct. Examples include:

- extremely challenging performance criteria and/or pressure to perform without adequate support or resources, which could lead to enhanced conduct-related risks;

- the execution risks generated by restructuring programmes and the risks these may pose to their conduct programmes;

- the risk of a lack of investment in conduct and controls programmes;

- the heightened employee-related risks in businesses that are being down-sized or exited;

- the risks posed by the behaviours of some clients and counterparties;

- failure of the firm's controls to support the desired behaviours.

'It seems to me that we can identify key drivers of culture at a firm. These include: setting the tone from the top; translating this into easily understood business practices; and supporting the right behaviours through performance management, employee development, and reinforcing through reward programmes.'

Source: 'The importance of culture in driving behaviours of firms and how the FCA will assess this', Clive Adamson, FCA Director of Supervision, at the Chartered Financial Advisors Society – UK Professionalism Conference (April 2013)

Conduct risk programmes

Approaches to implementing conduct risk management

9.4   The implementation of conduct risk programmes to manage conduct necessarily varies by firm. From industry research undertaken by Thomson Reuters Regulatory Intelligence it is clear there is no definitive or single approach.

- There is a mixed picture in terms of responsibility for implementing and embedding the conduct risk policy in an organisation. The compliance function has continued to take the lead in just under a third of firms (see **6.6** above).

183

- Firms were also asked whether they have a named senior manager responsible for conduct risk and culture. Whilst half of firms (51%) have a named senior manager responsible for conduct risk, just over a third (37%) have a named senior manager for culture.

- Only a quarter of firms (22%) have a formal risk appetite agreed by the board which includes culture and conduct risk.

William C Dudley, President and CEO of the Federal Reserve Bank of New York, echoed this view in November 2015, saying: 'It is the culture within the firm that influences the behavior of its staff. While regulators can set rules on what is permissible, it is not possible to impose rules to promote a certain corporate culture. The changes have to come from within.'

Conduct risk framework

9.5   In 2018, the FSB published a 'toolkit' for both firms and supervisors with the aim of strengthening governance frameworks to mitigate misconduct risk. It is a comprehensive set of recommendations, suggestions and options, rather than formal guidance, and has set a future benchmark for both firms and supervisors in seeking to raise standards in the financial services sector.

All firms should have a robust conduct risk framework in place which is relevant and proportionate to their size and the risks they face. Similarly, the conduct risk programmes designed to implement the ongoing framework should be tailored to the needs of the firm based on its:

- size and complexity;
- business lines and model; and
- jurisdiction and geographic reach.

Good practices in risk management

9.6   While there is no correct approach, there are industry-wide good practices in risk management which firms should consider as well as specific features that the regulator has highlighted that firms have found most effective as summarised below.

Governance and accountability

- Clear lines of responsibility and accountability for conduct risk established.
- The appointment of a specific head of conduct risk or a specific conduct risk committee.

19 tools for firms mitigating cultural drivers of misconduct

For firms mitigating cultural drivers of misconduct

1 Senior leadership of the firm articulate desired cultural features that mitigate the risk of misconduct.

2 Identify significant cultural drivers of misconduct by reviewing a broad set of information and using multidisciplinary techniques.

3 Act to shift behavioural norms to mitigate cultural drivers of misconduct. Senior leadership could take actions to shift attitudes and behaviours within the firm toward its cultural vision and to reinforce the governance frameworks designed to mitigate misconduct risk. Actions could be selected with reference to the most significant cultural drivers of misconduct identified by the firm (tool 2) and based on the firm's operations.

For national authorities mitigating cultural drivers of misconduct

4 Build a supervisory programme focused on culture to mitigate the risk of misconduct.

5 Use a risk-based approach to prioritise for review the firms or groups of firms that display significant cultural drivers of misconduct. A risk-based approach to reviews could prioritise firms according to a comparative assessment of the cultural drivers of misconduct risk present within each firm. The depth of review could depend upon both the size and complexity of a firm or groups of firms under review, as well as the authority's own resources and the magnitude of misconduct.

6 Use a broad range of information and techniques to assess the cultural drivers of misconduct at firms.

7 Engage firms' leadership with respect to observations on culture and misconduct.

For firms strengthening individual responsibility and accountability

8 Identify key responsibilities, including mitigation of the risk of misconduct, and assign them. Identifying key responsibilities and clearly assigning them to the holder of various positions within a firm promotes individual accountability and increased transparency both within a firm and to relevant stakeholders. The identification and assignment of key responsibilities may be achieved through legislative or regulatory requirements, firm driven decisions on the preferred structure, or both.

9 Hold individuals accountable.

19 tools for firms mitigating cultural drivers of misconduct

10 Assess the suitability of individuals assigned key responsibilities.

For national authorities strengthening individual responsibility and accountability

11 Develop and monitor a responsibility and accountability framework.

12 Coordinate with other authorities. Supervisory techniques that aim to strengthen individual accountability through clearly assigned responsibilities could be deployed by more than one authority in the same jurisdiction. Approaches applied by one authority may have consequences for approaches that other authorities are considering. As such, national authorities could engage and coordinate with those authorities to understand their approaches to individual accountability.

For firms addressing the rolling bad apples phenomenon

13 Communicate conduct expectations early and consistently in recruitment and hiring processes.

14 Enhance interviewing techniques.

15 Leverage multiple sources of available information before hiring.

16 Reassess employee conduct regularly.

For national authorities addressing the rolling bad apples phenomenon

17 Conduct "exit reviews".

18 Supervise firms' practices for screening prospective employees and monitoring current employees.

19 Promote compliance with legal or regulatory requirements regarding conduct-related information about applicable employees, where these exist. Authorities could provide methods for firms to exchange meaningful information on employees. This could include promoting consistent and more comprehensive information in databases of financial service professional, where they exist.

Source: Corlytics Barometer – Conduct 2018 (www.corlytics.com/wp-content/uploads/2018/06/Corlytics_barometer_conduct_2018.pdf) based on 'Strengthening Governance Frameworks to Mitigate Misconduct Risk: A Toolkit for Firms and Supervisors', Financial Stability Board (April 2018)

- Responsibility for the overall culture of firms sitting with senior management who set the tone for how their staff behave.

- Prominent executive committee level involvement including:

  o actively supporting the status and visibility of the programme within the organisation;

  o highly visible CEO sponsorship;

  o engagement and challenge by the board;

  o senior executives taking leading roles in programme design;

  o clear ownership and responsibility for programme implementation by senior executives, sometimes supported by conduct specialists within the organisation as opposed to compliance or the chief operations officer (COO) being the primary driver of the programme;

  o regular discussion at board level of conduct, culture and programme implementation;

  o periodic reporting to the board.

A holistic scope

Firm-wide programmes which allow for the cross-comparison of risks in recognition that risks identified in one business may manifest, albeit in a slightly different form, in other businesses.

- All front, middle and back office and control, operational and support functions included.

- Joined up and coordinated efforts including:

  o a forum to compare conduct risk across business lines and functions. This enables examination of whether conduct risk arising in one area could arise in another;

  o performing 'read-across' exercises around conduct risk incidents and comparing the conduct risks identified.

- Detailed roll-out plans with clearly defined short-term and long-term goals.

- Integration within strategic or operational risk management frameworks.

- A standardised conduct risk self-assessment process across the firm.

- A firm-wide taxonomy for conduct risk types, enabling consistent data capture and risk reporting.

- Active engagement by internal audit, including monitoring the programme's effectiveness at an early stage.

- A top-down, rather than compliance-led, process and approach.

- Training, promotion, performance management and remuneration all linked to conduct and culture objectives.

- Long-term conduct risk initiatives becoming fully embedded in business as usual.

- Adoption or support for local programmes from the head office of international organisations.

Focus on tone in the middle

The focus on accountability at the most senior levels of management plus at the induction and onboarding stage of new people joining the industry, is enabling particular progress in conduct at the top and bottom layers of organisations. Attention and progress still needs to be made in the middle layer where many individuals entered the industry during times when the perception of what was acceptable may have been different.

Clear definition

- A clear and consistent definition of what conduct risk means for the firm.

- A clear understanding of conduct risk embedded throughout all levels of the firm and on a global basis.

Assessment

- An assessment of what conduct risks the firm is exposed to. Key risks can range from conflicts of interest through to product design, data security through to mis-selling due to inappropriate incentives and targets.

- Periodic update of the conduct risk assessment.

- Controls established to monitor and mitigate conduct risks on an ongoing basis. Ongoing review and assessment to ensure those controls remain fit for purpose.

Strategy

- A direct relationship between conduct risk and business strategy needs to be established. The FCA will expect firms to be able to demonstrate and evidence how conduct risk matters are driving business strategy and decision making.

- 75% of firms in Thomson Reuters' research said they consider, or in part consider, conduct risk factors when discussing business strategy. Conduct risk and culture are inherent in all firms, and they need to consider the conduct risk implications of any new, revised or existing business strategy.

- To test the practical ramifications of the regulatory focus on culture and conduct risk, Thomson Reuters' research asked whether culture or conduct risk concerns had affected decision making with regard to potentially profitable business opportunities. Almost a third of all firms (28%) responded that they had declined a potentially profitable business proposition due to culture and/ or conduct risk concerns.

- The stated supervisory stance is the need to drive consistently better customer outcomes and more risk-aware behaviours, and the response may be an early indicator of the policy starting to take effect in practice. Reviewing any decisions taken to step away from a potentially lucrative deal for such reasons and discussing them with regulators is a practical example of regulatory risk management in action.

Risk appetite

- A clearly articulated risk appetite informed by the conduct risk assessment and the firm's strategy.

- Linked to FCA's key objectives of good customer outcomes and market integrity.

Embedding

- Conduct risk matters embedded into existing processes, procedures and practices through a conduct risk policy, specific conduct risk training and awareness raising initiatives.

- Incentivise and reward employees in a way that encourages good customer outcomes.

- Remuneration, recruitment, performance management and promotion policies which reinforce the right values and embedding good behaviour.

- HR practices in both the hiring stage and for promotions to reinforce good conduct.

> '...why you – as a business – should be treating conduct risk as seriously as any other risk on your balance sheet, and managing it accordingly'.
>
> Source: Speech by Tracey McDermott, Director of Supervision, Investment, Wholesale and Specialists, FCA, delivered at the British Bankers' Association Conference, 'Wholesale Markets and Risk: FEMR and beyond', London (July 2015)

Measurement and metrics

> 'I hear in boardrooms relentless discussion of culture and am often asked how senior managers should measure their culture and how we, the FCA, measure and set targets for their culture. My response is that culture may not be measurable but it is manageable.'
>
> Jonathan Davidson, FCA Director of Supervision – Retail and Authorisations, City and Financial Summit, London (September 2017)

9.7   Management information requires continuing attention and firms have more work to do on metrics for conduct risk. Metrics will also need to continually evolve as conduct risks change and employee behaviour adapts in response to what is being measured. In general, quantitative measures are usually easily repeatable and require limited context to deliver their findings.

This is not the case with qualitative measures, which need extensive evidence and documentation on parameters, assumptions and data sets to ensure that the resulting management information is fit for purpose. An example is complaints analysis: a simple quantitative measure would be the number of complaints received. The assessment of culture and conduct risk in terms of complaints is an entirely different data set covering everything from timeliness of response, customer satisfaction, product governance issues, review of sales process, training needs and compensation implications.

There is no single measure of conduct risk and culture which requires firms to monitor, collate and assess a wide range of indicators from a variety of sources. The sources of information that firms are relying on include:

Customer survey results and feedback

Internal audit results   Results of mystery shopping
Complaints analysis
Internal attestations on culture and conduct risk **Staff opinion survey results**
Compliance monitoring results
Individual performance objectives
None – we are still developing any meaningful qualitative indicators

Results of HR disciplinary action   Use of compensation adjustments/clawback

Source: Thomson Reuters Regulatory Intelligence – Culture and Conduct Risk 2018 survey

Misconduct risk monitoring

9.8   Many firms have conduct-related quantitative metrics embedded in their risk assessment frameworks to enable monitoring and assessment.

The metrics commonly referenced by firms include:

(1) operational losses, including:

   (a) actual and expected losses due to misconduct;

   (b) the market value of investment products sold to high-risk clients; and

   (c) reputation risk on the franchise value or brand;

(2) number of cases of market abuse or customer complaints, such as:

    (a) number of monthly trade surveillance escalations;

    (b) percent of favourable versus unfavourable;

    (c) volume of comments;

    (d) number of serious incidents or significant conduct investigations underway; and

    (e) regulator fines as a percentage of prior year pre-tax income;

(3) performance/training indicators, such as:

    (a) number of employees who receive code of conduct training; or

    (b) alternatively those who miss mandatory training sessions;

    (c) embedding conduct metrics or objectives into variable compensation; and

    (d) a number of involuntary employee terminations and disciplinary actions due to misconduct;

(4) qualitative statements on conduct included in risk assessments include:

    (a) adherence to laws and regulations;

    (b) meeting compliance obligations; and

    (c) acting on compliance breaches.

> Source: Stocktake of efforts to strengthen governance frameworks
> to mitigate misconduct risks, FSB (May 2017)

Many firms have developed dashboards capturing conduct risk management information for business areas, produced centrally, with metrics about individuals' conduct and policy breaches. Dashboards are regularly discussed with supervisors.

Examples of metrics included on dashboards relate to:

- late completion of tasks;
- travel and expense-related matters;
- exception-based trades;
- delinquent compliance training reports;
- gifts and entertainment policy exceptions;
- policy breaches;
- personal account and trading reviews;
- personal account dealing breaches;

- missed or late training;
- excessive hours worked;
- lateness for work;
- limit breaches;
- late trades;
- expense policy breaches;
- suspicious transaction reports;
- word and voice surveillance reports;
- customer complaint analysis;
- most profitable trades;
- high client entertainment;
- clients earning the firm the most money;
- compliance exceptions;
- HR reports.

'...rules cannot simply be put in place that paper over cultural deficits; rules can actually encourage people to abdicate responsibility – if the rule book doesn't say it's forbidden, it must be OK.'

Source: Speech by Tracey McDermott, former Director of Enforcement and Financial Crime, FCA, at the FCA's Enforcement Conference, London (December 2014)

Checklist

9.9   The checklist below offers practical questions for all financial service firms to consider.

Checklist

- What is the firm's culture? How would this be described by people working at various levels of the business and by people outside of the business? Is there a clear definition of what good conduct and culture means to the firm?
- Are all staff aware of conduct-related expectations – through training, awareness and the behaviour demonstrated by senior management?

- How are conduct risks identified, managed and mitigated? Are there measures in place to assess and monitor culture and culture?

- Is culture and conduct embedded in HR processes from onboarding and performance reviews to promotion and reward? Does employee reward and incentives encourage the right behaviours?

- How engaged is the firm's management with culture and conduct issues?

Chapter 10

Other areas personal liability can arise

Chapter summary

Personal liability can arise in all manner of areas for senior managers operating in or from the UK. There are general laws designed to protect the public from fraud, negligence, financial crime and other malpractice. For financial services firms there are also specific laws and regulations related to investor protection and the preservation of an orderly market.

This chapter covers some of the key requirements which are pertinent to financial services firms and their senior managers including:

- The prevention of money laundering

- Bribery and corruption

- Market abuse

- Corporate governance

Money laundering

10.1 The need to detect and prevent financial crime in all its forms is a high priority for governments and regulators around the world. The prevention of money laundering and counter terrorist financing (AML/CTF) has spawned numerous legal and regulatory updates, all of which need to be tracked, implemented, embedded and tested as working effectively in firms.

In simple terms, money laundering is the process by which the proceeds of crime are channelled into ostensibly legitimate activities in such a way that the link between the two cannot be discovered. There are considered to be three stages to money laundering, each of which may comprise numerous transactions by the launderers, as follows:

(1) Placement – the disposal of (often) cash proceeds from illegal activity;

(2) Layering – disguising the audit trail by creating multiple complex layers of financial transactions; and

(3) Integration – placing the funds back into the economy in such a way that it appears legitimate.

In the UK there are four main acts of primary legislation which make up the AML/CTF legislation – the Terrorism Act 2000, the Anti-terrorism, Crime and Security Act 2001, the Proceeds of Crime Act 2002 and the Serious Organised Crime and Police Act 2005. The primary legislation is supplemented by a series of regulations the most recent of which, the Money Laundering Regulation, Terrorist Financing and Transfer of Funds (Information on the Payer) Regulations 2017, SI 2017/692, came into force in June 2017 and, among other things, enacted the European Union's Fourth Money Laundering Directive (see www.legislation.gov.uk/uksi/2017/692/pdfs/uksi_20170692_en.pdf).

At its heart, the UK regulatory and legal requirements oblige firms to put in place anti-money laundering systems and procedures (which include the appointment of a money laundering reporting officer) and report suspicions of money laundering to the National Crime Agency (www.nationalcrimeagency.gov.uk). The NCA was formed in 2013 as a non-ministerial government department and aggregated a number of law enforcement agencies including the Serious Organised Crime Agency. The NCA is the UK's lead agency against organised crime; human, weapon and drug trafficking; cybercrime; and economic crime that goes across regional and international borders, but can be tasked to investigate any crime. The NCA has a strategic role in which it looks at the bigger picture across the UK, analysing how criminals are operating and how they can be disrupted.

It is a measure of how seriously the regulatory bodies view the fight against financial crime that the money laundering reporting officer (or MLRO) for a firm is a named senior management function (designation SMR17) with all of the associated fitness and propriety and other obligations. The FCA describes the MLRO's job as being 'to act as the focal point for all activity within the firm relating to AML'.

While the ultimate responsibility for a firm's AML/CTF controls lies with the MLRO, there are a number of expectations expressly placed on senior managers. In addition to the sanctions available to the FCA and PRA, substantive money laundering offences carry a maximum penalty of 14 years' imprisonment and the offence of failing to report a suspicion of money laundering by another person carries a maximum penalty of five years' imprisonment.

The 2017 Regulations

10.2   The 2017 Regulations stipulate express senior manager involvement in the creation of policies, controls and procedures to identify, mitigate and manage any and all AML/CTF risks identified.

Extract from the Money Laundering Regulation, Terrorist Financing and Transfer of Funds (Information on the Payer) Regulations 2017, Pt 2, Ch 2, reg 19: Risk Assessment and Controls (author's emphasis added):

'19 Policies, controls and procedures

(1) A relevant person must—

  (a) establish and maintain policies, controls and procedures to mitigate and manage effectively the risks of money laundering and terrorist financing identified in any risk assessment undertaken by the relevant person under regulation 18(1);

  (b) regularly review and update the policies, controls and procedures established under sub-paragraph (a);

  (c) maintain a record in writing of—

    (i) the policies, controls and procedures established under sub-paragraph (a);

    (ii) any changes to those policies, controls and procedures made as a result of the review and update required by sub-paragraph (b); and

    (iii) the steps taken to communicate those policies, controls and procedures, or any changes to them, within the relevant person's business.

(2) The policies, controls and procedures adopted by a relevant person under paragraph (1) must be—

  (a) proportionate with regard to the size and nature of the relevant person's business, and

  (b) **approved by its senior management.**

(3) The policies, controls and procedures referred to in paragraph (1) must include—

  (a) risk management practices;

  (b) internal controls (see regulations 21 to 24);

  (c) customer due diligence (see regulations 27 to 38);

  (d) reliance and record keeping (see regulations 39 to 40);

  (e) the monitoring and management of compliance with, and the internal communication of, such policies, controls and procedures.

(4) The policies, controls and procedures referred to in paragraph (1) must include policies, controls and procedures—

  (a) which provide for the identification and scrutiny of—

(i) any case where—

(aa) a transaction is complex and unusually large or there is an unusual pattern of transactions, and

(bb) the transaction or transactions have no apparent economic or legal purpose, and

(ii) any other activity or situation which the relevant person regards as particularly likely by its nature to be related to money laundering or terrorist financing;

(b) which specify the taking of additional measures, where appropriate, to prevent the use for money laundering or terrorist financing of products and transactions which might favour anonymity;

(c) which ensure that when new technology is adopted by the relevant person, appropriate measures are taken to assess and if necessary mitigate any money laundering or terrorist financing risks this may cause;

(d) under which anyone in the relevant person's organisation who knows or suspects (or has reasonable grounds for knowing or suspecting) that a person is engaged in money laundering or terrorist financing as a result of information received in the course of the business or otherwise through carrying on that business is required to comply with—

(i) Part 3 of the Terrorism Act 2000; or

(ii) Part 7 of the Proceeds of Crime Act 2002;

(e) which, in the case of a money service business which uses agents for the purpose of its business, ensure that appropriate measures are taken by the business to assess—

(i) whether an agent used by the business would satisfy the fit and proper test provided for in regulation 58; and

(ii) the extent of the risk that the agent may be used for money laundering or terrorist financing.

(5) In determining what is appropriate or proportionate with regard to the size and nature of its business, a relevant person may take into account any guidance which has been—

(a) issued by the FCA; or

(b) issued by any other supervisory authority or appropriate body and approved by the Treasury.

(6) A relevant person must, where relevant, communicate the policies, controls and procedures which it establishes and maintains in accordance with this regulation to its branches and subsidiary undertakings which are located outside the United Kingdom.'

> For the purposes of this regulation 'appropriate body' means any body which regulates or is representative of any trade, profession, business or employment carried on by the relevant person (regulation 3).
>
> 'Senior management' means an officer or employee of the relevant person with sufficient knowledge of the relevant person's money laundering and terrorist financing risk exposure, and of sufficient authority, to take decisions affecting its risk exposure.

Senior managers do not need to be AML/CTF experts but they do need to have sufficient detailed skills, knowledge and awareness to fulfil their prevention of money laundering obligations. As part of the FCA's responsibility to ensure the integrity of the UK financial markets, it requires all authorised firms to have systems and controls in place to mitigate the risk that they might be used to commit financial crime.

Governance

10.3   Firms must satisfy the FCA that they have robust governance, effective risk procedures and adequate internal control mechanisms to manage their financial crime risk. A firm's systems need to be appropriate and proportionate to the nature and scale of its business. As with so much of regulation, there is no 'one size fits all' approach. It will vary, for example, between large firms and small firms, firms operating in products or areas of high risk, and those offering products to customers where the firm assesses there is less financial crime risk.

The FCA has made crystal clear that 'senior management should take clear responsibility for managing financial crime risks and be actively engaged in addressing these risks'. The FCA expects a firm to:

- have a thorough understanding of its financial crime risks in order to apply proportionate systems and controls;

- have an organisational structure that promotes coordination and information sharing across the business;

- have appropriate up-to-date policies and procedures in place that can be easily accessed and understood by all staff;

- employ staff who have the skills and expertise to do their jobs effectively;

- review employees' competence and take appropriate action to ensure they remain competent for their role;

- manage the risk of staff being rewarded for taking unacceptable financial crime risks; and

- be able to provide evidence to demonstrate that it has adequate systems and controls to prevent the risk that it might be used to further financial crime.

In parallel with the obligations placed on senior managers by the 2017 Regulations, the FCA has stated that not only should senior managers ensure that appropriate policies and procedures are in place, but also that they are monitored as being followed through robust internal audit and compliance processes that routinely test the firm's defences against specific financial crime threats.

In April 2015, the FCA produced guidance entitled 'Financial crime: a guide for firms' which consolidates the FCA's guidance on financial crime (at www. handbook.fca.org.uk/handbook/FC/link/?view=chapter). As guidance it does not contain rules and its contents are not binding, but it does give practical suggestions on how firms can reduce their financial crime risk. There are self-assessment questions together with examples of good and poor practice covering governance, structure, risk assessment, policies and procedures, recruitment, vetting, training, awareness and remuneration and quality of oversight. Of particular pertinence for senior managers is the guidance around governance.

On governance, the FCA expects senior managers to take clear responsibility for managing financial crime risks, which should be treated in the same manner as other risks faced by the business. There should be evidence that senior managers are actively engaged in the firm's approach to addressing the risks. The governance self-assessment questions are:

- When did senior management, including the board or appropriate sub-committees, last consider financial crime issues? What action followed discussions?

- How are senior management kept up to date on financial crime issues? (This may include receiving reports on the firm's performance in this area as well as ad hoc briefings on individual cases or emerging threats.)

- Is there evidence that issues have been escalated where warranted?

Examples of governance good practice from which the FCA would 'draw comfort' from seeing evidence of include:

- Senior managers set the right tone and demonstrate leadership on financial crime issues.

- A firm takes active steps to prevent criminals taking advantage of its services.

- There are clear criteria for escalating financial crime issues.

Examples of governance poor practice include:

- There is little evidence of senior staff involvement and challenge in practice.

- A firm concentrates on narrow compliance with minimum regulatory standards and has little engagement with the issues.

- Financial crime issues are dealt with on a purely reactive basis.

- There is no meaningful record or evidence of senior managers considering financial crime risks.

Bribery and corruption

'Corruption is an insidious plague that has a wide range of corrosive effects on societies. It undermines democracy and the rule of law, leads to violations of human rights, distorts markets, erodes the quality of life, and allows organised crime, terrorism and other threats to human security to flourish.'

Source: Kofi Annan, UN Secretary-General, Statement on the adoption by the General Assembly of the United Nations Convention Against Corruption (October 2003)

10.4   The UK Bribery Act 2010 came into force in July 2011 and was a transformation of the UK's stance on bribery and corruption. The reach of the Act, by design, extends far beyond the UK and covers any organisation with a UK presence, regardless of where it was formed or incorporated.

The Act has a deliberately wide-ranging scope specifically designed to aid the Serious Fraud Office (SFO) in achieving successful prosecutions. The SFO intends to enforce the Act not only in the UK but also internationally, wherever British firms or individuals are in breach. The Act specifies four offences:

- the general offence of offering, promising or giving a bribe;
- the general offence of requesting or agreeing to receive a bribe;
- a separate offence of bribery of a foreign public official; and
- a new corporate offence of failing to prevent bribery.

The Bribery Act 2010 is designed to have the maximum deterrent effect. The definition of what constitutes a bribe is drawn very broadly and covers any financial or other advantage offered to someone to induce them to act improperly. Similarly, the penalties for those found guilty of an offence under the Act can be severe, including unlimited fines and up to 10 years' imprisonment.

The corporate offence of failing to prevent bribery is significant because it expands the scope of the Act beyond an individual transaction or event to consider the corporate environment in which the bribery took place. The full defence available to an organisation is one of having 'adequate procedures' in place to prevent bribery. What constitutes 'adequate procedures' is not clearly defined and only time will tell how the courts will respond to this and other issues, such as precise scope and jurisdiction.

On paper, the Bribery Act creates arguably the toughest regulatory regime applicable in any jurisdiction, and it presents issues not just for lawyers but also for senior managers. The actual challenges lie in implementing and overseeing comprehensive and demonstrable anti-bribery and corruption policies, procedures, systems and controls, and in instilling an appropriate culture.

'Adequate procedures'

10.5 2018 brought the first court case in which a company sought to rely on having 'adequate procedures' in place, the case concluded with a small British company, Skansen Interiors, being found guilty of a 'failure to prevent bribery'. Skansen is now dormant, but the case was tried in the public interest and the findings send a clear message that companies of all sizes should (re)consider whether or not they have appropriate adequate procedures in place to prevent bribery.

The numbers involved are not huge compared to some of the headline grabbing bribes prosecuted. In this instance, the former managing director of Skansen Interiors paid a bribe of £10,000 to a former project manager and another bribe, which was not in the end paid, to seek to secure contracts worth £6m.

Skansen's defence was that it had adequate procedures in place. The firm argued that since it operated a small business out of an open-plan office with no more than 30 staff, it did not require an elaborate control infrastructure. Skansen did not have a separate anti-bribery and corruption policy, but it did have policies stating that all business dealings were to be conducted in an ethical, open and honest way. In addition, Skansen argued that its financial controls inherently had checks and balances in place in relation to bribery.

> In April 2018, the Crown Prosecution Service reported that two people had been jailed for bribery:
>
> 'Stephen Banks, former managing director of Skansen Interiors Limited, gave Graham Deakin, of DTZ Ltd, £10,000 and promised him a further £29,000 in return for confidential information in 2012 and 2013. Banks was intending to use the information to help Skansen Interiors Limited gain contracts through DTZ. Skansen won contracts in excess of £6m.
>
> Banks and Deakin pleaded guilty to bribery at an earlier hearing. Banks was sentenced to 12 months' imprisonment and was disqualified as a director for six years and Deakin was sentenced to 20 months' imprisonment and was disqualified as a director for seven years at Southwark Crown Court today.
>
> Deakin was also ordered to pay £10,697 within three months or face a further seven months in prison. Skansen Interiors Limited was previously convicted of failing to have in place adequate procedures to prevent bribery.'

The case gives a clear sense of what the court considered to be poor practice and, by association, what inadequate procedures might look like. From there, firms and their senior managers can build a picture of the reverse of what good or better practice might look like for 'adequate procedures', including the need for the following:

- No matter what the size or shape of the company the need to create a comprehensive, standalone anti-bribery and corruption policy which reflects both the Bribery Act and the associated guidance, ideally with a named senior manager responsible for its maintenance and roll-out throughout the business. The assessed potential risk of bribery and/or corruption should be used to design robust and proportionate policies, procedures and controls.

- As part of the overall review of business activities a regular risk assessment to seek to identify business locations, operations and people that may present an increased bribery and corruption risk. The risk assessments should then be used to inform the firm's risk register or appetite and determine the extent to which bribery and corruption should be included in the firm's compliance, risk and internal audit monitoring programs.

- A whistleblowing mechanism through which suspected wrongdoing can be reported in a safe (anonymous and confidential) way that is appropriately communicated and seen to be championed by senior managers. In some smaller firms this is outsourced to help to minimise possible conflicts of interest.

- As part of the overall suite of mandatory training provided, there should be a regular update and reminder on bribery and corruption. Equally, the issue can be usefully included in managers' briefings and other internal communications.

- Firms need to stay up to date with evolving good and better practice in the sphere of bribery and corruption compliance and should seek to benchmark their approach on a regular basis. In particular, senior managers should expect to receive a periodic update on the latest bribery cases and their ramifications.

Foreign Corrupt Practices Act

10.6   Senior managers also need to be aware of the potential extra-territorial impact of overseas legislation on those doing business in the UK. The US Foreign Corrupt Practices Act of 1977 (FCPA) has global reach and, alongside the UK Bribery Act 2010, is another key piece of bribery and corruption legislation which could impact senior managers.

The FCPA addresses the problem of international corruption in two ways: first by prohibiting individuals and businesses from bribing foreign government officials in order to obtain or retain business; and second, through the accounting provisions which impose certain record keeping and internal control requirements on issuers, and prohibit individuals and companies from knowingly falsifying an issuer's books and records or circumventing or failing to implement an issuer's system of internal controls. Violations of the FCPA can lead to civil and criminal penalties, sanctions, and remedies, including fines, disgorgement, and/or imprisonment.

In general, the FCPA prohibits offering to pay, paying, promising to pay, or authorising the payment of money or anything of value to a foreign official in order to influence any act or decision of the foreign official in his or her official capacity or to secure any other improper advantage in order to obtain or retain business.

The FCPA's anti-bribery provisions apply broadly to three categories of persons and entities:

(1) *'Issuers' and their officers, directors, employees, agents, and shareholders.* An 'issuer' is defined as a company that is listed on a national securities exchange in the United States (either stock or American Depository Receipts) or the company's stock trades in the over-the-counter market in the US and the company is required to file SEC reports. The definition makes clear that a company does not have to be US domiciled to be caught by the provisions of the FCPA and its officers, directors, employees, agents, and shareholders can be foreign nationals.

(2) *'Domestic concerns' and their officers, directors, employees, agents, and shareholders.* A domestic concern is any individual who is a citizen, national, or resident of the US, or any corporation, partnership, association, joint-stock company, business trust, unincorporated organisation, or sole proprietorship that is organised under the laws of the US or its states, territories, possessions, or commonwealths or that has its principal place of business in the US. Officers, directors, employees, agents, or stockholders acting on behalf of a domestic concern, including foreign nationals or companies, are also covered.

(3) *Certain persons and entities, other than issuers and domestic concerns, acting while in the territory of the United States.* The FCPA also applies to certain foreign nationals or entities that are not issuers or domestic concerns. Since 1998, the FCPA's anti-bribery provisions have applied to foreign persons and foreign non-issuer entities that, either directly or through an agent, engage in *any* act in furtherance of a corrupt payment (or an offer, promise, or authorisation to pay) while in the territory of the US. Also, officers, directors, employees, agents, or stockholders acting on behalf of such persons or entities may be subject to the FCPA's anti-bribery prohibitions.

The FCPA's anti-bribery provisions can apply to conduct both inside and outside the US. Issuers and domestic concerns – as well as their officers, directors, employees, agents, or stockholders – may be prosecuted for using the US mails or any means or instrumentality of interstate commerce in furtherance of a corrupt payment to a foreign official. The Act defines 'interstate commerce' as:

> 'trade, commerce, transportation, or communication among the several States, or between any foreign country and any State or between any State and any place or ship outside thereof ....'

The term also includes the *intrastate* use of any interstate means of communication, or any other interstate instrumentality. Thus, placing a telephone call or sending an email, text message, or fax from, to, or through the US involves interstate commerce – as does sending a wire transfer from or to a US bank or otherwise using the US banking system, or travelling across state borders or internationally to or from the US.

Those who are not issuers or domestic concerns may be prosecuted under the FCPA if they directly, or through an agent, engage in *any* act in furtherance of a corrupt payment while in the territory of the US, regardless of whether they utilise the US mails or a means or instrumentality of interstate commerce. Thus, for example, a foreign national who attends a meeting in the US that furthers a foreign bribery scheme may be subject to prosecution, as may any co-conspirators, even if they did not themselves attend the meeting. A foreign national or company may also be liable under the FCPA if it aids and abets, conspires with, or acts as an agent of an issuer or domestic concern, regardless of whether the foreign national or company itself takes any action in the US.

In addition, under the 'alternative jurisdiction' provision of the FCPA enacted in 1998, US companies or persons may be subject to the anti-bribery provisions even if they act outside the US. The 1998 amendments to the FCPA expanded the jurisdictional coverage of the Act by establishing an alternative basis for jurisdiction, that is, jurisdiction based on the nationality principle. In particular, the 1998 amendments removed the requirement that there be a use of interstate commerce (eg wire, email, telephone call) for acts in furtherance of a corrupt payment to a foreign official by US companies and persons occurring wholly outside of the US.

In terms of the type of actions or business covered by the FCPA, the FCPA applies only to payments intended to induce or influence a foreign official to use his or her position 'in order to assist ... in obtaining or retaining business for or with, or directing business to, any person'. This requirement is known as the 'business purpose test' and is broadly interpreted.

The FCPA has been summed up as:

'In short, while the FCPA does not cover every type of bribe paid around the world for every purpose, it does apply broadly to bribes paid to help obtain or retain business, which can include payments made to secure a wide variety of unfair business advantages.'

The definitive detailed guide to FCPA was produced jointly in 2012 by the criminal division of the US Department of Justice and the enforcement division of the US Securities and Exchange Commission and can be found at www.justice.gov/sites/default/files/criminal-fraud/legacy/2015/01/16/guide.pdf.

Market abuse

'I'll start with the definition of inside information – something which is central to the market abuse regime – its very definition is both fluid and situational. The information must be of a precise nature, not have been made public, relate directly or indirectly to one or more issuers or financial instruments and fundamentally, if made public, be likely to have a significant effect on the prices of those financial instruments or related derivatives.

Even applying that statement in practice requires a set of situational judgements to be made by relevant parties across the industry (and indeed those who might not even consider themselves to be in the industry at all). Defining inside information cannot be just a set of rules, therefore, it must be a state of mind, a vigilance to identify the potential for such information and the skill to have the capacity to make the assessment as to whether the conditions are met and then, simply put, the awareness of what to do next. There is a risk therefore that systems and controls will only go so far if that critical thinking has not taken place.'

Source: 'Effective compliance with the Market Abuse Regulation – a state of mind', speech delivered by Julia Hoggett, Director of Market Oversight at the FCA, at the 'Recent Developments in the Market Abuse Regime' Conference (November 2017)

10.7 The prevention, detection and punishment of market abuse is a high priority for the UK regulators and the FCA in particular. Specifically, it is important in fulfilling the FCA's statutory objectives of protecting consumers, enhancing market integrity and promoting competition.

Certain types of behaviour, such as insider dealing and market manipulation, can amount to market abuse. Firms are required to have safeguards in place to identify and reduce the risk of market abuse and other financial crime. The UK's current market abuse obligations are derived from the EU Regulation No 596/2014 of 16 April 2014 on market abuse ('the Market Abuse Regulation' or MAR) which took effect across the EU on 3 July 2016 (available at http://eur-lex.europa.eu/legal-content/EN/TXT/PDF/?uri=CELEX:32014R0596&from=EN).

MAR makes insider dealing, unlawful disclosure, market manipulation and attempted manipulation civil offences and gives the regulator powers and responsibilities for preventing and detecting market abuse. For breaches of MAR the FCA can impose unlimited fines, order injunctions, or prohibit regulated firms or approved persons.

Criminal insider dealing is an offence under Part V of the Criminal Justice Act 1993, and criminal market manipulation is an offence under sections 89–91 of the Financial Services Act 2012. Criminal sanctions for insider dealing and market manipulation can incur custodial sentences of up to seven years and unlimited fines.

The FCA undertakes surveillance of financial markets and has systems in place for identifying insider dealing and market manipulation in various financial markets. This includes analysing transaction-reporting data, order book data, benchmark submission and other market data, which significantly helps the FCA in detecting market abuse. The regulator's ability to identify market abuse is also assisted by the requirement that firms and operators of a trading venue must identify and reduce the risk of market abuse, report it to the FCA under the suspicious transaction and order reporting (STOR) regime and other relevant rules.

In addition to the required STOR disclosures, under MAR, firms and individuals must make the following notifications to the FCA:

- Persons discharging managerial responsibilities (PDMRs) within issuers, and persons closely associated with them, must notify the FCA and the issuer of relevant personal transactions they undertake in the issuer's shares, debt instruments, derivatives or other linked financial instruments if the total amount of transactions per calendar year has reached €5,000. The issuer in turn must make that information public within three business days. PDMRs are also prohibited from conducting certain personal transactions during a closed period.

- Delaying disclosure of inside information – under MAR, inside information must be announced as soon as possible and may only be delayed where certain conditions are met. Where an issuer has delayed disclosing inside information in accordance with MAR, Article 17, the issuer must notify the FCA of the delay immediately after publicly disclosing the information.

- Buy-back transactions and stabilisation activity notifications.

MAR applies to:

(a) financial instruments admitted to trading on a regulated market or for which a request for admission to trading on a regulated market has been made;

(b) financial instruments traded on a multilateral trading facility (MTF), admitted to trading on an MTF, or for which a request for admission to trading on an MTF has been made;

(c) financial instruments traded on an organised trading facility (OTF)

(d) financial instruments not covered by point (a), (b) or (c), the price or value of which depends on, or has an effect on, the price or value of a financial instrument referred to in those points, including, but not limited to, credit default swaps and contracts for difference.

MAR also applies to behaviour or transactions, including bids, relating to the auctioning on an auction platform authorised as a regulated market of emission allowances or other auctioned products based thereon, including when auctioned products are not financial instruments. Without prejudice to any specific provisions referring to bids submitted in the context of an auction, any requirements and prohibitions in MAR referring to orders to trade shall apply to such bids.

Market abuse offences and how the new and old regimes compare

Inside information – the definition of 'inside information' is broadly unchanged in MAR from the previous definition, but is wider to capture inside information for spot commodity contracts. There is also a new definition of 'inside information' for emission allowances and auction products based on these.

Insider dealing and unlawful disclosure – MAR clarifies that the use of inside information to amend or cancel an existing order constitutes insider dealing. It also prohibits persons in possession of inside information from using that information to deal, or attempt to deal, in financial instruments or to recommend or induce another person to transact on the basis of inside information.

Market soundings – MAR introduces a framework to make legitimate disclosures of inside information in the course of market soundings. Provided certain requirements are met, disclosing market participants are protected from an allegation of unlawful disclosure of inside information.

Market manipulation – MAR defines and prohibits market manipulation. This offence has been extended to capture attempted manipulation, benchmarks and, in some situations, spot commodity contracts.

There are some exemptions to the activities deemed to be market abuse including buy-back programmes and stabilisation measures. Providing certain requirements are met, trading in securities or associated instruments for the stabilisation of securities or trading in own shares in buy-back programmes are exempt from the prohibitions against market abuse.

Insider lists – MAR places an obligation on issuers to maintain a list of all persons working for them that have access to inside information. Firms subject to MAR, Article 18 will be required to transmit their insider lists to the FCA on request.

Investment recommendations – persons producing or providing investment recommendations must ensure information is objectively presented, and disclose any conflicts of interest.

Whistleblowing – MAR places requirements on regulators and firms to be able to receive whistleblowing notifications related to suspected market abuse. The FCA has proposed that there should be a 'single home' in SYSC 18 which covers the requirement that firms must establish, implement and maintain appropriate and effective arrangements for the disclosure of reportable concerns by whistleblowers [see www.handbook.fca.org.uk/handbook/SYSC/18/?view=chapter]. Recognising that each piece of EU legislation had its own whistleblowing requirements with slight variations, it was also proposed that each whistleblowing requirement should be signposted in a 'single home' in SYSC 18.

Case study 1: Personal liability under the UK market abuse regime

In November 2017, the FCA fined Paul Walter, a former Bank of America Merrill Lynch International Limited (BAML) bond trader, a financial penalty of £60,090 for engaging in market abuse.

Following an investigation, the FCA found that Mr Walter, an experienced trader, engaged in market abuse by creating a false and misleading impression as to supply and demand in the market for Dutch State Loans (DSL) on 12 occasions in July and August 2014.

On 11 occasions, Mr Walter entered a series of quotes that became the best bids on BrokerTec, an electronic trading platform, giving the impression that he was a buyer in a DSL. Other market participants who were tracking his quotes with algorithms followed him in response and raised their bids. Mr Walter then sold to those other participants and cancelled his own quote. Despite placing quotes that suggested he wanted to buy, he actually sold the DSL. On one further occasion, Mr Walter did the opposite by attracting market participants to follow him with the result he purchased the DSL from the market participants who had recently lowered their offer price and then cancelled his own quote.

Critically, while the FCA did not find that Mr Walter knew his conduct amounted to market abuse, the FCA considered he was negligent in not realising this.

Market participants were affected by Mr Walter's trading because his trading strategy manipulated their prices and led to them either buying or selling DSLs at worse prices than they could otherwise have done. Mr Walter's abusive trading resulted in a profit of €22,000 to his trading book.

Mr Walter's behaviour constituted market abuse in that it gave a false and misleading impression as to the price and supply or demand of the DSLs and it also secured the price at an artificial level.

The FCA therefore imposed a £60,090 financial penalty on Mr Walters.

Case study 2: Corporate and personal liability under the UK market abuse regime

In March 2017, the FCA announced that Tesco plc and Tesco Stores Limited ('Tesco') had agreed that they committed market abuse in relation to a trading update published on 29 August 2014, which gave a false or misleading impression about the value of publicly traded Tesco shares and bonds. Tesco have agreed to pay compensation to investors who purchased Tesco shares and bonds on or after 29 August 2014 and who still held those securities when the statement was corrected on 22 September 2014.

The Tesco case was the first time the FCA used its powers under section 384 of the Financial Services and Markets Act to require a listed company to pay compensation for market abuse.

Andrew Bailey, Chief Executive of the FCA, said:

'Dissemination of information that gives a false or misleading impression as to traded securities harms the integrity of our markets. The FCA is committed to UK markets being fair, transparent and thus competitive. Tesco and its board are doing the right thing here, taking appropriate responsibility and agreeing to rectify the consequences of the misconduct. They have cooperated fully with us and this sets a good example for the market and so is a good outcome for Tesco and investors.'

By way of background, on 29 August 2014, Tesco plc published a trading update in which it stated that it expected trading profit for the six months ending 23 August 2014 to be in the region of £1.1bn. On 22 September 2014, Tesco plc published a further trading update in which it announced that it had 'identified an overstatement of its expected profit for the half year, principally due to the accelerated recognition of commercial income and delayed accrual of costs'. Tesco knew, or could reasonably have been expected to know, that the information in the 29 August 2014 announcement was false or misleading. In making this finding, the FCA did not suggest that the Tesco plc board knew or could reasonably have been expected to know that the information was false or misleading.

As a result of the false or misleading information within the 29 August 2014 announcement, the market price for Tesco shares and bonds was inflated. This continued until Tesco issued a corrective statement on 22 September 2014. Purchasers of shares and bonds between these dates paid a higher price than they would have paid had the false impression not been created.

Under the compensation scheme, Tesco will pay an amount to each purchaser of Tesco shares and bonds who makes a claim under the proposed scheme that is equal to the inflated amount for each share or bond. The inflated amount has been established with the assistance of an independent expert engaged by the FCA.

The FCA estimates the total amount of compensation that may be payable under the scheme will be approximately £85m, plus interest.

The FCA considers the outcome is in the public interest because Tesco has accepted responsibility for market abuse and has agreed to remediate the consequences in an appropriate way that tackles directly the loss caused by the market abuse, avoiding the costs and burden on investors of litigation.

In addition, Tesco entered into a deferred prosecution agreement with the Serious Fraud Office (SFO) relating to false accounting, pursuant to which it will pay a fine of £128,992,500. As a result, the FCA does not propose to impose a separate additional sanction.

The SFO has instituted criminal proceedings in relation to other parties, specifically three ex-Tesco senior executives, all three of which deny the charges of false accounting and fraud. As of March 2018, the SFO announced a re-trial, a five-month criminal trial having been abandoned in February 2018 after one of the defendants had a heart attack.

As of summer 2018, no date had been confirmed for the re-trial.

Corporate governance

'For culture, the lessons I take from these examples are about the power of simple ideas, responsibility and commitment as represented by skin in the game, accountability. None of these big ideas is new, in fact quite the opposite. Nor do they require sophisticated tools to apply and monitor. They go with the grain of good incentives, and they act to support the public interest and its objectives. But they do require effective and consistent implementation. This is where good governance comes in, a strong role for senior management and particularly boards.'

Source: 'Transforming culture in financial services', speech by
Andrew Bailey, Chief Executive of the FCA (March 2018)

10.8   Senior managers are an inherent and fundamental part of the approach to, and focus on, the corporate governance of firms. While many of the statements and principles for good corporate governance are aimed at boards and directors, they are equally applicable to all senior managers whether or not they are also a director. Recent developments in corporate governance cover not only the systems and controls, checks and balances and approach to risk management for the business itself, but also the role, remit and responsibilities (and hence potential personal liability) of senior individuals.

'Codes put forward principles for best practice that make bad behaviour less likely to occur; and public reporting can make it harder to conceal such behaviour. But, by itself, a code does not prevent inappropriate behaviour, strategies or decisions. Only people, particularly the leaders within a business, can do that. In order to establish an appropriate governance structure, a board must define the purpose of the company and what type of behaviours it wishes to promote in order to deliver its business strategy. It involves establishing a company specific corporate culture, asking questions and making choices: how to align values and purpose to the company's strategy; how to integrate new leaders into that culture, particularly at times of a merger or acquisition; how to maintain a healthy governance under pressure; how to decide whether different parts of the business should operate different cultures, and how actively to communicate values, purpose and behaviours in order for shareholders to engage in constructive discussion.'

Source: Board briefing on culture indicators by Tracy Vegro Executive Director,
Strategy and Resources Division Financial Reporting Council (March 2018)

For UK firms there are a number of sources of guidance and expectation on corporate governance with the most prominent being the 'UK Corporate Governance Code', published in April 2016 by the Financial Reporting Council (available at www.frc.org.uk/document-library/corporate-governance/2016/uk-corporate-governance-code-april-2016). The Code operates on the principle of 'comply or explain'. Choosing to explain where a company does not comply enhances transparency for shareholders and wider stakeholders as well as recognising that one type of approach does not necessarily fit all companies. By design, the 'comply or explain' approach offers flexibility and means that it is possible to expect more demanding standards than can be achieved through legislation. In addition, requiring companies to report to shareholders rather than regulators means that the decision on whether a company's governance is adequate is taken by those in whose interest the board is meant to act.

The main principles of the Code cover good practice on:

- **Leadership** – every company should be headed by an effective board which is collectively responsible for the long-term success of the company. There should be a clear division of responsibilities at the head of the company between the running of the board and the executive responsibility for the running of the company's business. No one individual should have unfettered powers of decision. The chairman is responsible for leadership of the board and ensuring its effectiveness on all aspects of its role. As part of their role as members of a unitary board, non-executive directors should constructively challenge and help develop proposals on strategy.

- **Effectiveness** – the board and its committees should have the appropriate balance of skills, experience, independence and knowledge of the company to enable them to discharge their respective duties and responsibilities effectively. There should be a formal, rigorous and transparent procedure for the appointment of new directors to the board. All directors should be able to allocate sufficient time to the company to discharge their responsibilities effectively. All directors should receive induction on joining the board and should regularly update and refresh their skills and knowledge. The board should be supplied in a timely manner with information in a form and of a quality appropriate to enable it to discharge its duties. The board should undertake a formal and rigorous annual evaluation of its own performance and that of its committees and individual directors. All directors should be submitted for re-election at regular intervals, subject to continued satisfactory performance.

- **Accountability** – the board should present a fair, balanced and understandable assessment of the company's position and prospects. The board is responsible for determining the nature and extent of the principal risks it is willing to take in achieving its strategic objectives. The board should maintain sound risk management and internal control systems. The board should establish formal and transparent arrangements for considering how they should apply the corporate reporting, risk management and internal control principles and for maintaining an appropriate relationship with the company's auditors.

- **Remuneration** – executive directors' remuneration should be designed to promote the long-term success of the company. Performance-related elements should be transparent, stretching and rigorously applied. There should be a formal and transparent procedure for developing policy on executive remuneration and for fixing the remuneration packages of individual directors. No director should be involved in deciding his or her own remuneration.

- **Relations with shareholders** – there should be a dialogue with shareholders based on the mutual understanding of objectives. The board as a whole has responsibility for ensuring that a satisfactory dialogue with shareholders takes place. The board should use general meetings to communicate with investors and to encourage their participation.

The Code is the widely acknowledged benchmark for corporate governance in UK firms with premium listed companies being required under the FCA Listing Rules either to comply with the provisions of the Code or explain to investors reasons for not doing so. This approach allows shareholders to consider the explanation and discuss this with the company where necessary. If shareholders are not content, or they consider that the explanation is unsatisfactory, they can use their rights – including the power to appoint and remove directors – to hold the company to account.

The Listing Rules (and associated expected standards of corporate governance) are one of the very few areas where the UK has chosen to 'gold plate' the relevant EU requirements as it seeks to ensure that the UK is seen as a safe place to invest.

In the summer of 2018, the FRC announced that an updated version of the Code (which can be found at www.frc.org.uk/getattachment/88bd8c45-50ea-4841-95b0-d2f4f48069a2/2018-UK-Corporate-Governance-Code-FINAL.pdf) will be introduced with effect from 1 January 2019.

There are a number of other international, but still relevant, sources of guidance on corporate governance and the role of senior managers. The Organisation for Economic Co-operation and Development (OECD) and the Basel Committee on Banking Supervision are two such sources.

OECD/G20 Principles of Corporate Governance

'Corporate governance is not an end in itself. It is a means. It is a means to create market confidence and business integrity, which in turn is essential for companies that need access to equity capital for long-term investment. Under current circumstances, it is particularly important to ensure access to equity capital for future oriented growth companies to support investment as a powerful driver of growth and to balance any increase in leveraging ... To put

> it differently, corporate governance is about the way in which board members oversee the running of a company by its management, and how board members are in turn accountable to shareholders and other stakeholders.'
>
> Source: Speech by Rintaro Tamaki, Deputy Secretary-General, OECD on the new G20/OECD Principles of Corporate Governance (December 2015)

10.9   The mission of the OECD is to promote policies that will improve the economic and social well-being of people around the world. The OECD provides a forum in which governments can work together to share experiences and seek solutions to common problems. The common thread of the OECD's work is a shared commitment to market economies backed by democratic institutions and focused on the well-being of all citizens with a particular current focus on helping governments around the world to restore confidence in markets and the institutions that make them function.

The OECD in conjunction with G20 have developed and updated their 'G20/OECD Principles of Corporate Governance' to provide not only an international benchmark but also to identify the key building blocks for a sound corporate governance framework and offer practical guidance for implementation at a national level (available at www.oecd-ilibrary.org/docserver/9789264236882-en.pdf?expires=1522920126&id=id&accname=guest&checksum=D6B7DB018C08516B6C0ED9917BDDF03B).

The OECD/G20 Principles of Corporate Governance cover:

* ensuring the basis for an effective corporate governance framework;

* the rights and equitable treatment of shareholders and key ownership functions;

* institutional investors, stock markets and intermediaries;

* disclosure and transparency; and

* the responsibilities of the board.

BCBS Corporate Governance Principles for Banks

10.10   Effective corporate governance is seen as critical to the proper functioning of the banking sector and the economy as a whole.

The international policy setting body for the banking sector is the Basel Committee on Banking Supervision (BCBS) and in July 2015 the BCBS published the latest iteration of 'Guidelines: Corporate Governance Principles for Banks' ('the guidance') available at www.bis.org/bcbs/publ/d328.pdf.

While there is no single approach to good corporate governance, the BCBS principles provide a framework within which banks and supervisors should operate to achieve robust and transparent risk management and decision making and, in doing so, promote public confidence and uphold the safety and soundness of the banking system. Supervisors have a keen interest in sound corporate governance, as it is an essential element in the safe and sound functioning of a bank and may adversely affect the bank's risk profile if not operating effectively. Well-governed banks contribute to the maintenance of an efficient and cost-effective supervisory process, as there is less need for supervisory intervention.

The revised guidance emphasises the critical importance of effective corporate governance for the safe and sound functioning of banks. It stresses the importance of risk governance as part of a bank's overall corporate governance framework and promotes the value of strong boards and board committees together with effective control functions. More specifically, the revised principles:

- expand the guidance on the role of the board of directors in overseeing the implementation of effective risk management systems;

- emphasise the importance of the board's collective competence as well as the obligation of individual board members to dedicate sufficient time to their mandates and to keep abreast of developments in banking;

- strengthen the guidance on risk governance, including the risk management roles played by business units, risk management teams, and internal audit and control functions (the three lines of defence), as well as underline the importance of a sound risk culture to drive risk management within a bank;

- provide guidance for bank supervisors in evaluating the processes used by banks to select board members and senior management; and

- recognise that compensation systems form a key component of the governance and incentive structure through which the board and senior management of a bank convey acceptable risk-taking behaviour and reinforce the bank's operating and risk culture.

To illustrate how the international policy initiatives on corporate governance are interlinked, the BCBS principles draw explicitly on those published by the OECD.

Checklist

10.11   The checklist below offers practical questions for senior managers to consider.

> ### Checklist
>
> - Can you explain how your firm's AML/CTF policies and procedures apply to your business area and, in practice, mitigate the risks arising?
>
> - Are you aware of your obligations and potential liabilities under the relevant prevention of bribery legislation?

- How up to date is your knowledge and awareness of market abuse or manipulation?
- Can you explain how you fit into, and discharge your obligations under, your firm's corporate governance framework?

Chapter 11

Enforcement

Chapter summary
This chapter covers:
• The purpose of enforcement and regulatory priorities
• Enforcement and the SM&CR – duty of responsibility and reasonable steps
• Penalties
• Learning lessons from enforcement cases

> 'Deterrence occurs when persons who are contemplating engaging in misconduct are dissuaded from doing so because they have an expectation of detection and that detection will be rigorously investigated, vigorously prosecuted and punished with robust and proportionate sanctions.'
>
> Source: Credible Deterrence in the Enforcement of Securities Regulation, International Organization of Securities Commissions (IOSCO) (June 2015)

11.1 In the era before the financial crisis, regulators around the world were largely content to punish regulatory breaches by imposing fines on the firm concerned. Whilst the imposition of financial penalties grew immensely, with monetary fines routinely in billions rather than millions, it failed to drive much needed changes in underlying behaviour. Equally, a flaw emerged in the trend for supersize fines in that they ultimately lost the power to shock, and being fined no longer created the level of reputational damage it once did. We are now in an era where the number of banks fined makes it increasingly difficult for end customers, investors and other stakeholders to distinguish, and choose to do business with, firms with an unblemished record.

> '"Global banks" misconduct costs have now reached over $320 billion – capital that could otherwise have supported up to $5 trillion of lending to households

and businesses. But there is a bigger cost. An industry the scale and importance of finance needs social capital as well as economic capital. It requires the consent of society in order to operate, innovate and grow.'

Source: 'Worthy of Trust? Law, Ethics and Culture in Banking', Mark Carney, Governor of the Bank of England at the Banking Standards Board Panel (March 2017)

In the post-crisis world, both the regulators and the approach taken changed as they were criticised for failing to establish liability for misconduct, and faced political and public pressure to hold those responsible to account. At the heart of the accountability regime in the UK and those being developed around the world, is making clear to those at the top of firms that in accepting their role and the rewards it brings, they also take on personal accountability. Although regulators have not discarded the use of monetary penalties against firms, they have changed their approach, deliberately and significantly to focus on individuals and the penalties that will have the greatest impact.

'If allowed to continue, this kind of compliance model could also compromise banks' condition. Losses due to fines, settlements and restitution now exceed credit losses. Penalties for breaches continue to escalate. Consequently, stress tests now routinely require banks to keep capital now against the fines and settlements they are likely to incur over the next three to five years.'

Source: COLUMN: 'Meeting supervisory expectations – Four questions banks must answer in 2016', Dr Thomas Huertas, EY Partner, Thomson Reuters Regulatory Intelligence (January 2016)

Purpose of enforcement and priorities

11.2   Regulatory enforcement is a fundamental method for changing behaviour and conduct in financial services. Making it clear that there are real and meaningful consequences and sanctions for firms and individuals who do not follow the rules, and the knowledge that they will be held to account is predominantly intended to be a deterrent to other wrongdoers operating in the industry.

The FCA's enforcement priorities are aligned to its overall strategic objectives. The issues it regards as priorities drive the focus of its supervisory and enforcement resources making it more likely to identify breaches and take enforcement action in these priority areas than non-priority areas. In the FCA's business plan for 2018/19 it sets out its number one cross-sector priority as 'firm's culture and governance' which includes its key work on the extension of the Senior Managers and Certification Regime. It states its expectation of firms to be able to demonstrate that their purpose, leadership, governance arrangements and approach to rewarding and managing staff do not lead to avoidable or unnecessary harm to their customers (see www.fca.org.uk/publication/business-plans/business-plan-2018-19.pdf). Equally, conduct, governance and accountability must also be at the top of the agenda for every senior manager in financial services.

Enforcement is invariably a disruptive, resource-intensive and intrusive process for the firm and individuals involved. The consequences are usually significant and detrimental for firms and individuals both financially and reputationally. Regulators will take enforcement action for a range of reasons from deterrence to providing protection and justice. They include:

(1) deterring wrongdoers from repeating their behaviour;

(2) serving as a strong reminder to other firms and individuals of what will happen if they break the rules;

(3) changing behaviour and raising standards in the broader financial services industry;

(4) publicly reinforcing the regulatory requirements in priority areas;

(5) holding those responsible for very serious breaches to account with proportionate penalties and sanctions; and

(6) removing wrongdoers from the industry or imposing other restrictions where appropriate.

> 'The real reason we exited [an area of business] was often because of the extraordinary legal risk if we were to make a mistake. In many of these places, it simply is impossible to meet the new requirements, and if you make just one mistake, the regulatory and legal consequences can be severe and disproportionate.'
>
> Source: Jamie Dimon, Chairman and Chief Executive Officer at JPMorgan Chase & Co, in his 2015 Chairman & CEO letter to shareholders

Suspected misconduct issues can be identified or referred to the FCA's Enforcement Division through several routes:

(a) The FCA's internal divisions:

- the Supervision Division following a visit to a firm or other supervisory activity;

- the Market Oversight, Authorisation and Competition Divisions;

- financial crime, intelligence and whistleblowing teams.

(b) Issues can also come to light via external channels including:

- whistleblowers;

- other market participants;

- customers;

- the Financial Ombudsman Service;
- consumer bodies;
- other UK and international regulators.

(c) The regulator also uses the intelligence and data it collects including:

- market data;
- information from firms (including self-reporting of breaches by firms);
- information from consumers;
- information from public databases;
- information from whistleblowers.

(www.fca.org.uk/publication/corporate/our-approach-enforcement.pdf)

Enforcement and the SM&CR

Duty of responsibility

11.3   Whilst the SM&CR does not specifically provide the FCA or the PRA with new enforcement powers to make it easier from a legal point of view to take enforcement action against individuals, it does bring much improved clarity regarding who is responsible for what. The Statements of Responsibilities and Management Responsibilities Maps are now an important enforcement tool for regulators enabling them to determine who was responsible for what within a firm at any time, when things go wrong.

The duty of responsibility introduced by the SM&CR requires senior managers to take reasonable steps to prevent regulatory breaches in the area for which they are responsible. The FCA and PRA can take enforcement action against senior managers if:

- there has been (or continues to be) a contravention of a relevant requirement by the senior manager's firm;
- at the time of the contravention, the senior manager was responsible for the management of any of the firm's activities in relation to which the contravention occurred; and
- the senior manager did not take such steps as a person in their position could reasonably be expected to take to avoid the contravention by the firm occurring or continuing.

Reasonable steps

11.4   The duty of responsibility applies not only to acts, but also to omissions, so failing to be aware of what a senior manager could reasonably be expected to know may constitute a breach. The regulators have set out guidance on how they will determine whether or not a senior manager has taken reasonable steps. The guidance reflects the regulators' specific objectives so there is some overlap. There are a wide range of considerations that are neither exhaustive nor prescriptive but which senior managers must be aware of.

Where action is taken against a senior manager, the onus is on the regulator to demonstrate that the senior manager has been guilty of misconduct including showing that the senior manager did not take reasonable steps to avoid the breach occurring or continuing.

Whilst the burden of proof lies with the regulator, firms and individuals should keep clear and accessible records of minutes of board, committee and internal meetings, Statements of Responsibilities and Management Responsibilities Maps along with other organisation charts and reporting lines, plus any relevant internal materials including reviews, audits and management information. On one hand, the FCA said that the duty of responsibility 'imposes no additional obligation on a senior manager to explain or justify to us the relevant steps they took and/or did not take, nor to keep records supporting such an explanation or justification' (at www.fca.org.uk/publication/policy/ps18-16.pdf). However, it also notes that:

'It may, however, be in the interests of a senior manager to keep records of relevant steps they take, in case questions are raised, whether by their firm, its lawyers, auditors, insurers or customers, the FCA or another regulator.'

Inadequate record keeping will certainly be detrimental to the individual and the firm in an enforcement investigation.

Based on the FCA's guidance in DEPP 6.2.9-EG the following considerations will be taken into account:

(1) the senior manager's **role and responsibilities** (for example, the steps a senior manager in a non-executive role could reasonably be expected to take may differ from those in an executive role);

(2) whether the senior manager exercised reasonable care when **considering the information available** to them;

(3) whether the senior manager **reached a reasonable conclusion** on which to act;

(4) the **nature, scale and complexity** of the firm's business;

(5) the **knowledge** the senior manager had, or should have had, of regulatory concerns, if any, relating to his or her role and responsibilities;

(6) whether the senior manager (where he or she was aware of, or should have been aware of issues) took reasonable steps to **ensure issues were dealt with** in a timely and appropriate manner;

---

(7) whether the senior manager acted **in accordance with his or her statutory, common law and other legal obligations**;

(8) whether the senior manager took reasonable steps to ensure that any **delegation of his or her responsibilities** was:

- reasonable;

- to an appropriate person with the necessary capacity, competence, knowledge, seniority and skill; and

- effectively overseen;

(9) whether the senior manager took reasonable steps to ensure that **reporting lines** (in the UK or overseas), in relation to the firm's activities for which he or she was responsible, were clear to staff and operated effectively;

(10) whether the senior manager took reasonable steps to satisfy themselves that, for the activities for which he or she was responsible, the firm had appropriate **policies and procedures for reviewing the competence, knowledge, skills and performance** of each individual member of staff to assess their suitability to fulfil their duties;

(11) whether the senior manager took reasonable steps to:

- **assess**, on taking up each of their responsibilities; and

- **monitor**, where reasonable, the governance, operational and risk management arrangements in place for the *firm's* activities for which he or she was responsible (including, where appropriate, corroborating, challenging and considering the wider implications of the information available to them);

- **deal with any actual or suspected issues** identified as a result in a timely and appropriate manner;

(12) whether the senior manager took reasonable steps to ensure an **orderly transition** when another senior manager under his or her oversight or responsibility was replaced;

(13) whether the senior manager took reasonable steps to ensure an **orderly transition when he or she was replaced** in the performance of his or her function by someone else;

(14) whether the senior manager **failed to take reasonable steps to understand and inform himself or herself about the firm's activities** for which he or she was responsible, including, but not limited to, whether he or she:

(a) **failed to ensure adequate reporting or seek an adequate explanation of** issues within a business area, whether from people within that business area, or elsewhere within or outside the firm, if he or she was not an expert in that area; or

(b) **failed to maintain an appropriate level of understanding** about an issue or a responsibility that he or she delegated to an individual or individuals; or

(c) **failed to obtain independent, expert opinion where appropriate** from within or outside the firm as appropriate; or

(d) **permitted the expansion or restructuring of the business without reasonably assessing the potential risks**; or

(e) **inadequately monitored highly profitable transactions, business practices, unusual transactions, or individuals** who contributed significantly to the profitability of a business area or who had significant influence over the operation of a business area;

(15) whether the senior manager took reasonable steps to ensure that, where he or she was involved in a **collective decision** affecting the firm's activities for which he or she was responsible, and it was reasonable for the decision to be taken collectively, he or she informed himself or herself of the relevant matters before taking part in the decision, and exercised reasonable care, skill and diligence in contributing to it;

(16) whether the senior manager took reasonable steps to **follow the firm's procedures**, where this was itself appropriate;

(17) how long the senior manager had been in the role with his or her responsibilities and whether there was an orderly transition and handover when he or she took up the role and responsibilities;

(18) whether the senior manager took reasonable steps to implement (either personally or through a compliance department or other departments) **adequate and appropriate systems and controls to comply with the relevant requirements and standards of the regulatory system** for the activities of the firm.

(www.handbook.fca.org.uk/handbook/DEPP/6/2.html)

Based on the PRA's SS28/15, the PRA will assess:

(i) the steps that the specific Senior Manager actually took; against

(ii) such steps as the PRA considers that a Senior Manager, in that position, could reasonably have been expected to take to avoid the contravention occurring (or continuing).

Examples of the considerations that the PRA may consider in forming its view of (ii) above include:

(1) the size, scale and complexity of the firm;

(2) what the senior manager actually knew, or a senior manager in that position ought to have known (taking into account, among other factors, the

length of time he or she had been in the role and handover arrangements to those new in a role);

(3) what expertise and competence the senior manager had, or ought to have possessed, at the time to perform his or her specific Senior Management Function;

(4) what steps the senior manager could have taken, considering what alternative actions might have been open to the senior manager at the time and the timeliness within which he or she could have acted;

(5) the actual responsibilities of that senior manager and the relationship between those responsibilities and the responsibilities of other senior managers in the firm (including in relation to any joint responsibilities or matrix-management structures);

(6) whether the senior manager delegated any functions, taking into account that any such delegation should be appropriately arranged, managed and monitored;

(7) the overall circumstances and environment at the firm and more widely, in which the senior manager was operating at the time. For example, the PRA may consider whether the way in which he or she prioritised matters was informed by an appropriate risk assessment and how he or she responded to new developments.

(www.bankofengland.co.uk/-/media/boe/files/prudential-regulation/ supervisory-statement/2018/ss2815update.pdf?la=en&hash=39EC46AE5FD2 17724BB307C420B80A4E09F42A24)

When the PRA assesses the steps that the specific senior manager actually took to avoid the contravention occurring or continuing, examples of the actions it might consider reasonable actions include the following.

Examples of reasonable actions might include:

(1) **pre-emptive actions** to prevent a breach occurring, including any **initial reviews** of the business or business area on taking up a senior manager function;

(2) implementing, policing and reviewing appropriate **policies and procedures**;

(3) **awareness** of relevant requirements and standards of the regulatory system;

(4) **investigations or reviews** of the senior manager's area of responsibilities;

(5) where a breach is continuing, any **response taken to that breach**;

(6) **structuring and control of day-to-day operations**, including ensuring any delegations are managed and reviewed appropriately. This includes in relation to any 'matrix-management' arrangements;

(7) obtaining appropriate internal **management information**, and critically interrogating and monitoring that information;

(8) **raising issues**, reviewing issues, and following them up with relevant staff, committees and boards;

(9) seeking and obtaining appropriate **expert advice or assurance**, whether internal or external;

(10) ensuring that the firm and/or relevant area has **adequate resources**, and that these are appropriately deployed, including for risk and control functions; and

(11) awareness of **relevant external developments**, including key risks.

Evidence that the PRA might review includes:

- board and board committee minutes;

- minutes of other internal meetings;

- Statements of Responsibilities and Management Responsibilities Maps;

- organisation charts and information on reporting lines;

- any other internal materials, for example, emails or telephone recordings; and

- regulatory correspondence and interviews.

Conduct Rules

11.5   The Conduct Rules apply to all employees within a financial services firm and set the minimum standards for every individual's behaviour. Employees are expected to:

(i)   act with integrity;

(ii)   act with due care, skill and diligence;

(iii)   be open and cooperative with regulators;

(iv)   pay due regard to the interests of customers and treat them fairly; and

(v)   observe proper standards of market conduct.

As the rules set out what are essentially common sense expectations of how employees should conduct themselves, there is a risk that firms will overlook how they apply in practice to different jobs. The new requirement to train all employees on what the Conduct Rules might mean for individuals will be an important step for firms in being able to demonstrate to regulators that employees understand both the spirit, as well as the letter of the rules. Maintenance of records to demonstrate that employees have undertaken and understood relevant and effective training will be critical evidence in the event of a breach.

Penalties

11.6   Regulators' investigation and enforcement powers are wide-ranging. When deciding whether to appoint enforcement investigators the FCA will consider what other tools are available, including:

- agreeing with firms what action they need to take through regular **supervisory correspondence**;

- appointing a **skilled person** to obtain an independent view of aspects of a firm's activities that cause concern or require further analysis, eg of a past business review or remedial action. Skilled persons' reports are typically undertaken by a consultancy, accountancy or law firms;

- preventing firms from conducting **particular activities**;

- **imposing requirements** on how firms conduct their activities;

- making firms pay **redress** to customers where they have caused loss/harm. Based on Corlytics data, one in three of the non-financial penalties imposed for misconduct include an element of remedial action and redress. In addition to the often significant operational impact of an enforcement action including the need for substantial senior manager involvement, in the last couple of years redress and restitution costs have added an additional third to the overall financial cost of misconduct penalties;

- ban or restrict particular products;

- ban or restrict misleading financial promotions.

The regulators have an extensive range of disciplinary, criminal and civil powers to take action against regulated and non-regulated firms and individuals who are failing, or have failed, to meet required standards. Examples of those powers include being able to:

- withdraw a firm's authorisation;

- prohibit an individual from operating in financial services;

- prevent an individual from undertaking specific regulated activities;

- suspend a firm for up to 12 months from undertaking specific regulated activities;

- suspend an individual for up to two years from undertaking specific controlled functions;

- censure firms and individuals through public statements;

- impose financial penalties;

- seek injunctions;

- apply to court to freeze assets;

- seek restitution orders;

- prosecute firms and individuals who undertake regulated activities without authorisation.

> 'We do not see Enforcement as an end in itself. It is simply one of the tools the FCA has at its disposal to encourage better behaviour. Yes, it is often the most newsworthy. Yes, it can be the most damaging to the reputation of a firm or individuals. Yes, it is unpopular with many within the industry.
>
> But it is only one tool.'
>
> Source: Tracey McDermott, FCA director of enforcement and financial crime at the FCA Enforcement Conference (December 2014)

Investigations and cases

11.7   Since 2017 there has been an increase in the number of investigations commenced by the FCA (see www.fca.org.uk/news/speeches/better-view). The purpose of investigations is predominantly diagnostic so that regulators can understand where there may be serious misconduct, what has happened and what actions needs to be taken. The increase has been significant as it represents approximately a 75% rise in the number of investigations underway.

> 'We need an approach to investigation that will meet the challenges of supporting the embedding of this culture. This means that generally where there are grounds for investigating a matter, there will be a need to investigate the role of senior management in the conduct issues that arise.'
>
> Source: Jamie Symington, FCA Director of Investigations, Legal Week Banking Litigation and Regulation Forum, London (June 2017)

Regulators are already taking action against individuals outside of the new accountability regimes. Of the 13 fines imposed by the FCA during 2017, eight were against individuals, and this trend of personal accountability is likely to continue as the UK regulators have made it clear it that it will hold individuals accountable for their actions. Worldwide the trend continues. Based on data from Corlytics, on average, at least one individual has been fined for misconduct every week for the last six years. This is set to increase substantially as individual accountability regimes are rolled out around the world (see www.corlytics.com/wp-content/uploads/2018/06/Corlytics_barometer_conduct_2018.pdf).

Regional variations
Total financial penalties for misconduct by regulatory body against individuals 2012 – (Q1) 2018

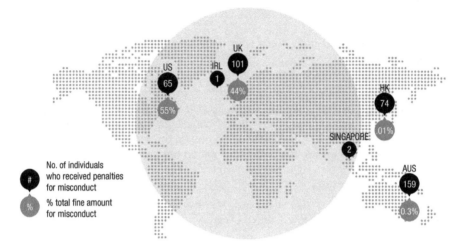

Source: © Corlytics 2018, Corlytics Barometer – Conduct 2018

> 'Holding individuals liable for wrongdoing is a core pillar of any strong enforcement program. A company, after all, can only act through its employees, and to have a strong deterrent effect on market participants, it is absolutely critical that responsible individuals be charged and that we pursue the evidence as high as it can take us.'
>
> Source: 'A New Model for SEC Enforcement Producing Bold and Unrelenting Results', speech by Mary Jo White, then Chair of the US Securities and Exchange Commission (SEC). New York University School of Law, Pollack Center for Law and Business (November 2016)

Publication of findings and learning the lessons

11.8   The UK regulators are required to publish statements of policy and procedure on its enforcement and investigation powers and in relation to the giving of statutory notices. The publication of enforcement actions is intended to act not only as a future deterrent to the firm or individual being disciplined but also to prevent others in the industry from making the same mistakes. The publications set out clear messages about the regulators' expectations about what is unacceptable behaviour.

Types of notice: information about enforcement action is published through:

- warning notices – issued when action is proposed;
- decision notices – issued when a decision has been made to take action;

- final notices – issued when action taken; plus
- supervisory notices, requirement notices, and cancellation notices.

Learning the lessons

11.9 It is critical that firms review the content of enforcement actions. Regulators expect firms to learn lessons from the experiences and reasons for action taken against industry peers. It enables firms to determine whether they may be exposed and at risk of making similar breaches. Regulators take a critical view of firms that fail to take notice of warnings and insight and who make the same breaches.

> 'And it should also be a tool for you – in the industry – a way of learning from the experiences of your peers. Our notices and the root causes that underpin the failings should inform your approach to consideration of the risks you face.
>
> Disappointingly, as illustrated by FOREX and by wave on wave of historic mis-selling issues, this is not yet second nature. The review of lessons is still, at times, too narrow and too literal. I get the impression that people say "this does not concern me because I don't sell UCIS or don't submit to LIBOR" rather than looking at whether the same drivers of behaviour might read across to other areas.
>
> ... it is vital that we, the regulator and the regulated, learn from the mistakes of the past. That is where I think enforcement action has its value; not just as a punishment but as a very public lesson from which all market participants can learn.'
>
> Source: Tracey McDermott, FCA director of enforcement and financial crime at the FCA Enforcement Conference (December 2014)

Review enforcement actions can also help firms to:

- identify emerging regulatory priorities and trends;
- make improvement to its compliance arrangements and controls;
- determine the areas of greatest risk and implement a program to manage and mitigate those risks to prevent similar violations and penalties; and
- incorporate lessons and weaknesses into the firm's training.

> **Factors the FCA uses to assess whether to take enforcement action:**
>
> **Deterring wrongdoers from repeating behaviours (specific deterrence)**
>
> - What was the reaction of the specific firm/individual to the breach?
> - What is the most efficient, effective and economic way to achieve the regulator's objectives for this firm?

- What would the impact of an enforcement investigation and enforcement action be on other steps the FCA and/or the firm itself is taking to improve its compliance with our requirements?

Changing behaviour and raising standards in the industry (general deterrence)

- Is the issue to be referred relevant to an FCA strategic priority, eg a specific area of focus as set out in the FCA's Business Plan?

- Do we know or suspect that the issues in this case may be widespread in the market?

- To what extent has the message to the market already been delivered in other ways?

- Does the suspected misconduct suggest poor culture and governance, such as:

  ○ misconduct by senior individuals?

  ○ repeat offending by firms, or firms who do the minimum to fix specific problems but do not address the root causes?

  ○ failing to cooperate with the FCA/other regulators, or firms not doing what they say they will do?

- If a number of firms could be subject to an enforcement investigation for similar failings, which cases are the most serious, have the most potential impact, and/or would send the strongest deterrent message across a range of different firms operating in the relevant market?

- For cases against senior individuals, would enforcement action deliver a strong message to senior individuals in the broader industry about the personal consequences of misconduct?

- Does the suspected misconduct involve an overseas jurisdiction? If so, would enforcement action materially further investor protection or market confidence in that jurisdiction?

Holding those responsible for very serious breaches to account with proportionate penalties and sanctions (justice)

- Are there actions or potential breaches that could undermine public confidence in the orderliness of financial markets?

- Has there been widespread harm or potential harm to consumers, market integrity or competition?

- How serious was the suspected misconduct, taking into account all relevant factors, including if appropriate:

  ○ Are there issues that indicate a widespread problem or weakness at the firm?

- ○ Is there evidence that the firm/individual has profited from the action or potential breaches?

- ○ Has the firm/individual failed to bring the actions or potential breaches to the attention of the FCA?

Removing wrongdoers from the industry or imposing restrictions where appropriate (protection)

- Are there circumstances that suggest an individual is not 'fit and proper'?

- Is, or was, the individual an approved person?

- Is the individual in the UK or were they in the UK?

- Is the individual still in the industry and, if so, at what level of seniority?

- A prohibition has protective and punitive purposes and holds individuals to account publicly. Would enforcement action be appropriate to achieve one of these aims?

(www.fca.org.uk/about/enforcement/referral-criteria)

Examples of enforcement action

11.10 Reviewing the published documentation relating to enforcement activity will provide firms with crucial insight into the risks of regulatory exposure that they and individuals must be alert to, as well as the priorities and expectations of regulators and the likely penalties for breaches.

Recent cases highlight the regulatory attention on the conduct of senior individuals:

- In the first case brought under the new SM&CR, the FCA and PRA jointly fined the Chief Executive of Barclays Group, Jes Staley, £642,430 in May 2018 for failing to act with due skill, care and diligence in the way he responded to a letter sent by a whistleblower to a Barclays Group Board member (see www.fca.org.uk/publication/final-notices/mr-james-edward-staley-2018.pdf). The letter raised concerns about a senior Barclays employee whose recruitment the CEO instigated and which led to Staley instructing investigations to identify the whistleblower. There has been public criticism of the regulators for not imposing a heavier penalty which would have sent a stronger message to the market (see www.bankofengland.co.uk/-/media/BoE/Files/prudential-regulation/regulatory-action/final-notice-from-pra-to-mr-staley).

- An FCA decision against Charles Palmer, the former Chief Executive of the Standard Financial Group, was upheld by the Upper Tribunal, which hears challenges against FCA disciplinary decisions. Palmer was banned from performing significant influence functions and received a financial penalty of £86,691. The tribunal agreed with the FCA finding that Palmer had failed to act with due skill, care and diligence in carrying out his roles as director.

Following previous disciplinary action, he had established systems and controls that would 'demonstrate to the Authority that the Group had implemented the kind of systems and controls that the Authority would consider appropriate'. However, the tribunal found this to be a matter of form over substance as the systems and controls were not implemented or operating effectively.

- The FCA's case against Bluefin Insurance Services centred on the existence and management of an inherent conflict of interest in Bluefin's business strategy. The broker held itself as truly independent but was owned by the insurance company AXA whose products were among those that its brokers had targets to recommend to clients. The case included a finding by the regulator that 'senior management promoted a culture that focused on compliance with Bluefin's business strategies, rather than responding to customers' individual demands and needs and ensuring that customers were in a position to make fully informed decisions'. The firm was fined £4,023,800.

- An Upper Tribunal decision in relation to Arif Hussein, a UBS trader who challenged the regulator's decision to ban him from financial services for engaging in activity that led to the manipulation of LIBOR submissions, included an observation about the lack of senior management accountability. The judge referred to 'troubling aspects' of the case in which a relatively junior trader had been singled out, noting 'This was against a background of widespread manipulation of LIBOR within UBS for which senior managers bear ultimate responsibility and which ... was widely condoned'. The FCA lawyer noted that 'senior people somehow manage to keep their fingerprints off relevant documents sometimes'. Clear responsibilities under the new accountability regime should help address this issue.

- Sonali Bank (UK) Ltd was fined £3,250,600 for failing to comply with its operational obligations in respect of customer due diligence, the identification and treatment of politically exposed persons, transaction and customer monitoring and making suspicious activity reports. A restriction was also imposed preventing it from accepting deposits from new customers for 168 days. Action was also taken against Steven Smith, its former money-laundering reporting officer and compliance officer, for failing to oversee the day-to-day operation of, and ensure the effectiveness of the bank's AML systems and controls, demonstrating a serious lack of competence and capability. He was fined £17,900 and prohibited from performing as the MLRO or compliance oversight functions at regulated firms.

Recent cases also reiterate the need to learn lessons from the firm's own or industry peers' contraventions:

- Merrill Lynch was fined £34,524,000 by the FCA in 2017 in relation to transaction reporting failings. The regulator stated that it considered the failings to be particularly serious given that the firm had been subject to two previous enforcement actions for transaction reporting breaches, and the regulator had publicised a number of enforcement actions taken in relation to similar failings by other firms. These factors were taken into account in determining the penalty (see www.fca.org.uk/publication/final-notices/merrill-lynch-international-2017.pdf).

- Deutsche Bank was fined £163,076,224 for serious failings in its anti-money laundering (AML) control framework (see www.fca.org.uk/publication/final-notices/deutsche-bank-2017.pdf). The case reinforces the need for firms to learn from both published information and industry failings. The final notice stated that:

  'Given the number and detailed nature of such publications, and past enforcement action taken by the Authority in respect of similar failings by other firms, Deutsche Bank should have been aware of the importance of appropriately assessing, managing and monitoring the money laundering risk associated with its CB&S division in the UK'.

  Mark Steward, the FCA's Director of Enforcement and Market Oversight reiterated the need for firms to learn lessons:

  'The size of the fine reflects the seriousness of Deutsche Bank's failings. We have repeatedly told firms how to comply with our AML requirements and the failings of Deutsche Bank are simply unacceptable. Other firms should take notice of today's fine and look again at their own AML procedures to ensure they do not face similar action' (www.fca.org.uk/news/press-releases/fca-fines-deutsche-bank-163-million-anti-money-laundering-controls-failure).

Case law also demonstrates the importance and consequences of how firms respond to enforcement action:

- In March 2017, the FCA took enforcement action against Tesco plc for market abuse in relation to a trading update which gave a false or misleading impression about the value of publicly traded Tesco shares and bonds. Tesco agreed to pay compensation to investors who purchased Tesco shares and bonds on or after the flawed trading update and who still held those securities when the statement was corrected a month later. The regulator has noted that Tesco's decision to co-operate, accept its findings and not contest the first compensation order sets a strong example of corporate responsibility. As a result, Tesco Stores Ltd was spared a further fine on top of the £129m it paid as part of a deferred prosecution agreement with the UK Serious Fraud Office.

Co-operation

11.11   The nature of a firm's relationship with the regulator is an important consideration in determining whether an investigation and enforcement action is taken forward. Enforcement is only one tool regulators use to achieve their objectives and it is less likely to be used if a firm has established a strong track record of taking its senior management responsibilities seriously and been open, transparent and co-operative with its regulators. Equally important is a firm's conduct in response to contraventions and issues which may give rise to potential disciplinary action. In the FCA's mission statement on its approach to enforcement, it sets out the factors taken into account when determining sanctions, which in extreme cases may determine whether a sanction is required at all (at www.fca.org.uk/publication/corporate/our-approach-enforcement.pdf).

Specifically these factors are:

- whether the individual(s) responsible has acknowledged responsibility;
- if voluntary redress, remediation or restorative steps have been taken in a timely and effective manner;
- the extent of cooperation with the regulator.

Firms and senior managers should be aware that where they fail to take steps to address harm or refuse to cooperate fully with the regulator it will be taken into account and may result in heavier sanctions.

> 'What we do expect, is it to get to the heart of the matter and the truth of what happened as quickly as possible. We will investigate with objectivity and rigour. Our response will be fair and proportionate in all circumstances.
>
> So we expect firms to appreciate that is it often also in their best interests that we do get to the heart of the matter quickly and support us in doing so.'
>
> Source: Jamie Symington, FCA Director of Investigations, Legal Week
> Banking Litigation and Regulation Forum, London (June 2017)

Checklist

11.12 The checklist below offers practical questions for financial services firms to consider.

Checklist

- Are all employees and senior managers aware of the regulatory consequences of misconduct?
- Do senior managers understand the regulatory expectations of, and need to evidence, 'reasonable steps'?
- Is there a culture of cooperation and open communication with regulators including processes to self-identify and report contraventions?
- Is there a process in place to learn the lessons from enforcement action within the industry?

Chapter 12

Overarching principles for how to manage personal regulatory risk

---

Chapter summary

This chapter considers the overarching considerations and principles for managing personal regulatory risk with reference to:

- The external and internal environment of a financial services firm

- The need to build and maintain a personal archive to evidence the discharge of all regulatory responsibilities

The extent to which each element discussed is relevant will depend on the particular circumstances of each senior manager, although it is likely that all senior managers will need to consider, in granular detail, the evolving external regulatory expectations regarding the assessment and potential re-design of incentives and compensation schemes.

Introduction

12.1   Senior managers operating in the financial services industry in or from the UK are likely to be all too familiar with the implications of the Senior Managers Regime (SMR) even if it has not, as yet, been rolled out to their particular sector. The application of SMR is fundamental to the increased focus on accountability and personal liability of senior managers but it is not the only factor that is contributing towards the need to be able to manage increased personal regulatory risk. Senior managers need to be able to take a holistic approach to their own personal risk management to help to ensure that all relevant areas are considered and all risks are identified, measured, managed and wherever possible, mitigated.

The qualitative areas of culture and conduct risk are discussed in detail in **Chapter 9**, with a key takeaway being the expectation that the regulatory focus on culture and conduct risk will increase the personal liability of senior managers.

The picture painted by the results from Thomson Reuters Regulatory Intelligence's annual survey on culture and conduct risk show that for globally systemically important financial institutions (G-SIFIs) as well as the wider population of all firms, more than two-thirds of respondents expect the liability of senior managers will increase due to culture and conduct risk concerns.

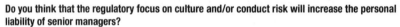

Do you think that the regulatory focus on culture and/or conduct risk will increase the personal liability of senior managers?

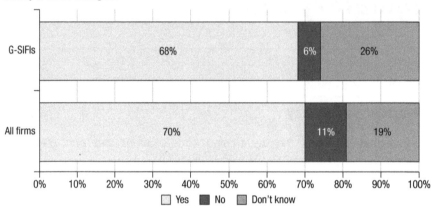

Source: Thomson Reuters Regulatory Intelligence – Culture and Conduct Risk 2018 survey

In addition to the formal governance requirements inherent in the SMR, senior managers need to consider how to best manage their personal regulatory risk. The challenge can be carved up in a number of ways but there are three main aspects to the consideration of personal regulatory risk management. The three considerations are the external environment, the internal environment and then the need for a personal archive.

The extent to which each area or issue is relevant will depend on the individual's role within the firm. The chief executive, for instance, is not expected to be an expert on the granular detail of risk and compliance but he or she must be aware of the issues, able to set an appropriate risk appetite, drive a strong compliant culture, understand and challenge all risk and compliance reports as well as engage appropriately with regulators.

External environment

12.2 The external environment for financial services firms has shifted profoundly as governments, supranational policy makers and regulators have acted to try to repair and rebuild economies and balance sheets. Blame for the crisis as well as subsequent London Interbank Offered Rate (or LIBOR) and foreign exchange (FX) scandals resulted in 'banker bashing' becoming a national pastime in many jurisdictions. As a result, financial services firms have, and continue to, face a complicated raft of changes to the rulebook and supervisory expectations with the stated intention of holding more individuals personally accountable for regulatory failings, particularly those which result in customer detriment.

In the increasingly harsh spotlight focused on senior individuals there needs to be a greater appreciation of the impact of the changes to both the rulebook and the more qualitative regulatory expectations. It remains critical for senior managers to stay abreast of the evolving external environment in order to have the best chance of staying in line with regulatory and other expectations and requirements.

The need to raise awareness of the external regulatory environment may mean changes to reporting and the inclusion of a standing update item on key meeting agendas. Firms need to be aware that it is not just mainstream domestic financial services regulatory changes which may have an impact on the business. A current example of which is the focus on the design and outcomes of incentives and compensation schemes as a key driver or influencer of persistent misconduct.

Misconduct and incentives

12.3   The explicit link between persistent misconduct and the design of incentive schemes was made by the Financial Stability Board (FSB) (a supranational body which operates as the global financial services policy-making arm of the G20). The issue of being seen to reward inappropriate risk taking first came to the fore in the wake of the financial crisis. Then the FSB first published in April 2009 the principles for sound compensation practices (at www.fsb.org/2009/04/principles-for-sound-compensation-practices-2) with the associated implementation standards following in September 2009 (at www.fsb.org/2009/09/principles-for-sound-compensation-practices-implementation-standards). As with other FSB initiatives, the policies percolate down to domestic regulators who are expected to implement rule changes as appropriate and oversee firms' compliance.

In recent years, the FSB has assessed the underlying cause(s) of the continuing misconduct by financial services firms, the impact of which was illustrated by Mark Carney, Governor of the Bank of England, who in March 2017 said, 'Global banks' misconduct costs have now reached $320 billion – capital that could otherwise have supported up to $5 trillion of lending to households and businesses'.

The FSB's work on policy approaches to tackle continuing misconduct by firms, significant institutions in particular, has come full circle to reassess the effectiveness of some of the first post crisis initiatives put in place. The original principles and standards on compensation did not specifically address the issue of misconduct or provide guidance on the operation of compensation tools in the event of misconduct but the role of compensation as an important influence on incentives was made clear. The G20 expressed its concern that costs may be imposed on firms and their customers not only by inappropriate risk-taking but also by misconduct resulting in harm to institutions and customers, and further impair trust in the financial system more generally.

The result of the FSB's work was the publication, in March 2018, of supplementary guidance to the FSB principles and standards on sound compensation practices (at www.fsb.org/wp-content/uploads/P090318-1.pdf).

The final guidance

12.4 The focus of the FSB's guidance is on the use of incentives as a means to address the continuing misconduct seen in financial services firms around the world. Compensation tools, along with other measures, are seen as having the potential to play an important role in addressing misconduct risk by providing both ex-ante incentives for good conduct and ex-post adjustment mechanisms that ensure appropriate accountability when misconduct occurs. The FSB, in collaboration with other standard-setting bodies, is seeking to supplement the principles and standards in the form of recommendations on better practice that specifically address the link between compensation and conduct.

The recommendations address:

- the full range of responsibility, from senior management to the front line, for conduct issues arising from firm culture and commitment to ethical conduct;

- the integration of non-financial considerations relating to conduct in a balanced approach to performance assessment and compensation;

- the alignment of compensation incentives to the longer time-frame misconduct risk may take to materialise;

- the use of transparent, consistent and fair compensation policies and procedures that establish clear expectations and accountability for conduct; and

- supervisory expectations that supervisors should, within the scope of their authority, monitor and assess the effectiveness of firms' compensation policies and procedures in managing misconduct risk.

The approach, which has implications for all senior managers, is predicated on the effective use of compensation tools as part of an embedded strong governance and management of misconduct risk framework in a firm, including robust performance management practices. The guidance is structured in three parts:

(a) the governance of compensation and misconduct risk;

(b) effective alignment of compensation with misconduct risk; and then

(c) the supervision of compensation and misconduct risk.

The final guidance, like the principles and standards, will apply to financial institutions that competent authorities consider significant for the purpose of the principles and standards.

The FSB is clear that the final guidance does not establish additional principles or standards beyond those already set out in the principles and standards and the guidance has been developed in the form of recommendations on better practices. The final guidance consists of eight recommendations for firms and supervisors:

(1) The board should oversee, and senior managers should implement, a compensation system designed to promote ethical behaviour and compliance with laws, regulations, and internal conduct standards.

(2) Sound governance, robust risk management frameworks and adequate involvement by control functions, including human resources, in compensation design and decision-making are critical to the effectiveness of compensation incentives in addressing misconduct risk.

(3) The ultimate responsibility for ensuring accountability for misconduct lies with the board of directors. Boards are accountable for overseeing compensation systems that promote prudent risk-taking behaviours and business practices. They should hold senior managers accountable for implementing and participating in the design of a compensation system that effectively delineates how compensation tools address misconduct risk.

(4) Senior managers should hold line of business management accountable for communicating, implementing and meeting expectations regarding ethical behaviour and business practices in compliance with laws, regulations, and internal conduct standards. Internal communications should ensure that the potential consequences of misconduct on compensation are clearly explained to all employees.

(5) Consistent with the principles and standards, compensation should be adjusted for all types of risk, including difficult to measure risks. These include risks associated with misconduct that can result in harm to firms, customers and other stakeholders. The processes for managing misconduct risk through compensation systems should include, at a minimum, ex-ante processes that embed non-financial assessment criteria such as the quality of risk management, degree of compliance with laws and regulations and the broader conduct objectives of the firm including fair treatment of customers, into individual performance management and compensation plans at all levels of the organisation and as part of the broader governance and risk management framework. Such processes should be supported by continuing programmes including formal training courses that reinforce appropriate standards of behaviour.

(6) To effectively accommodate the potentially longer term nature of misconduct risk, compensation systems should provide for mechanisms to adjust variable compensation, including, for instance, through in-year adjustment, and malus or clawback arrangements, which can reduce variable compensation after it is awarded or paid.

(7) Compensation policies and procedures are an important control on misconduct. To ensure consistency, fairness and transparency in the application of compensation adjustment, it is important that effective policies and procedures are in place to decide cases that may result in reductions to variable compensation, based on clear specification, ex ante, of the misconduct triggers or other mechanisms that may result in such reduction.

(8) Supervisors should, within the scope of their authority, monitor and assess the effectiveness of firms' compensation policies and procedures, including the application of compensation tools in addressing misconduct risk and related misconduct outcomes. National regulations and/or guidance should set out clear expectations, within the scope of applicable legislative and regulatory frameworks, on the use of compensation tools in addressing misconduct risk and related misconduct outcomes and the criteria for their application.

Throughout the final guidance there is further explanatory text from the FSB giving additional granular detail on the expected, better, approach and outcomes.

There are several elements for firms to consider when considering the final supplementary guidance. The first is that it is made crystal clear that the accountability for any and all misconduct 'lies first with the board of directors'. Firms must not, and cannot, simply push the management of misconduct and the associated governance and compensation expectations down and away from the board table.

Another element to consider is that the compensation governance expectations regarding the minimisation of misconduct are all pervasive and cover better practices on:

- the full range of responsibility, from boards to senior managers to the front line and control functions, for conduct issues arising from firms' risk culture and commitment to ethical conduct;

- the integration of non-financial considerations relating to conduct in a balanced approach to performance assessment and compensation;

- the alignment of compensation incentives to the longer time frame misconduct risk may take to materialise;

- the use of transparent, consistent and fair compensation policies and procedures that establish and promote clear expectations and accountability for conduct.

Supervisory expectations

12.5   The final guidance also frames the supervisory expectations that regulators should use, within the scope of their authority, to monitor and assess the effectiveness of firms' compensation policies and procedures in managing misconduct risk. Specifically, firms need to understand the practical ramifications of how the supervisory approach to the governance and use of compensation tools to address misconduct risks will change. Firms need a clear insight into the regulatory approach to the supervision of compensation practices to help them meet evolving supervisory expectations.

Supervisors are expressly required to analyse the use of compensation tools in mitigating misconduct risk, as part of overall assessments of compensation, corporate governance, risk culture or wider risk management practices in a firm.

With regard to supervisory assessments regulators will be expected to take into account:

- a firm's overall approach to governance, including the role of the board in overseeing misconduct risk management as well as appropriate linkage to the firm's wider risk management framework and risk appetite;

- whether compensation schemes include ex-ante criteria of non-financial risks, such as assessments of performance against conduct, and related compliance and risk management standards;

- whether performance management systems and communication to staff sufficiently reflect firms' expectations in respect of misconduct and its influence on staff's compensation;

- the effectiveness of compensation tools in aligning compensation paid and awarded with misconduct risk and related adverse outcomes; and

- disclosures that make clear the manner in which misconduct risk is managed, including through the use of compensation system and tools.

The FSB has also set out the need for the regular collection and evaluation of appropriate and consistent data to enable firms and supervisors to assess the effectiveness of compensation programs and to highlight potential areas of weakness. In the first instance, the recommendations are aimed at the supervision of significant financial institutions but may well be applied more universally by regulators. Equally, the recommendations are not intended to be prescriptive, but instead suggest certain categories of data that may be useful for supervisors when interacting with firms on misconduct risk.

Specifically, the FSB believes the recommendations will be useful in furthering a number of important FSB objectives, including development of comparative baselines, supporting accountability for adverse outcomes and identifying areas of weakness or emerging risks that could usefully be addressed through compensation and performance management processes. The use of compensation and performance management mechanisms should not only address misconduct – preventatively and when it occurs – but should also help to promote good conduct.

The proposed data set is designed to help firms and supervisors answer a number of important questions. These include whether governance and risk management processes surrounding compensation:

- appropriately include conduct considerations in the design of their compensation and incentive systems, including the setting of individual goals, ex-ante performance measurement mechanisms and ex-post compensation adjustments;

- support the effective use of compensation tools – in combination with other performance management tools such as training, promotion and disciplinary systems – to help promote good conduct or to remediate individual conduct that is not in line with the firm's expectations, including holding individuals accountable for any misconduct that occurs;

- promote wider risk management goals, including for conduct issues, consistent with the firm's strategy and risk tolerance; and

- support the effective identification of emerging misconduct risks and, where appropriate, review use of incentive systems and compensation decisions in response to conduct incidents to ensure alignment of incentives, risk and reward.

The detail of the 'core' data set proposed is divided into two parts: the first considers in part A the compensation frameworks to address misconduct risk and their governance and the second, in part B, the compensation actions taken in the event of misconduct. The core data set is supported by additional information which is designed to provide supervisors with additional context and may be useful, in particular, in the case of supervisory deep dives or horizontal reviews on compensation and misconduct risk.

The FSB is recommending that supervisors carry out an initial, comprehensive data gathering of the core data set for significant financial institutions, and then receive updates no less frequently than once a year. Since frameworks, policies and procedures do not usually change frequently, at least not in a material way, the updates on the information in part A related to the firms' policies and procedures generally should include only material changes or new elements that became relevant.

On the other hand, the information in part B on concrete compensation actions taken in response to misconduct generally should be updated annually.

The FSB is clear that the recommendations do not establish new principles or standards but rather should be seen as 'particularly important' for the supervision and monitoring of misconduct incidents and when considering trends and the related responses by firms. While the proposed core data set and additional information is fairly comprehensive, the FSB is clear that it represents the 'minimum set of information' that should ideally be available to supervisors.

In the past, senior managers may have had little to do with the design of incentives and compensation schemes in their firms, but that is set to change. In short, senior managers need to engage comprehensively with the compensation, remuneration and incentive setting processes in their firm and to be able to evidence that all are appropriately designed to ensure that they do not either encourage or reward inappropriate risk taking. Senior managers should also be prepared to devote appropriate skilled resources to the building and maintenance of the systems and processes likely to be required to fulfill the enhanced data-gathering requirements.

Lobbying

12.6   Lobbying is a way of senior managers and their firms being able to shape their external environment and hence their regulatory future. It is not a quick win and will require medium- to long-term investment, but it can be worth it to both shape policy and prevent the unintended (and often expensive) consequences of poor rule making. While the potential benefits are attractive, all too many UK firms will not have fond recent memories of lobbying. Large amounts of effort and resource were deployed in an attempt to get the European Securities and Markets Authority (ESMA) to change the granular detail of the implementing measures for the revised Markets in Financial Instruments Directive 2004/39/EC (MiFID II) and associated Regulation (MiFIR). This effort was in addition to the original consultation dating back to May 2014 – indeed, even if there had been nothing else going on, the MiFID II/R response process monopolised significant amounts of skilled senior manager and compliance resources to assess the potential impact of nearly 900 pages of policy proposals and 960 specific questions asked. It was therefore both disappointing and a matter of concern that ESMA's final report comprehensively rejected much of the feedback received from firms. Some minor drafting changes were made but overall ESMA reiterated its customer and investor-centric approach even where firms stated that compliance with the new requirements would prove unduly burdensome and, on occasion, 'very difficult'.

Brexit will change many things including the regulatory landscape for financial services and firms can use the possibly painful memories of the challenges associated with crafting responses to the MiFID II/ MiFIR consultations to shape their lobbying strategy now that the UK will be taking back at least some of its own future. Exiting the EU will not result in an automatic lowering of regulatory standards in the UK but rather the UK may well be more in charge of its own regulatory destiny. There are some areas, such as the Listing Rules, where the UK has chosen, quite deliberately, to implement absolute best practice standards and could have been in danger of having to lower those requirements as part of future European moves towards a single rulebook.

The overarching supranational frameworks and financial services policy directions agreed by the G20, the FSB and other supranational policy makers such as Basel would apply to the UK no matter what its EU membership status. Outside of the EU the UK would, however, be able to interpret and implement the supranational requirements to suit its own economy – it is not that the UK's regulatory regime would end up completely different from that of the EU, but that it would be the UK's own view on common supranational policies. This may well be a key point for many firms and their revised lobbying strategy as the potential issues arising from the transposition of the EU requirements are set to become more acute as the number of regulations (which are directly applicable) were set to increase as the EU continued to seek to enshrine a single European rulebook.

The MiFID II/MiFIR experience showed there was little sympathy for firms at the European Supervisory Authority level but that does not mean that any policy maker (pan-European or not) can or should choose to wholly discount the views of financial services firms. It is in no-one's interests to have poor quality legislation or guidance. So, given the potential changes driving Brexit, what can UK firms, and their senior managers, do now to influence the future shape of UK regulatory policy?

- Firms still need to invest skilled resources in responding to consultations and discussion papers. Even if the apparent chances of getting a regulator to alter its approach are small, they will, by definition, be nil if firms do not respond. Firms may wish to coordinate further between themselves and/or trade bodies to add weight to key arguments where compliance will either be unduly onerous or the approach is unlikely to meet the required good customer outcomes.

- Firms also need to submit detailed written responses (preferably with practical examples) if they then wish to follow up with either domestic or supranational policymakers. Any firm approaching either body without having submitted a detailed, reasoned response to any formal consultation process will be given short shrift.

- A well-trodden lobbying path has been for firms to engage with relevant civil servants and/or members of Parliament to get key points across. Firms need to appreciate that MPs tend to deal at the legislative (rather than rulebook) level of proposed changes. That said, big picture concerns can be raised and discussed but any and all points made will need to cover relevant good customer outcome and investor protection issues.

- One key change in the wake of Brexit will be the potential ability of the Financial Conduct Authority and the Prudential Regulation Authority to shape and indeed reshape the granular detail of existing regulatory requirements. It has been made clear there will be no 'bonfire of the regulations' but there is now substantially more scope for the UK regulators to tailor changes to the UK marketplace. The deliberate strategy in pursuit of a single European rulebook has meant that where the regulatory requirements are in the form of a regulation there is no scope for change at all as the regulation went directly into national rulebooks. Even in the case of a directive, the level of detail now associated with the implementing technical standards meant that there was often very little room for manoeuver by individual jurisdictions. Where firms do have substantive concerns that particular EU-derived measures are unworkable, in conflict with other requirements, or are unlikely to lead to the required good customer outcomes, then those should be prioritised as part of any lobbying strategy.

- Board engagement is an essential part of any lobbying strategy. A post-Brexit world may lead some UK firms to restructure their business model and approach to take advantage of the new world order in financial services. The current uncertainty as to detailed practical ramifications, whilst of potential concern, is also an opportunity to seek to shape the new world to a firm's advantage. As a first step, firms need to think through the implications for their own business of the forthcoming changes in the UK/EU relationship and then take a senior level decision as to what good looks like for their business. 'Good' in this sense could include a scenario which is neutral for the firm itself but potentially a significant threat for its competitors. Equally, if a possible threat is bad for the firm, it might end up being worse for competitors leaving the firm in a relatively better position.

- One thread throughout the post-Brexit discussions is likely to be that of deemed 'equivalence' between the UK approach and that in the EU. Where rules and regulations are deemed to be equivalent to those in the EU then many of the onerous third country provisions imposed in many of the European financial services directives are waived. 'Equivalent' does not mean 'the same as' and it is entirely possible that the UK can remain in 'equivalence' whilst having the flexibility to amend practical details which do not sit well in the UK marketplace. Again, this is an area where firms can assess what would work best for them and their business model and lobby accordingly.

It is perhaps stating the obvious that Brexit will be a game changer for financial services in the UK, but it is a game changer which is ripe with opportunity for those firms and senior managers willing and able to invest in well thought through strategic lobbying. Wholesale rulebook change is unlikely but the lessons learned in responding to and seeking to influence European bodies should stand UK firms in good stead to build persuasive strategic approaches to lobbying and, as a result, be able to influence significantly their own regulatory futures.

Internal environment

12.7   In theory, senior individuals should have much more control over the internal environment of their firm than they do over the external environment. The levels of line of sight and control can, however, be illusory in a large complex firm. Senior managers need to be realistic about the implications of their accountability and their ability to discharge their role and responsibilities.

Tone from the top and mood in the middle

12.8   The regulatory focus on culture and conduct risk (discussed in detail in **Chapter 9**) has created the need to consider the 'how' of business as well as the 'what'. Firms need to ensure that the discussions on culture, risk appetite and setting the tone from the top have happened at a suitably senior level and that critically consensus has been reached. It is not necessarily a given that all senior individuals will agree on what 'good' looks like for the firm. Indeed, anecdotally there have been some widely differing opinions and views aired at board meetings where the subject was raised. Any discussion, challenge and constructive criticism should be documented and the final agreed position needs to be given, and be seen to be given, support from all senior managers.

As a key element on the governance around promulgating tone from the top, firms need to ensure comprehensive, robust and consistent documentation on all aspects of the development, implementation, embedding and testing of conduct risk. Senior managers are expected to be able to translate, interpret and implement board level tone from the top to ensure that it flows into the 'mood in the middle' accurately and completely before cascading down to everyone in the firm.

Understanding the business and its risks

12.9   All senior managers need to truly understand the business being conducted in their area of responsibility. It ought to be stating the obvious that a senior manager needs thorough in-depth understanding of all products, activities and processes, but all too often enforcement actions show that as people and businesses change, knowledge levels become severely depleted with the inevitable regulatory consequences. Particular care needs to be taken over any new areas of business or products whether the change is by acquisition or internal development.

A critical part of understanding the business of a financial services firm is the need to understand the risk and compliance obligations arising. Senior managers must have a baseline knowledge and understanding of risk management and the arrangements needed for an effective compliance regime are a required core competency. There are some basic questions which senior managers would be advised to keep under consideration and which they should expect to be able to discuss with regulators. The expectation is that senior managers should be able to evidence a 'yes' to each question with any areas where there is a lack of positive evidence or a 'no' being followed up for a possible weakness which could lead to poor or non-compliance. In other words, the questions can be used by senior managers to assess the quality of compliance arrangements in their business area and may help to prioritise or allocate time and resources to areas or processes which require the most urgent consideration and potential remediation.

The ten basic questions are based on a predecessor UK regulator's compliance arrangements scorecard and are as follows:

---

(1) Is your firm's compliance manual tailored to your firm's operations, up to date and understood by all staff?

(2) Are your firm's operational procedures documented clearly and linked to the requirements of all relevant regulators rules?

(3) Is your firm's compliance monitoring program risk-based and all embracing?

(4) Is your compliance monitoring program implemented properly and reported on?

(5) Are issues identified by either your compliance staff or others correctly and satisfactorily resolved?

(6) Is your firm's reporting chain and relationship with the compliance function effective?

(7) Are any rule breaches and complaints being identified properly and resolved promptly?

(8) Do your compliance staff have the appropriate experience?

(9) Are there dedicated compliance resources and are they adequate?

(10) Is there regular training about compliance for all staff?

While senior managers are not expected to be risk and compliance experts they are expected to know sufficient about the current risk and compliance issues facing their business. With regard to the ten basic questions, senior managers should feel free to keep asking questions or requiring clarification until they themselves are completely comfortable with the explanations and answers given together with the knowledge displayed by others and quality of the evidence to demonstrate compliant business activities.

Management information and evidence

12.10   As has been stated elsewhere in this book, good management information is the life blood of any firm and in the current regulatory environment management information could be seen as the need for evidence, evidence and more evidence that a firm and the senior managers running it have done all of the right things in all of the right ways. Part of high quality management information is the need to constructively challenge the assumptions, scope and limitations on all reporting. In today's world the challenge needs to extend to all areas of the business and not just those that are overtly or directly regulated.

One pertinent example is from the United States where, in May 2015, the Nationwide Life Assurance Company ended up being fined $8m by the US Securities and Exchange Commission for breaches regarding the processing and pricing of subsequent purchase payments and redemption orders for variable insurance contracts and underlying mutual funds (see www.sec.gov/litigation/admin/2015/ic-31601.pdf). The issue at the heart of the enforcement action was something as apparently mundane as the procedures around the collection of mail. Not an area directly covered by the rule books but, in this instance, an area where the procedures had not been reviewed or changed for almost six years, ended up leading to Nationwide Life being in breach of its regulatory obligations.

Personal archive

12.11   As has been made amply clear by the SMR, senior managers must not only contribute to their firm being compliant but be able to demonstrate their own discharge of their personal regulatory obligations and accountabilities.

The breadth of the required core competency of senior individuals has been extended to encompass the need to be able to evidence, robustly and consistently, the discharge of their responsibilities and hence be seen to have managed and mitigated their own personal regulatory risk. As with so much of regulation, there is no 'one size fits all' for how to build a personal archive of compliance but rather a number of elements for senior managers to consider.

Decision registers

12.12   In a somewhat different angle to the use of prescribed responsibilities and job descriptions as part of the internal environment, it is clear that the job descriptions (or equivalent) will now need to be significantly more detailed than those previously used and for the protection of both the individual and the firm. In particular, it is critical that all regulatory criteria and expectations are not only included but kept up to date.

As part of the daily management of the firm, senior managers will need to routinely collect and maintain the evidence to show how they discharged all of their obligations and responsibilities. Consideration may in particular be given to the need for a 'decision register' to facilitate all senior managers' ability to evidence not only the decision taken but also the evidence on which that decision was taken. Similarly, when roles change, detailed documented handovers need to become the norm to ensure that all concerned can manage their personal regulatory risk. It could easily be seen as a cottage industry, but the increased level of documentation has become an essential part of enabling senior managers to demonstrate the appropriate discharge of their responsibilities.

Skills

12.13   Another investment is in building knowledge and awareness of the implications of the changing regulatory environment. Engaging in a rolling regulatory training programme is one option – apart from anything else there is a significantly increased likelihood of enforcement action for any unprepared or unaware individual. Given the global political will and the changing regulatory approach, senior managers who ignore the brave new regulatory world are likely to feel the full brunt of supervisory enforcement. Even if a senior manager is not banned as part of any enforcement action it is unlikely that an individual who has 'only' been fined will work again in a senior capacity in financial services.

Evidence, evidence and more evidence

12.14   Senior managers need to build and maintain their own personal archive of evidence to demonstrate the full and complete discharge of their regulatory obligations. For some quantitative elements that process is likely to be relatively simple, but there are often challenges when culture is added into the mix. Akin to the potential for a 'decision register', one quick win could be to gather all board and other meeting minutes which evidence the challenge and engagement by the individual.

As part of the routine, collation of minutes should be an assessment as to whether there has been an appropriate level of detail captured from the discussions held. In the past, minutes of meetings were little more than confirmation that a particular item had been raised, discussed and an action agreed. In today's world, minutes need to capture the discussion in granular detail and then to be expressly agreed as an accurate record of the meeting.

Last, but not least, is a point on intellectual property. When a senior manager changes firms it is entirely reasonable that he or she should be able to maintain the suite of documents to support the compliant discharge of his or her regulatory responsibilities. This is not without its potential challenges given that at least some of the documents could be business sensitive and the intellectual property of the firm. Senior managers and their firms will need to come to sensible arrangements that will enable the senior manager to access (potentially sensitive) documents under certain circumstances as and when they are no longer employed by the firm.

Checklist

12.15   The checklist below offers practical questions for all senior managers to consider.

Checklist

- Have arrangements been put in place to build and maintain a personal archive to evidence the discharge of your personal regulatory risk?

- How have you satisfied yourself that the risk and compliance infrastructure is operating effectively in your part of the business?

- Are you completely satisfied that you have a thorough in-depth understanding of all products, activities and processes in the business area under your management?

- Has consideration been given to how the design and implementation of compensation and incentive schemes could lead to possible misconduct? And is your firm prepared for the possible additional data requirements on compensation?

Chapter 13

Regulatory relationship management

Chapter summary

A key part of any senior manager's role in a financial services firm is the knowledge and ability to be able to interact appropriately with all relevant regulators. This chapter covers:

- The considerations for senior managers dealing with regulators directly

- The approaches to both internal and external (supervisory) investigations including the potential for dawn raids

- The assessment of what senior managers need to consider when another group company is under regulatory investigation

---

Principle 11: relations with regulators – a firm must deal with its regulators in an open and cooperative way, and must disclose appropriately to the FCA anything relating to the firm of which that regulator would reasonably expect notice.

Source: FCA Principles for Businesses

Dealing with regulators

13.1   The nature and intensity of the relationship between regulators and authorised firms is dependent on the size and business of the firm. A large multinational bank is likely to have a close, continuous and often intrusive relationship with relevant regulators involving extensive reporting, additional information requests and frequent meetings. In contrast, a small mono-line firm is likely to have a much more 'hands off' relationship with the only regular contact being through the regulatory reporting and returns.

Senior managers need to be aware that the FCA's priority in supervising firms is to ensure consumers are at the centre of a firm's business and specifically it seeks to tackle risks before they can cause harm. In terms of conduct supervision, the FCA is responsible for supervising over 56,000 firms and has divided them up such that:

- Pillar 1 – proactive supervision for the biggest firms;

- Pillar 2 – event-driven, reactive supervision of actual or emerging risks according to our (ie the FCA's) risk appetite;

- Pillar 3 – thematic work that focuses on risks and issues affecting multiple firms or a sector as a whole.

The FCA will seek to intervene early where it sees poor behaviour, the regulator will also take action to prevent harm to consumers and markets, and get redress where appropriate.

A key line of sight for supervisors to the activities of a firm is regulatory reporting. The base plate reporting for all FCA firms includes the annual accounts and reports, annual controllers reporting, client asset reports, client money and assets reporting, market data reporting, product sales data reporting, remuneration data reporting and reporting complaints.

In the past, much of the building and maintaining of regulatory relationships was left to the compliance function. Nowadays, the regulator will choose to interact with a far wider range of senior managers and, during a routine visit or investigation, may also choose to speak to much more junior staff. Regulatory relationship management has reached a new level of importance with regulators around the world focusing more on outcomes, qualitative issues such as risk culture, using more judgement and choosing to interact far beyond the board room at financial services firms.

As part of the management of regulatory relationships, it needs to be acknowledged that issues can and do occur and this needs to be an inherent part of any distinct, agreed strategic plan to manage regulatory interactions, to ensure clarity regarding regulatory expectations and to allow, where possible, the positive management of regulatory investigations. The detailed elements of any regulatory relationship plan must be tailored precisely to the firm's business activities. One of the many lessons from the London Interbank Offered Rate (LIBOR) market failings is that firms would be wise to include all activities in the plan and not just those that are directly regulated.

All senior individuals need to be able to discuss all relevant regulatory issues with the regulator, and to understand the likely impact on the firm and its customers. Anyone meeting with, or speaking to, the regulator should be expected to make, maintain and share comprehensive notes of the discussion and should keep a record of any documents or other information exchanged. In particular, any requests or expectations stated by the regulator should be noted and, as a matter of best practice, confirmed in writing to ensure clarity of understanding. In particular, any possibility of an investigation or other regulatory scrutiny should be documented in detail and shared internally as soon as is feasible.

It goes without saying that all information provided to the regulator must be accurate and able to be substantiated, and that all actions and timescales agreed must be met and reported on both internally and externally. A useful benefit of a (global) regulatory relationship plan will be the development of a group-wide database of regulatory interactions enabling senior managers to spot trends, ensure a uniformity of information flows and enable pre-emptive briefings on emerging issues. Regulators speak to each other across borders and firms operating internationally need to ensure that regulatory relationships are managed on that basis.

One area that is often missed when compiling the elements of a regulatory relationship plan is that of regulatory approvals and registrations. It can be a bureaucratic resource-hungry process but it needs constant maintenance and in a large international firm it may well need significant investment. As a piece of best practice, firms may wish to ask certain regulators for a full list of all registered persons and licenses held to check that the records at the firm and the regulator can be reconciled; it is not, for instance, unheard of for a regulator to fail to update its own records even if it has been informed of changes. It is far better for both the individual and the firm to be active in undertaking such checks rather than discrepancies coming to light, for example as part of an intrusive supervisory visit and there being, say, a mismatch of understanding as to which senior manager is registered where, and responsible for what.

FCA ten supervision principles

The FCA's approach to supervision is built on ten principles which form the basis of the regulator's interaction with all firms:

(1) Ensuring fair outcomes for consumers and markets. This is the dual consideration that runs through all the FCA's work. The FCA assesses issues according to their impact on both consumers and market integrity.

(2) Being forward-looking and pre-emptive, identifying potential risks and taking action before they have a serious impact.

(3) Being focused on the big issues and causes of problems. The FCA concentrates its resources on issues that may have a significant impact on its objectives.

(4) Taking a judgment-based approach, with the emphasis on achieving the right outcomes.

(5) Ensuring firms act in the right spirit, which means they consider the impact of their actions on consumers and markets rather than just complying with the letter of the law.

(6) Examining business models and culture, and the impact they have on consumer and market outcomes. The FCA is interested in how a firm makes its money, as this can drive many potential risks.

---

(7) An emphasis on individual accountability, ensuring senior managers understand that they are personally responsible for their actions – and that the FCA will hold them to account when things go wrong.

(8) Being robust when things go wrong, making sure that problems are fixed, consumers are protected and compensated, and poor behaviour is rectified along with its root causes.

(9) Communicating openly with industry, firms and consumers to gain a deeper understanding of the issues they face.

(10) Having a joined-up approach, making sure firms get consistent messages from the FCA. The FCA also engages with the Prudential Regulation Authority to ensure effective independent supervision of dual-regulated firms, and work with other regulatory and advisory bodies including the Payment Systems Regulator, Financial Ombudsman Service, Financial Services Compensation Scheme, Money Advice Service and international regulators.

The detail of the regulator's evaluation of a firm is tailored by the supervisory approach and the nature of the business undertaken. Senior managers should expect a summary of the FCA's view of their firm or group, in which the regulator examines all the information it has about it, including all the work it has done in relation to the firm since the previous evaluation. This will include the business model and strategy assessment, deep dives, thematic issues and products work, events-based reactive work, sector analysis, and any specific risks relating to financial crime and client assets. The FCA will also make an assessment as to whether the firm is meeting its threshold conditions.

Taking all this into account, the FCA will set out the risks the firm poses and its view of their root causes together with the strategy and work program for the next supervision cycle, to address and mitigate these risks. The key supervisory messages are sent to the board of directors and the FCA will discuss its conclusions with the board and senior managers.

Senior managers should expect to make any risks or issues highlighted by the regulator a key priority and to be able to report back to both their board and the regulator on the timely mitigation or resolution of concerns raised.

Internal investigations

13.2 Senior managers may wish to trigger an internal investigation for a wide range of reasons made all the more pertinent with the need to take reasonable steps to prevent regulatory breaches from occurring or continuing. The need for an internal investigation will be a judgement call depending on the nature of the issue arising. Compliance or internal audit monitoring findings, the discovery of a fraud or other misconduct, allegations made by whistleblowers, complaints received from clients and issues raised with the firm by regulatory or law enforcement authorities could all be triggers for further work and a formal internal investigation.

Setting up an internal investigation is not to be taken lightly. Investigations are, by definition, disruptive with the potentially extensive need for management time not only during the investigation process itself, but also in terms of any follow-up remedial actions required. Other potential costs could include the need to reprioritise or reschedule other work, possible damage to staff morale and the need to employ external consultants or lawyers.

On the other hand, a failure to properly investigate could cause the firm and the senior manager(s) concerned additional regulatory, even enforcement, issues. There are no guarantees, but the FCA and the PRA are likely to take into (favourable) account the fact that the firm has carried out an effective and thorough investigation in determining any regulatory action to be taken.

In some cases, it may be that the issue is one that has a serious regulatory impact requiring the firm to notify the appropriate regulator immediately. The firm will need to have regard to its regulatory obligations under Principle 11 and senior managers should be aware that in these circumstances, the firm's ability to conduct its own internal investigation before involving the FCA and/or the PRA is likely to be very limited. If, however, the firm has a good relationship with its regulators and the relevant regulator or regulators are confident that the firm has efficient and robust internal systems and controls, the regulator may accept a proposal from the firm to carry out an initial investigation internally and to report to the regulator at a later date.

Where the firm has concluded that it will pursue an internal investigation it is critical that the key stakeholders discuss and agree the objectives and scope of the investigation. Depending on the nature of the issue the key stakeholders could include senior managers, directors, human resources, IT, legal, compliance and internal audit.

In general terms, the main objectives of any internal investigation should cover the need to:

- understand and assess the nature and scope of what has occurred together with the degree of knowledge and involvement of relevant individuals (including the extent to which individuals ought to have been aware even if, in fact, they were not);

- ensure that evidence is secured and preserved;

- assess the effect the issue will have on the firm's business and take appropriate steps to mitigate any continuing impact;

- identify any breakdown in systems and controls and/or breaches of internal processes and procedures;

- undertake root cause analysis and consider whether the issue could be systemic and, if so whether the original terms of the investigation need to be widened;

- identify whether customers have been disadvantaged and quantify any loss, or propose a methodology to do so;

- minimise the impact of an identified issue in order to give the firm time to propose a remedial course of action;

- report promptly at an appropriate level internally and externally;
- prevent adverse publicity as far as possible; and
- maintain a good relationship with the regulator(s).

Where an internal investigation is proposed in response to a concern expressed by the regulator, the objectives of the investigation are likely to be the same hallmarks of those for a firm-generated investigation. No matter the source of the original concerns, it is critical that the firm has sufficient skilled resources to be able to devote to any investigation in terms of both expertise to manage and oversee the work and the extent to which the investigation may distract the internal investigators from their usual day job.

Another potential benefit of up-front strategic management of an internal investigation is that if a firm can assure the FCA and/or PRA that it is properly handling an investigation, it may discourage the relevant regulator from appointing external investigators (or at least if it does so, it may help to limit the scope of such external investigation).

Once the objectives of the investigation have been agreed, senior managers should consider preparing an action or project plan to address the scope and timetable for the investigation. The complexity of the plan will depend largely upon the size of the firm, the nature of the matters under investigation and the timescales involved. At its simplest, the plan should deal with the following:

- the scope of the investigation, including relevant business areas and jurisdictions;
- which areas will be reviewed;
- tasks to be assigned to named individuals;
- whether any tasks may require the involvement of external parties such as professional advisers;
- an investigation timetable;
- anticipated interim reporting both internal and external; and
- identification of dependencies within the plan and clarification of timescales.

The development of a detailed project plan will help to ensure that no areas are missed and will be another means by which the firm can reassure the relevant regulators that the internal investigation is being handled efficiently and effectively. In addition, the plan should help any senior managers demonstrate the discharge of their regulatory obligations under the SMR.

The use of a detailed plan should facilitate the tracking of the progress of the investigation and to demonstrate that the investigation is being conducted within an agreed set of parameters. It may be necessary to amend the plan as the investigation proceeds to take account of any new developments. It will also be important to identify early on where immediate interim remedial measures may be taken to mitigate any potential loss, detriment to customers and/or the risk of any misconduct recurring. As a matter of course, the firm should keep the FCA and/or PRA fully informed on progress made, any amendments to the plan and interim remedial actions taken.

Senior managers will need to ensure that any internal investigation is followed through to completion. This is not only to ensure that all remedial actions identified are fully implemented and embedded, but also in the event that the regulator chooses to take action then reference can be made to the work already undertaken.

Practice note

Particular care will need to be taken with regard to the record keeping surrounding an investigation. It is essential to record the conclusions of the investigation, the remedial steps required and the process of reviewing the progress of remedial actions. Even if the information is not to be made immediately available to the regulator, it is important to establish an audit trail for the work undertaken, in case the problem recurs or becomes relevant at some later stage.

Documents created and collected during the investigation should be carefully reviewed at the conclusion and copied and retained where appropriate. The need to retain documentary evidence should be balanced against the requirements under relevant data protection legislation. Documents that may be legally privileged should be separated and identified to ensure that they are not disclosed at some later stage. This process can be particularly useful in preparing for a FCA and/or other supervision visit or even a dawn raid.

Other elements for senior managers to consider at the end of an internal investigation include the need to de-brief staff and other stakeholders. The firm should consider if, and how, the findings of an investigation should be communicated to staff and other stakeholders. The need to de-brief staff, and to communicate with other stakeholders, will depend upon the extent to which the investigation has been made known, its findings, and whether the matter has reached the public domain. The firm may wish to consider using a specialist public relations firm for this task.

Another element for post-investigation review is that of the governance infrastructure together with all relevant policies and procedures. In particular, critical evaluation should be given to the firm's approach to risk identification and the balance of preventative and detective controls in the areas subject to the investigation. It may be that in a potentially high-risk area additional preventative controls may need to be considered.

Overall it is critical that senior managers can personally satisfy themselves that all feasible reasonable steps towards assessing or verifying compliant activities in the areas under their control have been taken. Where compliance issues or breaches have been found, it is equally critical that all reasonable steps are seen to have been taken, where required, to investigate and remediate the problem, compensate customers and inform the regulator.

Regulatory (external) investigations

13.3   Mistakes can and do happen. How a firm and its senior managers handle those breaches will have a direct bearing on the regulatory outcome, including specifically the extent to which the senior manager concerned faces enforcement action as a result of his or her personal accountability.

The UK regulators operate a policy of credible deterrence on enforcement by making it clear that there are real and meaningful consequences for firms and individuals who do not follow the rules. Enforcement is discussed in more detail in **Chapter 11.**

The FCA for instance has a wide range of enforcement powers – criminal, civil and regulatory – to protect consumers and to take action against firms and individuals that do not meet the required standards. The FCA seeks to make the punishment fit the crime and can take action such as:

- withdrawing a firm's authorisation;

- prohibiting individuals from carrying on regulated activities;

- suspending firms and individuals from undertaking regulated activities;

- issuing fines against firms and individuals who breach the FCA's rules or commit market abuse;

- issuing fines against firms breaching competition laws;

- making a public announcement when the FCA begins disciplinary action and publishing details of warning, decision and final notices;

- applying to the courts for injunctions, restitution orders, winding-up and other insolvency orders;

- bringing criminal prosecutions to tackle financial crime, such as insider dealing, unauthorised business and false claims to be FCA authorised;

- issuing warnings and alerts about unauthorised firms and individuals and requesting that web hosts deactivate associated websites.

Senior managers need to be prepared to deal with regulators not only as part of the routine visits but also as part of any regulatory investigation or potential enforcement action. A usual part of any visit or investigation is the interviewing of senior managers. Being interviewed by the regulator can be daunting but there are a series of good or better practice tips which senior managers would be well advised to consider in order to fulfil the expected open and cooperative approach:

- *Do your homework* – ensure that you are fully briefed on all relevant correspondence with the regulator regarding the investigation. You should also review the latest firm evaluation. Equally ensure that you are fully up to date with all internal work on the area(s) concerned.

- *Only answer the question asked* – be clear and concise in responding to questions. If the question is in anyway unclear ask for clarification. Do not speculate and do not respond on any areas of which you are not completely certain. Assuming it is accurate, 'I don't know' is a perfectly acceptable answer though it will need follow up with those who *do* have the information.

- *Take notes (or have someone taking notes for you)* – there should be a detailed record kept of the conversation, any documentation handed over and specifically any issues raised.

- Ensure that any documents or follow ups promised to the regulator are followed up and completed and a record kept.

Extract from the PRA's approach to banking supervision, March 2016

Disciplinary action against individuals

While the PRA's preference is to use its statutory powers to secure ex ante, remedial action, it also has a set of disciplinary powers which it will use ex post if necessary.

The PRA has disciplinary powers over individuals approved to perform a Senior Management Function by the PRA or an equivalent function by the FCA (eg as a member of the governing body) and is empowered to use these where an individual fails to comply with the PRA's Conduct Rules, or has been knowingly involved in a contravention by their firm of a requirement imposed by the PRA. The powers enable the PRA, among other sanctions, to impose financial penalties, to censure an individual publicly, to withdraw approval from individuals holding Senior Management Functions, and to prohibit individuals from holding Senior Management Functions in the future.

In assessing whether to take disciplinary action against a Senior Manager or director, the PRA considers a variety of factors, including:

- the impact the individual's behaviour has had or is having on the PRA advancing its objectives, including the behaviour of other persons in the firm over whom the individual should exercise control, and thus whether that behaviour calls into question the person's fitness and properness (be it an isolated incident or a course of conduct);

- whether taking action will serve to deter the person who committed the breach, and others who are subject to the PRA's requirements, from committing similar or other breaches; and

- the individual's behaviour towards the PRA, including the level of co-operation and openness with which the individual deals with the PRA and the appropriateness of the individual's actions in response to concerns raised.

Dawn raids

13.4   Regulators around the world often need access to physical documents as well as IT systems as part of enforcement investigations. Dawn raids are not new but regulators (and other law enforcement agencies) are continuing to use them to gain access to the information and data needed to investigate and prosecute both firms and individuals.

Dawn raids are by definition a surprise, but many of the unduly damaging ramifications can be mitigated by training and awareness together with a robust suite of tested policies and procedures. Senior managers need to be prepared and involved in the creation of a policy for surprise inspections from a regulatory body or law enforcement agency. As with all policies it should be clearly documented and all members of staff should be both aware of the policy and familiar with its contents. Given the potential implications of a dawn raid it is a policy area where the board and all senior managers should not only be briefed in detail but also asked to expressly confirm their knowledge and understanding of the agreed approach. In addition:

- Firms may wish to have the dawn raids policy included as part of any annual re-affirmation of polices – this can be a useful means of ensuring the policy both remains up to date and staff are re-familiarised with the contents.

- The dawn raids policy should be included as part of any induction training or 'starter pack' for new joiners.

- The roll-out of any specific detail of a dawn raids policy should be included in any new office or branch opening checklist. Equally, any changes to the corporate approach to dawn raids must be rolled out, where relevant, to all parts of the group structure regardless of geography.

- Firms who share offices or who share reception staff or security guards should ensure that any policies and procedures for dawn raids (and indeed serving of legal or court notices) are communicated to all front desk staff. Where the office is shared, firms may wish to consider stipulating adherence to dawn raid and other relevant policies as part of the rental agreement or equivalent.

- Firms should be aware that dawn raid policies and procedures should be tailored to each legal jurisdiction in which the firm, or its assets or data, have a physical presence – when in any doubt a firm should seek specific legal opinion as to the detail of the local approach under the umbrella of an overarching group policy. Data protection issues should be expressly considered in any jurisdiction specific policy approach.

- The dawn raid policy should cover any outsourced operations and should be one of the policies agreed to in the outsourcing terms and conditions.

- Communication is a key part of the successful management of a dawn raid. The policy should clearly state who should be contacted and in what order. Whilst the local compliance officer should be one of the first people contacted, senior managers all the way to a very top of a firm should be included in the communication ladder. The firm's press office should also be high on the contact list with an agreed holding statement as a minimum – handling the PR of any dawn raid is a critical part of the process.

- Firms also need to consider communication to other regulators. This can take a couple of forms – in a single jurisdiction, firms should actively consider the need to inform their financial services regulator of any dawn raid by another authority, such as tax, data protection or competition bodies. For firms who are in multiple jurisdictions, a surprise inspection by any regulatory authority should be considered for reporting to the firm's lead financial services regulator.

- As a practical piece of procedure during a dawn raid, a firm should aim to keep as many records as possible in the form of copies of documents taken, notes of which sections of the firm were visited and which computers or other equipment (such as phone recordings) were removed. Where possible a firm should try to ascertain the information stored on any computers or hard drives taken to ensure it is aware of the detail of the information now in the possession of the authorities.

- Where a firm has claimed legal privilege over certain documents, it is important that those documents are separated from non-privileged material and that staff are clear about what to do in the event of a dawn raid or regulatory challenge. In anticipation of a dawn raid, firms may, for instance, wish to consider procedures to seal particular documents and deliver them to a third party until an issue has been resolved. This approach can be particularly useful not only for surprise inspections but also in the context of regulatory supervision visits.

- Last, but not least, is the need for a review process as and when a firm has been the subject of a raid. As experienced senior managers know, the only true test of a policy is once it has been used for real. Detailed jurisdiction specific policies and procedures may look great on paper but until they have been tested in the often controlled chaos of a dawn raid, then there is no way to know whether or not they were fit for purpose. A post-raid review should be used to refine and update any policy and to initiate a new round of training and awareness for the entire firm.

Dawn raids are never the easiest event for firms and their senior managers but a clearly documented and communicated policy should allow a potentially difficult situation to be managed as smoothly as possible. A lack of an effective and articulated policy increases the risk of poor scenario turning into a potential regulatory disaster.

What to do if another group company is under investigation

13.5   It might be tempting for senior managers to not prioritise or even to ignore when another part of their group has come under regulatory investigation. After all, the regulatory scrutiny is not in their jurisdiction and regulators are not looking into their area of responsibility. There is, however, a need both to be informed and to take action when any part of a financial services group has come under investigation. This is not a theoretical exercise as regulators regularly communicate and share information across borders and international firms can and should do the same to help manage the overall regulatory risks to the wider firm.

As with all the best risk management there are major benefits in anticipating the potential impact of a regulatory investigation anywhere in a financial services group and putting plans in place to enable all parts of the group to navigate ramifications as smoothly as possible. If nothing else, the plans in place should ensure that other parts of the group do not compound any regulatory issues.

There are a range of plans and proposed actions which firms should consider as part of the strategic approach to the mitigation of what is in effect contagion risk between the different parts of a regulated group. First and foremost is the need for strong working regulatory relationships in all jurisdictions where the firm holds a license. As has been noted previously, regulatory relationship management has reached a new level of importance with regulators around the world focusing more on outcomes, qualitative issues such as risk culture, using more judgement and choosing to interact with a far wider range of people at regulated firms.

The trigger for any action plan to be invoked will be the report of a regulatory investigation in part of the group. It is imperative that the details of any kind of regulatory visit or action out of the normal supervisory approach is reported internally to a pre-agreed list of senior individuals in all jurisdictions where licenses are held. Without knowledge of regulatory actions in other jurisdictions, the ability for the rest of a regulated group to manage its own regulatory risks is not only moot but could also be increased. Depending on the nature of the regulatory issue under investigation elsewhere, other parts of the group may need to consider the following:

- *Making a formal report to all relevant local regulators.*

  Even where there is no legal obligation consideration should be given to discussing the issue with local regulators and to inform them of the work being done to, for instance, ensure that the same issues do not arise locally.

- *Review whether there are any senior managers or directors in common.*

  Many large international firms have senior individuals who are directors and/or registered or authorised persons in more than one jurisdiction. Any individuals who are associated with both the jurisdiction under investigation and the local one will need to be briefed in detail. Specifically, any potential for cross contagion of personal liability for actions or inactions arising will need to be considered and potentially investigated further.

- *Review whether there are any products in common.*

  Many products are jurisdiction specific but this is not always the case. Consideration should be given to where similar or the same products are sold in both jurisdictions. If certain product features or sales approach are perceived as having given rise to poor customer outcomes in one jurisdiction then other parts of the group would be well advised to undertake a pre-emptive review.

- *Review whether there are any processes in common.*

  Most international firms have group policies which are by definition cross-border. Consideration should be given to whether the application of a group or indeed other widely used policy could give rise to the similar regulatory concerns locally. Anecdotally, areas where this has caused problems in the past include the approach to regulatory investigations themselves, customer complaints handling and the type of evidence gathered to fulfil 'know your customer' requirements.

- *Review whether there are any customers in common.*

  Firms and customers often deal with each other in multiple jurisdictions. Any issues involving a customer in one jurisdiction should be investigated locally to assess whether a similar breach could arise thus enabling prompt customer relationship management.

- *Consider the need to inform local stakeholders such as suppliers, public relations, insurers and external auditors.*

  Care will need to be taken if the mere fact of a non-public regulatory investigation elsewhere in the group could be considered in any way price sensitive.

- *Ensure all work undertaken is documented in detail with particular care given to the nature and timing of information shared.*

  Any instances where information has not for legal or regulatory reasons been shared will need a full explanation as well as clear additional mitigating steps wherever possible.

Last, but not least, take the time once the regulatory investigation has been concluded to assess how the strategic and action plans worked in practice and to consider whether any changes could or should be made. Firms and their senior managers would be well advised to learn any and all lessons to maximise the mitigation available for the next time any regulator is in enforcement mode.

Checklist

13.6 The checklist below offers practical questions for senior managers to consider.

Checklist

- Are you aware of your firm's approach to regulatory relationship management and do you understand your part in the approach?

- Can you explain how the lessons learned from investigations (whether internal or external) have been applied in your business?

- How recently have you refreshed your knowledge of the detail of your firm's policy on dawn raids?

Chapter 14

Technology

Chapter summary
Senior managers are familiar with technology in their day-to-day lives. Equally, they need to be familiar with the use and potential misuse of technology in their professional lives. The potential gamut of technology is huge and its influence on the financial services sector is potentially profound. This chapter considers the practical ramifications for senior managers including in particular:
•   Cyber resilience
•   Data protection, and
•   Fintech

'Overall, the financial services sector is poised for change. But it is hard to judge whether this will be more evolutionary or revolutionary. Policymaking will need to be nimble, experimental, and cooperative.

At the same time, regulatory authorities need to balance carefully efficiency and stability tradeoffs in the face of these rapid changes. They need to be assured that risks to stability and integrity – including from cyber-attacks, money-laundering and terrorism financing – can be effectively managed without stifling innovation. They need to ensure that trust is maintained in an evolving financial system.'

Source: International Monetary Fund Staff Discussion Note – 'Fintech and Financial Services: Initial Considerations', Dong He *et al* (June 2017)

Technology plays a pivotal role in the delivery of financial products and services bringing with it both challenges and opportunities for firms and their customers. The unprecedented pace and scale of innovation and development of new technologies can increase risk if not safely implemented and managed. In parallel firms need to ensure existing technology and systems are resilient to outages, data breaches and cyber-attacks to reduce the risk of disruption and harm to customers. Given both the increased scrutiny by regulators on the impact of technology, who are strengthening their focus on firms to understand current and planned use of technology and operational resilience, and the rise in personal accountability, technology needs to become a priority for senior managers.

Cyber resilience

'We are witnessing a whole succession of technological innovations, but none of them will do away with the need for integrity in the individual or the ability to think.'

> Source: Wesley Bricker, Chief Accountant, US SEC, Remarks to the
> Institute of Chartered Accountants in England and Wales: 'The
> intersection of financial reporting and innovation' (June 2018)

14.1 All things cyber, whether risk, attack, crime or resilience are never far from the headlines with companies of all shapes and sizes around the world vulnerable to attack in the online world. In terms of cyber resilience, cyber risk, cyber crime as well as headline grabbing cyber-attacks (Carphone Warehouse, British Airways and Ticketmaster being just a handful of recent UK examples), it is perhaps stating the obvious that good customer outcomes will be under threat in the event of a failure of cyber resilience.

The continued prominence of cyber resilience, together with data privacy and GDPR, as a practical challenge for firms was highlighted in the Thomson Reuters Regulatory Intelligence's ninth annual cost of compliance survey report in 2018 (available at https://risk.thomsonreuters.com/en/resources/special-report/cost-compliance-2018.html).

The greatest compliance challenges I expect to face in 2018 is/are:

Customer due diligence
Senior management buy-in Regulatory and political uncertainty MiFID II/R Vendor compliance Sanctions compliance
Enforcement actions Increased regulatory scrutiny Senior management accountability
Training staff Greater clarity on regulations
Corporate government Global reach and consistency Culture Data privacy and GDPR
Balancing compliance and business needs
Managing workload Meeting additional licence requirements
Continuing regulatory change Third Party Risk Internal and regulatory investigations
Anti-bribery and corruption More information requests Tone from the top Cyber resilience AML Outsourcing
Product lifecycle management
Automation
Enhanced monitoring and reporting requirements
Conflicts management Fintech/Regtech Adequacy and availability of skilled resources
Conduct Risk framework
Implementation of regulatory change
Coping with limited budget and resources

> Source: Thomson Reuters Regulatory Intelligence – Cost of Compliance 2018 survey

The concerns are borne out by the statistics around cyber-attacks which show the threat to be increasing, and increasing rapidly. In a January 2018 speech by Robin Jones, Head of Technology, Resilience & Cyber at the FCA, it was stated that:

'In the past 12 months, the National Cyber Security Centre recorded over 1100 reported attacks, with 590 regarded as significant. 30 of these required action by government bodies, a number of which included the Financial Sector. In real terms, the UK deals with more than 10 significant cyber-attacks every week. In 2017 we had 69 material attacks reported to us, an increase on the 38 last year and 24 the year before. Recent ONS statistics show about 1.9 million incidents of fraud were cyber related.'

'It is critical that business leaders understand what a cyber-attack could do, how to respond and recover. We understand this makes demands of already busy senior leaders. But we think it is important this is no longer confined to the technology department. It needs to move into the Board room. It needs to be understood as a significant risk to the operation of a business, its consumers and wider markets.'

Source: Speech by Robin Jones, Head of Technology, Resilience & Cyber, FCA, at the PIMFA Financial Crime Conference, 'Building Cyber Resilience', London (January 2018)

In June 2017, the FCA updated its policy approach to cyber resilience and its expectations such that firms should be aware of the threat, able to defend themselves effectively, and respond proportionately to cyber events. What had previously often been seen as simply an IT issue has become a key issue for senior managers, with the FCA stating its goal, in common with many other financial services regulators, to 'help firms become more resilient to cyber-attacks, while ensuring that consumers are protected and market integrity is upheld'.

Effective cyber security practice

Manage the risk:
You need to know what information you hold and why you hold it. *Is it classified? Do you review who has access to your most sensitive data? Do you understand your vulnerabilities?*

Encryption:
Protect your sensitive data. *Do you use encryption software to protect your critical information from unauthorised access?*

Disaster recovery:
Backup your critical systems and data, and test backup recovery processes regularly. *Do you know if you are able to restore services in the event of an attack?*

Network and computer security:
Keep systems, software and apps up-to-date and fully patched. *Do you make sure your computer network is configured to prevent unauthorised access?*

User and device credentials:
Ensure your staff use strong passwords when logging on to hardware and software. Change the default Administrator credentials for all devices. *Do you use two-factor authentication where the confidentiality of the data is most crucial?*

Awareness:
People are an integral part of the cyber security chain. *Do you educate your staff on cyber security risks?*

Accreditation:
Gaining a recognised accreditation, such as *Cyber Essentials*, could improve the security of your firm. *Do you align your firm to a recognised cyber scheme?*

Information sharing:
Sharing threat information with your peers, through networks such as the *Cyber Security Information Sharing Partnership (CiSP)*, is a vital tool in strengthening your cyber defences. *Are you a member of any information-sharing arrangements?*

Source: UK Financial Conduct Authority. Infographic: Good Cyber Security – the foundations (June 2017) extracted from https://www.fca.org.uk/publication/documents/cyber-security-infographic.pdf

Good and better practice cyber resilience

14.2   As with many aspects of the management of personal accountability and regulatory risk management, senior managers do not need to become technological experts overnight but they do need to ensure that cyber risks are effectively identified, managed, mitigated, monitored and reported on within their firm's corporate governance framework. For some senior managers, cyber risk may be outside their comfort zone, however, not only does it need to be considered but there is also evidence that simple steps implemented rigorously can go a long way towards protecting a firm and its customers.

The Verizon 2016 Data Breach Investigations Report provided an analysis of 2,260 data breaches and 64,199 security incidents from 61 countries. It found that ten vulnerabilities accounted for 85% of successful breaches. As part of the analysis it was found that the vast majority of the vulnerabilities exploited in the attacks were not only well known, but had fixes available at the time of attack. Furthermore, some of the attacks used vulnerabilities for which a fix had been available for over a decade.

In October 2017, the Financial Stability Board reported on a workshop on cybersecurity held between public and private sector participants which noted that:

> 'effective cybersecurity requires a strategic, forward looking, fluid and proactive approach. They noted that it is not sufficient to simply look to past incidents and known risks, but that one must evaluate potential future threats. At the same time, participants stated that up to 90% of threats can be mitigated by basic cybersecurity hygiene.'

There are some basic measures which senior managers and their firms need to consider, and indeed can expect increasing levels of regulatory interest in the following:

- *What information needs protecting?* Risk, compliance and IT control infrastructures can only be designed to protect the processes and assets that are known. Everything from customer data to operational networks, the use of the cloud, systems (outsourced as well as in-house), links to payment infrastructures and exchanges to levels of user access to information need to be mapped and included in the governance infrastructure. Care should be taken to ensure that manual workarounds, often a legacy of as yet unintegrated businesses acquired, are not excluded. The process may be manual and therefore not cyber, but the human factor may well be the entry point into the firm's wider systems.

- *What are the risks to information or data held and how much risk is the firm willing to accept?* Financial services firms are used to the concept of risk appetites which should, as a matter of course, be extended to all information assets. It is key that all assessments keep pace with technological advances.

- *What measures are needed?* Governance, management information and reporting are not a 'one size fits all' and must reflect the precise nature and activities of the relevant firm. A number of bodies have produced lists of precautionary measures which for financial services firms could be applied as follows:

○ information risk management regime – establish an effective governance structure and determine an appropriate risk appetite, maintain the board's engagement with cyber risk and produce supporting information risk management policies;

○ home and mobile working – develop a mobile working policy and train staff to adhere to it, apply the secure baseline build to all devices and protect data both in transit and at rest;

○ user education and awareness – produce user security policies covering the acceptable and secure use of the firm's systems, establish a staff training program and maintain use awareness of cyber risks;

○ incident management – establish an incident response and disaster recovery capability, produce and critically test incident management plans and where needed include them in recovery and resolution planning or living wills;

○ managing user privileges – establish account management processes, monitor user activity, control access to activity and audit logs and ensure a robust removal of access as part of leaving process;

○ removable media controls – develop and implement a policy to control all access to removable media;

○ monitoring – establish a robust monitoring program using external expertise where needed, for example, by employing hackers to test system firewalls and other access controls;

○ secure configuration – ensure that security patches are applied in a timely manner and that the secure configuration of all relevant systems is maintained and evidenced;

○ malware protection – establish and maintain robust anti-malware defences and ensure continuous scanning for malware across the firm;

○ network security – protect networks against external and internal attack, manage the network perimeter and regularly monitor and test all security controls.

• *Do security measures work?* A fundamental part of cyber resilience is testing that the measures in place work. Whilst it is not necessarily for senior managers to undertake in person, senior managers do need to ensure that the effectiveness and adherence to the control infrastructure is robustly tested and any gaps or issues followed up. As has been shown numerous times with physical disaster recovery plans, they look fine on paper but do not work as designed in practice. Firms also need to consider what they would do if the worst occurred and they became the victim of a full-blown cyber-attack. Carefully thought through and tested incident management and contingency plans need to be agreed, pre-emptively, at the highest levels of the firm including communication protocols (to media, regulators and customers as well as other stakeholders) and the authority levels needed to invoke disaster or recovery plans (such as, say, the switching of operating systems to a secure back-up location). An inherent part of testing whether planned security measures work is the follow up investigation to assess any attack and the lessons to be learned.

Board responsibility

14.3   Cyber security has hit the headlines around the world with numerous big name firms, some financial services, but not all, being targeted with literally millions of customers potentially impacted. As regulators focus on the need for consistently good customer outcomes delivered by firms who have strong compliance cultures and a robust approach to conduct risk, cyber risks have rapidly arrived on firms' risk radars. Senior managers need to ensure that cyber risks are expressly included in the range of risks considered by firms and that the board is prepared to discuss the actions taken to ensure that all reasonable steps have been taken to embed cyber resilience throughout the firm.

> 'The ICO has promoted privacy by design for years, and there's plenty of guidance on our website. But in this context it means building data privacy and security into every part of your information processing, from the hardware and software to the procedures, guidelines, standards, and policies that your organisation has or should have.
>
> And remember: security is a boardroom-level issue. We have seen too many major breaches where companies process data in a technical context, but security gets precious little airtime at board meetings.
>
> If left solely to the technology teams, security will fail through lack of attention and investment. These companies may have the best policies in the world – but if those policies are not enforced, and personal data sits on unpatched systems with unmanaged levels of employee access, then a breach is just waiting to happen.'
>
> Source: Speech by Elizabeth Denham, UK Information Commissioner at the
> National Cyber Security Centre's CYBERUK 2018 event (April 2018)

Case study: Ransomware attacks and what to do about them

14.4   There are different types of ransomware all of which will seek to prevent a firm or an individual from using their IT systems and will ask for something (usually payment of a ransom) to be done before access will be restored. There is, of course, no guarantee that paying the fine or doing what the ransomware attacker demands will restore full access to all IT systems, data or files. All too many firms have found that critical files often containing client data have been encrypted as part of an attack and large amounts of money are demanded for restoration. Encryption is in this instance used as a weapon and it can be practically impossible to reverse-engineer the encryption or 'crack' the files without the original encryption key – which is deliberately withheld by the cyber attackers.

The UK data protection regulator, the Information Commissioner's Office (ICO), has put out extensive guidance on basic cybersecurity hygiene aimed at protecting businesses from ransomware attacks.

The ICO has suggested that firms make full use of the wide range of resources available on cyber resilience, IT security and protecting against malware attacks. Good advice on the general prevention of a ransomware attack is to seek to ensure company confidential, sensitive client or other important files are securely and regularly backed up in a remote, unconnected back-up or storage facility. As with other aspects of risk management and compliance the basics done consistently well will go a long way towards providing firms and their clients with a reasonable level of cyber resilience. Equally good advice if the firm has been a victim of a ransomware attack is to use all possible means to regain access to IT systems and client files as swiftly and cleanly as possible which may mean paying any ransom demanded as a matter of urgency. The follow-up action is then to learn all possible lessons to prevent a recurrence of the attack.

The specific recommendations from the ICO on preventing ransomware attacks include:

- Checking the firm has basic protection against malware and it is up to date – the ICO has referenced the National Cyber Security Centre guidance on steps to prevent malware attacks (at www.ncsc.gov.uk/guidance/10-steps-malware-prevention). In summary, the NCSC guidance is aimed at malicious software, or 'malware' as an umbrella term to cover any code or content that could have a malicious, undesirable impact on systems.

- Ensuring all devices have the latest necessary security patches.

- Removing unnecessary user accounts (such as guest and unnecessary administrator accounts) and restrict user privileges to only what is necessary.

- Removing or disabling unnecessary software to reduce the number of potential routes of entry available to ransomware.

- Segmenting the network so that if an attack does take place the damage suffered is limited.

- Importantly, back-ups need to be protected from also being encrypted – make sure the firm has an offline and offsite back-up.

- Training staff to recognise a ransomware attack if it does manage to get past the firm's anti-malware protection.

Recovery from a ransomware attack is just as important, with the ICO recommending that:

- The firm has an effective back-up policy and process in place and that it is working. In particular, can the firm be sure the back-up will not be encrypted in the event of a successful attack?

- Making sure the firm can recover from a ransomware attack by testing its back-ups regularly.

- Once any ransomware has been removed, ensure that a full security scan and penetration test of all systems and network is carried out – if attackers were able to get the ransomware onto the firm's systems, they may have gained other access that has not yet been detected.

Data protection

> **UK enforcement action against Royal & Sun Alliance**
>
> In January 2017, the ICO fined Royal & Sun Alliance Insurance (RSA) £150,000 for losing a device containing personal data sets with nearly 60,000 customer names, addresses, bank account and sort code numbers and 20,000 customer names, addresses and credit card numbers.
>
> It was found that a portable 'Network Attached Storage' device was taken offline and stolen by a member of staff or contractor who was permitted to access a data server room. The device held (among other things) personal data sets containing 59,592 customer names, addresses, bank account and sort code numbers and 20,000 customer names, addresses and credit card 'Primary Account Numbers'. However, it did not hold expiry dates or CVV numbers.
>
> As a result, the ICO deemed RSA to be in 'serious contravention' of the seventh data protection principle which states that: 'appropriate technical and organizational measures shall be taken against unauthorized or unlawful processing of personal data and against accidental loss or destruction of, or damage to, personal data'. Portable devices have a high risk of loss or theft and therefore firms must put adequate security measures to protect any personal data. The need for appropriate security measures is enhanced whenever financial information is concerned and RSA's customers had the right to expect that their information would be held securely. As the ICO stated 'for no good reason, RSA appears to have overlooked the need to ensure that it had robust measures in place despite having the financial and staffing resources available'.
>
> Source: https://ico.org.uk/media/action-weve-taken/
> mpns/1625635/mpn-royal-sun-alliance-20170110.pdf

14.5 An inherent part of the consideration of technology is a firm's approach to data protection which has come into sharp focus with the May 2018 deadline for the implementation of the General Data Protection Regulation (EU) 2016/679 (GDPR). The GDPR is an EU requirement with a deliberately global reach and takes the obligations and expectations regarding data protection, the associated licenses, security and management to the next level.

> 'Those organizations which thrive in the changing environment will be the ones that look at the handling of personal information with a mindset that appreciates what citizens and consumers want and expect. That means moving away from looking at data protection as a tick box compliance exercise, to making a commitment to manage data sensitively and ethically. When you commit, compliance will follow.'
>
> Source: Speech by Elizabeth Denham, UK Information Commissioner,
> at the Institute of Directors Digital Summit (October 2017)

The implementation of the GDPR has myriad ramifications, not least of which is the reinforced recognition that the ownership of personal data remains with the individual concerned and not with the data controllers or processors. The GDPR applies to all online interactions with EU citizens no matter where in the world the business is taking place, and it also has enhanced requirements regarding accountability and governance, consent, enshrines a 'right be forgotten' and introduces substantially higher penalties for breaches with fines up to the higher of £17m or 4% of a firm's global annual turnover. GDPR is one of the few pieces of EU legislation which will be unaffected by Brexit with the UK already stating its commitment to the new approach to data protection.

The focus on accountability and governance and the additional obligations and expectations placed on senior managers has not gone unnoticed. At the March 2018 Thomson Reuters London customer summit, delegates were asked how the focus on accountability and governance for data privacy is likely to impact the personal liability of senior managers: 64% responded that there will be a huge increase in personal liability post GDPR with a further 30% expecting a minor increase in personal liability.

'I have no intention of changing our proportionate and pragmatic approach after 25 May. My aim is to prevent harm, and to place support and compliance at the heart of our regulatory action. Voluntary compliance is the preferred route.

But we will back this up by tough action where necessary; hefty fines can and will be levied on those organisations that persistently, deliberately or negligently flout the law. Report to us, engage with us. Show us effective accountability measures. Doing so will be a factor when we consider any regulatory action.'

Source: Keynote speech by Elizabeth Denham, Information Commissioner, ICO at the IAPP Europe Data Protection Intensive 2018, London (April 2018)

The sheer sweep of the new requirements and the enhanced expectations was highlighted by the ICO's preparations for the GDPR and summarised by the pre-GDPR '12 steps to take now'.

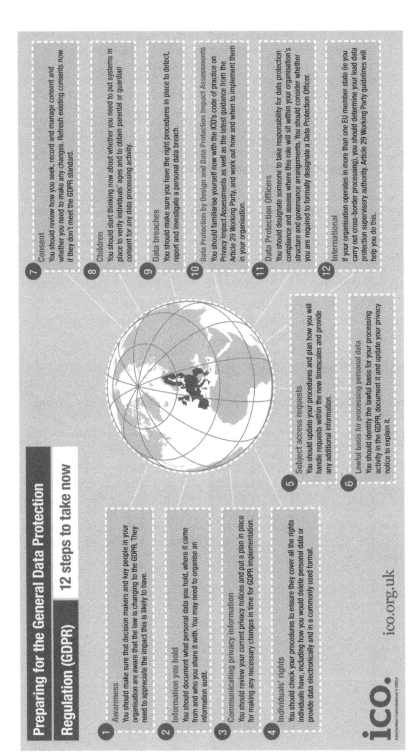

Source: UK Information Commissioner's Office, 'Guidance: Preparing for the General Data Protection Regulation' (https://ico.org.uk/media/for-organisations/documents/1624219/preparing-for-the-gdpr-12-steps.pdf)

> 'We want you to feel prepared, equipped and excited about the GDPR. I know many, many of you do. For those that still feel there is work to be done – and there are many of those too – I want to reassure you that there is no deadline.
>
> In fact, it's important that we all understand there is no deadline. 25 May is not the end. It is the beginning.'
>
> Source: Speech by Elizabeth Denham, Information Commissioner at the Data Protection Practitioners' Conference (April 2018)

Senior managers need to ensure that they have sufficient knowledge, awareness and understanding of how, in granular detail, the new data privacy requirements apply in their business. Specifically, senior managers need to be aware of the need to maintain up-to-date documentation on all aspects of data handling and to be prepared to share these with the ICO on request.

> **In February 2018 the FCA published an update on the GDPR:**
>
> 'Compliance with GDPR is now a board level responsibility, and firms must be able to produce evidence to demonstrate the steps that they have taken to comply. The requirement to treat customers fairly is also central to both data protection law and the current financial services regulatory framework. When the FCA makes rules, we take into account how our requirements will affect the privacy interests of individuals such as firms' customers and employees, and are open and transparent on why we have made rules in the way that we have.
>
> ....
>
> While the ICO will regulate the GDPR, complying with the GDPR requirements is also something the FCA will consider under their rules, for example, the requirements in the Senior Management Arrangements, Systems and Controls (SYSC) module. As part of their obligations under SYSC, firms should establish, maintain and improve appropriate technology and cyber resilience systems and controls.'

Nuisance calls

14.6   One area where senior managers will be held directly accountable for breaches is under the proposed changes to the nuisance calls regime, governed under the Privacy and Electronic Communications Regulation (PECR) and again regulated by the ICO.

As of summer 2018, the UK Government's Department for Digital, Culture, Media and Sport consulted on potential new rules in a document entitled 'Tackling nuisance calls and messages – Consultation on action against rogue directors' (https://assets.

publishing.service.gov.uk/government/uploads/system/uploads/attachment_data/file/711999/Nuisance_calls_and_texts_consultation__1_.pdf). The proposals, which closed for comments in August 2018, are aimed at introducing additional measures to curb 'those who intentionally and repeatedly flout the rules on nuisance calls'. The proposals had been expected for some time with the original announcement that the ICO would be given the power to fine directors individually up to £500,000 each for breaches of the PECR made in spring 2017.

The proposals are a further extension of the powers granted in April 2015 whereby the ICO was able to take wider action (with fines of up to £500,000) against firms found to have breached PECR rather than having to prove 'substantial' damage or distress.

The ICO has taken repeated enforcement action on nuisance calls. As part of one enforcement action taken in January 2018 in which a PPI claims firm was fined £350,000 for making 75 million nuisance calls, the ICO Enforcement Group Manager, Andy Curry, stated:

> 'The ICO will come down hard on rogue operators who want to treat the law and the UK public with contempt. We hope the Government will bring forward plans to introduce personal liability for directors as a matter of urgency, to stop them from escaping punishment after profiting from nuisance calls and texts. In the absence of a change in the law, the ICO will continue to face challenges in the recovery of penalties, and rogue directors will think they can get away with causing nuisance to members of the public.'

Given the plan to hold directors personally liable, senior managers need to track the progress of any updates. It would be a very rare firm that is not potentially caught by any new liability as PECR covers any electronic marketing messages whether by phone, fax, email or text.

Fintech, regtech and insurtech

14.7   The use of technology to enable the rapid and potentially disruptive development of new products and services has moved from a future concern to a current reality, with financial services firms across the spectrum now engaging with the potential opportunity to meet customers' needs (and indeed expectations) more efficiently and cheaply. Financial services firms and their senior managers have always not only embraced change, but also technological developments. The key difference with the current marketplace is the sheer pace and scale of that change.

There are no universally accepted definitions, but, at its simplest, fintech is an IT-enabled solution for the financial services industry.

The FSB's working definition of 'fintech' is:

> 'technologically enabled financial innovation that could result in new business models, applications, processes, or products with an associated material effect on financial markets and institutions and the provision of financial services'.

While the FCA has defined 'fintech' as:

'the intersection between finance and technology. It can refer to technical innovation applied in a traditional financial services context or to innovative financial services that disrupt the existing financial services market.'

It has further defined 'regtech' as the:

'sub-set of fintech that focuses on technologies that may facilitate the delivery of regulatory requirements more efficiently and effectively than existing capabilities.'

The International Association of Insurance Supervisors added to the developing lexicon in a March 2017 report on fintech developments in the insurance industry. The IAIS introduced the term 'insurtech' as a subset of fintech and defined it as:

'the variety of emerging technologies and innovative business models that have the potential to transform the insurance business.'

'London … has the most vibrant FinTech centre with revenues of £6.5 billion and employment of over 61,000, both of which are growing rapidly.'

Source: 'The high road to a responsible, open financial system', speech by Mark Carney, Governor of the Bank of England given at a Thomson Reuters Newsmaker (April 2017)

One area which remains under not only the regulatory but also the political spotlight is that of board and senior manager awareness of, and involvement in, technology. The scene was set by the January 2016 UK Treasury Committee response to a number of major bank IT system failures as part of which the Rt Hon Andrew Tyrie MP, then Chairman of the Treasury Committee, stated that:

'The current situation cannot be allowed to continue. IT risks need to be accorded the same status as credit, financial and conduct risk. They are every bit as serious a threat to customers and overall financial stability. More and higher quality investment is probably required.'

As a result, the Treasury Committee made three, what it has called, 'suggestions', which will, in effect, steer the future UK regulatory and supervisory approach to IT in financial services. In outline, the three suggestions are that:

- banks need greater IT expertise at main board and subsidiary board level;
- much greater resources should be put towards modernising, managing and securing banks' IT infrastructures;
- legal, regulatory, structural and cultural changes are needed in the way that banks manage their cyber security risks.

The PRA and FCA also outlined the six key themes arising from a review of critical infrastructure and technology resilience:

(1) Board accountability for critical infrastructure – several firms were found to not have a designated individual to oversee IT risk at board level.

(2) IT expertise on the board – in some firms, there was limited IT subject matter expertise on the board.

(3) Appreciation of conduct considerations within IT risk appetite statement needed to be improved.

(4) Maturity of three lines of defence model – IT risk management capabilities were found to be relatively immature across several firms. In particular, the FCA identified instances of inadequate delineation between the first and second line responsibilities, with substantial dependence on external consultancies to supplement second and third line capabilities. The FCA also observed that single points of failure and other risks inherent in IT architecture had been largely derived from external review, commissioned rather than through 'business as usual' risk assessments.

(5) Breath of IT resilience scenarios required improvement.

(6) A potential over-reliance on third party assurance.

'Regulation does not offer the answer to every fintech dilemma – yet it is certainly needed when distortions, excessive arbitrage, market abuse, and the risk of contagion pose a danger to consumers, investors and the broader financial system. Regulatory boundaries may need to be revised, given the cross-sector and cross-border growth of the crypto-asset sector – and that fact means that building a global consensus and consistent application of regulation is essential.'

Source: Remarks by Tobias Adrian, IMF Financial Counsellor and Director of the Monetary and Capital Markets Department, entitled 'Fintech – Building Trust Through Regulation' at the IMF Fintech Roundtable (April 2018)

To get the most out of fintech, senior managers need to understand the lifecycle of a solution. Senior managers need to be involved throughout in the evaluation of any and all technology solutions for their area of the business. Given that senior managers are responsible for continuing compliant activities, it follows that anything which may either aid compliance or have the potential to disrupt it should be carefully managed and evaluated.

Note that the diagram below is adapted from the lifecycle of a regtech solution in 'Fintech, regtech and the role of compliance' a special report from Thomson Reuters Regulatory Intelligence, also written by Stacey English and Susannah Hammond. The latest report can be downloaded from https://risk.thomsonreuters.com/en/resources/special-report/fintech-regtech-and-the-role-of-compliance-2017.html

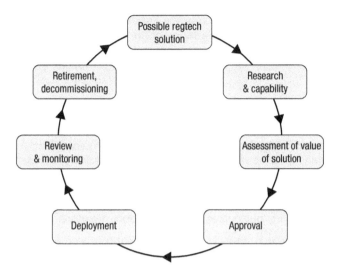

Source: Thomson Reuters Regulatory Intelligence – Fintech,
Regtech and the Role of Compliance 2017

Going around the lifecycle of a regtech solution:

- **Possible fintech or other solution**

  There are growing shopping lists of possible technological solutions for firms to choose from. One way of prioritising the range of solutions available may be to focus on the pinch points in existing business or compliance processes. This may include an easier way for customers to interface with the business, the need to speed up the full onboarding process for new clients, the ability to use 'big data' for business or compliance monitoring, the need to detect possible insider dealing or abuse of trading limits, the ability to evidence all elements of a discretionary sale or even to collate, assess and evidence the skills sets on corporate governance committees and the board.

- **Research and capability**

  Once a possible solution has been selected, due diligence will be needed to check the understanding of what it delivers, the assumptions in any data feeds, capture and processing, and its capacity to be integrated into the firm's existing systems (including the disaster recovery and business continuity plans). If the solution is to be provided by a third party (or even another group company), the due diligence protocols also need to include the usual steps for the assessment of a third-party outsourced provider. One practice step at this stage is to ensure all the research and due diligence is documented in detail, particularly with regard to the assumptions.

- **Assessment of value of solution**

  As with compliance, there is no 'one size fits all' approach to assessing the value of a solution. Unlike the implementation of regulatory change, which is compulsory, the evaluation of one solution over another (or to choose to

279

do nothing) is at the discretion of the firm. One good practice step is to seek to include the widest possible range of criteria to maximise the accuracy of the value proposition and any possible trade-offs. The costs, in terms of both money and other resources, of implementation, embedding and testing, are obvious for inclusion, as are any maintenance or upgrade costs.

Other elements to consider are: the value of any senior manager or compliance time potentially freed up; equally the additional need for senior manager care and attention during any transition or implementation period; the additional compliance or internal audit testing which may be required to ensure the efficacy of the solution; the need for additional skills and/or training; the use of an already crowded IT change schedule for implementation; the impact of any additional data protection, information security or other cyber risks; the need to change existing reporting to accommodate new information flows; and the need to add another third-party outsourcer to the compliance monitoring program.

As with the research stage, it is good practice to document the detail of the pros and cons considered as part of the assessment and the relative weighting given to each, and thereby support the final decision made. This is equally valuable if the decision is to do nothing and not invest in a solution, as the firm may be asked the question by its regulators as to why technology has not been employed.

- **Approval**

  Most firms have established approval processes involving sign-off by relevant stakeholders. Given the potentially hybrid nature of a fintech or regtech solution it may be that several different governance committees are involved in the sign-off and approval. Throughout the approval process, critical challenge needs to be in place to ensure all the potential additional risks are appropriately captured, measured and, where possible, offset. The approval process may also impose success criteria and stipulate the period in which, say, the risk committee will require a full review of the operational success (or otherwise) of the solution.

- **Deployment**

  The implementation and embedding of any solution is likely to be undertaken by the IT department within a firm, but it is critical that the relevant senior managers together with the compliance function have sufficient skill to engage with and, if need be, oversee the process. Firms may wish to consider 'parallel running' of existing protocols and any new solutions until they are satisfied with the operational results. This may be particularly useful if the solution relies on outsourced processing of data. Detailed records should be kept of the exact technical nature of the implementation process employed to allow for troubleshooting and any system or personnel changes.

- **Review and monitoring**

  As a matter of course, the efficacy of any solution deployed must be tested in and of itself. Wherever possible, testing should obtain independent third-party confirmation that the solution, system or process is operating as expected. Any discrepancies should be followed up as a matter of urgency and assessed to see if they provide indicators to any process or control issues or with the underlying data flow assumptions made. With many IT implementations there is a process of 'snagging' or 'user acceptance testing' whereby a series of small tweaks are made until the solution is operating as expected.

- **Retirement, decommissioning**

  As part of the overall planning and management process, firms should consider how the solution would be decommissioned. Particular care needs to be taken with any elements which have been outsourced to ensure, if required, an orderly and auditable return of data.

'To make things smoother – at least a bit – we need dialogue. Between experienced regulators and those regulators that are just beginning to tackle fintech. Between policymakers, investors, and financial services firms. And between countries.

Reaching across borders will be critical as the focus of regulation widens— from national entities to borderless activities, from your local bank branch to quantum-encrypted global transactions.'

Source: 'Central Banking and Fintech – A Brave New World?', speech by Christine Lagarde, IMF Managing Director at the Bank of England Conference (September 2017)

Senior managers should begin to see developing technological skills, knowledge and awareness as a core competency. Without a baseline of appropriate knowledge senior managers will struggle to be prepared to not only oversee the successful implementation of technological solutions to support business activities, but be unable to engage effectively with relevant regulators on the implications of all aspects of technology.

Checklist

14.8   The checklist below offers practical questions for senior managers to consider.

Checklist

- Are you confident you would know how to handle a ransomware attack on your business?

- Can you explain how the new data protection requirements apply in practice to your business activities?

- Have you built and maintained up-to-date skills to enable you to both understand and evaluate the ramifications of technological developments and possible solutions?

- Have you reviewed the process by which fintech or other technology solutions are evaluated for potential deployment?

Chapter 15

Overview of related global developments

Chapter summary

For some senior managers there is limited consideration needed of the regulatory regimes operating outside the UK. For others there may be a web of matrix management spanning the globe with the need to consider multiple regulatory regimes. It is a rare financial services firm that has no interaction with any entities or individuals outside of the UK and, as such, senior managers need to keep a weather eye on the expectations placed on senior managers in other jurisdictions.

This chapter is not a comprehensive look at all countries but a snapshot of some of the larger financial services regimes and covers:

- The accountability, governance and personal liability of senior managers

- The recent policy coming out of the FSB which is one of the bodies which sets the direction of regulatory change at a supranational level

The Financial Stability Board

15.1   In April 2018, the Financial Stability Board (FSB) published 'Strengthening Governance Frameworks to Mitigate Misconduct Risk: A Toolkit for Firms and Supervisors', a 'toolkit' for both firms and supervisors with the aim of strengthening governance frameworks to mitigate misconduct risk (available at www.fsb.org/wp-content/uploads/P200418.pdf). The toolkit, which is considered in more detail in **Chapter 9**, identifies 19 tools that firms and supervisors could use to address three overarching issues identified by the FSB as part of its earlier work on misconduct, namely:

- *Mitigating cultural drivers of misconduct* – including tools to effectively develop and communicate strategies for reducing misconduct in firms and for authorities to effectively supervise such approaches.

- *Strengthening individual responsibility and accountability* – including tools that seek to identify key responsibilities and functions in a firm and assign them to individuals to promote accountability and increase transparency.

283

- *Addressing the 'rolling bad apples' phenomenon* – including tools to improve interview processes and onboarding of new employees and for regular updates to background checks to avoid hiring individuals with a history of misconduct.

The toolkit is not guidance, but it does set the supranational benchmark for what and how jurisdictions, financial services regulators and firms could seek to mitigate persistent misconduct risk. A key thread throughout is the need for senior managers to be, and to be seen to be, accountable for their (in)actions.

Although the toolkit is a comprehensive set of suggestions, recommendations and options, it is a landmark publication and sets the benchmark for the consideration and management of governance, culture and (mis)conduct risk in financial services firms. The FSB's focus on misconduct has been driven by its sheer persistence in the marketplace. Specifically, misconduct may further indicate that firms are unable to get their employees to adhere to other standards, including those for sound risk management. Repeated and severe misconduct has implications for the financial system and has potential linkage to financial stability issues.

Many of the tools articulated are aimed at firms and what they could do to seek to improve their overarching governance frameworks and risk management. Of equal relevance are the tools aimed at national authorities which firms should also consider through the lens of how those suggestions may change the way they are supervised.

The FSB stops short of making definitive guidance that jurisdictions should introduce a responsibility and accountability regime for senior managers, but the implicit suggestion is there that national authorities could do worse than to consider a regime similar to the senior managers regime in the UK. Specifically, some of the additional detail is for jurisdictions to consider developing a responsibility and accountability framework that includes, inter alia:

- the identification of key responsibilities for individuals in the firm;
- allocation of those responsibilities to specific individuals; and/or
- holding individuals accountable for the responsibilities to which they have been assigned.

All of which will be very familiar to senior managers in UK financial services firms.

Asia

Hong Kong

'Under the Hong Kong MIC regime, firms are primarily required to identify those individuals in charge of core functions and map out their responsibilities and reporting lines. In other words, we are requiring firms to consider who is accountable for what within their firms to improve

> overall governance. This requirement would of course help enforcement identify responsible individuals when things go wrong. And you can assume that we will make use of this additional information to hold responsible individuals accountable.'
>
> Source: Speech by Thomas Atkinson, Executive Director, Enforcement Division, Hong Kong Securities and Futures Commission (October 2017)

15.2   Hong Kong operates a twin peaks regulatory system akin to that in the UK. The Hong Kong Monetary Authority (HKMA) and the Securities and Futures Commission (SFC) provide supervisory oversight of financial services activities in Hong Kong. Together they have a focus on the need for financial services firms to foster a sound corporate culture and to heighten their focus on governance and personal accountability.

The HKMA has sought to promote culture initiatives at banks, and it has supported supervisory initiatives that focus on risk culture and banking governance, culture and capacity building, and board of director empowerment. In March 2017, the HKMA issued guidance (at www.hkma.gov.hk/media/eng/doc/key-information/guidelines-and-circular/2017/20170302e2.pdf) on developing and promoting a sound corporate culture, emphasising that while there have been considerable efforts thus far, 'much more needs to be done'. The point was made that there is no 'one size fits all' approach to firm culture, but that a 'holistic and effective framework' should include what it labels as the 'three pillars' for promoting sound bank culture:

- governance;
- incentive systems; and
- assessment and feedback mechanisms.

The HKMA also outlined more specific factors to be considered. It requires banks to review their policies and procedures relevant to culture and to make any necessary enhancements within one year. While it does not go as far as to assign specific responsibilities to individuals under a UK-style accountability regime, the HKMA has advocated for the use of 'summary sheets' that make clear to staff the conduct that is expected of them.

In December 2016, the SFC implemented a 'Managers in Charge' (MIC) regime modelled on the UK's SMR (see 'Circular to Licensed Corporations Regarding Measures for Augmenting the Accountability of Senior Management' available at   www.sfc.hk/edistributionWeb/gateway/EN/circular/intermediaries/licensing/doc?refNo=16EC68). In so doing, it became the first Asian regulator to adopt a regime focusing on personal accountability. The SFC requires its licensed firms to identify the managers in charge for eight new core functions:

- Overall management oversight;
- Key business line;
- Operational control and review;

- Risk management;
- Finance and accounting;
- Information technology;
- Compliance;
- Anti-money laundering and counter-terrorist financing.

Further detail on the defined core functions can be found in Annex 1 and 2 to the December 2016 circular at www.sfc.hk/edistributionWeb/gateway/EN/circular/intermediaries/licensing/openAppendix?refNo=16EC68&appendix=0.

A key feature of the MIC regime is that a senior manager may live outside Hong Kong but can still be named as one of several MICs in charge of a core function. The MIC regime is designed to accommodate complex international matrix managed firms but senior managers not based in Hong Kong will still need to ensure they can comply, and evidence compliance with, all local regulatory requirements.

Singapore

'Clear accountability and proper conduct are important elements of good governance and sound business practice. Persistent misconduct and a lack of individual accountability by persons in charge will erode public confidence in our Financial Institutions (FIs). We expect the boards and senior management of FIs to instill a strong culture of responsibility and ethical conduct.'

Source: Mr Ong Chong Tee, Deputy Managing Director (Financial Supervision), Monetary Authority of Singapore (April 2018)

15.3   In April 2018, the Monetary Authority of Singapore (MAS) proposed guidelines to strengthen individual accountability of senior managers and raise standards of conduct in financial institutions (FIs). The guidelines are a key part of MAS's broader efforts to foster a culture of ethical behaviour and responsible risk-taking in the financial industry. The proposed guidelines set out the MAS's supervisory expectations of boards and senior management with respect to individual conduct and behaviours. They are not designed to be prescriptive. It is ultimately the responsibility of each FI to hold its senior managers accountable for their actions and ensure proper conduct amongst their employees.

The guidelines reinforce financial institutions' responsibilities in three key areas:

- *Promote individual accountability of senior managers* – FIs should identify senior managers who are responsible for core management functions and clearly specify their individual accountabilities. FIs should ensure that senior managers are fit and proper for their roles and hold them responsible for the actions of their staff and the conduct of the business under their purview. The FI's management structure and reporting relationships should be clear and transparent.

- *Strengthen oversight of employees in material risk functions* – FIs should identify employees who have the authority to make decisions or conduct activities that can significantly impact the FI's safety and soundness, or cause harm to a significant segment of the FI's customers or other stakeholders. FIs should ensure that such employees are fit and proper and are subject to an appropriate incentive structure and effective risk governance.

- *Embed standards of proper conduct among all employees* – FIs should have in place a framework that promotes and sustains the desired conduct among employees. The conduct framework should articulate the standards of conduct expected of all employees and be effectively communicated and enforced throughout the organisation. Policies and processes should be implemented to ensure regular monitoring and reporting of conduct issues to the board and senior management. There should also be appropriate incentive systems and effective feedback channels, such as whistleblowing mechanisms, in place.

The guidelines are designed to provide FIs with the operational flexibility to determine the most appropriate ways to achieve the desired outcomes of proper accountability and conduct. The MAS has made clear that it intends to monitor FIs' progress in implementing the guidelines through its regular supervisory engagements.

As of summer 2018, the MAS has not confirmed an implementation date for the proposed Guidelines on Individual Accountability and Conduct.

Australia

> 'Our regulatory system was not designed as a police state, and this is deliberate. Instead, our system was designed on the premise that participants should also do their part to ensure the system operates appropriately. I think "professionalism" is a good description of the role that is expected of participants.'
>
> Source: Speech by James Shipton, Chair of the Australian Securities
> & Investments Commission (ASIC) (April 2018)

15.4   Australia also operates a twin peaks regulatory approach with the Australian Prudential Regulatory Authority (APRA) and the Australian Securities and Investment Commission (ASIC) dividing up the regulation and supervision of financial services. While both APRA and ASIC have culture, conduct risk and the accountability of senior managers under review, the regulatory landscape in Australia is under critical scrutiny.

Widespread and persistent misconduct concerns led to the Royal Commission into misconduct in the banking, superannuation and financial services industry being established on 14 December 2017. The Commission will submit an interim report no later than 30 September 2018, and will provide a final report by 1 February 2019. The terms of reference for the Royal Commission can be found at https://financialservices.royalcommission.gov.au/Documents/Signed-Letters-Patent-Financial-Services-Royal-Commission.pdf.

Australia had already made substantive moves with regard to senior manager accountability with the Banking Executive Accountability Regime (BEAR) which came into effect in July 2018. The new regime has many of the hallmarks of the UK SMR and requires the registration of senior managers with APRA and introduces the need for responsibility mapping of roles and responsibilities. BEAR covers executives who have management or oversight functions as prescribed under the legislation or who otherwise have significant influence overall, or a material part of the bank's operation. The requirements also expressly cover non-executive directors.

BEAR will fundamentally extend APRA's ability to fine banks for misconduct, and to remove and disqualify the firms' board members and senior managers. APRA will also have stronger powers to review and adjust remuneration policies when it sees inappropriate outcomes. In April 2018, APRA published an Information Paper on 'Remuneration practices at large financial institutions' (available at www.apra.gov.au/sites/default/files/180328-Information-Paper-Remuneration-Practices.pdf). As part of its next steps, APRA concludes the paper:

> 'Ultimately, it remains the responsibility of boards and senior executives to ensure that the remuneration arrangements within their organisations are aligned with good risk management and long-term financial soundness. More needs to be done to achieve this outcome. While improvements to the regulatory framework will help provide a foundation for better remuneration structures that support and reinforce a strong risk culture within financial institutions, institutions should not wait for regulatory changes to address the scope for improvement that currently exist, nor regard the task as one of simply meeting minimum regulatory requirements.'

APRA Chairman, Wayne Byres discussed accountability in the financial sector and the implementation of the new Banking Executive Accountability Regime (BEAR). His comments included:

- The BEAR provides an important new framework for promoting stronger accountability in the banking sector, but more than the BEAR alone is needed. Financial institutions need to think beyond the necessities of BEAR if they wish to truly demonstrate accountability.

- The financial sector provides products which are, in many cases, not optional to consume, difficult to understand, and of great importance to an individual's overall financial well-being, now and into the future. That combination of compulsion, opacity and materiality generates, as a *quid pro quo*, a heightened expectation that financial institutions will exhibit high standards of behaviour in the way they operate.

- APRA ... has an interest in failings in governance, culture and accountability that indicate a lax attitude to risk-taking, which might ultimately impact the soundness of the financial institution itself (and thereby jeopardise the interests of depositors, policyholders and superannuation fund members).

- In many authorised deposit-taking institutions, there is often collective responsibility for various aspects of its business: for any given process or product, there are often hand-offs of responsibility (including, at times, to external partners and suppliers). But this creates the risk of collective responsibility leading to no individual accountability. Clarity of accountability – the foundation of the BEAR – goes to the heart of a strong risk culture.

- Organisational complexity and diffused responsibility have been at the heart of many of the issues that have damaged the standing of the banking industry in recent years. ... To the extent that BEAR provides a catalyst to untangle that complexity and provide clear accountability for putting things right, it can only be a good thing.

  Source: 'Beyond the BEAR Necessities', speech by Wayne Byres, Chairman of APRA (May 2018)

In its 2016–2017 plan, ASIC stated that it would integrate 'cultural indicators into our risk-based surveillances and use our findings to better understand how culture is driving conduct'. ASIC defines 'culture' as a set of shared values and assumptions within an organisation. It represents the 'unwritten rules' for how things really work.

To address cultural and conduct-related issues, it is imperative that ASIC-regulated firms focus first and foremost on setting the right tone from the top. It is also important to:

- cascade cultural values to the rest of the organisation;

- translate values into actual business practices; and

- ensure:

  - staff accountability;

  - effective communication and challenge;

  - recruitment, training and rewards; and

  - governance and controls.

ASIC has always looked at individual elements of culture such as remuneration, breach reporting and complaints handling. This helps the regulator to not only identify instances of misconduct, but also broader, more pervasive conduct problems. ASIC continues to undertake a suite of work in respect of culture and conduct in the markets area. In particular, it is reviewing attitudes to conduct risk, sound remuneration policies, management of confidential information and conflicts of interest, and supervisory frameworks and risk management. All of which are central to the governance and accountability expectations on senior managers.

Case study for compliance and prevention of money laundering breaches

15.5   The Commonwealth Bank of Australia (CBA) has become something of a cause célèbre in Australia and made headlines for numerous compliance and prevention of money laundering breaches.

Case study – CBA enforceable undertaking

In May 2018, the APRA released the final report of the prudential inquiry into CBA (at www.apra.gov.au/sites/default/files/CBA-Prudential-Inquiry_Final-Report_30042018.pdf).

The final report is comprehensive and contains a large number of findings and recommendations. It raised a number of matters of prudential concern which led to CBA offering an 'Enforceable Undertaking' under which CBA's remedial action in response to the report will be monitored (at www.apra.gov.au/sites/default/files/20180430-CBA-EU-Executed.pdf). APRA has also applied a AUS $1bn add-on to CBA's minimum capital requirement.

There was a key focus on senior managers' (in)ability to recognise, manage and mitigate the risks arising. The report stated:

'These risks were neither clearly understood nor owned, the frameworks for managing them were cumbersome and incomplete, and senior leadership was slow to recognise, and address, emerging threats to CBA's reputation. The consequences of this slowness were not grasped.'

Specifically, it was found that there was:

- inadequate oversight and challenge by the board and its committees of emerging non-financial risks;

- unclear accountabilities, starting with a lack of ownership of key risks at the executive committee level;

- weaknesses in how issues, incidents and risks were identified and escalated through the institution and a lack of urgency in their subsequent management and resolution;

- overly complex and bureaucratic decision-making processes that favoured collaboration over timely and effective outcomes and slowed the detection of risk failings;

- an operational risk management framework that worked better on paper than in practice, supported by an immature and under-resourced compliance function; and

- a remuneration framework that, at least until the AUSTRAC (the Australian Transaction Reports and Analysis Centre which is an Australian government financial intelligence agency set up to monitor financial transactions to identify money laundering, organised crime, tax evasion, welfare fraud

---

and terrorism) action, had little sting for senior managers and above when poor risk or customer outcomes materialised (and, until recently, provided incentives to staff that did not necessarily produce good customer outcomes).

The final report includes numerous recommendations for addressing these issues within CBA, focusing on five key levers:

- more rigorous board and executive committee level governance of non-financial risks;

- exacting accountability standards reinforced by remuneration practices;

- a substantial upgrading of the authority and capability of the operational risk management and compliance functions;

- injection into CBA's DNA of the 'should we' question in relation to all dealings with and decisions on customers; and

- cultural change that moves the dial from reactive and complacent to empowered, challenging and striving for best practice in risk identification and remediation.

APRA Chairman, Wayne Byres, said the Inquiry Panel's findings show CBA's governance, culture and accountability frameworks and practices are in need of considerable improvement.

It is a measure of how seriously the issues at CBA were viewed that it was made clear that given the nature of the issues identified in the report, all regulated financial institutions are expected to conduct a self-assessment to gauge whether similar issues might exist in their institutions. APRA supervisors will also be using the report to aid their supervision activities, and will expect institutions to be able to demonstrate how they have considered the issues within the report.

For the largest financial institutions, APRA will be seeking written assessments that have been reviewed and endorsed by their boards.

Europe

Holland

15.6   The financial services regulatory authorities in Holland have taken substantive policy steps towards addressing misconduct particularly in banks. The Dutch Central Bank (DNB) has put in place a supervisory framework for banks around behaviour and culture that is, by design, 'intrusive and decisive' in nature. The DNB has also sought to be forward looking in its supervisory approach considering that a focus on behaviour and culture, along with governance and integrity, and a financial institution's business models and strategies, provides a more forward-looking, and therefore more robust, model.

The Dutch have also taken the unique step of adopting a Bankers' Oath. In 2015, the Dutch Banking Code was revised to require about 90,000 Dutch bank employees to swear and sign an oath and adhere to a code of conduct or face disciplinary measures.

The Banker's Oath:

I swear / promise that, within the boundaries of my function in the banking sector, I will:

- Execute my function ethically and with care;

- Draw a careful balance between the interests of all parties associated with the business, being the customers, shareholders, employees and the society in which the business operates;

- When drawing that balance, making the customer's interests central;

- Will comply with the laws, regulations and codes that apply to me;

- Will keep confidential that which has been entrusted to me;

- Will not abuse my knowledge;

- Will act openly and accountably, knowing my responsibility to society;

- Will make every effort to improve and retain trust in the financial sector.

So help me God! / This I pledge and promise!

Republic of Ireland

'There are steps we can drive from the regulator's perch, in the face of concerns about culture, such as:

- Governance requirements around board-level awareness of ethical and cultural issues (including the establishment of a board standards sub-committee and a clearly defined role for internal audit in the review of culture).

- Providing feedback on what we see on inspections to build awareness in firms of the impact of, for example, their incentives policies.

- Requiring an increase in the formality of individual accountability at leadership level.'

Source: 'Transforming Culture in Regulated Financial Services in Ireland'
Martin Moloney, Special Advisor, Central Bank of Ireland (May 2018)

15.7   In line with regulators around the world, the Central Bank of Ireland (CBI) has been driving forward a suite of changes to seek to eradicate misconduct and the associated customer detriment. In January 2018, the CBI responded to the Law Reform Commission's Issues Paper on Regulatory Enforcement and Corporate Offences. The CBI's response set the updated the policy agenda for future regulatory reform together with some specific observations on criminal powers, individual responsibility for regulatory breaches and reckless decision making informed by recent enforcement actions.

The CBI has used its experience to respond to the issues paper, specifically the standardisation of regulatory powers, the use of civil financial sanctions, the coordination of regulators and jurisdiction for regulatory appeals. The response included a number of recommendations including:

- Reform strengthening the accountability of senior personnel in regulated entities should be adopted. Such reform would permit the CBI to require senior managers to submit a Statement of Responsibilities that clearly states the matters for which they are responsible and accountable. These requirements would assist in assigning responsibility to individuals in a regulatory context and decrease the ability of individuals to claim that the culpability for wrongdoing lay outside their sphere of responsibility.

- The extension of the period for which individuals can be suspended from senior positions in regulated firms as part of the fitness and probity regime.

- The legislative framework be strengthened to include a criminal offence of egregious recklessness by those in charge of financial firms that fail.

- The embedding of certain core common standards within a legislative framework. These standards would be used to guide regulated entities, and the individuals who exercise influence and authority over them, as to what is expected of them. Core standards can sit alongside prescriptive rules, and can be enforced where entities or individuals fall below them. Such core standards could include the requirement on entities and individuals that they conduct themselves with honesty and integrity, possess the competence and capability to conduct their business properly and cooperate with relevant regulatory authorities.

The CBI has also supported the creation of a dedicated division within an existing criminal agency to investigate white-collar crime which would allow for more effective investigation and prosecution of white-collar offences. In terms of a number of the other specific matters raised in the issues paper, the CBI:

- supports the enactment of a single act setting out the full suite of inspection and investigation powers of regulatory agencies;

- notes that, in its experience, civil financial sanctions act as a powerful deterrent to unlawful behaviour;

- supports measures designed to facilitate coordination and cooperation between regulators; and

- encourages the establishment of a specialised appeals body akin to the Competition Appeals Tribunal in the UK.

Overall, while acknowledging that any changes may be tempered by the European authorities, the blueprint for the next iteration of supervisory change in Ireland is taking shape. For senior individuals in firms, there are two major enhancements to their personal regulatory risk, one on fitness and probity and the other on individual responsibility.

Fitness and probity

15.8   As it currently stands, the CBI operates a fitness and probity regime as follows:

- a gatekeeper role which operates to prevent individuals from entering into senior positions in regulated firms;

- a standard setting role which imposes statutory standards of fitness and probity which individuals in the financial services industry are required to follow; and

- a supervisory role which allows the CBI to investigate, suspend, remove or prohibit individuals from senior positions in regulated firms.

The gatekeeper function of fitness and probity is seen as being 'robust and effective'. An example is given of fitness and/or probity concerns being raised by supervisors in relation to proposed appointments to certain pre-approval controlled functions following which the CBI prepared for 26 specific interviews (22 of which were conducted) with proposed appointees. Following contact from the CBI, ten proposed appointments were subsequently withdrawn and one proposed appointment was refused. The first prohibition notice and the first suspension notice in relation to individuals in controlled functions were issued in 2015.

In order to further enhance and strengthen the CBI's gatekeeper role, a power to publish the details of refusals to approve those who have applied to perform pre-approval controlled functions is seen as being of further assistance in protecting users of financial services. As part of a credible deterrent approach, transparency in regulatory outcomes plays a critical part in engendering confidence in the effectiveness of the regulatory system and demonstrating that the public are protected.

In addition, two further potential reforms are put forward:

- a broadening of the remit of the fitness and probity regime to include investigations into those individuals who performed controlled functions in the past. This would seek to ensure that the public were protected and that accountability lines are clear, and

- an extension to the current six-month time frame for suspending individuals under investigation. The potential intricacies of investigating in the financial services sector and the need for effective protection of the public justify an extension to the six-month time frame.

Individual responsibility

15.9   The CBI 'strongly recommends' that reforms to assign responsibility to senior personnel should be adopted and that such reforms 'should be modelled on the Senior Managers and Certification Regime in the UK'. The CBI noted that the Financial Conduct Authority has found the new approach 'effective' and that 'great benefit has been found in other jurisdictions in relation to the adoption of this policy'.

Such a reform would permit the CBI to require every senior manager to present a Statement of Responsibilities that clearly states the matters for which they are responsible and accountable. Firms could be obliged to provide maps setting out the responsibilities of their senior managers, and their management and governance arrangements. As already stated, it is believed that these requirements would assist in assigning responsibility to individuals in a regulatory context and decrease the ability of individuals to claim that the responsibility for wrongdoing lay outside their sphere of responsibility.

While the timescale has not been set, the direction of travel appears to be relatively clear with the CBI seeking changes, in particular how it can oversee the (in)actions and activities of senior managers with the aim of driving better, compliant and risk-aware behaviours.

Middle East

United Arab Emirates (UAE)

15.10   The UAE has set up a purpose built financial-free zone, the Dubai International Financial Centre (DIFC), with the Dubai Financial Services Authority (DFSA) as the independent regulator of financial services conducted in, or from, the DIFC. The DFSA is a full services regulator with a regulatory mandate that includes asset management, banking and credit services, securities, collective investment funds, custody and trust services, commodities futures trading, Islamic finance, insurance, an international equities exchange, and an international commodities derivatives exchange. In addition to regulating financial and ancillary services, the DFSA is responsible for supervising and enforcing anti-money laundering and counter-terrorist financing requirements in the DIFC.

The DFSA has established, and strives to maintain, an environment that fosters the DIFC guiding principles of integrity, transparency and efficiency. It has done so by embedding uncompromisingly high standards in a clear, succinct and flexible regulatory framework based on international best practices relevant to a modern international financial centre. The DFSA has a statutory obligation to pursue a number of objectives including the need to 'prevent, detect and restrain conduct that causes or may cause damage to the reputation of the DIFC or the financial services industry in the DIFC, through appropriate means including the imposition of sanctions'.

The approach to the imposition of sanctions applies equally to individuals as it does to firms.

Case study: Andrew Grimes – how not to be a SEO in the DIFC

In May 2018, the DFSA obtained a court judgment ordering the payment of a fine imposed on Andrew Grimes the previous year. Grimes, the former senior executive officer of Clements (Dubai) Limited, had been fined US$52,500 and banned from performing any function in connection with the provision of financial services in or from the DIFC.

The background to the Grimes case is intertwined with that of his former firm. In September 2016, the DFSA fined Clements (Dubai) Limited US$85,191, made up of US$17,191 disgorgement of benefit and a penalty amount of US$68,000. Clements agreed to settle at an early stage of the investigation without which the total fine would have been US$102,191.

The underlying facts of the two enforcement actions are the same. The DFSA's investigation into Clements was conducted in collaboration with the Insurance Authority of the United Arab Emirates and arose after Clements self-reported the breach. The investigation found that, from January 2014 to July 2014, Clements engaged in prohibited insurance activities in breach of DFSA-administered rules. As an insurance intermediary in the DIFC, Clements is restricted from acting in relation to a contract of insurance for a risk situated in the UAE, unless the risk is situated in the DIFC or the contract is one of re-insurance. In contravention of the restriction, Clements intermediated 21 contracts of insurance for customers with risks situated in the UAE but outside the DIFC.

The DFSA found that Clements operated its business in such a way that allowed prohibited insurance intermediation activities to occur and it failed to have in place adequate systems and controls to detect, monitor and prevent such Insurance Intermediation activities from occurring. In addition, Clements did not classify its customers, provide key information, enter into client agreements, conduct anti-money laundering customer risk assessments or undertake customer due diligence for its customers as required under the relevant DFSA Rules.

Specifically, Clements was deemed to have breached:

• Principle 2 – due skill, care and diligence – in that it failed to conduct its business activities with due skill, care and diligence; and

• Principle 3 – management, systems and controls – in that it failed to ensure that its affairs were managed effectively and responsibly and did not have adequate systems and controls to ensure, as far is reasonably practicable, that it complied with legislation applicable in the DIFC.

The DFSA made a point of crediting Clements' initiative to self-report the misconduct, taking steps to remediate its deficiencies and cooperating fully with the investigation. The DFSA also noted that Clements voluntarily

---

appointed a new senior executive officer together with a compliance and money-laundering reporting officer.

Andrew Grimes was the previous SEO, and in addition to being the most senior authorised individual at Clements, was found to have presided, in person, over the breaches despite being aware of all the relevant compliance obligations. Grimes compounded his own accountability by deliberately misleading the DFSA. No regulator has any tolerance for being misled and Grimes' actions were a direct contributory factor in his being banned. Grimes' fitness and propriety were called into serious question given he failed to be candid and truthful with the DFSA and although he is no longer working in financial services in the DIFC, the DFSA:

'... considers the Restriction appropriate to protect direct and indirect users and prospective users of the financial services industry in the DIFC should Mr Grimes seek to perform any functions in connection with the provision of Financial Services (eg by seeking employment with an authorised firm to perform such functions) in the DIFC in the future.'

For firms and senior managers seeking to learn the lessons from the sanctions imposed, the two enforcement actions and the following court case surrounding Grimes are a study in the contrast between cooperating with a regulator and misleading it. On the one hand, Clements itself chose to remediate the breaches and changed key personnel and although there is the potential for negative publicity from the enforcement action, its response should be seen as good practice for other firms who find themselves in breach of their regulatory requirements. The DFSA was explicit about taking into consideration the range of mitigating factors in determining the sanctions in the Clements case.

By way of complete contrast, Grimes knowingly engaged in non-compliant behaviour and then lied about it to the DFSA. The enforcement decision notice sets out the compliance training, notifications and advice received by Grimes and the fact that he had signed to confirm he had read and understood the firm's compliance manual. The sense is given that once the nature of Grimes' misconduct came to light he was exited from Clements who then sought to rebuild regulatory relations with the DFSA by, in part, cooperating fully with the investigation.

Grimes has then further compounded his misdeeds by failing to pay the fine to the DFSA. The DFSA is committed to credible deterrence in terms of enforcement action and a failure to pay a regulatory fine was never going to pass unchallenged. Grimes was already banned from financial services in the DIFC and his repeated failure to show any kind of compliant behaviour has made his chances of ever working in financial services anywhere in the world vanishingly small.

The contrast between the approach taken by Clements on the one hand and Grimes on the other is crystal clear. Equally clear is the difference in the response of the DFSA. Misleading the regulator is never a good idea and the DFSA's irritation for having been lied to by Grimes is a thread throughout the original decision notice. Misleading the regulator simply makes matters worse when the deception is exposed. It also makes the consequences of the breach potentially significantly worse as Grimes has found to his cost with both a fine and a ban. Indeed, the Grimes' case would make a useful example in compliance training on not only the responsibilities of senior authorised individuals, but also the personal liability associated with deliberate wrongdoing and, in particular, misleading the regulator.

On the flip side, the DFSA has made clear in the Clements case its appreciation for firms who are seen to take their regulatory obligations seriously and who engage promptly and positively with the regulator when an issue is found.

North America

Canada

'Many boards have improved their own self-governance. Yet there is more to be done. We have raised awareness of the importance of financial industry and risk management expertise on boards, and most boards have responded. Better still would be for boards to be more assiduous about assessing how their own requirements for different skills and experience have changed. Boards need to regularly take stock of industry developments and identify if the required expertise and knowledge is available on the board.

....

A board that does not have the requisite expertise, or is unwilling, to task senior management to provide it with suitably focused material is undermining its own effectiveness. There is clearly a risk that a board that allows itself to be immersed in overly detailed or sometimes inconsequential information will lose sight of important prudential risks.

Moreover, if the board cannot successfully assert itself with senior management on an issue as apparent and recurring as the volume of material that senior management provides the board, we have to wonder where else the board may be failing to gain traction with senior management.'

Source: 'Enabling More Effective Governance of Canadian Financial Institutions' – Remarks by Superintendent Jeremy Rudin, Office of the Superintendent of Financial Institutions (June 2016)

15.11 The Canadian regulatory approach is very much a top-down one with the focus on boards to ensure that there are consistently compliant behaviours throughout their firm. The Office of the Superintendent of Financial Institutions has enshrined this approach in the guidance on corporate governance which covers the role of the board of directors, risk governance and the role of the audit committee. In terms of the role of the board of directors, the board is seen as playing a 'pivotal role' in the success of a firm through the approval of the overall strategy and risk appetite together with oversight of the firm's senior managers and internal controls.

Specific expected board responsibilities are split into two – those requiring board approval and those which require review and discussion. The primary functions of a board are those which require approval and are therefore considered to be the main focus of the board's attention and activities, including:

• short-term and long-term enterprise-wide business objectives, strategy and plans (capital, financial, liquidity), including the risk appetite framework;

• significant strategic initiatives or transactions, such as mergers and acquisitions;

• internal control framework;

• appointment, performance review and compensation of the CEO and, where appropriate, other senior managers, including the heads of the oversight functions;

• succession plans with respect to the board, CEO and, where appropriate, other senior managers, including the heads of the oversight functions;

• mandate, resources and budgets for the oversight functions; and

• external audit plan, including audit fees and the scope of the audit engagement.

Those functions which are deemed the responsibility of senior managers are subject to 'thorough review and discussion' by the board which has a critical role in providing high-level guidance. The board should understand the decisions, plans and policies being undertaken by senior managers and their potential impact on the firm. It should probe, question and seek assurances from senior managers that these are consistent with the board-approved strategy and risk appetite, and that the corresponding internal controls are sound and implemented in an effective manner. The board should establish processes to periodically assess the assurances provided to it by senior managers. The matters considered in the continuing detailed day-to-day responsibility of senior managers but subject to review and discussion by the board include:

• significant operational and business policies;

• business and financial performance relative to the board-approved strategy and risk appetite framework;

• compensation policy for all human resources, to be consistent with FSB Principles for Sound Compensation and related Implementation Standards;

• implementation of internal controls, including their effectiveness;

• organisational structure; and

• compliance with applicable laws, regulations and guidelines.

USA

> 'Culture is often viewed as a "soft" topic, but I would disagree. The financial penalties associated with misconduct are anything but soft – with bank fines since the crisis estimated at more than $320 billion as of year-end 2016. The hit to a bank's reputation from misconduct can also be quantified through, for example, the associated impact on its share price or funding costs. Culture should be about concrete incentives and behaviors that help achieve specific goals, implying that it should not be viewed as a "soft" issue.'
>
> Source: William C Dudley, President and Chief Executive Officer
> of the Federal Reserve Bank of New York (March 2018)

15.12   Unlike many countries around the world, the US has not considered introducing a personal accountability regime in the same vein as the UK SMR. What the US regulators have done is to seek to drive cultural reform, and thereby a reduction in misconduct by senior managers, through industry-led initiatives primarily focused on corporate governance and incentive changes.

The US has a patchwork quilt of regulators which are, as of summer 2018, still in a state of transition under the Trump Administration. The Federal Reserve has had a focus on culture and (mis)conduct risk under its president and CEO William Dudley who made the overt connection between (poor) bank culture and conduct and systemic financial stability.

Conclusion from Federal Reserve Bank of New York white paper –'Misconduct Risk, Culture, and Supervision', December 2017

Bank supervisors and regulators promote the sustainable provision of financial products and services to the economy over time. This can be disrupted by employee misconduct, which hurts individual firms by diverting resources and attention, hurting reputations, and depleting their equity capital through large fines. Moreover, misconduct can hurt the industry more broadly by decreasing trust and confidence in the financial sector. As a result, supervisors have been increasing their focus on this critical area and working to promote appropriate investments in cultural capital that can mitigate misconduct risk. Supervisors should also recognise that the same underlying cultural dynamics that drive misconduct risk may also drive other equally consequential outcomes related to different risks and business decisions. Firms with a stronger culture may not only face lower misconduct risk, but may also exhibit greater resilience overall, higher customer satisfaction, better employee morale and well-being, and enhanced productivity over the long term. These benefits certainly accrue to the firm, and would likely also benefit the broader financial system and economy.

The Federal Reserve's shift in focus has expanded its supervisory approach to consider corporate governance and culture issues and to enhance its engagement with boards and senior managers at banks.

The Office of the Comptroller of the Currency (OCC) is the primary federal supervisor of many large US banks. The OCC's regulatory approach has evolved post financial crisis to include required standards for banks' risk governance frameworks and the responsibility of the board of directors to provide effective oversight. The expectations include the need for a risk appetite statement which articulates the risk culture of the firm together with its core values, the roles and responsibilities of the board and senior managers.

The US Securities and Exchange Commission also has a focus on culture and has set out its expectations with regard to a top-down approach to compliance and compliant behaviours. The identification and sanctioning of 'bad actors' and the need for individual accountability are hallmarks of the SEC stated approach.

> 'By being smart and resourceful in the Cyber arena, we hope to discourage misconduct before it takes root. And in a world of finite resources, it is imperative that enforcement actions advance goals of specific and general deterrence.
>
> One of the primary ways we do that is with a focus on identifying and charging culpable individuals. Bad actors undermine the hard-earned trust essential to the health and stability of our capital markets. I view individual accountability as perhaps the most effective general deterrent tool in our arsenal, because it can have a broad effect on corporate culture in a way that immeasurably benefits individual investors, preventing misconduct before it starts.'
>
> Source: Steven Peikin, Co-Director, Division of Enforcement at the US Securities and Exchange Commission (SEC). Keynote address to the UJA Federation, New York (May 2018)

FINRA's assessment of firm culture

15.13 The Financial Industry Regulatory Authority (FINRA) has formalised its assessment of firm culture, which it defined as 'the set of explicit and implicit norms, practices and expected behaviours that influence how employees make and carry out decisions in the course of conducting the firm's business'. In February 2016, FINRA took the assessment of culture and the role of senior managers a step further by undertaking a wide-ranging review in which it met with executive business, compliance, legal and risk management staff to discuss cultural values. In preparation for the meetings, FINRA asked for the following information, which gives an indication of the detailed nature of its focus.

FINRA's request for information:

(1) A summary of the key policies and processes by which the firm establishes cultural values. In the summary, include whether this is a board-level function at your broker-dealer or at the corporate parent of the firm. If it is a board-level function, describe the board's involvement. Also, provide a description of any steps you have initiated or completed in the past 24 months to promote, strengthen or change your firm's culture.

(2) A description of the processes employed by executive management, business unit leaders and control functions in establishing, communicating and implementing your firm's cultural values. Include a description of how executive management communicates, promotes and establishes a 'tone from the top' as it relates to cultural values (to the extent not covered by the previous question). Include a description of the firm's approach to ensure that its cultural values are adopted and applied by middle management.

(3) A description of how your firm assesses and measures the impact of cultural values (to the extent assessments and measures exist) and whether they have made a difference at your firm in achieving desired behaviours. Provide a summary of the policy statements, procedures, mission statements or other related documents that reflect your firm's assessments and measures.

(4) A summary of the processes your firm uses to identify policy breaches, including the types of reports or other documents your firm relies on, in determining whether a breach of its cultural values has occurred. Please focus your summary on those activities your firm considers to be directly related to reinforcing its culture.

(5) A description of how your firm addresses cultural value policy or process breaches once discovered. What efforts are used to promptly address these policy or process breaches? What is the escalation process to surface and resolve such breaches?

(6) A description of your firm's policies and processes, if any, to identify and address subcultures within the firm that may depart from or undermine the cultural values articulated by your board and senior management?

(7) A description of your firm's compensation practices and how they reinforce your firm's cultural values.

(8) A description of the cultural value criteria used to determine promotions, compensation or other rewards. Describe opportunities for promotion to the managing director or equivalent level available to personnel of your compliance, legal, risk and internal audit functions.

The aims of the review were to help FINRA to not only understand firms' practices, and the challenges they face, but to also help it develop potential guidance for the industry and determine other steps that could be taken. As of summer 2018, FINRA has not published a follow up to the review or anything further on culture and the associated role of senior managers.

Commodity Futures Trading Commission (CFTC) which seeks to ensure the integrity of the futures and swaps markets has put an emphasis on senior managers both self-reporting breaches and cooperating fully with any resulting investigation. In January 2017, the CFTC issued a pair of enforcement advisories (one aimed at firms and the other at individuals) designed to improve the quality and effectiveness of the cooperation the regulator receives. As a result, the enforcement division of the CFTC may, at its discretion, consider the following factors, over and above mere compliance with the law, in assessing whether a company's or individual's cooperation warrants credit:

- the value of the cooperation to the division's investigation(s) and enforcement action(s);

- the value of the cooperation to the CFTC's broader law enforcement interests;

- the culpability of the company or individual and other relevant factors; and

- uncooperative conduct that offsets or limits credit that the company or individual would otherwise receive.

The overall stance being that if senior managers identify, self-report and cooperate with regard to breaches then the sanction may well be lighter and more quickly settled.

Checklist

15.14 The checklist below offers practical questions for senior managers to consider.

Checklist

- Do you have clear line of sight to any and all international regulatory requirements which may apply to the business activities under your control?

- Are you satisfied with your firm's ability to track and assess the impact of all relevant global regulatory changes? And do you receive a regular update on all relevant regulatory change both domestic and international?

- Where you, as a senior manager, have responsibilities and obligations in jurisdictions outside the UK, do you have sufficient detail on what 'good' looks like in the discharge of those overseas requirements?

- When your firm is considering business in overseas jurisdictions, are the senior manager obligations and associated potential personal liability routinely considered as part of the decision-making process?

Appendix 1

Full timeline

The following outlines key events and developments as they have continuously unfolded over the decade.

The financial crisis

Late July/early August 2007: The credit crunch begins as banks begin to stop lending to each other due to fears over exposure to potential losses on high-risk US mortgages.

13 September 2007: The news that Northern Rock has sought emergency funding from the Bank of England sparks fears that it will shortly go bankrupt. Customers queue to withdraw savings causing the first run on a bank for 150 years.

17 February 2008: The UK Government announces that Northern Rock is to be temporarily nationalised.

14 March 2008: The investment bank, Bear Stearns, is bought out by JP Morgan.

14 July 2008: US authorities step in to assist America's two largest lenders, Fannie Mae and Freddie Mac, owners or guarantors of $5 trillion worth of home loans.

15 September 2008: American bank, Lehman Brothers, files for bankruptcy protection due to heavy exposure to the sub-prime mortgage market, creating global financial panic. Another US bank, Merrill Lynch, is taken over by the Bank of America.

17 September 2008: Lloyds TSB announces a £12bn deal to take over Britain's biggest mortgage lender, HBOS, after a run on its shares.

29 September 2008: The Government takes control of Bradford & Bingley's £50bn of mortgages and loans. Savings operations and branches are sold to Spain's Santander.

6 October 2008: Trading is suspended in several Icelandic banks. The Icelandic Government takes control of Landsbanki, the country's second largest bank.

Appendix 1 *Full timeline*

8 October 2008: The UK Government unveils an unprecedented £500bn rescue package for the banking industry including – £50bn to part-nationalise major UK banks, £200bn into a Special Liquidity Scheme and a further £250bn under a debt guarantee scheme.

13 October 2008: The Government announces a £37bn rescue package for RBS, Lloyds TSB and HBOS.

20 November 2008: The International Monetary Fund approves its first loan for a western European nation since 1976 with a £1.4bn loan for Iceland following the collapse of its banking system.

29 November 2008: The UK Government takes majority ownership of RBS. Its Chief Executive, Sir Fred Goodwin, steps down.

15 January 2009: The Irish Government announces it will nationalise the Anglo Irish Bank.

16 January 2009: The US Government provides the Bank of America with another $20bn dollars to help it with the losses incurred when it bought Merrill Lynch.

11 February 2009: The Irish Government announces it will inject €7bn into Bank of Ireland and Allied Irish in return for guarantees on lending, executive pay and mortgage arrears.

26 February 2009: RBS reports a loss of £24.1bn for 2008 – the biggest loss in British corporate history.

9 March 2009: The Tripartite review Preliminary Report is published which reviews the UK's Tripartite regulatory structure in relation to financial stability, requested by the Shadow Chancellor.

13 April 2010: The FSA fined and banned the former Northern Rock Deputy Chief Executive and Credit Director for concealing the scale of bad debts in the years before its nationalisation, followed by the former Finance Director in July.

16 April 2010: The Securities and Exchange Commission accuses Goldman of defrauding investors of more than $1bn through mis-marketing toxic sub-prime mortgage-related securities.

The reviews

16 June 2010: The UK Chancellor announces a review of the UK banking industry in his Mansion House speech by an independent commission chaired by Sir John Vickers and his intention to reform the UK regulatory system and replace the tripartite system made up of the Bank of England, HM Treasury and the Financial Services Authority.

24 September 2010: The Independent Commission on Banking (known as the Vickers' Commission) publishes initial thoughts in an issues paper.

12 April 2011: The Independent Commission on Banking publishes an interim report including proposals on ring-fencing.

13 September 2011: The Independent Commission on Banking publishes its final report – 'Changing banking for good'.

6 December 2011: The FSA publishes a report on the failure of the Royal Bank of Scotland, where it could not hold any senior executives to account.

The LIBOR scandal becomes public

27 June 2012: Manipulation of the London Interbank Offered Rate (LIBOR), a key interest rate which influences the cost of loans and mortgages, became public with the first fine against Barclays.

Reviews and recommendations

2 July 2012: The UK Chancellor announces action in response to the LIBOR scandal including the setting up of the Wheatley Committee to undertake a review of the structure and governance of LIBOR and determine legal reforms to incorporate into the Financial Services Bill.

5 July 2012: The House of Commons announces the establishment of the Parliamentary Commission on Banking Standards to review and report on professional standards and culture within banking, the lessons to be learned about corporate governance, transparency and conflicts of interest and recommend legislative and other action.

28 September 2012: The Wheatley Review publishes its final report, 'The Wheatley Review of LIBOR', following a discussion paper published on 10 August.

28 November 2012: The UK Government launches its public consultation on the regulation of LIBOR.

21 December 2012: The Parliamentary Commission on Banking Standards publishes its first report focused largely on the structural ring-fencing proposed by the Vickers Commission.

16 January 2013: The FCA publishes guidance on managing the risks and governance of incentive schemes and features that increase the risk of mis-selling.

New regulatory structure

1 April 2013: The new regulatory structures take effect with three new bodies: The Financial Policy Committee, The Prudential Regulation Authority (PRA) and the Financial Conduct Authority (FCA).

5 April 2013: The Parliamentary Commission on Banking Standards publishes a report on the collapse of Halifax Bank of Scotland (HBOS): 'An accident waiting to happen: The failure of HBOS', which informs the recommendations in their final report.

19 June 2013: The Parliamentary Commission on Banking Standards publishes its final report also called 'Changing Banking for Good', proposing a new framework for individuals including making senior individuals more accountable for their responsibilities.

14 February 2014: The Banking Standards Review consults on the scope, make-up and purpose of a new banking standards body to be set up following recommendations made by the Parliamentary Commission on Banking Standards.

12 June 2014: The Fair and Effective Markets Review is launched by the Chancellor and the Governor of the Bank of England to reinforce confidence in the wholesale Fixed Income, Currency and Commodities (FICC) markets following serious misconduct and to influence the international debate on trading practices.

1 July 2014: The PRA and the FCA issue joint proposals on 'Strengthening the alignment of risk and reward: new remuneration rules' to amend the Remuneration Code in areas considered weak from a risk/reward perspective and address recommendations from the Parliamentary Committee on Banking Standards.

Industry consultation on new accountability regime

30 July 2014: The FCA and PRA consult on proposals for the new Senior Managers Regime (SMR), Certification Regime and new Conduct Rules for UK banks, building societies, credit unions and PRA designated investment firms.

23 February 2015: The FCA and PRA consult on a revised approach to the approach of the new rules in relation to Non-Executive Directors in banking and Solvency II firms and the application of the presumption of responsibility to senior managers in banking firms.

23 February 2015: The FCA and PRA propose a package of measure to formalise firms' whistleblowing procedures with the aim to ensure that all employees are encouraged to blow the whistle where they suspect misconduct, with confidence that their concerns will be considered and they will not personally suffer as a consequence.

16 March 2015: The FCA provides feedback on the proposed regime, sets out near final rules and consults on guidance on the presumption of responsibility.

16 March 2015: Joint PRA and FCA consultation on the application of the regime to UK branches of third country banks.

23 March 2015: The PRA publishes a policy statement setting out the first set of final PRA rules to implement the SMR and Certification Regime for UK deposit-takers and PRA-designated investment firms and the Senior Insurance Managers Regime (SIMR) for Solvency II insurers.

25 March 2015: The PRA publishes a policy statement setting out near final rules and supervisory statements relating to the implementation of ring-fencing covering the legal structure, governance and the continuity of services and facilities.

10 June 2015: The Fair and Effective Markets Review publishes its final report, providing an analysis of the root causes of misconduct and other sources of perceived unfairness in FICC markets and evaluating the impact of the significant reforms. Recommendations were based on key principles to raise conduct standards including: individuals active in FICC markets should be more accountable for their actions; the UK authorities should extend the regulatory perimeter, broaden the regime to hold senior management to account and toughen sanctions against misconduct.

23 June 2015: The PRA and the FCA publishes new remuneration rules including changes to deferral and clawback of bonuses. The new framework aims to further align risk and individual reward in the banking sector to discourage irresponsible risk-taking and short-termism.

7 July 2015: The FCA publishes final rules on the Individual Accountability Regime and consults on extending the Certification Regime to wholesale market activities.

3 August 2015: Ex-UBS and Citigroup trader, Tom Hayes, sentenced to 14 years in prison after being found guilty of conspiring to rig Libor benchmark interest rates following a seven-year investigation. During his trial he said managers were aware of, and condoned, the trading methods which were common industry practice.

13 August 2015: The FCA publishes near final rules on the application of the new regime to UK branches of EEA and non-EEA banks. The PRA sets out final and near final rules on the application of the new regime to UK branches of non-EEA banks.

6 October 2015: The PRA consults on regulatory references following further recommendations from the Fair and Effective Markets Review (FEMR) in 2015 that 'the FCA and the PRA should consult on a mandatory form for regulatory references, to help firms prevent the "recycling" of individuals with poor conduct records between firms…'.

6 October 2015: The FCA publishes rules on whistleblowing in deposit-takers, PRA designated investment firms and insurers. The PRA publishes rules on whistleblowing in deposit takers, PRA-designated investment firms and insurers along with guidance on compliance with the rules.

15 October 2015: The UK Government publishes proposals and measures in the Bank of England and Financial Services Bill to extend the SM&CR to all sectors of the financial services industry and introduce a 'duty of responsibility', superseding the 'reverse burden of proof' in earlier SM&CR proposals for the banking sector.

9 December 2015: The FCA sets out amendments to the Decision Procedure and Penalties Manual and the Enforcement Guide.

16 December 2015: The FCA publishes final rules relating to UK branches of foreign banks. The PRA publishes final rules relating to UK branches of non-EEA banks.

1 January 2016: Aspects of the SIMR come into force on 1 January 2016 to align with Solvency II including: the requirement for firms to ensure all persons performing a key function are fit and proper, identification of key functions and compilation of a Governance Map.

6 January 2016: The FCA consults on implementing changes to rules following removal of the requirement to report known or suspected breaches of the Conduct Rules.

6 January 2016: The PRA consults on implementing changes to rules following removal of the requirement to report known or suspected breaches of the Conduct Rules.

15 January 2016: The PRA banned the former Chief Executive and former Managing Director of the Co-operative Bank from holding senior banking positions due to their role at the lender which came close to collapse.

4 February 2016: The FCA sets out final rules on extending the Certification Regime to wholesale market activities and interim rules on referencing.

The new Senior Managers Regime takes effect

7 March 2016: The Senior Managers Regime takes effect for banks. The requirement to assign responsibilities to a whistleblowers' champion takes effect.

7 September 2016: The FCA whistleblowing requirements take effect.

28 September 2016: The PRA proposes amendments and optimisations to the SM&CR and SIMR including making a specific individual responsible for ensuring the operational continuity and resilience of internal operations, systems and technology.

28 September 2016: The FCA and PRA publish their final rules on regulatory references.

1 September 2016: The FCA sets out proposals to extend the application of its Code of Conduct Sourcebook (COCON) to standard non-executive directors (NEDs), ie those without a designated responsibility and outside of the SMR, following changes to the Bank of England and Financial Services Act 2016 and new power for the regulators to apply individual rules of conduct to all directors.

3 May 2017: The FCA introduces final rules to extend its Code of Conduct Sourcebook to standard non-executive directors to help raise standards of conduct and reduce the risk of future misconduct and mis-selling in firms.

3 May 2017: The FCA publishes guidance on how it will enforce the 'duty of responsibility' and setting out how a senior manager may be held accountable for a firm's contravention of a regulatory requirement.

13 June 2017: The FCA publishes optimisations/expansion to the SIMR bringing the regime more closely in line with the SMR and including creating new Senior Insurance Management functions and Prescribed Responsibilities.

Extending the Senior Managers Regime to all firms

26 July 2017: The FCA and PRA publishes proposals on extending the SM&CR to insurers.

26 July 2017: The FCA publishes proposals to extend the senior manager regime to all firms, replacing the Approved Persons Regime applicable to those firms with the new Senior Managers and Certification Regime (CP17/25). The proposed regime has three levels to allow for proportionality: the core regime, the enhanced regime, and the limited scope regime.

29 January 2018: HM Treasury announces the effective date for the extension of the SM&CR to insurers.

10 December 2018: SM&CR effective for insurers.

9 December 2019: SM&CR implementation deadline for solo regulated firms.

9 December 2020: Conduct Rules apply to staff not holding a senior management function (SMF) or a certification function.

9 December 2020: Certification deadline for solo regulated firms.

Appendix 2

Useful sources for senior managers of UK financial services firms

Senior managers need to be aware of the wider regulatory environment and the bigger picture of the why and how of regulation. While senior managers do not need to track personally every publication by every regulator or policymaker, they do need to understand the objectives of regulators and the varying sources of evolving rules and requirements.

This appendix looks at UK regulators and policymakers, not in terms of detailed rules, but rather in terms of their scope, approach, funding and accountabilities. For the supranational policymakers and those bodies focused on financial crime, senior managers should be aware of the nature of their influence on the detailed requirements which are implemented on a domestic level.

Last, but not least, is the role of thought leadership. Given the focus on the holistic nature of culture and (mis)conduct risk, senior managers need to be able to benchmark their approach and be aware of emerging areas of potential concern.

UK regulators/policymakers

Financial Conduct Authority (FCA)

The FCA is the conduct regulator for 56,000 financial services firms and financial markets in the UK and the prudential regulator for over 18,000 of those firms. Its website (which among other things has the FCA handbook) can be found at www.fca.org.uk/.

The FCA's strategic objective is to ensure that the relevant markets function well and the operational objectives are to:

- protect consumers – by securing an appropriate degree of protection for consumers;

- protect financial markets – by protecting and enhancing the integrity of the UK financial system;

- promote competition – by promoting effective competition in the interests of consumers.

The FCA is an independent public body funded entirely by charging fees to the firms it regulates. It is accountable to the Treasury, which is responsible for the UK's financial system, and to Parliament.

At a high level, the work and purpose of the FCA is defined by the Financial Services and Markets Act 2000 (FSMA) (available at www.legislation.gov.uk/ukpga/2000/8/contents). The FCA works with consumer groups, trade associations and professional bodies, domestic regulators, EU legislators and a wide range of other stakeholders. The FCA seeks to use a proportionate approach to regulation, prioritising the areas and firms that pose a higher risk to its objectives.

The FCA also maintains the Financial Services Register which is a public record of firms, individuals and other bodies that are, or have been, regulated by the PRA and/or FCA. The Financial Services Register can be found at www.fca.org.uk/firms/financial-services-register. Searches can be made for information on a firm, individual or financial services product by entering its name, reference number (FRN) or postcode. Searches can also be made for certain investment exchanges.

As of summer 2018, the FCA is consulting on proposals to introduce a 'directory' which would be a new public register for checking the details of key individuals working in financial services. The intention is that the directory will include information available currently through the Financial Services Register, as well as information about a wider group of individuals. The consultation set out the FCA's proposals for how it plans to do this following the roll out of the SM&CR to all financial services firms on 9 December 2019 and sought feedback on which individuals to include, what information should be published and when firms need to submit and update information about their employees. It is expected that the final details on the new directory will be published in late autumn 2018.

Prudential Regulation Authority (PRA)

The PRA is the prudential regulator of around 1,500 UK banks, building societies, credit unions, insurers and major investment firms. The FCA is the regulator of those firms for conduct matters, so for around 1,500 firms they are dual regulated.

Specifically prudential regulation rules require financial firms to hold sufficient capital and have adequate risk controls in place. Close supervision of firms ensures that the PRA has a comprehensive overview of their activities so that it can step in if they are not being run in a safe and sound way or, in the case of insurers, if they are not protecting policyholders adequately. The PRA's website is at www.bankofengland.co.uk/prudential-regulation and the PRA Rulebook can be found at www.prarulebook.co.uk/.

The PRA has three objectives:

- to promote the safety and soundness of the firms it regulates;
- to contribute to securing an appropriate degree of protection for insurance policyholders;
- a secondary objective to facilitate effective competition between firms.

The PRA is particularly concerned about the harm that firms can cause to financial stability. A stable financial system is one in which firms continue to provide critical services to households and businesses.

Two key tools are used to advance PRA objectives: regulation and supervision. Through regulation, the PRA sets standards or policies that define what is expected of firms. Through supervision, the PRA assesses whether firms are meeting expectations, the risks that firms pose to the objectives and, where necessary, takes action to reduce those risks.

The PRA's approach to using regulation and supervision is judgement based, forward looking and focused. It does not aim for zero firm failure. Instead, the PRA aims to ensure that a financial firm that fails does so in a way that avoids significant disruption to critical financial services.

Structurally the PRA is part of the Bank of England and is accountable to Parliament. It is funded by the fees charged to firms. The fees depend on the size and type of firm, and the potential risk they could pose to financial stability. The FCA collects these fees on behalf of the PRA.

Financial Ombudsman Scheme (FOS)

The FOS was set up by Parliament to arbitrate complaints between financial services firms and their customers as an alternative dispute resolution mechanism to avoid customers having to pursue unresolved complaints through the court system. The FOS website is at www.financial-ombudsman.org.uk/.

The consumer factsheet on how customer complaints are handled by FOS gives a sense of how the process works (at www.financial-ombudsman.org.uk/publications/factsheets/how-we-deal-with-your-complaint.pdf). Senior managers need to be aware that FOS decisions are considered (bar rare exceptional circumstances) binding on firms.

The FOS is funded by levies and case fees which businesses that are covered pay. The FOS receives no government funding and consumers do not pay to bring a complaint to the ombudsman.

Financial Services Compensation Scheme (FSCS)

The FSCS is the UK's statutory fund of last resort for customers of financial services firms and, as such, the FSCS can pay compensation to consumers if a financial services firm is unable, or likely to be unable, to pay claims against it. The FSCS is an independent body, set up under FSMA. The FSCS website is at www.fscs.org.uk/. There are varying compensation limits depending on the type of business or activity that has failed. From 30 January 2017, the compensation limit for deposits made by private individuals and small businesses to any authorised firm is £85,000.

As with the FOS, the FSCS is funded by the financial services industry. Every firm authorised by the UK regulators is obliged to pay an annual levy, which goes towards running costs and any compensation payments made. Individual consumers are not charged for using the FSCS.

Information Commissioner's Office (ICO)

The ICO is the UK's independent body set up to uphold information rights. Its website can be found at https://ico.org.uk/. The ICO reports directly to Parliament and is sponsored by the Department for Digital, Culture, Media and Sport. It is the independent regulatory office supervising and enforcing the provisions of the Data Protection Act 2018 (available at www.legislation.gov.uk/ukpga/2018/12/pdfs/ukpga_20180012_en.pdf). Breaches of the Data Protection Act (which is derived for the most part from the European General Data Protection Regulation) can be punished with fines up to £17m or 4% of global annual turnover whichever is the higher.

Among other things, the ICO also oversees the Privacy and Electronic Communications (EC Directive) Regulations 2003, SI 2003/2426 (PECR) across the UK which sit alongside the Data Protection Act. They give people specific privacy rights in relation to electronic communications.

There are specific rules on:

- marketing calls, emails, texts and faxes;
- cookies (and similar technologies);
- keeping communications services secure; and
- customer privacy as regards traffic and location data, itemised billing, line identification, and directory listings.

The ICO aims to help organisations comply with PECR and promote good practice by offering advice and guidance (at https://ico.org.uk/for-organisations/guide-to-pecr/). The ICO will take enforcement action against organisations that persistently ignore their obligations, starting with those that generate the most complaints. The ICO can fine firms up to £500,000 for breaches of PECR and consideration is, as of summer 2018, underway to grant additional powers to fine directors up to £500,000 each for breaches of PECR.

Financial Reporting Council (FRC)

The FRC regulates auditors, accountants and actuaries, and sets the UK's Corporate Governance Code which articulates standards of good practice in relation to board leadership and effectiveness, remuneration, accountability and relations with shareholders (available at www.frc.org.uk/document-library/corporate-governance/2016/uk-corporate-governance-code-april-2016).

The FRC also sets the Stewardship Code which aims to enhance the quality of engagement between investors and companies to help improve long-term risk-adjusted returns to shareholders (at www.frc.org.uk/document-library/corporate-governance/2012/uk-stewardship-code-september-2012).

The FRC seeks to promote transparency and integrity in business with work aimed at investors and others who rely on company reports, audit and high-quality risk management.

The FRC's functions derive from a number of sources. It has direct statutory powers in relation to audit regulation, as well as some statutory powers delegated by the Secretary of State. Some of the functions are supported by statutory obligations on other parties to meet our requirements and/or participate in arrangements provided by the FRC. Other of the functions have no statutory backing but derive their authority from widespread support from, and voluntary arrangements with, stakeholders.

As of summer 2018, the FRC's roles and responsibilities were under review.

Banking Standards Board (BSB)

The BSB was established to promote high standards of behaviour and competence across UK banks and building societies. The BSB website is at www.bankingstandardsboard.org.uk/.

The BSB began its work in April 2015. It is a private sector body funded by membership subscriptions and open to all banks and building societies operating in the UK. It is neither a regulator nor a trade association; it has no statutory powers, and it will not speak or lobby for the industry. It will, instead, provide challenge, support and scrutiny for firms committed to rebuilding the sector's reputation, and it will provide impartial and objective assessments of the industry's progress.

Among other things, the BSB undertakes a regular assessment and benchmark of behaviour, competence and culture in UK banking. It does not measure or rank culture as such; rather, it examines how far a firm demonstrates characteristics (honesty, respect, openness, accountability, competence, reliability, responsiveness, personal and organisational resilience and shared purpose) that the BSB expects to be associated with any good culture in banking.

Supranational policy makers

The supranational policy makers operate at an international level and should be considered as 'upstream' from domestic regulators in terms of policy making.

G20

The G20 is an international forum for the governments and central bank governors from Argentina, Australia, Brazil, Canada, China, France, Germany, India, Indonesia,

Italy, Japan, Mexico, the Republic of Korea, the Russian Federation, Saudi Arabia, South Africa, Turkey, the United Kingdom, the United States, and the European Union, (plus Spain as a permanent guest member). The G20 website is at www. g20.org/en.

The prominence of the G20 in supranational policy making stems from the global financial crisis when there was a need for new consensus-building at the highest political level. Since then, the G20 summits have been attended by heads of state or government, and the G20 was seen as being instrumental in stabilising the world economy with its agenda expanded to include additional issues affecting financial markets, trade, and development.

The presidency of the G20 rotates annually with priorities set, reports received (from bodies such as the Financial Stability Board) and policies communicated. The 2018 G20 summit was held in Argentina, and for 2019 it will be held in Japan and 2020 in Saudi Arabia.

Financial Stability Board (FSB)

The FSB operates under the aegis of the G20. The FSB was created in the wake of the global financial crisis out of the Financial Stability Forum and given much expanded powers, resources and remit with regard to the international financial system. The FSB website is at www.fsb.org/.

The FSB's central mandate is to promote international financial stability which it does by coordinating national financial authorities and international standard-setting bodies as they work toward developing strong regulatory, supervisory and other financial sector policies. It seeks to foster a level playing field by encouraging coherent implementation of these policies across sectors and jurisdictions.

The FSB has a broad mandate which includes a requirement to:

- assess vulnerabilities affecting the global financial system as well as to identify and review, on a timely and ongoing basis within a macroprudential perspective, the regulatory, supervisory and related actions needed to address these vulnerabilities, and their outcomes;
- promote coordination and information exchange among authorities responsible for financial stability;
- monitor and advise on market developments and their implications for regulatory policy;
- monitor and advise with regard to best practice in meeting regulatory standards;
- undertake joint strategic reviews of the international standard setting bodies and coordinate their respective policy development work to ensure this work is timely, coordinated, focused on priorities and addresses gaps;
- set guidelines for establishing and supporting supervisory colleges;

- support contingency planning for cross-border crisis management, particularly with regard to systemically important firms;

- collaborate with the International Monetary Fund (IMF) to conduct Early Warning Exercises;

- promote member jurisdictions' implementation of agreed commitments, standards and policy recommendations, through monitoring of implementation, peer review and disclosure.

The FSB is the genesis of many of the detailed policy changes which filter down to domestic rulebooks. For any senior managers wishing to engage in lobbying, it is likely that they will choose to engage with the FSB. That said, senior managers also need to understand that policies agreed by the FSB are not legally binding, nor are they intended to replace the normal national and regional regulatory process. Instead, the FSB acts as a coordinating body, to drive forward the policy agenda to strengthen financial stability. It operates by moral suasion and peer pressure, to set internationally agreed policies and minimum standards that its members (the G20 countries plus Hong Kong, Singapore, Spain and Switzerland) commit to implement at national level.

There is a trio of sector-specific standard setting bodies which work closely with the FSB:

- for banking, the Basel Committee on Banking Supervision;

- for securities, the International Organisation of Securities Commissions; and

- for insurance, the International Association of Insurance Supervisors.

Bank for International Settlements (BIS) and the Basel Committee on Banking Supervision (BCBS or Basel)

The Bank for International Settlements' mission is to serve central banks in their pursuit of monetary and financial stability, to foster international cooperation in those areas and to act as a bank for central banks. BIS, which has its head office in Basel, Switzerland, is owned by 60 central banks, representing countries from around the world that together account for about 95% of world GDP.

BIS has a number of key committees one of which is the BCBS which acts as the primary global standard setter for the prudential regulation of banks and provides a forum for regular cooperation on banking supervisory matters. The BCBS website is at www.bis.org/bcbs/index.htm. Its mandate is to strengthen the regulation, supervision and practices of banks worldwide with the purpose of enhancing financial stability. In doing so, the BCBS is a key figure in promulgating the next level of practical detail of those FSB policies which relate specifically to banks.

The BCBS seeks to achieve its mandate through the following activities:

- exchanging information on developments in the banking sector and financial markets, to help identify current or emerging risks for the global financial system;

- sharing supervisory issues, approaches and techniques to promote common understanding and to improve cross-border cooperation;

- establishing and promoting global standards for the regulation and supervision of banks as well as guidelines and sound practices;

- addressing regulatory and supervisory gaps that pose risks to financial stability;

- monitoring the implementation of BCBS standards in member countries and beyond with the purpose of ensuring their timely, consistent and effective implementation and contributing to a 'level playing field' among internationally-active banks;

- consulting with central banks and bank supervisory authorities which are not members of the BCBS to benefit from their input into the BCBS policy formulation process and to promote the implementation of BCBS standards, guidelines and sound practices beyond BCBS member countries; and

- coordinating and cooperating with other financial sector standard setters and international bodies, particularly those involved in promoting financial stability.

The BCBS does not possess any formal supranational authority. Its decisions do not have legal force but it has become the de facto source of global prudential banking regulation through its members' commitments to implement and embed the agreed policies.

International Organisation of Securities Commissions (IOSCO)

IOSCO is the international body that brings together the world's securities regulators and is recognised as the global standard setter for the securities sector. The IOSCO website is at www.iosco.org/.

IOSCO develops, implements and promotes adherence to internationally recognised standards for securities regulation. It works 'intensively' with the G20 and the FSB on the global regulatory reform agenda. Specifically, IOSCO's objectives and principles of securities regulation (updated May 2017 and available at www.iosco.org/library/pubdocs/pdf/IOSCOPD561.pdf) have been endorsed by both the G20 and the FSB as the relevant standards in this area.

IOSCO members, which regulate more than 95% of the world's securities markets in more than 115 jurisdictions, have resolved to:

- cooperate in developing, implementing and promoting adherence to internationally recognised and consistent standards of regulation, oversight and enforcement in order to protect investors, maintain fair, efficient and transparent markets, and seek to address systemic risks;

- enhance investor protection and promote investor confidence in the integrity of securities markets, through strengthened information exchange and cooperation in enforcement against misconduct and in supervision of markets and market intermediaries; and

- exchange information at both global and regional levels on their respective experiences in order to assist the development of markets, strengthen market infrastructure and implement appropriate regulation.

International Association of Insurance Supervisors (IAIS)

The IAIS is a voluntary membership organisation of insurance supervisors and regulators from more than 200 jurisdictions, constituting 97% of the world's insurance premiums. Its mission is to promote effective and globally consistent supervision of the insurance industry in order to develop and maintain fair, safe and stable insurance markets for the benefit and protection of policyholders and to contribute to global financial stability. The IAIS website is at www.iaisweb.org/home.

The IAIS produces the Insurance Core Principles which set out a globally accepted framework for the supervision of the insurance sector (updated November 2017 and available at www.iaisweb.org/page/supervisory-material/insurance-core-principles/file/70028/all-adopted-icps-updated-november-2017).

As with IOSCO and the BCBS, the IAIS coordinates its work with other international financial policymakers and associations of supervisors or regulators, and assists in shaping financial systems globally. In particular, the IAIS works with the FSB with regard to insurance issues as well as on issues related to the regulation and supervision of the global financial sector.

Organisation for Economic Co-operation and Development (OECD)

The mission of the OECD is to promote policies that will improve the economic and social well-being of people around the world. The OECD website is at www.oecd.org. One of the OECD's many areas of interest is that of governance, specifically corporate governance.

The G20/OECD Principles of Corporate Governance are designed to help policy makers evaluate and improve the legal, regulatory, and institutional framework for corporate governance. They also provide guidance for stock exchanges, investors, corporations, and others that have a role in the process of developing good corporate governance. First issued in 1999, the principles have become the international benchmark in corporate governance. They have been adopted as one of the FSB's Key Standards for Sound Financial Systems and endorsed by the G20. The 2015 edition takes into account developments in both the financial and corporate sectors that may influence the efficiency and relevance of corporate governance policies and practices (available at http://dx.doi.org/10.1787/9789264236882-en).

Financial Crime

There are two key supranational bodies for the evolution of global policy initiatives to seek to prevent financial crime including money laundering.

Financial Action Task Force (FATF)

FATF is an inter-governmental body established to set standards and promote effective implementation of legal, regulatory and operational measures for combating money laundering, terrorist financing and other related threats to the integrity of the international financial system. The FATF website is at www.fatf-gafi.org. FATF sees itself as a policy-making body which works to generate the necessary political will to bring about national legislative and regulatory reforms in these areas.

FATF developed the International Standards on Combating Money Laundering and the Financing of Terrorism & Proliferation – the FATF Recommendations are recognised as the international standard for combating of money laundering and the financing of terrorism and proliferation of weapons of mass destruction and are available at www.fatf-gafi.org/recommendations.html. They form the basis for a coordinated response to these threats to the integrity of the financial system and help ensure a level playing field.

FATF monitors the progress of its members in implementing necessary measures, reviews money laundering and terrorist financing techniques and counter-measures, and promotes the adoption and implementation of appropriate measures globally. In collaboration with other international stakeholders, FATF also works to identify national-level vulnerabilities with the aim of protecting the international financial system from misuse.

FATF is due to visit the UK in 2018 and, as with other assessment visits carried out, will review the UK's adherence to the recommendations and publish a detailed report.

The Wolfsberg Group

The Wolfsberg Group is an association of thirteen global banks which aims to develop frameworks and guidance for the management of financial crime risks, particularly with respect to know your customer, anti-money laundering and counter terrorist financing policies. The Wolfsberg Group website is at www. wolfsberg-principles.com.

Materials published by the Wolfsberg Group are designed to provide financial institutions with an industry perspective on effective financial crime risk management. Senior managers should be aware that the Wolfsberg Group publications and guidance are detailed and practical and aim to give firms the tools with which to seek to mitigate their own specific financial crime risk.

Specifically, the Wolfsberg Group does not advocate that firms simply adopt each publication, but rather senior managers should consider the risks described, the applicable regulatory standards and their own defined risk management strategy. The materials published by the Wolfsberg Group offer a perspective through which firms may identify gaps or new insights and consider to what extent these gaps or insights require attention. This is a matter for each firm. For example, a firm may identify alternative controls or other compensating measures to the ones suggested, for as long as the risks in question are adequately managed. Furthermore, the risks may indeed be different in different businesses, regions or countries.

The Wolfsberg Group has published a significant number of documents, whether in the form of principles, guidance, frequently asked questions (FAQs) or statements covering topics such as private banking, anti-money laundering principles for correspondent banking, guidance on a risk-based approach for managing money laundering risks, FAQs on politically exposed persons and guidance on anti-bribery and corruption compliance programmes.

European bodies

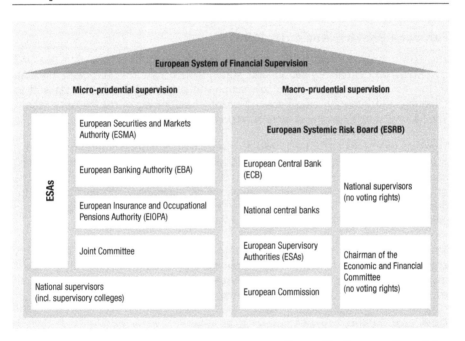

Source: The European Commission

Despite separation of the UK and EU after March 2019, there is likely to be at least some equivalence of regulatory approach on financial services post Brexit. If nothing else the UK regulators are likely to maintain their open lines of communication with the European supervisory bodies:

European Central Bank (ECB)

The ECB's stated main aim is to maintain price stability, ie to safeguard the value of the euro. The ECB website is at www.ecb.europa.eu. Price stability is essential for economic growth and job creation – two of the European Union's objectives – and it represents the most important contribution monetary policy can make in that area. The ECB operates the Eurosystem which is responsible for:

- defining and implementing monetary policy;
- conducting foreign exchange operations;
- holding and managing the euro area's foreign currency reserves;
- promoting the smooth operation of payment systems.

The ECB carries out specific tasks in the areas of banking supervision, banknotes, statistics, macroprudential policy and financial stability as well as international and European cooperation.

European Banking Authority (EBA)

The EBA is an independent EU Authority which works to ensure effective and consistent prudential regulation and supervision across the European banking sector. Its overall objectives are to maintain financial stability in the EU and to safeguard the integrity, efficiency and orderly functioning of the banking sector. The EBA website is at www.eba.europa.eu.

The main task of the EBA is to contribute, through the adoption of binding technical standards (which are legally binding and directly applicable in all member states) and guidelines, to the creation of the European single rulebook in banking. The single rulebook aims to provide a single set of harmonised prudential rules for financial institutions throughout the EU, helping create a level playing field and providing high protection to depositors, investors and consumers.

The EBA also plays an important role in promoting convergence of supervisory practices to ensure a harmonised application of prudential rules. The EBA is mandated to assess risks and vulnerabilities in the EU banking sector through, in particular, regular risk assessment reports and pan-European stress tests.

Other tasks set out in the EBA's mandate include:

- investigating alleged incorrect or insufficient application of EU law by national authorities;
- taking decisions directed at individual competent authorities or financial institutions in emergency situations;
- mediating to resolve disagreements between competent authorities in cross-border situations;
- acting as an independent advisory body to the European Parliament, the Council or the Commission;
- taking a leading role in promoting transparency, simplicity and fairness in the market for consumer financial products or services across the internal market.

European Securities and Markets Authority (ESMA)

ESMA is an independent EU Authority that contributes to safeguarding the stability of the European Union's financial system by enhancing the protection of investors and promoting stable and orderly financial markets. ESMA's website is https://www.esma.europa.eu.

ESMA achieves its mission and objectives by assessing risks to investors, markets and financial stability, completing a single rulebook for EU financial markets, promoting supervisory convergence and directly supervising credit rating agencies and trade repositories.

ESMA is also acts as the direct supervisor of credit rating agencies (CRAs) and trade repositories (TRs) which form essential parts of the EU's market infrastructure.

ESMA's activities are closely interlinked. Insights gained from risk assessment feed into the work on the single rulebook, supervisory convergence and direct supervision, and vice versa. ESMA considers supervisory convergence to be the main outcome of the implementation and application of the single rulebook. The direct supervision of CRAs and TRs benefits from and also feeds into the risk assessment and single rulebook activities.

European Insurance and Occupational Pensions Authority (EIOPA)

Like the EBA and ESMA, EIOPA is an independent EU Authority with a core responsibility to support the stability of the financial system, transparency of markets and financial products as well as the protection of policyholders, pension scheme members and beneficiaries. EIOPA's website is at https://eiopa.europa.eu.

EIOPA's main goals are:

- protecting consumers, rebuilding trust in the financial system;

- ensuring a high, effective and consistent level of regulation and supervision taking account of the varying interests of all member states and the different nature of financial institutions;

- greater harmonisation and coherent application of rules for financial institutions and markets across the European Union;

- strengthening oversight of cross-border groups;

- EIOPA is also commissioned to monitor and identify trends, potential risks and vulnerabilities stemming from the micro-prudential level, across borders and across sectors.

Thought leadership

The focus on culture and conduct risk has increased the need for senior managers to consider relevant thought leadership as well as all the applicable regulatory requirements. A key thought leader is Thomson Reuters Regulatory Intelligence which, in addition to tracking over 900 global regulatory bodies and providing daily news and analysis on regulatory developments, produces a number of free special reports, white papers, expert talks and infographics. These are summarised below.

Culture and Conduct Risk 2018: benchmarking five years of implementation

'Culture and Conduct Risk 2018' is Thomson Reuters Regulatory Intelligence's fifth annual survey on how firms around the world are managing the challenges presented by the regulatory focus on culture and conduct risk (available at https:// risk.thomsonreuters.com/en/resources/special-report/culture-and-conduct-risk-2018.html). As in previous years, the research provides an opportunity for firms, and specifically compliance practitioners, to give their views and opinions on how they manage culture and mitigate conduct risk in the financial services industry. Since its inception, the survey has highlighted distinct industry-wide and year-on-year trends against which firms can benchmark their own progress and has proved to be a valuable and trusted resource for firms and their compliance officers. Last year's report was read by more than 5,000 entities including global systemically important financial institutions (G-SIFIs), regulators, local government, law firms and consultancies.

State of Regulatory Reform 2018

The State of Regulatory Reform annual report covers Thomson Reuters' predictions and highlights what regulatory events will shape the year and how to best stay prepared.

For 2018 it was going to be the year that theory became practice for many compliance officers and regulatory professionals, and a year in which the post-financial crisis push for regulatory harmony yielded to international divergence. 'State of Regulatory Reform 2018: A Special Report' is available at https://risk. thomsonreuters.com/en/resources/special-report/state-of-regulatory-reform-2018-special-report.html.

Cost of Compliance 2018

The 'Cost of Compliance Report: 2018' written by Stacey English and Susannah Hammond is Thomson Reuters Regulatory Intelligence's annual survey on the cost of compliance and the challenges financial services firms expect to face in the year ahead (available at https://risk.thomsonreuters.com/en/resources/special-report/cost-compliance-2018.html). The survey is now in its ninth year and has become the trusted voice for risk and compliance practitioners around the world. Last year's report was read by nearly 9,000 entities including firms, G-SIFIs, regulators, law firms, domestic governments and consultancies. The unparalleled insight into the frank concerns and issues shared by practitioners have, once again, given a wealth of information into the reality and challenges faced across all industry sectors.

The survey findings aim to help regulated firms with planning and resourcing, while allowing them to benchmark their own practices and experiences to determine whether their strategy and expectations are in line with the wider industry. The experiences of G-SIFIs are analysed where these can provide a sense of the approach taken by the world's largest financial services firms.

In the last couple of years, the cost of compliance survey reports have highlighted emerging resource constraints which, combined with continuing regulatory uncertainty, suggested something of a pivot point for firms and their approach to risk and compliance. This year what is beginning to emerge is, in addition to firms seeking more creative solutions to risk and compliance challenges, a sense of increasing pressure on senior managers to both understand and cope with evolving regulatory expectations.

Five key risks for 2018

Each year Susannah Hammond analyses the five key risks for financial services firms around the world. It is perhaps stating the obvious but while the detailed risks run by firms are, by their very nature, firm specific and unique, there are a series of high-level risks applicable to all financial services firms irrespective of geography or sector. For 2018 the risks considered were cyber resilience, incentives and remuneration, vulnerable customers, the implementation and embedding of regulatory change and, last but not least, technology risk.

'Five Key Risks for Firms in 2018' by Susannah Hammond is available at https://risk. thomsonreuters.com/en/resources/expert-talk/expert-talk-five-key-risks-2018.html.

327

Index

[All references are to paragraph number]

Accountability
background context,
Approved Persons regime, 1.12
financial crisis, 1.1–1.2
regulatory reform, 1.3–1.11
corporate governance, and, 10.8
organisational culture, 9.6
purpose, 1.13
timeline, 1.2
Anti-money laundering regime
approval by senior management, 10.2
generally, 10.1
governance, 10.3
integration, 10.1
layering, 10.1
legislative framework
generally, 10.1
Regulations (2017), 10.2
meaning, 10.1
National Crime Agency, 10.1
placement, 10.1
policies, controls and procedures, 10.2
regulatory framework, 10.2
role of FCA, 10.3
stages, 10.1
Approved Persons Regime
generally, 1.12
Australia
case study, 15.5
generally, 15.4
Basel Committee on Banking Supervision (BCBS)
corporate governance, and, 10.10
overview, Appendix 2
Banking Standards Board
fit and proper requirement, and, 2.7
generally, 1.7
overview, Appendix 2
Senior Managers and Certification
Regime, and, 2.7

Banking Standards Commission (PCBS)
generally, 1.6
Banking Standards Review Council
generally, 1.7
Banking Standards Rules
introduction, 1.13
Bribery
adequate procedures, 10.5
generally, 10.4
legislative framework, 10.4
offences, 10.4
US legislation, and, 10.6
Canada
generally, 15.11
Certification Regime
application, 3.9
background, 1.10
change of functions during the year, 3.19
content of certificates, 3.18
emergency appointments, 3.21
employees affected, 3.9
fit and proper
generally, 3.15–3.16
mandatory template for regulatory references, 3.17
FCA significant harm functions
introduction, 3.13
specified, 3.14
financial services firms, for
fit and proper requirement, 5.7
functions, 5.8
generally, 5.8
insurers, for
application, 4.15
fitness and propriety requirements, 4.17
functions, 4.16

329

Certification Regime – *contd*
  insurers, for – *contd*
    introduction, 4.14
    outsourcing, 4.22
    regulatory references, 4.18
    training and notification, 4.21
  introduction, 3.8
  overview, 3.1
  PRA functions
    introduction, 3.11
    material risk takers, 3.12
  refusal of certificate, 3.20
  scope, 3.9
  temporary UK role, 3.22
  territorial scope, 3.10
Capability
  fit and proper requirement, and, 2.4
  Senior Managers Regime, and, 3.4
Competence
  fit and proper requirement, and, 2.4
  Senior Managers Regime, and, 3.4
Compliance
  reasonable steps requirement, and,
    2.11
Conduct risk
  components, 9.2–9.3
  framework
    generally, 9.5
    good practices, 9.6
    measurement and metrics, 9.7
    risk monitoring, 9.8
  generally, 9.1
  programmes, 9.4
Conduct Rules
  compliance with requirements and
    standards, 2.11
  co-operation with regulators, 2.13
  delegation, 2.12
  effective control, 2.10
  enforcement, and, 11.5
  financial services firms, and, 5.9
  insurers, and
    Individual, 4.20
    introduction, 4.19
  Senior Manager, 4.20
Conflicts of interest
  practical issues, 8.3
Control
  Individual Conduct Rules, and, 2.10

Co-operation with regulators
  enforcement, and, 11.11
  Individual Conduct Rules, and, 2.17
  reasonable steps requirement, and,
    2.13
Core firms
  See also **Financial services firms**
  generally, 5.11
  introduction, 5.2
  meaning, 5.2
  transition from AP regime, 5.14
Corporate governance
  accountability, 10.8
  BCBS Governance Principles for
    Banks, 10.10
  culture of an organisation, and
    generally, 9.3
    good practices, 9.6
    introduction, 9.2
  effectiveness, 10.8
  generally, 10.8
  G20 Principles, 10.9
  leadership, 10.8
  money laundering, and, 10.3
  OECD Principles, 10.9
  principles, 10.8
  remuneration, 10.8
  shareholder relations, 10.8
  UK Code, 10.8
Corporation
  adequate procedures, 10.5
  generally, 10.4
  legislative framework, 10.4
  offences, 10.4
  US legislation, and, 10.6
Culture of an organisation
  accountability, 9.6
  behavioural role, 9.1
  conduct risk
    components, 9.2–9.3
    framework, 9.5–9.8
    generally, 9.1
    programmes, 9.4
  corporate governance
    generally, 9.3
    good practices, 9.6
    introduction, 9.2
  definitions, 9.2
  good practices, 9.6

Culture of an organisation – *contd*
governance
  generally, 9.3
  good practices, 9.6
  introduction, 9.2
holistic scope, 9.6
implementation of SM&C regime,
  and, 6.12
internal environments, and, 12.8
introduction, 9.1
measurement and metrics, 9.7
misconduct risk monitoring, 9.8
people-related practices, 9.3
regulatory expectations, 9.1–9.3
remuneration practices, 9.3
role, 9.1–9.2
senior manager behaviours, 9.3
terminology, 9.2
true purpose of business, 9.3
USA, and, 15.13
Cyber resilience
board responsibility 14.3
case study, 14.4
generally, 14.1
good practice, 14.2
ransomware, 14.4
Data protection
GDPR, 14.5
generally, 14.5
Dawn raids
regulatory relationship management,
  and, 13.4
Delegation
reasonable steps requirement, and,
  2.12
Due diligence
fit and proper requirement, and,
  2.6
Individual Conduct Rules, and, 2.16
Due skill and care
Individual Conduct Rules, and, 2.16
Documentation
discharge of regulatory obligations,
  and
decision registers, 12.12
evidence, 12.14
introduction, 12.11
skills, 12.13
fit and proper requirement, and, 2.6

Duty of responsibility
enforcement, and, 11.2
financial services firms, and 5.5
insurers, for
  generally, 4.9
  introduction, 4.5
  overview, 4.3
Effective control
Individual Conduct Rules, and, 2.10
Enforcement
Conduct Rules, 11.5
co-operation with regulators, 11.11
criteria, 11.9
duty of responsibility, 11.2
effect, 11.9
examples, 11.10
FCA objectives and priorities, 11.2
introduction, 11.1
investigations, 11.7
penalties, 11.6
publication of findings, 11.8
purpose, 11.2
reasonable steps, 11.4
regulatory relationship management,
  and, 13.3
review, 11.9
Senior Managers Regime, 11.3–11.4
Enhanced firms
See also **Financial services firms**
generally, 5.12
introduction, 5.2
meaning, 5.2
transition from AP regime, 5.15
European bodies
overview, Appendix 2
External environment
generally, 12.2
External investigations
regulatory relationship management,
  and, 13.3
**Fair and Effective Markets Review
(2015)**
generally, 1.8
Financial Action Task Force (FATF)
overview, Appendix 2
Financial Conduct Authority (FCA)
Certification Regime
  see also **Certification Regime**
  generally, 3.8–3.22

Financial Conduct Authority (FCA)
 – *contd*
 financial crisis, and, 1.2
 fit and proper requirement
  see also **Fit and proper
   requirement**
  generally, 2.2–2.7
 generally, 1.10
 Individual Conduct Rules
  see also **Individual Conduct
   Rules**
  generally, 2.14–2.19
 overview, Appendix 2
 Senior Manager Conduct Rules
  see also **Senior Manager
   Conduct Rules**
  generally, 2.8–2.13
 Senior Managers Regime
  see also **Senior Managers
   Regime**
  generally, 3.3–3.7
 significant harm functions
  introduction, 3.13
  specified, 3.14
**Financial Ombudsman Service
 (FOS)**
 overview, Appendix 2
Financial Reporting Council (FRC)
 overview, Appendix 2
**Financial Services Compensation
 Scheme (FSCS)**
 overview, Appendix 2
Financial services firms
 categorisation, 5.2
 certification functions, 5.8
 Certification Regime
  fit and proper requirement, 5.7
  functions, 5.8
  generally, 5.8
 Conduct Rules, 5.9
 core firms
  generally, 5.11
  introduction, 5.2
  meaning, 5.2
  transition from AP regime, 5.14
 duty of responsibility, 5.5
 enhanced firms
  generally, 5.12
  introduction, 5.2

Financial services firms – *contd*
 enhanced firms – *contd*
  meaning, 5.2
  transition from AP regime, 5.15
 exempt firms, 5.2
 fit and proper requirement, 5.7
 implementation of regime
  challenges for business, 6.2
  human resources, 6.7
  internal audit, 6.9–6.11
  introduction, 6.1
  key functions in oversight, 6.4–6.5
  legal function, 6.13
  liaison between control functions,
   6.6
  non-executive directors, 6.8
  organisational culture, 6.12
  risk management and assurance,
   6.3
 Individual Conduct Rules, 5.9
 introduction, 5.1
 limited permission consumer credit
  firms, 5.2
 limited scope firms
  generally, 5.10
  introduction, 5.2
  meaning, 5.2
  transition from AP regime, 5.14
 prescribed responsibilities
  core firms, 5.11
  enhanced firms, 5.12
  generally, 5.6
 senior management functions
  core firms, 5.11
  enhanced firms, 5.12
  generally, 5.3
  limited scope firms, 5.10
 Senior Manager Conduct Rules, 5.9
 Senior Managers Regime
  duty of responsibility, 5.5
  fit and proper requirement, 5.7
  functions, 5.3
  generally, 5.3
  prescribed responsibilities, 5.6
  statements of responsibility, 5.4
  territorial scope, 5.3
 solo-regulated firms, 5.1
 statements of responsibility, 5.4
 transition from AP regime, 5.13–5.15

Financial soundness
fit and proper requirement, and, 2.5
Senior Managers Regime, and, 3.4
Financial Stability Board (FSB)
generally, 15.1
introduction, 1.11
overview, Appendix 2
Fintech
generally, 14.7
Fit and proper requirement
BSB Statement of Good Practice, 2.7
Certification Regime
generally, 3.15–3.16
mandatory template for regulatory
references, 3.17
competence and capability, 2.4
due diligence and documentation,
2.6
financial services firms, and, 5.7
financial soundness, 2.5
generally, 2.2
honesty, integrity and reputation, 2.3
Senior Insurance Managers Regime,
and, 4.17
Senior Managers Regime, and, 3.4
Governance
accountability, 10.8
BCBS Governance Principles for
Banks, 10.10
culture of an organisation, and
generally, 9.3
good practices, 9.6
introduction, 9.2
effectiveness, 10.8
generally, 10.8
G20 Principles, 10.9
leadership, 10.8
money laundering, and, 10.3
OECD Principles, 10.9
principles, 10.8
remuneration, 10.8
shareholder relations, 10.8
UK Code, 10.8
Group companies
regulatory relationship management,
and, 13.5
G20
corporate governance, 10.9
overview, Appendix 2

Handover
Senior Insurance Managers Regime,
and, 4.8
Honesty
fit and proper requirement, and, 2.3
Senior Managers Regime, and, 3.4
Hong Kong
generally, 15.2–15.3
Human resources
implementation of SM&C regime,
and, 6.7
Implementation of SM&C regime
challenges for business, 6.2
human resources, 6.7
internal audit
evidence, 6.10
generally, 6.9
good practices, 6.10
organisational culture, 6.12
regulatory relationship
management, 6.10
reporting, 6.10
reviews, 6.11
scope of work programmes, 6.10
skills and resources, 6.10
terms of reference, 6.10
introduction, 6.1
key functions in oversight, 6.4–6.5
legal function, 6.13
liaison between control functions,
6.6
'lines of defence'
introduction, 6.3
practice, in, 6.5
roles, 6.4
non-executive directors, 6.8
organisational culture, 6.12
risk management and assurance, 6.3
Incentives
see also **Remuneration**
misconduct, and
generally, 12.3
guidance, 12.4
supervisory expectations, 12.5
**Independent Commission on
Banking (2011)**
generally, 1.4
Individual Conduct Rules
co-operation with regulators, 2.17

Individual Conduct Rules – *contd*
due skill, care and diligence, 2.16
financial services firms, and, 5.9
generally, 2.14
insurers, for, 4.20
integrity, 2.15
openness with regulators, 2.17
proper market conduct, 2.19
treating customers fairly, 2.18
Information Commissioners Office (ICO)
overview, Appendix 2
Insider dealing
market abuse, and, 10.7
Insurers
affected employees, 4.3
application, 4.1
certification functions, 4.16
Certification Regime
application, 4.15
fitness and propriety requirements, 4.17
functions, 4.16
introduction, 4.14
outsourcing, 4.22
regulatory references, 4.18
training and notification, 4.21
changes, 4.4
Conduct Rules
Individual, 4.20
introduction, 4.19
Senior Manager, 4.20
duty of responsibility
generally, 4.9
introduction, 4.5
overview, 4.3
EU Solvency II Directive, 4.1
fit and proper requirement, 4.17
functions
generally, 4.6
practical implementation, 4.7
generally, 4.5
handover, 4.8
implementation of regime
challenges for business, 6.2
human resources, 6.7
internal audit, 6.9–6.11
introduction, 6.1
key functions in oversight, 6.4–6.5

Insurers – *contd*
implementation of regime – *contd*
legal function, 6.13
liaison between control functions, 6.6
non-executive directors, 6.8
organisational culture, 6.12
risk management and assurance, 6.3
Individual Conduct Rules, 4.20
introduction, 4.1
management responsibilities map, 4.13
managing agents, 4.2
multiple roles, 4.7
outsourcing, 4.22
overall responsibility, 4.7
overview, 4.3
prescribed responsibilities
generally, 4.10
introduction, 4.5
overview, 4.3
practical implementation, 4.11
regulatory references, 4.18
scope, 4.2
Senior Management Functions
generally, 4.6
practical implementation, 4.7
Senior Manager Conduct Rules, 4.20
separation of roles, 4.7
small NDFs, 4.2
statements of responsibilities
generally, 4.12
introduction, 4.5
overview, 4.3
temporary cover, 4.7
training and notification, 4.21
Insurtech
generally, 14.7
Integrity
fit and proper requirement, and, 2.3
Individual Conduct Rules, and, 2.15
Senior Managers Regime, and, 3.4
Internal audit
evidence, 6.10
generally, 6.9
good practices, 6.10
organisational culture, 6.12

Internal audit – *contd*
  regulatory relationship management,
    6.10
  reporting, 6.10
  reviews, 6.11
  scope of work programmes, 6.10
  skills and resources, 6.10
  terms of reference, 6.10
Internal environment
  introduction, 12.7
  management information, 12.10
  organisational culture, 12.8
  understanding the business and its
    risks, 12.9
Internal investigations
  regulatory relationship management,
    and, 13.2
International Association of
  Insurance Supervisors (IAIS)
  overview, Appendix 2
International Organisation of
  Securities Commissions (IOSCO)
  overview, Appendix 2
Investigations
  enforcement, and, 11.7
  regulatory relationship management,
    and
    external investigations, 13.3
    internal investigations, 13.2
Legal function
  implementation of SM&C regime,
    and, 6.13
Liaison between control functions
  implementation of SM&C regime,
    and, 6.6
LIBOR
  PCBS review, and, 1.13
Licensing Regime
  generally, 1.13
Limited scope firms
  See also **Financial services firms**
  generally, 5.10
  introduction, 5.2
  meaning, 5.2
  transition from AP regime, 5.14
'Line of sight'
  generally, 8.2
  regulatory relationship management,
    and, 13.1

Lobbying
  generally, 12.6
Management information
  internal environments, and, 12.10
Management responsibilities
  map
  generally, 3.1
  insurers, for, 4.13
  practical issues, 7.3
Managing agents
  Senior Insurance Managers Regime,
    and, 4.2
Market abuse
  generally, 10.7
  insider dealing, 10.7
  inside information, 10.7
  market manipulation, 10.7
  notifications, 10.7
  offences, 10.7
  regulatory framework, 10.7
  unlawful disclosure, 10.7
  whistleblowing, 10.7
Market conduct
  Individual Conduct Rules, and, 2.19
Misconduct
  incentives, and
    generally, 12.3
    guidance, 12.4
    supervisory expectations, 12.5
Money laundering
  approval by senior management,
    10.2
  generally, 10.1
  governance, 10.3
  integration, 10.1
  layering, 10.1
  legislative framework
    generally, 10.1
    Regulations (2017), 10.2
  meaning, 10.1
  National Crime Agency, 10.1
  placement, 10.1
  policies, controls and procedures,
    10.2
  regulatory framework, 10.2
  role of FCA, 10.3
  stages, 10.1
Netherlands
  generally, 15.6

Non-executive directors
implementation of SM&C regime,
and, 6.8
Nuisance calls
generally, 14.6
PECR, 14.6
**Organisation for Economic Co-
operation and Development
(OECD)**
corporate governance, and, 10.9
overview, Appendix 2
Organisational culture
accountability, 9.6
behavioural role, 9.1
conduct risk
components, 9.2–9.3
framework, 9.5–9.8
generally, 9.1
programmes, 9.4
corporate governance
generally, 9.3
good practices, 9.6
introduction, 9.2
definitions, 9.2
good practices, 9.6
governance
generally, 9.3
good practices, 9.6
introduction, 9.2
holistic scope, 9.6
implementation of SM&C regime,
and, 6.12
internal environments, and,
12.8
introduction, 9.1
measurement and metrics, 9.7
misconduct risk monitoring,
9.8
people-related practices, 9.3
regulatory expectations, 9.1–9.3
remuneration practices, 9.3
role, 9.1–9.2
senior manager behaviours, 9.3
terminology, 9.2
true purpose of business, 9.3
USA, and, 15.13
Outsourcing
insurers, and, 4.22
practical issues, 8.4

**Parliamentary Commission on
Banking Standards (PCBS)**
generally, 1.6
Penalties
enforcement, and, 11.6
Personal archive
decision registers, 12.12
evidence, 12.14
introduction, 12.11
skills, 12.13
Practical aspects
allocation of responsibilities, 7.4
challenges to come
conflicts of interest, 8.3
introduction, 8.1
'line of sight', 8.2
outsourcing, 8.4
qualitative risk management, 8.6
skill sets, 8.5
conflicts of interest, 8.3
introduction, 7.1
LIBOR, and, 8.2
'line of sight', 8.2
management responsibilities map, 7.3
outsourcing, 8.4
prescribed responsibilities
generally, 7.4
smaller firms, 7.5
qualitative risk management, 8.6
reasonable steps
evidencing, 7.7
generally, 7.6
senior management functions, 7.2
skill sets, 8.5
smaller firms, and, 7.5
statements of responsibility, 7.2
training for boards and senior
managers, 7.8
Prescribed responsibilities
financial services firms, and
core firms, 5.11
enhanced firms, 5.12
generally, 5.6
generally, 3.6
insurers, and
generally, 4.10
introduction, 4.5
overview, 4.3
practical implementation, 4.11

Prescribed responsibilities – *contd*
introduction, 3.1
practical issues, 7.4
smaller firms, 7.5
Proper market conduct
Individual Conduct Rules, and, 2.19
Prudential Regulation Authority (PRA)
certification functions
introduction, 3.11
material risk takers, 3.12
Certification Regime
see also **Certification Regime**
generally, 3.8–3.22
fit and proper requirement
see also **Fit and proper requirement**
generally, 2.2–2.7
generally, 1.10
Individual Conduct Rules
see also **Individual Conduct Rules**
generally, 2.14–2.19
overview, Appendix 2
Senior Manager Conduct Rules
see also **Senior Manager Conduct Rules**
generally, 2.8–2.13
Senior Managers Regime
see also **Senior Managers Regime**
generally, 3.3–3.7
Ransomware
generally, 14.4
Reasonable steps requirement
compliance, 2.11
co-operation with regulators, 2.13
delegation, 2.12
effective control, 2.10
enforcement, and, 11.4
evidencing, 7.7
introduction, 2.8
practical issues
evidencing, 7.7
generally, 7.6
Senior Manager Conduct Rules, and, 2.8–2.13
Regtech
generally, 14.7

Regulators
generally, 1.10
Regulatory relationship management
approvals and registrations, 13.1
'dawn raids', 13.4
enforcement, and, 13.3
external investigations, 13.3
group companies under investigation, and, 13.5
internal audit, and, 6.10
internal investigations, 13.2
introduction, 13.1
'line of sight', and, 13.1
role and priorities of FCA, 13.1
supervision principles, 13.1
Remuneration
corporate governance, and, 10.8
general practices, 9.3
Republic of Ireland
fitness and probity, 15.8
generally, 15.7
individual responsibility, 15.9
Reputation
fit and proper requirement, and, 2.3
Senior Managers Regime, and, 3.4
Risk management and assurance
implementation of SM&C regime, and, 6.3
practical issues, and, 8.6
Risk mitigation
allocation of responsibilities, 7.4
introduction, 7.1
management responsibilities map, 7.3
prescribed responsibilities, 7.4
statements of responsibility, 7.2
Sassoon Review (2009)
generally, 1.9
Senior Insurance Managers Regime (SIMR)
affected employees, 4.3
application, 4.1
certification functions, 4.16
Certification Regime
application, 4.15
fitness and propriety requirements, 4.17
functions, 4.16

Senior Insurance Managers Regime (SIMR) – *contd*
Certification Regime – *contd*
introduction, 4.14
outsourcing, 4.22
regulatory references, 4.18
training and notification, 4.21
changes, 4.4
Conduct Rules
Individual, 4.20
introduction, 4.19
Senior Manager, 4.20
duty of responsibility
generally, 4.9
introduction, 4.5
overview, 4.3
EU Solvency II Directive, 4.1
fit and proper requirement, 4.17
functions
generally, 4.6
practical implementation, 4.7
generally, 4.5
handover, 4.8
implementation
challenges for business, 6.2
human resources, 6.7
internal audit, 6.9–6.11
introduction, 6.1
key functions in oversight, 6.4–6.5
legal function, 6.13
liaison between control functions, 6.6
non-executive directors, 6.8
organisational culture, 6.12
risk management and assurance, 6.3
Individual Conduct Rules, 4.20
introduction, 4.1
management responsibilities map, 4.13
managing agents, 4.2
multiple roles, 4.7
outsourcing, 4.22
overall responsibility, 4.7
overview, 4.3
prescribed responsibilities
generally, 4.10
introduction, 4.5
overview, 4.3
practical implementation, 4.11
regulatory references, 4.18

Senior Insurance Managers Regime (SIMR) – *contd*
scope, 4.2
Senior Management Functions
generally, 4.6
practical implementation, 4.7
Senior Manager Conduct Rules, 4.20
separation of roles, 4.7
small NDFs, 4.2
statements of responsibilities
generally, 4.12
introduction, 4.5
overview, 4.3
temporary cover, 4.7
training and notification, 4.21
Senior Management Functions
financial services firms, and
core firms, 5.11
enhanced firms, 5.12
generally, 5.3
limited scope firms, 5.10
generally, 3.3–3.4
insurers, and
generally, 4.6
practical implementation, 4.7
introduction, 3.1
practical issues, 7.2
Senior Manager Conduct Rules
compliance with requirements and standards, 2.11
co-operation with regulators, 2.13
delegation, 2.12
effective control, 2.10
enforcement, and, 11.5
financial services firms, and, 5.9
insurers, and
Individual, 4.20
introduction, 4.19
Senior Manager, 4.20
Senior Managers and Certification Regime (SM&CR)
See also **Senior Insurance Managers Regime**
accountability, and, 1.13
background, 1.10
Banking Standards Board, and, 2.7
Certification Regime
see also **Certification Regime**
generally, 3.8–3.22

**Senior Managers and
Certification Regime (SM&CR)**
 – *contd*
Conduct Rules, and
  compliance with requirements and
    standards, 2.11
  co-operation with regulators, 2.13
  delegation, 2.12
  effective control, 2.10
  generally, 2.9
  introduction, 2.8
elements, 3.1
financial services firms, and
  See also **Financial services firms**
  categorisation of firms, 5.2
  Certification Regime, 5.8
  Conduct Rules, 5.9
  core firms, 5.11
  enhanced firms, 5.12
  introduction, 5.1
  limited scope firms, 5.10
  Senior Managers Regime, 5.3–5.7
  transition from AP regime, 5.13–
    5.15
fit and proper requirement
  BSB Statement of Good Practice,
    2.7
  competence and capability, 2.4
  due diligence and documentation,
    2.6
  financial soundness, 2.5
  generally, 2.2
  honesty, integrity and reputation,
    2.3
implementation
  challenges for business, 6.2
  human resources, 6.7
  internal audit, 6.9–6.11
  introduction, 6.1
  key functions in oversight, 6.4–6.5
  legal function, 6.13
  liaison between control functions,
    6.6
  non-executive directors, 6.8
  organisational culture, 6.12
  risk management and assurance,
    6.3
Individual Conduct Rules
  co-operation with regulators, 2.17

**Senior Managers and
Certification Regime (SM&CR)**
 – *contd*
Individual Conduct Rules – *contd*
  due skill, care and diligence, 2.16
  generally, 2.14
  integrity, 2.15
  openness with regulators, 2.17
  proper market conduct, 2.19
  treating customers fairly, 2.18
insurers, for
  See also **Senior Insurance
    Managers Regime**
  affected employees, 4.3
  Certification Regime, 4.14–4.18
  changes, 4.4
  Conduct Rules, 4.19–4.22
  introduction, 4.1
  scope, 4.2
  Senior Managers Regime, 4.5–4.13
introduction, 2.1
reasonable steps requirement
  compliance, 2.11
  co-operation with regulators, 2.13
  delegation, 2.12
  effective control, 2.10
  introduction, 2.8
  Senior Manager Conduct Rules,
    and, 2.8–2.13
'senior manager', 3.2
Senior Managers Regime
  see also **Senior Managers
    Regime**
  generally, 3.3–3.7
specific issues, 3.1
structure, 3.1
timeline, 1.2
Senior Managers Regime (SMR)
certification functions, 3.2
competence and capability, 3.4
conditional approval, 3.5
enforcement, and, 11.3–11.4
FCA significant harm functions, 3.2
financial services firms, and
  See also **Financial services firms**
  duty of responsibility, 5.5
  fit and proper requirement, 5.7
  functions, 5.3
  generally, 5.3

Senior Managers Regime (SMR) –
contd
prescribed responsibilities, 5.6
statements of responsibility, 5.4
territorial scope, 5.3
financial soundness. 3.4
fit and proper requirement, 3.4
functions
generally, 3.3---3.4
introduction, 3.1
honesty, integrity and reputation,
3.4
insurers, for
See also **Senior Insurance
Managers Regime**
duty of responsibility, 4.9
functions, 4.6–4.7
generally, 4.5
handover, 4.8
management responsibilities map,
4.13
prescribed responsibilities, 4.10–
4.11
statements of responsibilities, 4.12
overview, 3.1
PRA certification functions, 3.2
prescribed responsibilities
generally, 3.6
introduction, 3.1
purpose, 1.13
regulatory approval, 3.5
responsibilities maps, 3.1
'senior manager', 3.2
significant harm functions, 3.2
smaller firms, and, 3.7
statement of responsibilities
generally, 3.6
introduction, 3.1
time-limited approval, 3.5
timeline, 1.2
Significant harm functions
introduction, 3.13
Senior Managers Regime, and, 3.2
specified, 3.14
Skill sets
practical issues, 8.5
Smaller firms
generally, 3.7
prescribed responsibilities, 7.5

Statements of Principles
generally, 1.13
Statements of responsibility
financial services firms, and, 5.4
generally, 3.6
insurers, and
generally, 4.12
introduction, 4.5
overview, 4.3
introduction, 3.1
practical issues, 7.2
Technology
cyber resilience
case study, 14.4
generally, 14.1
good practice, 14.2
data protection
GDPR, 14.5
generally, 14.5
fintech, 14.7
insurtech, 14.7
nuisance calls
generally, 14.6
PECR, 14.6
ransomware, 14.4
rectech, 14.7
Temporary cover
Senior Insurance Managers Regime,
and, 4.7
Training
boards and senior managers, for, 7.8
insurers, and, 4.21
Treating customers fairly
Individual Conduct Rules, and, 2.18 ·
United Arab Emirates (UAE)
generally, 15.10
Unlawful disclosure
market abuse, and, 10.7
USA
assessment of firm culture, 15.13
generally, 15.12
Vickers Commission (2011)
generally, 1.4
Wheatley Committee (2012)
generally, 1.5
Whistleblowing
market abuse, and, 10.7
Wolfsberg Group
overview, Appendix 2